Manchester Medieval Sources Series

series advisers Rosemary Horrox and Simon MacLean

This series aims to meet a growing need amongst students and teachers of medieval history for translations of key sources that are directly usable in students' own work. It provides texts central to medieval studies courses and focuses upon the diverse cultural and social as well as political conditions that affected the functioning of all levels of medieval society. The basic premise of the series is that translations must be accompanied by sufficient introductory and explanatory material and each volume therefore includes a comprehensive guide to the sources' interpretation, including discussion of critical linguistic problems and an assessment of the most recent research on the topics being covered.

also available in the series

John H. Arnold and Pete Biller *Heresy and inquisition in France, 1200–1300*

Andrew Brown and Graeme Small *Court and civic society in the Burgundian Low Countries c. 1420–1520*

Martin Heale *Monasticism in late medieval England, c. 1300–1535*

David Jones *Friars' Tales: Thirteenth-century exempla from the British Isles*

Graham Loud *Roger II and the making of the Kingdom of Sicily*

T. J. H. McCarthy *Chronicles of the Investiture Contest: Frutolf of Michelsberg and his continuators*

A. K. McHardy *The reign of Richard II*

Simon MacLean *History and Politics in Late Carolingian and Ottonian Europe: The Chronicle of Regino of Prüm and Adalbert of Magdeburg*

Anthony Musson and Edward Powell *Crime, law and society in the later Middle Ages*

Andrew Rabin *The political writings of Archbishop Wulfstan of York*

I. S. Robinson *Eleventh-century Germany: The Swabian Chronicles*

I. S. Robinson *The Annals of Lampert of Hersfeld*

Rachel Stone and Charles West *Hincmar of Rheims: On the divorce of King Lothar and Queen Theutberga*

Craig Taylor *Joan of Arc: La Pucelle*

Diana Webb *Saints and cities in medieval Italy*

JACOPO DA VARAGINE'S *CHRONICLE OF THE CITY OF GENOA*

Manchester University Press

Medieval Sources*online*

Complementing the printed editions of the Medieval Sources series, Manchester University Press has developed a web-based learning resource which is now available on a yearly subscription basis.

Medieval Sources*online* brings quality history source material to the desktops of students and teachers and allows them open and unrestricted access throughout the entire college or university campus. Designed to be fully integrated with academic courses, this is a one-stop answer for many medieval history students, academics and researchers keeping thousands of pages of source material 'in print' over the Internet for research and teaching.

titles available now at Medieval Sources*online include*

Trevor Dean *The towns of Italy in the later Middle Ages*

John Edwards *The Jews in Western Europe, 1400–1600*

Paul Fouracre and Richard A. Gerberding *Late Merovingian France: History and hagiography 640–720*

Chris Given-Wilson *Chronicles of the Revolution 1397–1400: The reign of Richard II*

P. J. P. Goldberg *Women in England, c. 1275–1525*

Janet Hamilton and Bernard Hamilton *Christian dualist heresies in the Byzantine world, c. 650–c. 1450*

Rosemary Horrox *The Black Death*

David Jones *Friars' Tales: Thirteenth-century exempla from the British Isles*

Graham A. Loud and Thomas Wiedemann *The history of the tyrants of Sicily by 'Hugo Falcandus', 1153–69*

A. K. McHardy *The reign of Richard II: From minority to tyranny 1377-97*

Simon MacLean *History and politics in late Carolingian and Ottonian Europe: The Chronicle of Regino of Prüm and Adalbert of Magdeburg*

Anthony Musson with Edward Powell *Crime, law and society in the later Middle Ages*

Janet L. Nelson *The Annals of St-Bertin: Ninth-century histories, volume I*

Timothy Reuter *The Annals of Fulda: Ninth-century histories, volume II*

R. N. Swanson *Catholic England: Faith, religion and observance before the Reformation*

Elisabeth van Houts *The Normans in Europe*

Jennifer Ward *Women of the English nobility and gentry 1066–1500*

For further information and subscription prices, see www.manchesteruniversitypress.co.uk/manchester-medieval-sources-online

JACOPO DA VARAGINE'S
CHRONICLE OF THE CITY OF GENOA

translated and annotated
by C. E. Beneš

Manchester University Press

Copyright © C. E. Beneš 2020

The right of C. E. Beneš to be identified as the author of this work has been asserted by her in accordance with the Copyright, Designs and Patents Act 1988.

Published by Manchester University Press
Oxford Road, Manchester M13 9PL
www.manchesteruniversitypress.co.uk

British Library Cataloguing-in-Publication Data
A catalogue record for this book is available from the British Library

ISBN   978 0 7190 9940 3   hardback
ISBN   978 1 5261 6439 1   paperback

First published 2020
Paperback published 2022

The publisher has no responsibility for the persistence or accuracy of URLs for any external or third-party internet websites referred to in this book, and does not guarantee that any content on such websites is, or will remain, accurate or appropriate.

Typeset
by Toppan Best-set Premedia Limited

CONTENTS

Acknowledgements	*page* vi
Abbreviations	viii
Maps and images	xi
Introduction	1
Jacopo da Varagine, *Chronicle of the city of Genoa*	39
Prologue	41
Part one: On the foundation of Genoa	45
Part two: On the early history of Genoa	57
Part three: On the name of Genoa	64
Part four: On the Christianisation of Genoa	72
Part five: On the growth of the city	82
Part six: On government	100
Part seven: On rulers	109
Part eight: On citizenship	123
Part nine: On domestic life	143
Part ten: On the Genoese church	160
Part eleven: The history of Genoa under the bishops	166
Part twelve: The history of Genoa under the archbishops	212
Appendix	255
References	258
Index	272

ACKNOWLEDGEMENTS

This translation originated in a conversation in a conference book exhibit where I was lamenting the fact that the only full medieval Italian chronicles—not excerpts—available in English translation were Florentine: this was not only giving my students a skewed sense of the practice of historiography in late medieval Italy, but also contributing to larger misapprehensions about the place of Florence in the late medieval urban network. A colleague suggested that perhaps *I* should fill that gap, and Jacopo's chronicle—with which I was already familiar—seemed like the ideal candidate. My first thanks are therefore due to that now-nameless colleague and everyone who encouraged me to undertake this translation, as well as my husband, Dr Thomas McCarthy, who offered the benefits of his expertise with medieval historiography and suggested the Manchester Medieval Sources series as an appropriate venue.

I would like to express my gratitude to Emma Brennan and Meredith Carroll at Manchester University Press for their enthusiasm, support, and patience with the delays that came inevitably with writing two books while first having and then raising two small children. Carol Lansing and two anonymous readers for Manchester University Press offered useful comments on the translation, while Laura Morreale and Samantha Herrick contributed both helpful feedback and incisive questions about the introduction. Edward Coleman, Joanna Drell, Steven Epstein, Lezlie Knox, Paolo Maggioni, Michèle Mulchahey, Bill North, Paola Guglielmotti, and others advised on particular points. I must also thank the participants in two sessions I organised about Jacopo at the 2018 Leeds International Medieval Congress for profoundly shaping my thinking about Jacopo's background and oeuvre.

My students at New College of Florida also merit thanks, first for their curiosity, engagement, and humour in my seminar on late medieval Italy and my Medieval Cities survey; and second, for offering their thoughts on early parts of the translation. Special appreciation goes to Victoria Deal '17 for taking time to work through parts 6–8. Kana Hummel, Andrew Maldonado, Adilyne McKinlay, Nicole Rockower, and Rory Sharp all contributed to my GIS project on medieval Genoa; while it was more directly aimed at my other current book project (*A companion to medieval Genoa*, 2018), the process made me think about Jacopo's relation to geography and landscape in unaccustomed and intriguing ways. The GIS database from that project also produced the maps for this book.

The New College Provost's Office and Division of Social Sciences supplied funding for research and travel, while the staff of Cook Library processed mountains of interlibrary loan requests with their usual quiet efficiency. Finally, I am grateful to Prof. Dr Martina Hartmann, Präsidentin of the MGH, as well as Christian Löhmer, Benedikt Marxreiter, the Vohrer family, and everyone else in Munich for their warm welcome during the 2018 residency in which this translation was finished.

In a sense, this translation is a pendant to the *Companion to medieval Genoa*: I agreed to edit that volume since I was already doing this translation, and working on the two in tandem—while sometimes exhausting—has taught me more than I ever expected about both project management and medieval Genoa. Like all good research projects, it has also piqued my interest in a wide variety of new topics. Since these two projects together span the earliest years of Tancred (p. 225) and Beatrice (p. 222), this book—like the *Companion*—is dedicated to them.

ABBREVIATIONS

Works by Jacopo da Varagine

CCG	*Cronaca della città di Genova dalle origini al 1297*, trans. S. Bertini Guidetti (Genoa, 1995)
GL	*The golden legend: Readings on the saints*, trans W.G. Ryan, rev. ed. (Princeton, 2012)
HLT	*Historia sive legenda translationis sancti Iohannis Baptistae*, ed. A. Vigna in 'Due opuscoli di Jacopo da Varagine', *ASLSP* 10 (1874–76): 455–91, at pp. 480–91
JVC	*Chronica civitatis ianuensis* = *Jacopo da Varagine e la sua cronaca di Genova dalle origini al MCCXCVII*, ed. G. Monleone, *FSI* 84–6 (Rome, 1941)
LA	*Legenda aurea*, ed. G.P. Maggioni, 2nd ed. (Florence, 1998)
LSS	*Legenda seu vita sancti Syri episcopi Ianuensis*, ed. V. Promis in 'Leggenda e inni sacri di S. Siro, vescovo di Genova', *ASLSP* 10 (1874): 355–83, at pp. 355–77
Mariale	*Mariale sive sermones de beata Maria virgine*, ed. G.P. Maggioni et al., Sermones.net (http://sermones.net/thesaurus/list.php?coll=voragine%2Fmariale) (2018); Italian trans. *Mariale aureo*, trans. V. Ferrua (Genoa, 2006)
SD	[*Sermones dominicales de evangeliis*] *Sermones dominicales per totum annum* (Venice, 1586)
SQ	*Sermones quadragesimales*, ed. G.P. Maggioni (Florence, 2005)
SS	*Sermones de sanctis per anni totius circulum* (Venice, 1573)

Other works

AASS	*Acta sanctorum*, 68 vols. (Paris, 1863–1940)
ASLSP	*Annali della Società Ligure di storia patria* (NS: Nuova serie), www.storiapatriagenova.it (Biblioteche digitali)
CCSL	*Corpus Christianorum, Series latina*
CCCM	*Corpus Christianorum, Continuatio mediaevalis*

ABBREVIATIONS

CGA	Caffaro di Caschifellone, *Genoese annals* = *Annales ianuenses* for 1099–1163, in *GA* 1, pp. 3–75; trans. *HP*, pp. 49–101*
CMG	*A companion to medieval Genoa*, ed. C.E. Beneš (Leiden, 2018)
CSEL	*Corpus scriptorum ecclesiasticorum Latinorum*
DBI	*Dizionario biografico degli italiani* (1960–)
DGA	Jacopo Doria, *Genoese annals* = *Annales ianuenses* for 1280–94, in *GA* 5, pp. 3–176; pp. 3–12 trans. *JD*, pp. 78–85
FSI	*Fonti per la storia d'Italia*
GA	*Genoese annals* = *Annali genovesi di Caffaro e de' suoi continuatori*, ed. L.T. Belgrano and C. Imperiale di Sant'Angelo, 5 vols., *FSI* 11–14bis (Rome, 1890–1929)
HP	Hall, M. and J. Phillips, ed. and trans., *Caffaro, Genoa, and the twelfth-century crusades* (Ashgate, 2013)*
JD	Dotson, J., 'The Genoese civic annals: Caffaro and his continuators', in S. Dale, A.W. Lewin, and D.J. Osheim (eds.), *Chronicling history: Chroniclers and historians in medieval and Renaissance Italy* (University Park, PA, 2007), pp. 55–85
LCO	Caffaro, *De liberatione civitatum orientis*, in *GA* 1, pp. 97–124; trans. *HP*, pp. 107–25*
MGH	*Monumenta Germaniae Historica*, http://dmgh.de
DD FII	*Friderici II diplomata*
DD KIII	*Diplomata Conradi III et filius eius Heinrici*
Fontes iuris	*Fontes iuris Germanici antiqui in usum scholarum separatim editi*
Ldl	*Libelli de lite imperatorum et pontificum*
Poetae	*Poetae latini aevi Carolini*
SS	*Scriptores* (in folio)
SSrG	*Scriptores rerum Germanicarum in usum scholarum separatim editi*
MO	Martin of Opava (Martinus Polonus), *Chronicon pontificum et imperatorum*, ed. L. Weiland, *MGH SS* 22, pp. 377–475
NCMH	*New Cambridge medieval history* (Cambridge, 1995–2005)
PG	*Patrologia graeca*, ed. J.-P. Migne, 161 vols. (Paris, 1856–66)
PL	*Patrologia latina*, ed. J.-P. Migne, 217 vols. (Paris, 1841–55)

RC	*Il registro della curia arcivescovile di Genova*, ed. L.T. Belgrano, *ASLSP* 2.2 (1862)
RC2	*Il secondo registro della curia arcivescovile di Genova*, ed. L.T. Belgrano and L. Beretta, *ASLSP* 18 (1887)
RIS, RIS2	*Rerum italicarum scriptores*, ed. L. Muratori (Milan, 1723–38); partly re-edited in *RIS2* (1900–)
RIBH	*Regni Iherosolymitani brevis historia*, in *GA* 1, pp. 127–49; trans. *HP*, pp. 151–67*
TIE	F.C. Tubach, *Index exemplorum: A handbook of medieval religious tales* (Helsinki, 1981)
YCAT	Caffaro, *Ystoria captionis Almarie et Turtuose*, in *GA* 1, pp. 79–89; trans. *HP*, pp. 127–35*

* Since Hall and Phillips' translation incorporates *GA* page numbers, references in this translation cite *GA* pages only, as these can be used to consult either *GA* or *HP*.

Also noted

Biblical citations in the text are given in italics; references are according to the Vulgate. Also, while the translation reflects Jacopo's use of the term 'Ecclesiasticus' for the book of Sirach, the footnotes use the name Sirach to avoid confusion with the book of Ecclesiastes.

All dates are AD unless otherwise indicated.

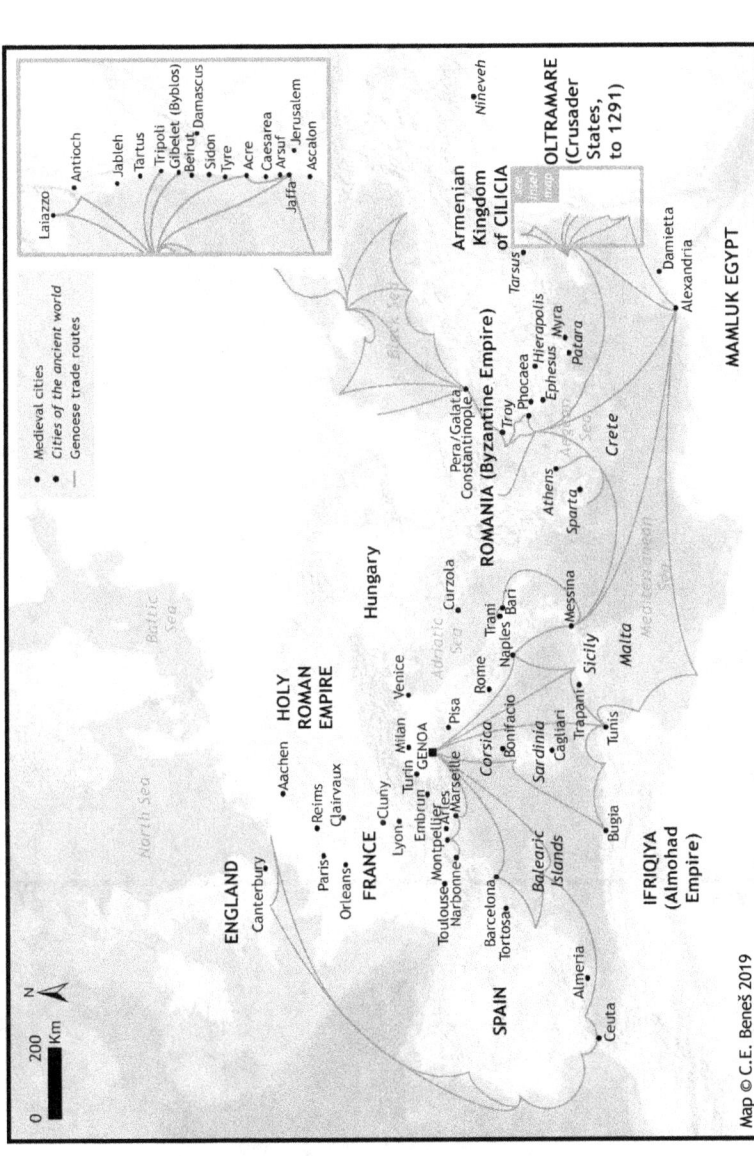

1 Late thirteenth-century Europe and the Mediterranean: places mentioned in the text.

2 Late thirteenth-century Italy and Liguria: places mentioned in the text.

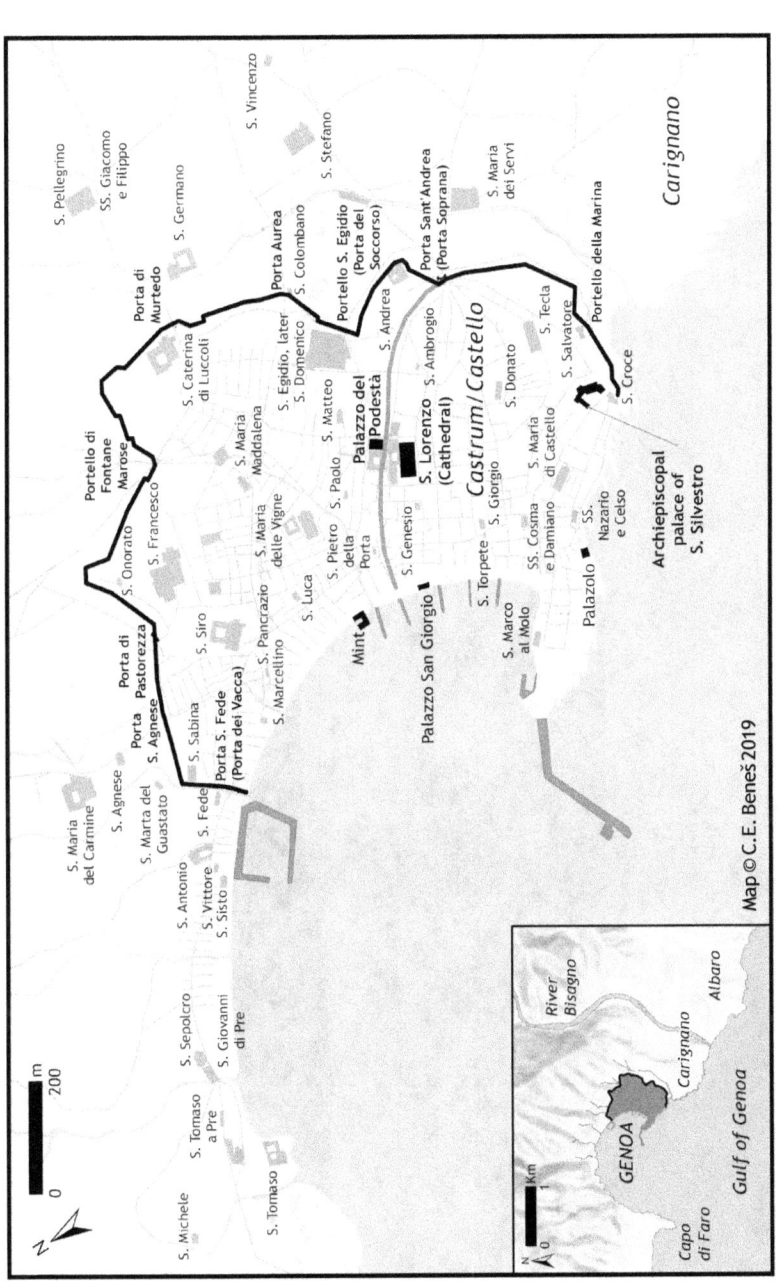

3 Late thirteenth-century Genoa.

4 Tomb effigy of Jacopo da Varagine. Museo di Sant'Agostino, Genoa. Photo by author.

5 Cathedral of San Lorenzo, Genoa. Jensens / Wikimedia public domain.

INTRODUCTION

Paradoxically, Jacopo da Varagine may be one of the least-known authors of the Middle Ages. As *Jacobus de Voragine*—the commonest Latin form of his name[1]—the collection of saints' lives he compiled in the 1260s, which came to be known as the *Golden legend* (*GL*), became one of the great medieval 'bestsellers'. The work was translated into most of the European vernaculars, survives in over a thousand medieval manuscript copies, and almost single-handedly determined how many Catholic saints are remembered and characterised even today. The stories that Jacopo related in the *GL* inspired countless sermons, literary imitations, and fresco cycles, and explanations of how and why saints are depicted in a certain way in the late medieval or early modern periods almost inevitably lead back to the *GL*.[2]

Yet Jacobus de Voragine has no real existence beyond the *GL*. This Latinate form of his name—supposedly taken from *vorago* (chasm) to suggest the boundless depths of his knowledge—only became standard long after his death. Instead, Jacopo refers to himself as *Jacobus de Varagine*, that is, James from Varazze, a small town on the Ligurian coast about twenty-three miles west of Genoa.[3] The modern Italian forms of his name, *Jacopo da Varazze* and *Jacopo da Varagine*, reflect those origins.[4] As Jacopo da Varagine, he was a Genoese native who rose through the ranks of the new Dominican order to become archbishop of Genoa, while at the same time maintaining a prolific writing career as the author of not only the *GL* but also hundreds of sermons, several relic treatises, and the *Chronicle of Genoa* translated here.[5]

---

1 Most English-language library catalogues redirect all searches on Jacopo da Varagine and Jacopo da Varazze to Jacobus de Voragine.

2 On the *GL* and its reception, see most recently Duffy's 2012 introduction to the *GL*; Le Goff (2014); and Epstein (2016), chaps. 2–3.

3 *Chronicle of the city of Genoa*, part 12.8, below.

4 His first name can appear as Jacobus/Iacobus, Jacopo/Iacopo, or Giacomo—more rarely in their English equivalents Jacob or James—and his toponym as Varazze, Varagine, or Voragine. Adding to the confusion, these can appear in almost any combination.

5 The Order of Preachers, a new order of mendicant friars founded by Saint Dominic (1170–1221), was approved by Pope Honorius III in 1216.

The popularity of the *GL*, therefore, has made Jacopo not only one of the best-known medieval authors but also one of the least-known, because his diligent work as a preacher, archbishop, historian, Dominican official, and citizen of late thirteenth-century Genoa is usually eclipsed by the *GL*'s enduring fame and influence. Eamon Duffy's 2012 introduction to the *GL*, for example, contains only a single—not very complimentary—sentence about Jacopo's existence beyond the *GL*: he excuses some of the more inaccessible or 'old-fashioned' aspects of the work by explaining that Jacopo was a 'man of his own times'.[6]

Similarly, Jacopo's work and career often slip through the cracks of contemporary academic scholarship because of the ways in which the medieval period is usually divided up and studied today. Those who study theology, literature, and art tend to focus on the *GL* to the exclusion of the circumstances in which it was created: in this, Duffy is hardly unusual.[7] At the same time, historians have not generally connected medieval Genoa with great cultural achievements—unlike Florence or Venice, or even Genoa's arch-rival Pisa. For many years, especially in the English-speaking world, scholarship on medieval Genoa has focused on the city's economic life, relying on documentary evidence such as treaties, statutes, charters, and, above all, notarial registers.[8] Historians of medieval Genoa have thus traditionally been less interested in Jacopo's highly literate perspective on Genoese history than in the more straightforward *Genoese annals* (*GA*) or the city's wealth of archival documentation, much of which is still unexplored.[9] Hence the abyss between the well-known and extensively analysed *GL* and the much less well studied career of its author.

A few efforts over the years have attempted to bring the two back into alignment. In 1935, E.C. Richardson published two volumes of *Materials for a life of Jacopo da Varagine*, without ever actually writing the biography implied in their title. Shortly thereafter, Giovanni Monleone published a full-length study of Jacopo as part of his edition of the *Chronicle* (*JVC*); the monograph and the edition remain major resources for the study

---

6 *GL*, pp. xix–xx.

7 As noted by Epstein (2016), p. 4 n. 13, Le Goff's recent book on the *GL* (2014) considers neither its Genoese context nor its place within Jacopo's larger body of work.

8 See my recent *Companion to medieval Genoa* (2018; *CMG*), especially the assessments of the field by Rovere/Macchiavello, Müller, Petti Balbi, and Stantchev/Miner.

9 Recent studies, however, have emphasised the ideological strategies underlying the *GA*'s seemingly factual narrative: Inguscio (2015) and Haug (2015). On the Genoese archives: *CMG*, chap. 1 (Macchiavello/Rovere).

of Jacopo and his work.[10] In 1988 Gabriella Airaldi published the short *Jacopo da Varagine: Tra santi e mercanti* ('between saints and merchants'), but it eschews footnotes in favour of a narrative accessible to non-academics. Little other research focused on Jacopo until the late 1990s, when Stefania Bertini Guidetti published an Italian translation of the chronicle (*CCG*) followed by an important series of studies.[11] Since then Giovanni Paolo Maggioni, who began by working on the *GL*, has shifted focus to Jacopo's sermons, with published editions and an extensive website providing both analysis and electronic versions.[12] Most recently, Steven A. Epstein, whose 1996 *Genoa and the Genoese* introduced medieval Genoa to a new generation of scholars, has written what he calls a study of Jacopo's 'mental world' (*The talents of Jacopo da Varagine*), analysing a broad range of Jacopo's work for its underlying attitudes, assumptions, and cultural values.[13]

The present translation of Jacopo's *Chronicle of the city of Genoa* contributes to such efforts to close the gap between the renowned writer of saints' lives, Jacobus de Voragine, and the less famous prelate Jacopo da Varagine (as he will be referred to here). It reveals Jacopo in historical context as a Dominican and an archbishop, born and raised in the bustling cities of late medieval Italy—most particularly Genoa, with its peculiar mix of cutthroat commerce and deep Christian piety. While material from the *GL* and his many sermons permeates Jacopo's *Chronicle*, the chronicle differs from them in that its narrative is historical and its focus is determinedly local, urban, and civic; it is thus a prime example of the civic chronicle, many hundreds of which were written in the cities of Italy during the Middle Ages.

The remainder of this introduction will introduce the reader to the genre of the Italian civic chronicle and the history of medieval Genoa as well as to Jacopo da Varagine, his career, and his literary corpus, all of which are necessary to understand why Jacopo's chronicle works the way it does and what Jacopo was trying to do in writing it. The chronicle's

---

10 *JVC* = *Jacopo da Varagine e la sua cronaca di Genova*, comprising Monleone's study of Jacopo and his chronicle (vol. 1), his edition of the *Chronicle* (vol. 2), and indices (vol. 3).

11 Bertini Guidetti (2001a) on Jacopo, (1998a) on the sermons, and (1998b) for a more general study of late thirteenth-century Genoa that incorporates much of her work on Jacopo. See also Bertini Guidetti (1997a, 1997b, 2001b).

12 www.sermones.net, which contains electronic editions of Jacopo's *Lenten sermons* (*SQ*) and *Mariale*. On the *GL*, see Maggioni (1997) and his edition of the *Legenda aurea* (*LA*); also his edition of the *SQ*.

13 Epstein (2016), p. 197.

present status as one of Jacopo's 'minor works'—quoted mainly for what Jacopo says in part twelve about his own scholarly output—sadly undervalues its contributions, not only to the civic historiography of late medieval Italy but also to a broader understanding of Jacopo's oeuvre. Read carefully, Jacopo's *Chronicle* is an invaluable resource for the urban history of medieval Italy, literary and historiographical practices within that milieu, ecclesiastical and political history, and the history of the later medieval Mediterranean.

Italian cities and their chronicles

The demographic landscape of medieval Italy (fig. 2) differed from most of the rest of Europe in its relatively high percentage of urban-dwellers, even after the end of the Roman Empire. Economic growth, especially from trade, from the eleventh century on expanded the urban middle classes, while the decline of imperial authority in Italy at the end of the eleventh century made room for the rise of communes: citizen-run governments of what became essentially independent city-states all across northern Italy. While they generally thought of themselves as republican, they were hardly democratic, and usually favoured the political participation of the local nobility and/or wealthy urban elites.[14]

Nonetheless, the combination of economic growth, political autonomy, and clear physical demarcation—i.e. by city walls—fostered the development among these cities' inhabitants of a particularly urban group identity or civic consciousness: a sense of collective identity focused on citizenship in, or at least belonging to, the urban community; a sense of ownership pertaining to the city, including its physical space and monuments; and a sense of the importance of one's own city on the broader stage of human history.[15] Increasing literacy and the significance of the profession of notary within these cities—a legacy of the Roman Empire, maintained and revived in an economy that thrived on written documentation—fostered an intellectual culture that both reflected and contributed to this sense of civic consciousness, with the production and preservation not only of civic treaties and council minutes but also poetry, plays, and histories, all on civic themes.[16]

---

14 Wickham (2015), Waley/Dean (2013), and Abulafia (2004).

15 Beneš (2011a) and Cassidy (2007), among others. The Italian-language literature on *coscienza civica* is also substantial.

16 On notaries, Kleinhenz (2004), pp. 780–4. On literacy in late medieval Italy: Petrucci (1995) and Cornish (2011). For civic poetry, see the early medieval 'Laudes

INTRODUCTION 5

Historical writing was one of the most popular and most variable genres, with annals, chronicles, hagiographies (saints' lives), and histories all celebrating urban life and communal achievements.[17] Some of the earliest are relatively simple annals recording notable events on a year-by-year basis; such annals survive from the tenth to twelfth centuries for most of the major towns in northern Italy, including Bergamo, Brescia, Como, Cremona, Genoa, Lodi, Milan, Piacenza, and Pisa.[18] Yet civic chronicles—more elaborately constructed and broader-ranging in scope than annals—were not far behind, such as Landulf Senior's late eleventh-century chronicle of Milan or Bernardo Maragone's mid-twelfth century *Pisan annals* (not a simple set of annals, despite its name).[19] Unlike earlier annals, the authors of such chronicles tended to be more concerned with civic origins, and with integrating their chosen cities into a universal narrative: they envisioned their chronicles as filling in gaps left by earlier historians, or correcting their underappreciation of cities that had since risen to greatness.[20] This focus is clearly a product of Italy's unusually high levels of urbanism, strong sense of civic identity, and competitiveness (*campanilismo*, 'belltower-ism') combined with widespread literacy. While the civic chronicle is not a genre exclusive to Italy, therefore, Italy's unique political and demographic situation meant that it was unusual in the sheer volume of chronicles produced, especially in the twelfth to fourteenth centuries.[21]

The official status of such chronicles varied widely: some (like the Perugian *Eulistea*) were commissioned by city councils, while others (like Giovanni Villani's well-known chronicle of Florence) were written by private citizens for no official purpose.[22] Sometimes—as with the *GA* or the thirteenth-century *Chronicle* of Rolandino of Padua—a previously written work was endorsed as 'official' by an approving city council.[23] As we

---

Mediolanensis' and 'Versus de Verona'—on which see Hyde (1966) and Zanna (1991)—or the late eleventh-century *Carmen in victoriam Pisanorum*, in Cowdrey (1977). For plays, see Albertino Mussato's late thirteenth-century Senecan tragedy *Ecerinis*.

17 Van Houts (1995), pp. 42–9; Kleinhenz (2004), pp. 215–18; and Dale/Lewin/Osheim (2007), including cited bibliography.
18 Coleman (2007).
19 Landulf Senior, *Historia Mediolanensis*; Bernardo Maragone, *Annales pisani*.
20 Bettini (2010), Beneš (2011a), and Campopiano (2014); see also Jacopo's prologue.
21 Dale/Lewin/Osheim (2007), p. ix.
22 Villani, *Nuova cronica*; on the *Eulistea*, see Beneš (2011a), chap. 5.
23 On the *GA* in brief, see *JD* or the introduction to *HP*. For Rolandino's *Chronica*, see also Andrews (2004).

shall see in Jacopo's case, rather than conforming to a static, standardised 'type' the genre of the civic chronicle borrowed from and incorporated numerous related types of literary and documentary composition, and each chronicle was different depending on its author and audience (real or imagined). In almost all cases, however, one stated purpose of the work was to encourage and admonish a city's inhabitants to the practice of active, virtuous citizenship. The writing of history, with its moral purpose, was thus believed to contribute to the development of a stable commonwealth, and it is no accident that the heyday of the medieval commune in Italy coincided with the production of innumerable civic chronicles in cities both large and small.

Over time, the chronicles of Florence—from Sanzanome in the early thirteenth century, to Dino Compagni and the Villani family in the fourteenth—have received the lion's share of scholars' attention.[24] This has created a scholarly feedback loop whereby a small number of well-known chronicles receive repeated scholarly attention, therefore they are more accessible, and thus they remain better known. As a recent sourcebook by Dale, Lewin, and Osheim seeks to demonstrate, however, the genre is enormous and diverse in a way that is hard for students to appreciate: most such chronicles are not available in English, and many remain unedited.[25] Alternatively, some appear only in eighteenth-century collections such as Muratori's *Rerum italicarum scriptores* (*RIS*), although the re-editing project *RIS2* is aimed at correcting that. Of those that have received modern editions, just a small sample of contemporary examples include Francesco di Andrea's *Chronicles of Viterbo* (c. 1250), Riccobaldo of Ferrara's *Short chronicle of Ferrara* (late thirteenth century), the anonymous *Chronicles of Todi*, and Martino da Canal's *Histories of Venice* (c. 1267–75).[26] Early fourteenth-century examples include multiple chronicles by the Visconti chancellor of Milan, Galvano Fiamma; the anonymous *Parmesan chronicle* (a chronicle of Parma, not a history of cheese); the chronicle of Ferreto de' Ferreti on Vicenza; and that of Ptolemy of Lucca on Lucca.[27] Jacopo's chronicle of Genoa fits

---

24 For Florentine chronicles, see e.g. Beneš (2011a), chap. 1, and Bornstein's introduction to Dino Compagni, *Chronicle*.

25 Dale/Lewin/Osheim (2007), introduction, esp. pp. ix–x.

26 Francesco d'Andrea, *Cronica*; Riccobaldo of Ferrara, *Chronica parva*; the anonymous *Cronache di Todi*; and Martino da Canal, *Estoires de Venise*.

27 Galvano Fiamma, *Chronicon maius*, *Manipulus florum*, and others; *Chronicon parmense*; Ferreto de' Ferreti, *Historia*; and Ptolemy, *Annales*.

INTRODUCTION 7

into this long tradition of civic historiography, and—as we shall see—his chronicle draws from a number of different approaches to writing history within the larger umbrella of 'civic history'. Furthermore, his chronicle features a medieval city not generally known for its intellectual culture or humanist engagement.[28] The present translation seeks to enlarge students' and scholars' understanding of the breadth and depth of the Italian civic chronicle as a genre in ways that have not previously been possible in English translation.

Genoa in the late thirteenth century

In some ways, the city-state of Genoa (fig. 3) was at its peak in the late thirteenth century.[29] From a modest regional existence in the early Middle Ages, the city had rapidly expanded its naval and economic reach in the tenth and eleventh centuries to become one of the great commercial powerhouses of the medieval Mediterranean, a role it would retain well into the early modern era.[30] The city's economic rise occurred in tandem with its fortunes in the crusades: even its early commercial expansion in the western Mediterranean brought it into military and economic conflict with the Muslim empires of north Africa and Spain, while its major contributions to the First Crusade (especially at Antioch, Jerusalem, and Caesarea) brought it great wealth and gave its merchants favoured status in the new crusader state.[31] The Genoese later played major roles in the Second, Third, Fifth, and Seventh Crusades as well. In the course of this expansion of its trade routes, the city's major Italian competitors were first Pisa (on the coast south of Genoa) and then Venice (across the peninsula on the Adriatic Sea; fig. 2): regular cycles of competition, conflict, and negotiation with these two rival communes occupied much of the later twelfth and thirteenth centuries.[32]

While a Pisan–Venetian alliance inflicted a major defeat on the Genoese in the War of Saint Sabas, fought in the Holy Land in 1256–58, the

---

28 See *CMG*, chap. 11 (Petti Balbi)—esp. pp. 322–3, 341–2—and Steven Epstein's forthcoming work on Giovanni Balbi, but also Cigni (2006) on French-language composition in Genoese prisons.
29 For an overview, see Epstein (1996), chaps. 3–4.
30 See Dauverd (2015) or Salonia (2017).
31 *CMG*, especially chaps. 14 (Stantchev/Miner) and 17 (Mack).
32 *CMG*, chap. 16 (Kirk).

situation quickly improved for the Genoese after they assisted Michael VIII Palaiologos to regain Constantinople from the French and their Venetian allies, who had occupied it since the Fourth Crusade in 1204.[33] Michael's gratitude gave the Genoese a major advantage over the Venetians in trade with Constantinople and into the Black Sea. Furthermore, the Genoese effectively eliminated the Pisans as commercial rivals at the battle of Meloria in 1284 (described by Jacopo in part 5.3). Soon thereafter, the collapse of the mainland crusader states with the fall of Acre in 1291 made the Genoese-controlled routes through Constantinople and the Black Sea even more important for eastern trade. In the 1290s, therefore, Genoa was a major entrepôt of international commerce, with trade networks stretching from Caffa on the Black Sea to Cyprus, Egypt, north Africa, Spain, and increasingly into the English Channel, the North Sea, and the Baltic (fig. 1).[34]

Historians have made much of the parallels between Genoa's economic rise and its political independence: the first pages of the city's official annals, begun by Caffaro in 1099, commemorate not only the fleet assembled to assist the new Kingdom of Jerusalem but also the establishment of the *compagna*, a sworn association generally understood to form the nucleus of the Genoese commune—an autonomous semi-republican government by which the city was governed until the Napoleonic invasion of 1797.[35] Jacopo explains that the city of Genoa 'is subject to no one—except God in all things and the emperor in a few' (part 10.2): as discussed above, while Genoa was technically part of the 'kingdom of Italy', which encompassed northern Italy down to Rome, the collapse of imperial power in the eleventh century had opened a political vacuum that came to be filled by many such autonomous city-states, or communes.[36]

Backed by their wealth from trade and occasional alliances such as the Lombard League, the Genoese more or less successfully resisted efforts by Charlemagne's German heirs to re-establish imperial sovereignty in Italy.[37] The emperors often had to content themselves with official—but functionally meaningless—recognition of their suzerainty. A major complicating factor was the contemporary conflict between the empire

---

33 *CMG*, pp. 403–4, 490, 507–8.
34 *CMG*, especially chaps. 10 (Müller), 14 (Stantchev/Miner), and 18 (Origone).
35 See the introduction to *HP* and *CMG*, chap. 4 (Filangieri).
36 Wickham (2015).
37 Raccagni (2010); also Duggan/Clarke (2016) for the papal perspective and Freed (2016) for the imperial view.

INTRODUCTION

and the papacy: at the same time that emperors such as Frederick I Barbarossa (r. 1155–90) were seeking to reimpose imperial authority in Italy, they were also clashing with the papacy over the respective rights of each as well as over temporal rule in the Patrimony of Saint Peter (the traditional papal lands in central Italy). The communes played these two adversaries against one another, fostering a broader antagonism often called the conflict between Guelfs (papal partisans) and Ghibellines (imperial partisans): while particular cities tended to support one side as a general rule (Genoa tended Guelf, Pisa Ghibelline), each city had partisans on both sides, and city governments changed alliances as it suited them.[38]

For these external reasons as well as internal ones, the political situation in Genoa became more and more volatile as it neared the end of the thirteenth century.[39] The commune as originally constituted had featured two executive magistrates called consuls, elected from the Genoese citizenry, as was the custom in such regimes. As Jacopo narrates in part 6.1, the rule of consuls lasted until 1190, when competition and factionalism caused the city to change to a podestarial regime on the eve of the Third Crusade. Podestà (the form is both singular and plural) were non-citizen professional magistrates elected annually; at least theoretically, their professional status and lack of local bias would improve their impartiality. By the side of the podestà, however, the same consular aristocracy retained the reins of political authority. In 1257, the wealthy non-aristocrats or *popolo* (an association called 'the people', which was nonetheless not remotely democratic) staged a coup, which replaced the podestà with a new chief magistrate, the *capitano del popolo* ('captain of the people') Guglielmo Boccanegra. Boccanegra's policies were unpopular, however, and he was ousted in 1262.

As the Genoese solidified their dominance of the Mediterranean's main trade routes and successfully bested their Pisan and Venetian rivals in the second half of the thirteenth century, then, the commune of Genoa was beset by increasingly serious political instability, with the rule of podestà and *capitani* alternating as regimes were established and quickly replaced. The most successful of these was the double captaincy of Oberto Doria and Oberto Spinola between 1270 and 1291 (with the former replaced by his son Corrado 1285–91), but this ended just before Jacopo's election as archbishop. The commune then tried another dual

---

38 See Waley/Dean (2013), chap. 5.
39 *CMG*, chaps. 4 (Filangieri) and 5 (Musarra).

regime with both *capitani* and podestà (1291–96), but, as Jacopo recounts, this ended in riots and a conflagration—both metaphorical and literal—at the end of 1295, during which Jacopo's cathedral of San Lorenzo (fig. 5) and archiepiscopal palace were both badly damaged by fire.[40] Jacopo's tenure as archbishop was therefore a time of increasing anxiety about political instability and social unrest in medieval Genoa. While the dangers of political instability are a common trope in medieval Italian historical writing, the vivid detail with which chroniclers like Jacopo treat the subject demonstrates that those dangers were personal and concrete rather than theoretical.[41]

Theoretically the archbishop of Genoa should be above such earthly conflicts, and in fact Jacopo oversaw a great civic peace-making ceremony early in 1295 (narrated in part 12.8).[42] Yet as a prelate he had his own concerns and spheres of responsibility: while Genoa was originally a bishopric subject to the archbishopric of Milan, in 1133 it had been raised to an archbishopric and given five suffragan (subject) bishoprics of its own: two in mainland Liguria (Bobbio and Brugnato) and three on the island of Corsica (Accia, Nebbio, and Mariana) (fig. 2).[43] Genoa's growing economic and political prominence was thus matched by its new ecclesiastical status, one gained at the expense of its neighbours Milan—which lost the three suffragan bishoprics of Genoa, Bobbio, and Brugnato—and Pisa, which lost the three suffragan bishoprics on Corsica now reassigned to Genoa. Later decrees of 1162 and 1239 gained Genoa two more suffragan bishoprics: Albenga and Noli, both in the western Riviera.[44]

The Genoese archbishopric was therefore relatively young, with borders that approximated (with some important exceptions) the mainland Genoese *districtus* or secular sphere of influence, which ran from

---

40 Epstein (1996), p. 325.

41 Here Jacopo's comments on virtuous government and citizenship (especially parts 6–8 of the *Chronicle*) may be usefully compared with the much better known chronicles of the Florentines Dino Compagni and Giovanni Villani.

42 On medieval Italian peace-making as socio-political theatre, see Kumhera (2017) and Jansen (2018).

43 Bobbio: a city about 75 km inland from Genoa, which grew up around the site of the abbey founded by Columbanus; Brugnato: a city in the Ligurian interior about 15 km northwest of La Spezia. Nebbio, Mariana, and Accia were small bishoprics at the northern end of Corsica.

44 See *Chronicle*, part 10; also *CMG*, chaps. 2 (Guglielmotti), 12 (Rosser), and 13 (Polonio).

INTRODUCTION

Monaco and Ventimiglia in the west to Portovenere and the gulf of La Spezia in the east—roughly the outlines of the modern Italian region of Liguria, and also its Roman predecessor as Jacopo points out in part 10.2 (fig. 2). But the overlapping borders and jurisdictions of the commune, the archbishopric, and the holdings of the city's noble families often caused friction, if not outright conflict (as Jacopo narrates regarding Archbishop Otto, part 12.4). Likewise, Genoa's ancient monasteries—such as San Siro and Santa Maria di Castello—often came into conflict with the cathedral chapter or the city's more recent foundations—Santa Maria delle Vigne, the Franciscan convent of Santa Caterina di Luccoli, or the Dominican priory at San Domenico—so the archbishop was needed to mediate those disputes as well.

Jacopo's job accordingly required not only a sharp intellect and a ready pen but talents on numerous fronts. While Genoese merchants were welcomed across the Mediterranean, the city itself was increasingly insecure. Jacopo had to manage complex relationships between the archdiocese, Genoa's prominent families, the commune, the *districtus*, and Genoa's far-flung trade outposts. During his tenure, the city (including Jacopo, by virtue of his office) was involved in diplomatic negotiations involving the papacy, the Venetians, and the struggle over Sicily and Sardinia between the Aragonese and the Angevin rulers of Naples. Relations were fractious between the city's families and its various ecclesiastical entities—most notably the struggle between the cathedral chapter and the monks of San Siro over the relics of Saint Syrus. In all of this, Genoa's citizens were confronting—as were their fellow citizens in other Italian cities of the day—fundamental questions of citizenship, sovereignty, economic exchange, and social harmony: What is the most effective sort of government that respects its citizens' rights and privileges? How much profit constitutes usury? What are a citizen's responsibilities to his fellow citizens and human beings? Jacopo's *Chronicle* seeks to help the citizens of Genoa answer such questions.

Jacopo da Varagine (1228/9 to 1298)

Given that Jacopo was a prominent archbishop, preacher, and author, oddly little is known about his life. Most of what we know, in fact, comes from what he tells us in his *Chronicle of Genoa*, but—unlike his Franciscan contemporary Salimbene de Adam, for example—he is notoriously reticent about his own life, and relatively few surviving records mention him.⁴⁵ As Epstein observes, 'a standard biography simply will not work'.⁴⁶

Jacopo was born in 1228 or 1229, probably in Genoa. While the 'da Varazze/Varagine' form of his name may indicate that he was born in Varazze, scholarly consensus seems to be that it is more likely he grew up in Genoa, where the existence of a 'da Varagine' family originally from Varazze is separately attested. Three titbits from the *Chronicle* comprise the extent of our knowledge of his early life: that he was a child (*anni pueriles*) during the eclipse of 1239 (part 12.4), that he entered the Dominican order in 1244 (part 12.5), and that he observed the great comet of 1264 (part 12.6), which was visible between July and September of that year. Everything else before Jacopo's election as Dominican prior for Lombardy in 1267 is speculation.

As Casagrande points out, however, prior for Lombardy—elected chief officer of one of the most important early Dominican provinces—was a prominent and influential position, so Jacopo must have had a fairly successful career up to that point. The Dominican community in Genoa was young but thriving: dating from around 1217–19, it was reputedly established by Saint Dominic himself.⁴⁷ While early friars were based in the small church of Sant'Egidio along the city walls, by 1250 the large complex that would become San Domenico was already under construction. When Jacopo joined the order in 1244, therefore, the community and its parent order were both less than thirty years old, but already vibrant and flourishing.

Since the Dominican order prioritised education—having been founded to preach the Gospel, encourage penitence, and combat heresy—Dominican convents or priories almost always included schools.⁴⁸ Thus

---

45 Salimbene de Adam of Parma (1221–*c.* 1289) wrote a chronicle contemporary to but very different from Jacopo's in its much broader scope and wealth of personal (sometimes scurrilous) observation; see the introduction to the Baird/Baglivi/Kane translation and Lewin's chapter on it in Dale/Lewin/Osheim (2007).

46 Epstein (2016), pp. 4–5. Most of the information presented in the following section comes from Epstein's introduction, plus the biography of Jacopo by Casagrande (*DBI* 62.92–102, under 'Jacopo da Varazze'), with additional details from Airaldi (1988) and the introductions to *JVC* and *CCG*.

47 Bertini Guidetti, introduction to *CCG*, pp. 9–10; Di Fabio/Besta (1998), pp. 122–6.

48 'Convent' is used here in its generic sense of 'religious community'. The usual terms for a Dominican community are that or 'priory' (since it was ruled by a prior). These are used instead of 'monastery' and 'abbot', since Dominican friars were not cloistered monks but rather priests sworn to lives of preaching and poverty (i.e. mendicants). On the formation and importance of the mendicant orders in medieval cities, see Little (1983).

INTRODUCTION

Jacopo was probably first educated in the Dominican convent in Genoa, and later at its *studium generale*, equivalent to a university. Bertini Guidetti has suggested that he studied in the late 1240s at Bologna, the main Italian site of Dominican higher education; it is also possible that he studied at Paris, then the centre of Dominican education in Europe—the great Dominican Thomas Aquinas, for example, was regent master in theology at Paris during 1256–59.[49] In the course of his education, Jacopo would have attained the degrees of *lector* (reader, i.e. teacher) and *magister theologiae* (master of theology, a higher degree); he may also have served as prior of a Dominican house or houses in northern Italy: both Genoa and Asti have been suggested. There is, however, no definite evidence for any of this.

We begin to know more after Jacopo's election as prior of Lombardy in 1267, the point at which he began to take a more prominent role in the management of the Dominican order.[50] The Dominican order was then divided into twelve different provinces; rather like the annual meetings held by professional organisations today, representatives from each of these provinces convened annually at a General Chapter, which was held at a different site each year. The province of Lombardy was one of the most influential of these early provinces, since it encompassed the entirety of northern Italy including Bologna, where the Dominicans maintained a strong presence at the university and where Saint Dominic himself was buried.

Jacopo was prior of the province of Lombardy for ten years, during which he attended the General Chapters held at Bologna (1267), Montpellier (1271), Budapest (1273), Lyons (1274), and Bordeaux (1277); at the last of these he was 'absolved' of his office. During most of this time he would have been based in Milan, although he would have spent much of his time travelling, either to the General Chapters or on official visits to the Dominican convents of the province. Managing such a large, growing, and often contentious, order was not easy: according to a later source Jacopo survived two assassination attempts by disgruntled friars in the course of his duties.[51] He was nonetheless re-elected provincial prior for 1281–86; between 1283 and 1285, he also served briefly as regent of the entire order while it was between masters general. His

---

49 On early Dominican education, see Mulchahey (1998).
50 Hinnebusch (1966), 1.172–87; on the office of provincial prior, 1.205–7.
51 Hieronymus de Bursellis, *Cronica magistrorum generalium Ordinis Praedicatorum* (Bologna, Biblioteca Universitaria, MS 1999), fol. 6. I am grateful to G.P. Maggioni for this reference.

last official position with the Dominicans was *diffinitor* (provincial representative) at the General Chapter held at Lucca in 1288.

Throughout his peripatetic life, Jacopo maintained close ties to Genoa and its Dominican communities. On two occasions—as he himself reports—he presented relics to the Genoese convent of Dominican nuns, Santi Giacomo e Filippo: in the 1260s, he donated to the sisters a finger of Saint Philip that he had detached from its hand in a reliquary in Venice, and in the 1280s he presented to them the head of one of the virgin companions of Saint Ursula, brought from Cologne. In 1288, Jacopo was one of four candidates considered for the Genoese archbishopric, but the election proved so contentious that no one was elected and the pope appointed a regent or administrator, Opizzo Fieschi (from the noble Genoese family). In 1292, however, in response to a new request by the Genoese, Pope Nicholas IV named Jacopo archbishop of Genoa, an office in which he served until his death in 1298. Since Nicholas IV had died by the time Jacopo travelled to Rome to be invested with his office, Jacopo was consecrated as archbishop by the cardinal bishop of Ostia on the octave of Easter (14 April) 1292 (part 12.8).

Continuing the pattern of little surviving evidence, there is almost none for Jacopo's tenure as archbishop apart from a few papal letters, a handful of notarial acts, and what he tells us himself in the *Chronicle of Genoa* (and even that, as we shall see, is inconsistently reported). We have no archiepiscopal letters written by Jacopo himself, and the official archiepiscopal registers from his tenure do not survive, if indeed they ever existed. For reasons that historians do not understand, the official *Genoese annals*—which had been maintained continuously since their inception in 1099—ended in 1293, and the last annalist Jacopo Doria does not even mention Jacopo da Varagine's election as archbishop. Thus Jacopo's *Chronicle of the city of Genoa*, written during his archiepiscopate (1292–98), is valuable not only for its eyewitness perspective on events in which Jacopo himself played a major role, but also because it is the only surviving contemporary source for Genoa in the 1290s.

By his own account, Jacopo was a dedicated, active, and involved archbishop, who made valiant efforts to mediate and resolve disputes among the Genoese, took a personal hand in administering the patrimony of his church, and helped maintain the city's diplomatic relations. The chief accomplishments of his tenure as he presents them in the *Chronicle of Genoa* are three. First, shortly after his election he held a provincial council for all the clerics in his archdiocese, during which he supervised an investigation of the relics of the early local bishop Saint Syrus in the Genoese cathedral of San Lorenzo (part 12.8; fig. 5). The cathedral canons and the monks of the ancient monastery of San Siro had been arguing over these relics for some years, and Jacopo hoped—in vain, as it turned out—that his intervention would settle the matter. Secondly, Jacopo spent six months in 1295 as part of a Genoese embassy to the papal court, which was attempting to negotiate a peace with the Venetians, with whom the Genoese had been intermittently at war for nearly fifty years. The negotiations failed, but Jacopo expends a great deal of ink extolling the naval preparations made by the Genoese as a backup plan (part 5.3). Thirdly, Jacopo mediated a general peace in Genoa in January 1295 between the city's main factions, the Rampini and Mascherati. This was nominally an opposition of Guelfs v. Ghibellines—supporters of the papal and imperial parties respectively—but it was exacerbated by more immediate local disputes of neighbourhood and kinship; as Jacopo reports: 'these dissensions, divisions, and factions persisted for fifty-five years and more'. Jacopo's intervention led to the establishment of a general peace with civic celebrations, a solemn celebratory mass, the singing of a *Te Deum*, a great feast, and a procession through the entire city (part 12.8).

While none of Jacopo's chief projects as archbishop bore as much fruit as he might have hoped, he seems to have taken the failure of this last effort most personally. In December 1295 the peace he had arranged and described with such enthusiasm collapsed, and unrest variously described as 'riots' or 'civil war' consumed the city for over a month: the Genoese 'clashed in hand to hand combat through the alleys and piazzas, and for many days they contended angrily against one another. From this followed the slaying of men, the wounding of many, the burning of houses, the looting and plunder of many things'. Even the cathedral and Jacopo's archiepiscopal palace were badly damaged, and Jacopo had to apply to Pope Boniface VIII for extra funds with which to replace his lost possessions.[52] At this point—although Jacopo remained archbishop for another two and a half years—the *Chronicle* peters out, with only three further entries: two on clashes with the Venetians in 1296 and 1297, and one on Boniface VIII's conflict with the Colonna in 1297. One can only speculate either that Jacopo was so downcast by the failure of his efforts to establish civic concord that he abandoned his historical work, or that, more proactively, he decided that his energies were needed more elsewhere.

52 Part 12.8 n. 219.

He was probably also feeling his age. He would have been nearly seventy years old at this point, past the point of retirement today and long-lived compared to most of his contemporaries. Again, little is known of Jacopo's final years: he must have written the treatise on the Genoese relics of Saint John the Baptist, which he stated in the *Chronicle* that he was planning to write, because it survives. He died in the night between 13 and 14 July 1298 and was buried in the church of San Domenico in Genoa. Due to his local reputation as archbishop and his broad fame as the author of the *GL*, his tomb became the site of a cult, so when San Domenico was demolished in the late eighteenth century Jacopo's bones and tomb effigy (fig. 4) were moved to the church of Santa Maria di Castello (then also a Dominican house).[53] He was beatified by Pope Pius VII in 1816.

Jacopo's works

The relatively little extant evidence for Jacopo's life stands in stark contrast to his body of work as an author, which by any calculation runs to thousands of pages written over the course of his life. In fact, Jacopo gives a convenient accounting of his work in part 12.8 of the *Chronicle*. The easiest to categorise, and one of the earliest, is the *Golden legend* (*Legenda aurea*, *GL* and *LA*), which Jacopo calls simply *Legends of the saints* (*Legende sanctorum*).[54] The title *Golden legend* was invented later as a description of the value of the work's contents, but the work appears in its many medieval copies by many different names, including *Historia lombardica* (from the excursus on Lombard history attached to its life of Pope Pelagius). The *GL* was Jacopo's first major work, written 1260–67; while it is generally known as a compilation of saints' lives, technically it is organised around the feasts of the church year, so along with the approximately 153 saints whose lives are recounted, there are chapters on the Nativity and Circumcision of Christ, the Birth, Purification, and Assumption of the Virgin Mary, the feasts of Pentecost, All Saints', and so on—including some little-known feasts like the 'Chair of Saint Peter', an *apologia* for the primacy of the Roman church. Most of the saints whose stories are recounted are traditional or 'ancient' ones: figures from the New Testament (the apostles, Mary Magdalen), the church fathers (Augustine, Ambrose), early popes

---

53 Bertini Guidetti, introduction to *CCG*, p. 9.
54 See n. 2, above.

(Sylvester, Gregory the Great), fathers of monasticism (Anthony, Benedict), and martyr saints (Agnes, Cecilia, Lawrence). Jacopo includes only four 'contemporary' saints, chiefly those associated with the mendicant orders: Francis of Assisi (d. 1217), Dominic (d. 1221), Peter Martyr (an early Dominican martyred in 1252), and Elisabeth of Hungary (d. 1231).[55]

Jacopo's genius was in collecting these legends and the miracles connected with them, then compiling all the information into engaging stories written in simple, clear Latin. While the volume was originally intended as 'an aid for busy priests and preachers in need of a handy source of vivid anecdote, instruction, and edification to bulk out their sermons and catecheses', its popularity soon expanded far beyond Dominican homiletics: within fifty years of its compilation, it was the dominant collection of saints' lives in Europe.[56] Over a thousand manuscript copies still survive in multiple formats and languages, which has led some to suggest that it was the most-read book of the later Middle Ages after the Bible. Another useful index of the *GL*'s wide dissemination and audience is its robust presence in early printing: between 1455 and 1500, nearly ninety editions of the Latin text are known to have been printed, along with seventy different vernacular translations.

Unsurprisingly given the collection's didactic purpose, many of the stories in the *GL* also appear (sometimes multiple times) in Jacopo's hundreds of sermons: anywhere from 725 to 1,200 depending on one's counting method.[57] These are not full texts such as could be read straight from a pulpit but model sermons constructed according to a standardised, characteristically Dominican logic and format: a preacher adopting one for some occasion would be expected to fill in situational asides, anecdotes, examples, and analogies appropriate to his audience.[58]

Jacopo wrote these sermons over the course of his career (*c.* 1250–98), but he assembled them for public dissemination into three main collections,

---

55 The first three are unsurprising for a Dominican author, but Elisabeth's inclusion (*GL*, pp. 688–704) is more mysterious: while some have connected her presence with a particular affinity for her cult in Genoa (Bertini Guidetti, 2001b), others have dismissed her *vita* as a later interpolation to the collection (Duffy, introduction to the *GL*, xv). She is also connected to the mendicant orders as patron of Franciscan tertiaries.

56 Duffy, introduction to the *GL*, pp. xi–xiii.

57 Epstein (2016), p. 11 n. 2.

58 On Dominican homiletics, see Wenzel, *Art of preaching*, and Corbari (2013).

identified in part 12.8 of the *Chronicle*. The first collection echoes his work in the *GL*: 'sermons on all the saints, by which their feasts may be celebrated according to the cycle of the church year'. These are the *Sermones de sanctis* (*SS*): two volumes of sermons organised by saint or feast, with anywhere from two to nine model sermons offered for each. The second collection—the *Sunday sermons on the Gospels* (*Sermones dominicales de evangeliis, SD*)—follows the Gospel readings proper to every Sunday in the church year, with three sermons offered for each Gospel reading. Finally, the third collection—the *Lenten sermons* (*Sermones quadragesimales, SQ*)—does the same for the Gospel readings proper to each day in Lent. A fourth collection, the *Sermones de tempore* or *Sermons for the liturgical year*, is not mentioned directly by Jacopo and overlaps significantly with the other three collections. All of the collections offer multiple model sermons on any given topic. Some of the sermons overlap considerably in content, and many of the editions published in the fifteenth to eighteenth centuries reorganise or combine the collections, which is why it is difficult to track their numbers. The only collection thus far to have benefited from a modern critical edition is *SQ*, although its editor, G.P. Maggioni, is working on both an edition of *SS* and a full categorisation of Jacopo's sermons on his website, www.sermones.net.

Related to the sermon collections is one of Jacopo's last works, the *Book of Mary* (*Liber Marialis* or simply *Mariale*), a collection of homiletic meditations on various attributes of the Virgin Mary organised according to the letters of the alphabet. For example, the entries under O include reflections on the ideas of 'sweet-smelling' (*odorifera*), olives (*oliva*: two separate entries), the 'best part' (*optima pars*) chosen by Mary in Luke 10.42, the 'garden of delights' (*ortus deliciarum*), and being a 'sheep of God' (*ovis Dei*). While scholars debate whether these are 'real' model sermons, their rhetorical and exegetical structure closely resembles Jacopo's other homiletic work.

The *GL*, the four collections of sermons, and the *Chronicle of the city of Genoa* are the works Jacopo claims by name in part 12.8 of the *Chronicle*, but scholars also regard as authentic (either via internal evidence or reference by Jacopo himself) six hagiographical treatises, most of which have to do with relics held in Genoa in Jacopo's time. First, in connection with his investigation into the relics of Saint Syrus of Genoa, Jacopo wrote a 'new' legend of Saint Syrus (*Legenda seu vita sancti Syri episcopi Ianuensis, LSS*). Second, he composed an account of the translation of the relics of Saint John the Baptist from the Holy

Land to Genoa (the *Historia sive legenda translationis sancti Iohannis Baptistae, HLT*); this is the treatise he summarises in part 11.16 of the *Chronicle*, promising to expand upon it later in a separate work. Third, he wrote a history of the relics which he himself donated (or at least facilitated the translation of) to the Dominican women's community of Santi Giacomo e Filippo (*Historia reliquiarum que sunt in monasterio sororum SS. Philippi et Iacobi de Ianua*). Beyond these, he wrote two treatises on the relics of Saint Florentius, bishop of Orange and patron saint of Fiorenzuola d'Arda near Piacenza (*Tractatus miraculorum reliquiarum sancti Florentii* and *Historia translationis reliquiarum eiusdem*), and a passion narrative of Saint Cassian (*Passio sancti Cassiani*) for the bishop of Imola, who had recently (1271) consecrated his new cathedral to that saint. In all of these treatises, Jacopo engages his audience by using local landscapes (of Genoa, Liguria, and beyond) to create a sense of immediacy for the reader; the associations that his narrative builds between landscape, object, and history give not only physical manifestation to a glorious civic past, but also meaning to the spaces and objects encountered by his readers in the course of their everyday existence.

Viewed from the perspective of thirteenth-century Genoa, Dominican homiletics, and the conventions of late medieval historical writing, Jacopo's body of work is remarkably coherent: the same exempla and moral lessons reappear across his chronicle, sermons, and saints' lives, and his entire oeuvre demonstrates the hierarchical logic characteristic of late medieval Dominican rhetoric. At the same time, Jacopo's work reveals a keen awareness of his audience: while his Genoese works (the *Chronicle* and relic treatises) are clearly grounded in local history and landscape, his sermons and the *GL* are just as clearly stripped of such immediate details to improve their usefulness for any preacher in search of material.

The *Chronicle of the city of Genoa*

In part 12.8 of the *Chronicle*, Jacopo refers to his work as 'the present chronicle' (*presens cronica*), and the incipits of the earliest manuscripts identify it as the 'chronicle of the city of Genoa' (*cronica civitatis Ianue*), so we must suppose that the title is more or less original, and in accord with Jacopo's own intention. While the *Chronicle* cannot match the *GL*'s thousand-plus manuscripts, the text survives in an impressive number of approximately forty-five manuscript copies, many of them from the fourteenth and fifteenth centuries.[59] (Many contemporary civic chronicles, by contrast, survive in only one or two copies.) Most of the early copies on which Monleone based his edition are codices of fairly high quality produced in Genoa itself—while not elaborately illustrated, they tend to be written on parchment rather than paper, and in Gothic book script (*littera textualis*) instead of more cursive *mercantesca* or notarial hands. Most contain headings and paragraph marks, known as rubrication, in one or more colours. Finally—and perhaps most revealingly—most contain marginal annotations, additions, and/or indices, some of them quite extensive, which confirm they were read and/or used for reference, both for the historical information they contain and for the stories they recount, which could be used separately as exempla. In one manuscript (now in Turin) a scribe has continued the chronicle up to the year 1332. These comments, interpolations, and additions suggest that a sizable number of readers found Jacopo's account of Genoese history both interesting and useful.[60] (In fact, it was probably the only narrative of Genoese history in circulation, since the Genoese commune tightly controlled access to the official city annals.)

At the same time, Jacopo's obvious Genoese bias and the development of more critical practices in the writing of history by humanists such as Coluccio Salutati (1331–1406) meant that some of the *Chronicle*'s more imaginative claims were soon challenged. The Milanese chancellor Benzo d'Alessandria (*c.* 1250–*c.* 1330), for example, writing about twenty years after Jacopo, skewered Jacopo's claim that Genoa was founded by a Trojan escapee named Janus: 'I have found nothing in any authoritative writings of the city being either built or expanded by a Trojan Janus'. Furthermore—he continues—since the Roman historian Livy always refers to the city as *Genua*, 'it appears that the ancient city was called *Genua* rather than *Janua*, and thus it was neither founded by nor named after Janus, even if it is known as *Janua* today'.[61] Salutati himself refers dismissively to Jacopo's entire effort in a letter to the Genoese historian Giorgio Stella: 'in the chronicle in which he wrote a great many stupid things, your Jacopo accepts as if they were of undoubted truth [certain facts] which are known to be quite otherwise ... In these matters he neither proves anything to me by the testimony of witnesses nor convinces me by persuasion'.[62]

---

59 Monleone, *JVC* 1.341–509.
60 See my discussion of one manuscript's extensive indices in Beneš (2011a), pp. 84–5.
61 Benzo d'Alessandria, *Chronicon* 14.155, p. 187; discussed in Beneš (2011b), pp. 9–10. See part 3 of the *Chronicle* for Jacopo's explanation of Genoa's origins.
62 Coluccio Salutati, letter 14.13 (1405), *Epistolario* 4.91–8 at pp. 93–4.

INTRODUCTION 21

Perhaps for these reasons, Jacopo's *Chronicle* fell into anonymity in the early modern period until it was partly edited along with so many other 'lost' medieval narrative sources by Ludovico Muratori for his *Rerum italicarum scriptores* in 1726.[63] Muratori explained, however, that the partial nature of his edition was due to the implausibility of many of Jacopo's claims: 'I have been unable to make myself edit the entirety of this Jacopo's chronicle, for who can bear reading with mental tranquillity so many ridiculous ideas, fables, and unfounded leaps of logic which this good writer has stuffed into this work, which he seems to have forgotten he called a history?'[64] Muratori's contemptuous comments stood as normative until the extensive critical edition and study by Giovanni Monleone in 1941 (*JVC*), which remain standard. Against Salutati and Muratori, Monleone recognised that the real value of Jacopo's chronicle lies in his careful organisation of his material and what it reveals about attitudes and beliefs in late thirteenth-century Genoa. As mentioned above, an Italian translation with an extensive introduction by Stefania Bertini Guidetti (1995; here *CCG*) contributed to a late twentieth-century revival of interest in Jacopo and his non-*GL* works.

The *Chronicle* claims to recount the history of Genoa from its foundation up to Jacopo's own time because—as Jacopo explains in the prologue— 'considering how there are many cities in Italy of which the ancient historians make much mention, we are amazed that so very little can be found written by them about the city of Genoa, as renowned, noble, and powerful as it is'.[65] Jacopo has resolved to remedy that lack by compiling the various details he has learned from the civic annals and other chroniclers into a history of Genoa. The chronicle narrates events up to the year 1295, but (as discussed above) it then peters out without a real conclusion, and with only three entries for the years 1296–97. Yet as a whole the work has the single goal of civic exhortation—that is, it is designed to teach the Genoese citizenry about their glorious past, to inspire them to civic virtue by the good example of their ancestors, and to instruct them in how to maintain that glory in the present. Jacopo's focus is urban; his goals unity, peace, and concord. Furthermore, as the previous sections of this introduction have shown, he was very conscious of the challenges facing his efforts. The purpose of Jacopo's entire historical enterprise was therefore to remind the Genoese of their collective past, present, and future, and to demonstrate how to translate past achievement into future glory.

63 *RIS* 9.1–56.
64 *RIS* 9.4.
65 *Chronicle*, prologue.

Author and audience are thus the main differences between Jacopo's chronicle and the *GA*, the Genoese annals first begun by Caffaro in 1099, adopted officially in 1152, and continued under communal sponsorship until 1293. In a sense, both are products of institutional sponsorship: the annals were sponsored by the commune, while Jacopo wrote from a position of authority as archbishop. Yet the annals were written by a series of officially appointed annalists—beginning with Caffaro in 1099 and ending with Jacopo Doria in 1293—so they have a chronological year-by-year format, and their tone and the interests of their multiple authors vary considerably. Jacopo da Varagine, by contrast, imagined and designed his chronicle as a holistic whole, so its approach and purpose are more coherent and targeted, even if its methods are more variable.

Secondly, the Genoese annals were meant as an official record of Genoese triumphs—whether political, military, territorial, diplomatic, or economic—so there was only one authorised copy of the text, which at least by Jacopo's time was closely guarded by communal officials.[66] The many passages in Jacopo's *Chronicle* that parallel those in the *GA* attest that Jacopo had access to the official manuscript while he was writing his own chronicle, but his status as archbishop gave him access to documents inaccessible to others. In a sense, the audience of the *GA* was posterity rather than anyone alive at the time, while the audience of Jacopo's chronicle was a much broader spectrum of literate Genoese citizens, particularly the clerics and communal officials who could benefit from its lessons and expound them to their less-literate fellow citizens. In other words, in intent and execution the *GA* was an archival document, while Jacopo's chronicle was a practical guide to Genoese citizenship.

That guide is divided into twelve parts, or books, which are diverse in their methodology or approach, and which in their turn are divided into multiple chapters. They demonstrate not one but three genres of socio-historical writing typical of the communes of late medieval Italy, all of which feature a clear and consistent civic focus: their intended audience is the citizenry; their priorities are those of the city, commune, or urban population; and they discuss broader historical events mainly insofar as they influenced or reflected events in the city.

Section 1: parts 1–5 and 10. The first section of the chronicle, comprising parts 1–5, constitutes what we might call civic history. (Part 10

---

66 The *GA* survives in only three copies: the 'authentic original'—Paris, Bibliothèque Nationale MS Lat. 10136—and two copies made from it in the thirteenth and fifteenth centuries respectively: *CMG*, pp. 37–8 (Macchiavello/Rovere).

also falls into this category, but occurs later as a lead-in to parts 11 and 12; see 'Section 3', below.) Section 1 focuses on Genoa's origins, with parts devoted to 1) the foundation of Genoa; 2) the city's early history; 3) its name (i.e. etymology); 4) its conversion to Christianity; and 5) its growth 'up to now, at the time of its perfection' (rubric, part 5). Part 10, on the growth of the church in Genoa, serves as a kind of pendant to part 5. These six parts establish Genoa's prestigious ancient origin and founding principles, integrating the city's history into the universal narrative of Creation and the ancient world: a refugee from the Trojan War is one of the founders of Genoa, and the city takes part in the Second Punic War as an ally of Rome. This material was mostly ignored by the *GA*: Caffaro started the annals in 1099 *in medias res* with the Genoese expedition to Caesarea during the First Crusade, and only the last annalist, Jacopo Doria, made any attempt to go back and record what was known about the city's origins.[67]

These sections draw first from the somewhat earlier tradition of the universal chronicle, efforts to narrate the entire history of the world that built on each other as time went on. Saint Jerome's translation of Eusebius of Caesarea's *Chronicle* served as the basis for Paul the Deacon's *Historia romana*, which served as the basis for countless later chronicles that simply started with Paul's text and continued where it left off.[68] Other compilations, such as Peter Comestor's *Historia scholastica*, began with biblical history, but were likewise incorporated into the universal narrative. In the thirteenth century, this tradition produced general chronicles such as Martin of Opava's *Chronicle of the popes and emperors* (*MO*), which Jacopo knew and used, but also numerous civic chronicles which began with Creation and simply narrowed their focus to their chosen city in the course of the chronicle, thereby imparting a sense of significance and destiny to the local events narrated in the later parts of the chronicle.

These early sections of Jacopo's work also draw from a genre known as *laus civitatis*, or 'praise of a city': set-pieces of prose or poetry extolling the virtues of a particular city. The earliest of these in Italy date from the ninth and tenth centuries, in works that recount the prestigious founders of cities such as Verona and Milan, compare them favourably to great ancient cities such as Rome and Jerusalem, and describe their

---

67 For a comparison, see Beneš (2011a), pp. 72–87.
68 Eusebius/Jerome, *Chronica*, and Paul the Deacon, *Historia romana*. The latter was continued by Landolfus Sagax, and Landolfus' text was continued in turn by other historians: see Allen (2003).

present greatness in more and more numerically explicit terms over time: while early *laudes* are more abstract, by the end of the thirteenth century works such as Bonvesin da la Riva's *Marvels of Milan* list the impressive numbers of the city's churches, blacksmiths, and communal trumpeters.[69] What the universal chronicle and civic-praise traditions have in common—at least in their Italian manifestations—is their apologetic and epideictic nature: they use history to contextualise and promote their own city, to explain its greatness and present success. These early parts of Jacopo's chronicle are, therefore, very similar to the early parts of other civic chronicles such as Giovanni Villani's (on Florence) and Galvano Fiamma's (on Milan) in: their reliance on myth and etymology; their enthusiasm for ancient Rome, in particular any perceived connections between it and their own cities; and finally, their emphasis on the noble roots and great virtues of their early citizens—in a sense, providing an idealised original community for later citizens to emulate.[70]

Section 2: parts 6–9. Parts 6 to 9 of Jacopo's chronicle provide rules or advice for good citizenship, discussed hierarchically: beginning with government in general (part 6), he addresses good and bad rulership in part 7, good and bad citizenship in part 8, and advice for domestic life in part 9. Part 9 goes further, starting from the relationship between husbands and wives, extending to that between parents and children, and finally addressing that between masters and servants or slaves. In these four parts Jacopo covers the entire social structure of medieval Genoa, from the highest members of the community to the lowest, the most powerful to the least. While the inclusion of this material in a work of history may not be intuitive, this section is packed with the same sorts of exempla and moral commentary that one sees in the more chronologically oriented parts of the *Chronicle*. As we see, anecdotes about Alexander the Great fit equally well into universal history and discussions of the importance of prioritising the common good over self-interest.[71]

---

69 See the poems on Milan and Verona cited in n. 16, above; also Bonvesin da la Riva, *De magnalibus Mediolani*, excerpts of which are translated in Dean, *Towns of Italy*, pp. 11–15.

70 Compare Giovanni Villani, *Chronicle* 1.1–39 (ed. Selfe/Wicksteed [1906], pp. 1–30), and Galvano Fiamma, *Manipulus florum* 3–10 (*RIS* 11.539–44), as well as the works cited in nn. 19 and 20, above.

71 A common theme: see Kempshall (1999) as well as the political works of Remigio de' Girolami and Ptolemy of Lucca (both Dominicans).

In fact, these sections are a fairly standard example of the larger medieval genre of 'advice for rulers': while there are numerous examples across the full span of the Middle Ages (often aimed at kings and princes), the version most common in the communes of medieval Italy was the variation aimed at republican magistrates.[72] As Chris Wickham has recently stressed, the political structure of the early Italian communes was often *ad hoc*, based on immediate needs and Roman precedent—because authors like Cicero and Livy were often the only available guides to how a republic ought to be organised and run.[73] That, combined with the fact that the Romans were considered virtuous citizens and excellent rhetoricians, made ancient history a one-stop source for everything to do with running a republican city-state or participating in its civic discourse. Drawing from it, advice for magistrates and citizens of such republics came in multiple forms: historical (e.g. civic histories), moral or practical (e.g. guidebooks to behaviour), and even visual (e.g. the many thirteenth- and fourteenth-century frescoes which decorate the Palazzo Pubblico in Siena).[74]

Moreover, these were not clearly defined categories: manuscripts had images illustrating their points; frescoes had extensive captions explaining their moral lessons; histories contained extensive moral excursuses and model speeches. Brunetto Latini's *Tresor* (written in French) is an excellent example of a didactic work straddling the genres of moral advice, rhetorical advice, and history—all in the service of instructing people who were not previously educated for the task of public citizenship and republican rule.[75] The fact that a third of Jacopo's supposed 'chronicle of Genoa' is actually moral advice—as much of which derives from his sermons as from Aquinas's treatise *On the government of rulers*[76]—is therefore not only unsurprising but fairly typical of the period.

Aside from the organisation of section 2, which so carefully reflects the social hierarchy of the city, two points make Jacopo's manual of advice for civic stewardship stand out from its contemporaries. First, most such manuals are polemical in the sense that they convey a very clear

---

72 Hertter (1973); Milner (2011).
73 Wickham (2015); see also Beneš (2011a), pp. 31–5.
74 Starn/Partridge (1992), chap. 1.
75 Brunetto Latini, *Li livres dou tresor*; see also Cornish (2011), chap. 5, and Beneš (2011a), chap. 1.
76 *De regimine principum*, translated by Blythe as Ptolemy of Lucca, *On the government of rulers*, and by Dyson as Thomas Aquinas, *On the rule of princes*; I prefer Blythe's translation of the title phrase.

opinion regarding the nature of the ideal political structure: republican or monarchic. These positions can be loosely linked to Guelf v. Ghibelline rivalries—an insistence on the fundamental autonomy of northern Italy's many city-states (typically the Guelf position, where it was easier to ignore the thorny question of papal authority in the secular realm), versus a willingness to recognise imperial sovereignty (typically the Ghibelline position).[77] Jacopo, by contrast, says very clearly that he does not care what type of government or rulers a city has as long as they work for the common good: 'there is no objection to any ruler—of whatever status he might be—while he governs the commonwealth justly and commendably ... The status of a person should not be considered in [choosing] a ruler: rather, the uprightness of his character, the even-handedness of his justice, the mature discernment of his heart, and the greatness of his soul' (part 6.1). Moreover, this firm statement comes directly after a quick review of all the different kinds of rulers Genoa has had over the last couple of hundred years—consuls, podestà, *capitani*, abbots, and so on—and Jacopo's only comment is: 'whether the regime will change again, we do not know; but we ask God that if it must be changed at some point, it should always be exchanged for something better'. With this he takes a firm stand above the kinds of petty politicking that led Genoa's citizens to favour one kind of government over another (the consuls were seen as too aristocratic, the *capitani* as too Ghibelline, and so forth) and emphasises the moral principles behind all good rulership.

The universal reach of those principles is also on clear display in part 9, where Jacopo advises Genoa's citizens on their personal relationships. While Jacopo's advice on how to choose a good wife may now strike us as sexist, if not morally repugnant ('he who has a beautiful wife will always be afraid but he who has a repulsive wife will always be depressed': part 9.1), Steven Epstein has recently observed that Jacopo's inclusion of servants and slaves in this survey—that is, his acknowledgement that a good citizen's moral responsibility extends even to the lowest members of society—is essentially unprecedented.[78] For Jacopo, responsible civic behaviour is not just for the elite members of society, but everyone, in both public and private.

77 Dante's *De monarchia*, written in the early years of the fourteenth century, is a major statement of the latter position; see also Lee (2018). For the republican position, see Milner (2011).
78 For this reason Epstein (2016) labels Jacopo a 'father of social history' (p. 6). Chapter 5 of Epstein's study contains an extensive analysis of part 9 of the *Chronicle*, which he sees as one of the most original parts of the work.

INTRODUCTION

Section 3: parts 11–12. The final section of the chronicle, comprising parts 11 and 12, is by far the longest section of the work, about 40 percent of the whole. It consists of twenty-seven chapters of historical narrative (nineteen chapters in part 11, and eight in part 12) in annalistic form, organised by the tenure of the bishop (part 11) or archbishop (part 12) in which they occurred. In the earlier sections, where Jacopo is frank about the sketchiness of his sources, he often resorts to vague approximations such as 'in the time of this bishop', but later sections often present events year by year. Jacopo's account is not strictly annalistic—he often skips years and sometimes gives events out of order—but the overall effect is fairly linear. This approach follows the well-established tradition of the annalistic civic chronicles discussed above, which originally derived from annual lists such as Easter tables calculating the date of Easter (which changed every year), or the election of Roman consuls (as one sees in Livy).[79]

Part 10, which precedes this section, stylistically falls more into the category of civic history (parts 1–5, discussed as section 1 above), since it summarises a number of disparate events according to a particular civic theme: the growth of the Genoese church, in particular the bishopric and archbishopric. Placed here, however, it provides a foundation for the ecclesiastical framework of the annalistic section that follows: having established in part 10 the moral and institutional authority of the bishops and archbishops of Genoa, both on a civic level and within the broader scheme of the universal church, Jacopo can then use their episcopates (and then archiepiscopates) as a convenient chronological scaffold to drive his narrative of events, from the legendary first bishop of Genoa up to his own time.

Within this framework, he includes a wide variety of reports—from summaries of saints' lives and translations of their relics to elaborate set pieces describing crucial battles, reports of contentious (and not so contentious) papal elections, and key moments in Genoa's continuing conflicts with Pisa and Venice, as well as quick notes about comets, earthquakes, and other unusual natural phenomena. Understandably, his accounts become more precise and less legendary as his narrative approaches his own time. But even within this supposedly more 'factual' section of the chronicle he still finds space for moralising and instruction, as in his account of the career of Pope Joan in part 11.8 (an exemplum of the foolish and presumptuous nature of women) or that of the great

---

79 Coleman (2007).

flagellant movement of 1260 in part 12.6 (a demonstration of God's grace and the moral benefits of repentance). Even here, his focus is civic: only some papal elections are reported, and we hear very little of the careers of Emperor Frederick I Barbarossa or his grandson Frederick II except as they affected the Genoese. Instead, Jacopo records the details of important Genoese treaties (for example, with the Byzantine emperors or the judges of Sardinia) and explains particular local customs and monuments (for example, the origin of the local place name Fontanella in the Muslim sack of Genoa in 934–35).

Jacopo's chronicle thus combines multiple medieval genres—the annal, the universal chronicle, civic praise or encomium, and handbooks of moral and political advice—into a coherent whole, recognisable as such despite its lack of a grand conclusion.[80] This mixing of genres and chronologies results in occasional repetition; parts 4, 5, and 10 highlight particular glorious moments in Genoese history, which then reappear at their proper chronological places in the annals of parts 11 and 12. Sometimes Jacopo provides verbal cross-references, as with the sack of Genoa in 934–35, but more often he does not: the battle of Meloria, a great victory over Pisa in 1284, appears in both part 5.3 and part 12.7 without further comment. The *Chronicle* thus provides Jacopo's Genoese audience with a model for proper citizenship in multiple formats—historical, moral, military, political, and so on. Rhetorically and structurally, it is a *speculum civitatis* (mirror of the city)—one of many works of the period, like Brunetto Latini's *Tresor*, that sought to educate citizens by a mixture of local history, ethics, political advice, and moral exempla. At the same time, Jacopo's careful paralleling of the particular and the universal demonstrates that he thought of the civic realm not as an isolated local environment but as a kind of microcosm paralleling the broader moral continuum of God's Creation.

Jacopo's sources

One major difference between Brunetto Latini's *Tresor* and Jacopo's *Chronicle* is that Latini's work is in the vernacular—French, in fact, although its intended audience was Italian.[81] While civic chronicles were increasingly being written in the vernacular in this period (like Martino

---

80 See above, p. 15.
81 Cornish (2011), p. 77.

da Canal's *Estoires de Venise*, also in French, or Villani's chronicle of Florence, written in Tuscan), Jacopo's *Chronicle* maintains the convention of writing in Latin. While one might think this was simply because of his status as a cleric and archbishop, it also had to do with his cultural formation and surroundings: Latinate culture persisted in Genoa longer than in other cities.[82] Perhaps predictably, then, most of the sources that we can recognise Jacopo consulting and incorporating into his work are also in Latin, whether they are documentary sources such as treaties or more literary ones such as saints' lives.

Identifying the sources used by a medieval author is challenging, particularly for such a many-faceted work as the *Chronicle*. Medieval authors placed no great value on originality or intellectual property; in fact, literary works chiefly convinced their readers by *not* seeming original, but rather appealing to named or unnamed 'authorities', earlier authors accepted as knowledgeable and reliable.[83] Compilation was seen as a natural form of composition, even a high art. Our first challenge, therefore, is that Jacopo only tends to name his sources when doing so makes his narrative more authoritative, i.e. when citing the Bible, patristic authors such as Saint Augustine or Gregory the Great, classical sources such as Cicero or Livy, or recognised authorities such as Bernard of Clairvaux, Peter Comestor, or Sigebert of Gembloux. Citations or borrowings from other sources are either vaguely referenced ('as the chronicler says') or incorporated without any comment at all. Even cited authorities are not a fail-safe source of attribution due to the related practice of increasing the perceived value of later texts by attributing them to well-known authors such as Ambrose or John Chrysostom. A work that Jacopo attributes to Saint Ambrose may therefore not be by Ambrose at all, but rather Pseudo-Ambrose (as we now identify such authors): either an author who claimed to be Ambrose, or an anonymous author whose work was later given that attribution.

The second challenge to identifying Jacopo's sources is the tendency—by medieval authors generally, but by thirteenth-century Dominicans in particular—to compile and then use enormous encyclopaedias of citations and quotations from such authoritative sources. Examples of this phenomenon exist from as far back as late antiquity, with authors such as Valerius Maximus (first century), Solinus (third century), and even Isidore, bishop of Seville (seventh century) compiling information from

82 *CMG*, p. 327 (Petti Balbi).
83 See Epstein (2016), pp. 7–9.

ancient authors into popular compendia. The phenomenon reached its peak with the late thirteenth-century interest in compiling *summae*, of which the works of Vincent of Beauvais, Thomas Aquinas, and Jacopo himself are some of the most famous examples.[84] It is therefore extremely difficult to determine Jacopo's source for a particular fact or exemplum: when offering an anecdote originally found in Caesar's *Gallic wars*, for example, he might be citing Caesar from memory; quoting it from an actual copy of Caesar's *Gallic wars*; or simply adopting the anecdote from an intermediary source such as Valerius Maximus or Vincent of Beauvais.

That said, we can make certain assumptions about the books Jacopo had available to him, and the books he would have come to know well in the course of his education as a Dominican. As Jacopo himself might observe, we can divide these into seven categories:

1. **Local documents.** These are the civic records to which Jacopo himself, as archbishop, would have had personal access: the *Genoese annals* (*GA*) and the books of communal treaties and privileges known as the *Libri iurium*, plus the equivalent registers of privileges pertaining to the (arch)bishopric: the *Liber privilegiorum ecclesiae Ianuensis* (*Book of privileges of the Genoese church*) and the two episcopal registers (*RC* and *RC2*). While they do not constitute documentary evidence from a modern perspective, legends of the early bishops and accounts of relic translations may also be included here, since Jacopo would not have distinguished between these and more 'factual' documents.[85]
2. **Christian authorities.** Probably the most-cited work in Jacopo's *Chronicle* is the Bible, which he would have come to know profoundly in his years of prayer, preaching, and liturgy. While he certainly would have had copies of the Bible (or of individual books of the Bible) around him, he probably quoted most of the biblical citations in the *Chronicle* from memory. (This is the most likely explanation when the words Jacopo quotes do not precisely match the verse in

---

[84] Vincent of Beauvais, *Speculum maius* (*Great mirror*), c. 1235–64, on which see the excellent website www.vincentiusbelvacensis.eu; Thomas Aquinas, *Summa theologiae*, c. 1265–74; and Jacopo, *GL/LA*, c. 1260–67. While the textual tradition of Vincent of Beauvais's *Speculum maius* is complicated, the work is usually divided into the *Speculum doctrinalis* (*Mirror of doctrine*), *Speculum historiale* (*Mirror of history*), and *Speculum naturale* (*Mirror of nature*); I have used these as the basis of citations in this translation.

[85] For example, the legend of Saint Syrus (*LSS*) or account of the translation of the relics of John the Baptist (*HLT*).

the Vulgate—as happens fairly often—or when he conflates two or more verses.) The depth of his theological training is also visible in the broad range of patristic authors he cites, chief among them the Fathers of the Latin church (Augustine, Ambrose, Jerome, and Gregory) but also authors such as Isidore of Seville and the Venerable Bede, as well as Greek Fathers such as John Chrysostom and John of Damascus, whose works he would have known either in Latin translation or by quotation.

3. **Scholastic authorities.** Jacopo cites a range of scholastic authors whose works would have been common in school and university settings: these vary from compendia such as Peter Comestor's *Scholastic history* (a schoolboy-friendly universal-chronicle retelling of the Bible) and Gratian's *Decretum* to the authors of sermons and treatises on particular topics such as Bernard of Clairvaux, Lanfranc of Pavia, and John of Salisbury (chiefly the *Policraticus*).

4. **Jacopo's own previous work.** Especially in the more hagiographical and moralising parts of the *Chronicle*, Jacopo extensively reuses his own material, from both the *GL* and his various collections of sermons. (In some passages the words in the *Chronicle*, the *GL*, and one or more sermons are nearly identical.) This borrowing may be limited to an individual exemplum or it may embrace whole paragraphs or discussions of a topic.

5. **Other encyclopaedias, exemplum collections, and textual compendia.** As mentioned above, Jacopo made regular use of other encyclopaedias and scholarly compilations, especially those by his fellow Dominicans. These include Vincent of Beauvais's *Speculum maius*, the *Summa theologiae* and *On the government of rulers* of Thomas Aquinas, and Martin of Opava's *Chronicle of the popes and emperors* (*MO*). We may also place in this category the dictionaries of Huguccio (twelfth century) and Jacopo's contemporary and fellow Genoese Dominican Giovanni Balbi. Compendia of aphorisms and *sententiae*— most of them late antique—are also included here, such as the collections by or attributed to Varro, Publilius Syrus, Caecilius Balbus, Isidore of Seville, and Sedulius Scottus.

6. **Classical sources.** Jacopo cites a broad range of classical authors in a variety of contexts—from Varro on animal husbandry and Vegetius on military affairs to a whole section on the Punic Wars derived from Livy (part 2.3). While this makes his historical writing different from the *GL*, most of them do not occur in such density as to suggest that Jacopo was working with an extensive library of

classical texts.[86] He was not especially interested in them for either rhetorical or historical purposes, as some of his contemporaries were.[87] Livy and Cicero are the two authors upon which he relied most heavily—Livy for ancient history and Cicero for moral citizenship (chiefly *De officiis / On duties*)—but one can also recognise quotations from Caesar, Horace, Juvenal, Ovid, Seneca, Varro, and Vegetius, along with the compendia of Valerius Maximus and Solinus.

7. **Works of history both ancient and contemporary.** Finally, Jacopo drew on numerous works of late antique and contemporary historiography. First, he used the late antique chronologies of Eusebius/Jerome and Cassiodorus (the *Tripartite history*). The *origo gentis* works of Gregory of Tours (*History of the Franks*) and Paul the Deacon (*History of the Lombards*) also appear. Beyond that, he clearly had access to numerous examples of the universal-chronicle tradition, including the *Roman history* begun by Paul the Deacon and continued by Landolfus Sagax and others, as well as the *Chronicle* of Sigebert of Gembloux (and multiple continuations thereof). Finally, Jacopo seems to have had access to numerous examples of local history and civic chronicle (including Liudprand of Cremona, Landulf Senior on Milan, several histories of Venice, and a few other local chronicles such as the *Chronicon parmense*). With regard to the Crusades and Genoa's interests in the East, he mainly relied upon the *GA*, but seems to have supplemented this with other accounts, such as those of Ralph of Caen and William of Tyre.

Within a work that spans multiple genres and integrates an immense number of disparate sources, however, Jacopo maintains fairly exacting control over a coherent agenda, which makes his chronicle quite different from, for example, that of his Franciscan contemporary Salimbene (1221–c. 1290). While modern scholars have generally characterised Salimbene's as the 'better' or 'more interesting' chronicle, this may be because Salimbene's chronicle is more personal and, in a sense, uncritical: he is quite willing to sacrifice coherent narrative in favour of including juicy bits of gossip. By contrast, Jacopo's chronicle is strictly focused on the city of Genoa and its inhabitants, and a reading of the entire chronicle reveals a number of key themes to which Jacopo regularly returns.

86 Epstein (2016, pp. 38–9, 69), discusses the rarity of references to classical authors in the *GL*.
87 See, for example, the works of Witt (2000, 2012) on early humanism.

INTRODUCTION

First, and perhaps most important, is Genoese independence. Jacopo uses the mythical, ancient, and etymological material in part 1 along with more contemporary material to stress Genoa's natural autonomy and freedom from unnecessary overlordship. He records Genoa's independent foundation by Janus, a Trojan escaping the Trojan War (part 1.3) and the city's later association (entirely voluntary, he assures us) with the Roman republic (part 2.3), and claims that it was one of the earliest fully Christian cities in Italy (part 4.2–3). His insistence therefore spans both secular/political and sacred/ecclesiastical spheres: he not only narrates the proud refusal of the Genoese to grovel before Emperor Frederick Barbarossa (parts 5.3 and 12.1), but also legitimates the emancipation of the diocese of Genoese from the archdiocese of Milan by reclaiming the Milanese saints Nazarius and Celsus for Genoa after their martyrdom by the still-pagan Milanese (part 4.2). Part 10 even ends with an excursus in which Jacopo justifies Genoese regional hegemony (and rebuts outside interference) by linking the borders of the ancient Roman province of Liguria to the contemporary archdiocese.[88] As he says at the beginning of part 10.2, 'just as the city of Genoa rules over many cities, commands many peoples, and is subject to no one—except God in all things and to the emperor in a few—thus it was also fitting that its archbishop should be suffragan to no primate, subject to no one except the highest pontiff'.

Jacopo's claims for the archdiocese are closely related to broader assertions about the orthodox piety of the Genoese and their unwavering support of Mother Church. While this comes out most obviously in part 4 on the Christianisation of Genoa—in which he asserts brazenly that the Genoese adopted Christianity before any other city in Italy, and that there has never been any heresy in the city (part 4.3)—it also comes out in more subtle ways. The recurrent role of the Genoese as gallant rescuers of popes in distress (parts 5.3, 10.2, 11.18, 12.1, and 12.5) contrasts strongly with the perfidious behaviour of the Ghibelline Pisans, who constantly work against the papacy, usually but not always on behalf of the emperor. Likewise, the Milanese generally appear as either pagans or heretics (part 4.3).

The Genoese, by contrast, demonstrate their faith and orthodoxy in their civic devotions (in the care and attention which they devote to patron saints and their relics, for example), in their intimate relations

---

88 Fig. 2 shows the outlines of the modern Italian region of Liguria, which roughly corresponds to the two territories discussed by Jacopo.

with numerous popes, and in their enthusiastic participation in campaigns against the Muslims, whether of the western Mediterranean (north Africa, the Balearics, Spain) or the eastern (the Crusades). The crusading sections of the *Chronicle*, in fact, sometimes read like a litany of exotic places liberated from the infidel by the Genoese. For example, Jacopo's summary of the First Crusade (1095–99) reads: 'thus the Genoese, inspired to avenge such a great injury to Christ and to seize the tomb of Christ out of the hands of the Saracens, valiantly armed forty galleys and took Jerusalem and made Godfrey of Bouillon king. They then took Acre and Gibelet, and also Cersona, Arsuf, and Tartus. Jerusalem was captured in the year of the Lord 1099' (part 5.2). While not exactly inaccurate, the passage may qualify as one of the most biased accounts of the campaign ever written.

Jacopo is also very clear about what he sees as the moral superiority of the Genoese character. Some of this is innate—for example, when he acknowledges that a particular naval defeat occurred because the Genoese had enlisted 'the people of Lombardy' as crews on their ships, who proved to be incompetent landlubbers: 'unfamiliar with the nautical art and inexperienced in naval warfare, they were just as ignorant of rowing as they were useless in fighting ... beset by stomach upset and headache'. Henceforth the Genoese only employed 'their own people and those of their own region, and thus they have subsequently had many victories over the Venetians and Pisans and their galleys' (part 5.3). But according to Jacopo the Genoese could also claim moral superiority through their adherence to honour, which distinguished them from the Pisans (who break treaties, part 12.2) and the Venetians (who are lying and underhanded, part 5.3). Particularly when speaking of the Pisans, Venetians, and Milanese, Jacopo can often be quite snide—as, for example, when he narrates the arrival of the Trojan refugee Antenor in the Adriatic (part 1.3). While Livy simply notes that Antenor founded Padua, and contemporary Venetian accounts such as that of Marco (*Prima edificacio*, 1292) appropriated that story to claim that Antenor must have founded Venice first, Jacopo places his own twist on the narrative: 'when Antenor arrived in the Venetian lands and found swampy places, he did not wish to live there', so 'sailing between the islands and up a certain river called the Brenta, he found a pleasing plain, and, deciding to make his home there, built a certain city in that place which he called Padua'.

Finally, we should note the role played by miracles in the *Chronicle*. As the author of the *Golden legend* and several relic treatises, Jacopo places great importance on miracles in his narrative of Genoese history. For example, of four pirates condemned to hanging in Genoa in 1230, the two who commended their souls to the protection of Genoa's patron saint John the Baptist were saved and eventually set free (part 12.4). However, while they demonstrate the omnipotence of God and the benefits of piety, these miracles do not just serve a religious or devotional purpose; rather, they also act as physical manifestations of the divine favour bestowed upon the Genoese. The two pirates who appeal to Genoa's patron saint are saved; or, in another case (part 12.3), a Pisan pirate who had stolen a piece of the True Cross from Saladin is miraculously forced to hand it over to the Genoese—not to mention the many miracles performed by the saintly early bishops of Genoa, whose bones are preserved in the cathedral of San Lorenzo. Miracles—and the saints and relics who work them—therefore serve a civic function as well here, as physical and/or historical proof of God's great favour toward the Genoese.

Jacopo's *Chronicle* thus demonstrates the didactic purpose of history as it was imagined in the Middle Ages. As articulated by Livy, 'what chiefly makes the study of history wholesome and useful is that one sees the lessons of every kind of experience set forth as on a visible monument; from these one may choose for oneself and for one's own state what to imitate, and to mark for avoidance what is shameful in both conception and result'.[89] Jacopo's chronicle recalls the city's glorious past for his Genoese audience, reassures them of God's favour toward them, and urges them to honour God and their ancestors by continuing in the same manner. In cases where the past was not so glorious (such as the Venetian defeat), he explains what happened and how citizens may avoid such disasters in future (avoid hiring Lombards).

In particular, Jacopo's chronicle encourages peace and concord among the notoriously fractious Genoese. Wherever possible, he stresses the virtues of unity and collective action. This sense of united purpose is most visible when Jacopo is recounting potential threats to Genoese autonomy—for example, its reinforcement of the city's defences against Frederick Barbarossa (part 12.1) or the preparations for war with Venice (part 5.3): 'then the son followed the father, the father the son, and the brother the brother, all with wondrous eagerness. The entire nobility of the city joined this renowned naval force: all the flower of its youth, all its popular officials, all the strength of the Riviera'.

---

89 Livy, *Ab urbe condita*, prologue 10.

Yet Jacopo does the same in less fraught circumstances, emphasising the achievements of the collectivity over the exploits of the individual. His account of the construction of the new cathedral of San Lorenzo (fig. 5; part 11.18), for instance, notes not only that the church is 'of great sanctity, dignity, and authority' but 'furthermore, we believe that the commune of Genoa created a work as sumptuous as the noble church of San Lorenzo, rather than any particular person'. Even when recounting individual exploits that redound to the honour of the city, Jacopo stresses that such heroes are acting as leaders of 'the Genoese' on behalf of the commune. Guglielmo Embriaco, hero of the siege of Caesarea during the First Crusade, is described as the *consul* (leader) of the Genoese force there: while his daring encourages the rest of his crew, the victory is nonetheless a collective one, 'and thus they took the city' (part 11.17). The same is true of Jacopo's account of Oberto Doria's victory at the battle of Meloria (part 11.6), which Jacopo concludes by noting that 'the Genoese displayed no ostentation or arrogance on account of this victory; rather, they praised the mighty works of God, who alone creates great wonders' (part 5.3).

As Stefania Bertini Guidetti has observed, one of the keys to Jacopo's approach is his own conception of the office of archbishop: to lead by example, to instruct his flock in the paths of virtue, and to serve as a link between the Genoese and God.[90] In particular, in his role as archbishop he could provide the kind of continuity in civic leadership that Genoa's shifting political system ('consuls or podestà or *capitani* or abbots', part 6.1) could not. I would extend Bertini Guidetti's argument to suggest that Jacopo took an Augustinian view of his role, mediating between the earthly city of Genoa and the heavenly city of God. While the traditional reading of Augustine's great metaphor of the 'city of God' is that people should abandon concern for the present material life ('the earthly city') in favour of fixing their attention on life after death ('the heavenly city'), the preachers and moralists of late medieval Italy often encouraged urban denizens to shape their own cities—the urban community in both its material and human forms—in the image of the New Jerusalem: a heavenly city here on earth.[91] According to Jacopo, therefore, Genoa had a strong foundation—architectural, economic, historical, saintly—but it also had much work to do, and his *Chronicle* was intended to help its citizens build the best *civitas* that they

---

90 Bertini Guidetti (1997a).
91 Frugoni (1991); Lilley (2009). Jansen (2018), p. 27, and Lee (2018), p. 105, note from different perspectives the heavenly benefits linked to earthly peacemaking.

could, 'to the honour of the commune of Genoa' (parts 12.5, 12.8, and elsewhere).

Note on the text and translation

This translation is based on the Latin text of Monleone's 1941 edition (*JVC*), correlated with Bertini Guidetti's 1995 Italian translation (*CCG*). I have deviated from Monleone's 'official' text only by including the appendix, a description of the events of 1298 inserted at the end of part 5 in one manuscript by a later scribe. Where appropriate, I have also consulted the Latin text of the *GA* (*FSI* 11–14 bis) as well as its several partial English translations (*HP*, *JD*) and recent Italian translation.[92] I have sought to create a translation that is close enough to the literal meaning of Jacopo's Latin to retain the feel of thirteenth-century Dominican composition—which is highly structured and repetitive—while still producing a narrative that is readable in twenty-first-century English.

While, like all translation, this is in some ways an impossible task, I hope I have achieved a reasonably successful balance between two very different idioms. In practice, this has meant, first, occasionally breaking up Jacopo's longer, more periodic sentences into shorter sentences that make more sense in English, since English cannot sustain the same weight of multiple dependent clauses that Latin can. Secondly, it has also meant varying conjunctions and connecting phrases, since when translated literally, Jacopo's near-constant use of conjunctions—especially *vero* ('indeed'), *enim* ('also'), *nam* ('for' or 'accordingly'), *et ideo* ('and therefore'), *unde* ('whence'), and *quapropter* ('by reason of which')—makes for repetitive and exhausting English prose. Some degree of editorial interpretation is also inevitable when some of those conjunctions have multiple, sometimes contradictory meanings (e.g. *autem*, which can mean 'and also' or 'however'). I have similarly sometimes varied or omitted the many instances of reference words such as *dicta/supradicta* ('aforesaid'), and substituted names for pronouns (or vice versa), since the grammatical differences between Latin and English can make those references either superfluous or newly necessary.

As much as possible, however, I have attempted to retain features of the *Chronicle*'s language, such as Jacopo's grammatical parallelism—for example, in the table of contents in the *Chronicle*'s prologue—because

---

92 In the series *Memorie genovesi*, edited by Gabriella Airaldi (2000–).

it is a key part of his Latin style, and highly representative of late medieval Dominican composition (homiletic or otherwise). I have also indicated certain potentially difficult or revealing Latin terms in parentheses in the text, seeking to be as transparent as possible about Jacopo's original word choices and my own translation choices based on them. My translation reflects Jacopo's inconsistent use of the first person (both 'I' and 'we'). Finally, I have retained the convention of rendering initial I as J—thus Jacopo, Janua, and Janus instead of Iacopo, Ianua, and Ianus—with the single exception of the Latin noun *ianua* (gate).

The division of the chronicle into parts and chapters is Jacopo's own work. Similarly—as far as we can ascertain from the earliest manuscripts—the headings and subheadings (rubrics) are all original to the chronicle, although the precise words of those headings often vary between manuscripts. Within each chapter, however, the paragraph divisions are my own, to increase ease of reading.

JACOPO DA VARAGINE
CHRONICLE OF THE CITY OF GENOA

PROLOGUE

Here begins the chronicle of the city of Genoa.

By the wisdom of the Gospel we are instructed not to hide beneath laziness or idleness that talent of intelligence which is entrusted to us by God; rather, let us return to God the profit of interest multiplied, presenting it at the table of the Holy Scriptures.[1] For the Lord rewards those who multiply their talents, but condemns the servant who dawdles at his task. Therefore, although we have been brought back from the solitude of the cloister to public office—by the will of the Lord, or at least with his permission—we must not always devote ourselves to public matters, nor continually involve ourselves in secular causes, because it is not always appropriate to pursue things destined to perish; rather is it better to cultivate in the fields those things whose fruits will persist in heaven, as the Lord says: *Do not work for food that perishes but for that which endures in eternal life.*[2] It is therefore fitting to take refuge occasionally in the tranquillity of the mind and *to see* with the mind's eye *how sweet the Lord is.*[3]

Furthermore, from time to time it is useful to commit to writing certain things that can assist the education of their readers and the edification of their hearers.[4] Thinking, therefore, and considering with careful

---

1 An extended economic pun on the Latin word *talentum*, used here both literally (a unit of currency) and figuratively ('aptitude'), echoing the parable in Matthew 25.14–30. While Epstein asserts that *talentum* did not acquire its figurative meaning until later (2016, pp. 176–7), dictionaries of medieval Latin (Du Cange, Niermeyer) provide numerous examples of figurative use. The notion of applying financial strategies—especially interest, banned under canon law—to the spiritual gifts of God seems particularly apt for the archbishop of a great mercantile city.

2 John 6.27. Jacopo's statement that he was reluctantly 'brought back' into the world is a common literary trope (cf. Gregory the Great, *Dialogues* 1.1). It may also be accurate: Jacopo reportedly refused the nomination in 1286, only accepting when nominated a third time in 1292.

3 An amalgam of Psalm 33.9 and 1 Peter 2.3. On the former, see Augustine, *City of God* 21.24.

4 This distinction between readers and hearers suggests that Jacopo's intended audience included both the educated and the illiterate to whom it might be read. On the didactic purpose of history: Smalley (1974), pp. 15–20; Allen (2003), pp. 35–9.

thought how there are many cities in Italy of which the ancient historians make much mention, we are amazed that so very little can be found written by them about the city of Genoa [fig. 3], as renowned, noble, and powerful as it is. We believe that the reason for this is the fact that the city of Genoa, although now very great and powerful, was in the beginning only small and modest. The historians who wrote in antiquity did not care to make extensive mention of villages and small settlements, but only exerted themselves to describe large and famous cities.[5]

In reading the histories of the commune of Genoa and considering various chronicles while also investigating the words of other authors, however, we have found certain details about the city of Genoa that we have decided to transcribe in the present fashion: among these are expressed something of the city of Genoa, as well as its age and founder; a rationale for its name is given, and many useful things are explained.[6] And since we mentioned the form of government by which Genoa is ruled and administered, we have accordingly included some general examples of the government and its rulers, wherein is also placed a general exhortation by which citizens may be usefully instructed. Finally, at the end of this work we have placed the names and dates of the bishops and archbishops who have presided in the city of Genoa up to our own times.[7] And so that whatever is wished for may be more easily found, we have arranged to divide the present chronicle into twelve parts and multiple chapters.

The chapters of part one. Part one describes those by whom the city of Genoa was founded and constructed. This part has four chapters: chapter one explains who the first founders and builders of the city were. Chapter two relates how Janus, first king of Italy, constructed and built Genoa. Chapter three relates how Janus, a citizen of Troy, later expanded this foundation and improved it. Chapter four relates how the god Janus, an idol of the Romans, was once venerated in Genoa.

The chapters of part two. Part two describes the age and great antiquity of the construction of Genoa. This part has three chapters:

---

5 See the similar passage in the official annals of Genoa (*GA*) by Jacopo's contemporary Jacopo Doria: *DGA*, pp. 3–4. Jacopo Doria (*DBI* 41.391–6) was the archivist brother of the naval heroes Oberto and Lamba Doria (parts 5.3 and 12.8, below).

6 'Histories of the commune' probably denotes the *GA*, which were begun by Caffaro di Rustico in 1099 and continued up to Jacopo's time (see previous note). Portions of the *GA* have been translated in *HP* and *JD*.

7 This paragraph offers an abstract of Jacopo's history followed by a summary of each of the twelve books of the work. Its methodical, hierarchic structure is the trademark of a Dominican trained in the *ars praedicandi* (art of preaching), which emphasised logic, categorisation, and numbered examples: Murphy (1974), pp. 310–55; Mulchahey (1998), pp. 400–79; Wenzel, *Art of preaching*, pp. 37–41, 243–5.

PROLOGUE   43

the first chapter discusses the era in which the city was built; the second, the era in which it was expanded; and the third, how it was destroyed by the Carthaginians or Africans but rebuilt by the Romans, and when these events occurred.

The chapters of part three. Part three describes how the city came to be distinguished with such a name. This part has four chapters: chapter one gives the opinion of those who say that Janua [Genoa] is named after Janus, king of Italy, who built it, or else after Janus the citizen of Troy, who improved it. Chapter two gives the opinion of those who say that Janua is called after Janus, an idol of the Romans who was venerated in Genoa in antiquity. Chapter three gives the opinion of those who say that Janua is so named because it is the port or entrance into Lombardy. Chapter four explains why it bears the name of Genua in all the books of the ancients.[8]

The chapters of part four. Part four describes the time in which the city of Genoa was converted to the faith of Christ. This part has three chapters: the first explains how the whole world was enslaved to idolatry; the second explains how Genoa was the first city, or one of the first cities in Italy, to convert to the faith of Christ; and the third supports this same assertion through reason.

The chapters of part five. Part five describes the three different states in which the city of Genoa has existed according to the vagaries of time. This part has three chapters: the first discusses the city's nature and size (*qualis et quanta*) at the time of its founding; the second discusses its nature and size during the time of its growth, and the third discusses its nature and size as it was and is now at the time of its perfection.

The chapters of part six. Part six describes and addresses the secular government of the city of Genoa. This part has three chapters: the first relates how the city of Genoa has been governed by a variety of regimes; the second explains that it is safer to be ruled by one than by the many, unless that many should be united for good; and the third explains the danger that arises from a bad government, and the profit that arises from a good one.

The chapters of part seven. Part seven describes how the rulers of a city should act. This part has four chapters: the first explains that those rulers should be powerful and magnanimous so that they can

---

8 Genoa appears in the classical sources as *Genua*, but by the eleventh century the standard Latin form was *Janua*. This is why Jacopo's legends all involve founders named Janus, and also why Jacopo needs to explain the earlier form *Genua* (part 3.4, below).

govern without fear; the second, that they ought to be God-fearing; the third, that they ought to be truthful in everything; and the fourth, that they ought to hate all avarice and cupidity.

The chapters of part eight. Part eight describes how the citizens and inhabitants of the city ought to act. This part has three chapters: the first demonstrates that citizens ought to be thoughtful and prudent in making decisions; the second, that they should not be subject to vice but disciplined in virtue; and the third, that they ought to exhibit the greatest zeal for the commonwealth.

The chapters of part nine. Part nine describes familial and domestic matters. This part has six chapters: the first addresses how a wife should be guided, and how one may know if she is good or not; the second, how she should be looked after; the third, how both spouses ought to love one another; the fourth, how they ought to live in peace; the fifth, how parents ought to behave toward their children and children toward their parents; the sixth, how masters ought to behave toward their servants or slaves, and servants toward their masters.

The chapters of part ten. Part ten describes and addresses the spiritual governance of the city of Genoa. This part has two chapters: the first explains the time in which the city was awarded the honour of a bishopric, while the second explains the time in which it was raised to the dignity of an archbishopric.

The chapters of part eleven. Part eleven describes the dates, names, and orders of all the bishops who are recorded as having existed in the city of Genoa; this part has as many chapters as the names of the bishops who are included there.

The chapters of part twelve. Part twelve describes the dates, names, and orders of all the archbishops who have presided in the city of Genoa up to our own time; this part has as many chapters as there are names of archbishops.

Now that these things have been introduced and summarised, the entire contents of this chronicle are accessible and manifest. It is said that the word 'chronicle' comes from the Greek *cronicon*, which is 'time' (*tempus*) in Latin; thus a book which describes the doings of many different times is called a chronicle.[9]

---

9 Isidore of Seville, *Etymologies* 5.28. The encyclopaedic *Etymologies* was a standard medieval reference work. On the importance of Isidore, Jerome, and Bede for historians in the Middle Ages: Allen (2003).

PART ONE: ON THE FOUNDATION OF GENOA

Part one, as stated above, describes those by whom the city of Genoa was founded and constructed. This part has four chapters: chapter one explains who the first founders and builders of the city were. Chapter two relates how Janus, the first king of Italy, constructed and built Genoa. Chapter three relates how Janus, a citizen of Troy, later expanded this foundation and improved it. Chapter four relates how Janus, who was a god of the Romans, was once venerated in Genoa.

Here begins the chronicle of the city of Genoa, which was compiled by the venerable father and lord Brother Jacopo of the Order of Preachers, archbishop of Genoa.

Chapter one: Those who were the first founders of the city. God, who created all things out of nothing, daily constructs new cities for the care of men, and protects these edifices by the ministry of heavenly spirits. For he protects individual people through the care of the angels; he protects cities and specific places through the care of the archangels; and he protects kingdoms and provinces through the care of the principalities,[1] according to the word of the prophet, who says: *Unless the Lord protects the city, he who protects it watches in vain. Unless the Lord builds the house, he who builds it labours in vain.*[2] Therefore every city has a dual founder: a principal one, namely God himself, and a secondary one, namely an earthly man.

For the first man who built a city before the Flood was Cain, son of Adam, who built a city that he called by the name of his son Enoch, as is reported in Genesis.[3] From this it is manifestly clear that at this time there were many men on the earth, although their genealogy is not recorded. For Cain would not have been able to build the city unless many people already existed who helped him and who lived in the city.

---

1 Angels, archangels, and principalities are the lowest of nine orders of angels in Pseudo-Dionysius' fifth-century *De coelesti hierarchia*; cf. Isidore, *Etymologies* 7.5 or Thomas Aquinas, *Summa theologiae* 1.108.

2 Psalm 126.1, inverted.

3 Genesis 4.17, paraphrased.

And this Cain amassed riches from the robbery of men and taught his sons to plunder likewise. Out of envy, this Cain killed his brother [Abel]; their father Adam is said to have mourned his death for one hundred years.[4] And because Cain was hated by all—first because he had killed his brother out of malice, and afterward because he committed robbery— he built a city and fortified it with walls so that he might be safe.

Later, after the Flood, the first man who built a city was Nimrod the great-grandson of Noah, who was a giant.[5] He was one hundred cubits in height, as it says in the *Scholastic history*.[6] This man, after the Flood, was the first to wish to rule among men. He taught his sons not to worship God, but rather to venerate fire, telling them that human happiness does not come from God, but rather that man may acquire it through his own virtue.[7] This Nimrod first built Babylon and began to reign there. He consulted among those of his own kind in order to build a very tall tower up to the heavens, so that they would be safe from every flood. There was only one language at that time, but God confused their tongues and divided them into eighty-two languages, so that when they could no longer understand one another, they totally abandoned the construction of this tower.[8]

For before this all men spoke in the single language of Adam, which was the Hebrew tongue, and Abraham, Isaac, and Jacob and the rest who were born of their line—that is, the Jewish people—all spoke this language; and thus as there was a single first language, so shall there be a single final language, according to the saying of the Apostle [Paul]: *After the Judgment, all tongues shall cease.*[9] Indeed, Saint Isidore says that after the Judgment all tongues will cease, and only the Hebrew tongue will remain; as it was in the beginning, so shall it remain at the

---

4 Most of Jacopo's narrative of Creation and early human history comes from the *Historia scholastica* by Paris schoolmaster Peter Comestor (d. *c.* 1178): *PL* 198.1045–1722. A prose work of sacred history intended for students, the *Historia scholastica* follows the narrative of the Bible while incorporating information from many other sources both Christian and pagan. Here Jacopo includes Comestor's statement (*Historia scholastica* 1.25, *PL* 198.1076) that Adam mourned Abel for one hundred years, which is not in Genesis but entered other Creation narratives during late antiquity.

5 Genesis 10.1–10; 1 Chronicles 1.10.

6 *Historia scholastica* 1.37 (*PL* 198.1088), although Comestor actually says that Nimrod was ten cubits high (a cubit was the distance from the elbow to the fingertips).

7 As in n. 4 above, Nimrod's connection with fire worship appeared in Creation narratives in late antiquity.

8 Genesis 11.1–9.

9 1 Corinthians 13.8.

end.[10] For this reason, indeed, some say that this language is natural to man, because Adam acquired it at his creation. And thus they say that if an infant is reared in a separate place where he cannot hear others speaking, when he has grown up he will speak the Hebrew language. But this is a falsehood, because such a boy would speak no language at all, from which we learn that speaking another language is not accomplished by nature, but by human art.[11]

So, with the passage of time after the construction of Babylon, many others built cities—such as Ninus, who built Nineveh, and many others after him.[12] Furthermore, many of these came by boat to Italy and there they built many cities; among their number was Janus. It must be noted, however, that there were supposedly three Januses. The first is the Janus who came from eastern lands to Italy, and reigned there first. The second is a certain prince who was a citizen of Troy, who came to Italy after the destruction of Troy. The third is the king of the Epirotes,[13] who came to Rome, and after whose death the Romans deified and venerated as a god. We will proceed briefly and in order with the stories of these three Januses.[14]

Chapter two: How Janus, first king of Italy, built Genoa. The first Janus was a certain prince who came to Italy from eastern lands. For after the Flood, the number of men in the East multiplied and cities were constructed, and of these many came into Italy, among them three princes who are said to have arrived. The first was Nimrod, the second was Janus, and the third was Saturn.[15] Nimrod was the great-grandson of Noah, because Noah begat Ham, Ham begat Cush, and Cush begat Nimrod, as it is written in the book of Genesis.[16] And this Nimrod was

10 Isidore, *Etymologies* 9.1.13, or Pseudo-Bede, *De linguis gentium* (*PL* 90.1179–82).
11 According to Salimbene, Emperor Frederick II conducted language-acquisition experiments of this sort: *Chronicle* 510, p. 535.
12 Augustine, *City of God* 16.3; also Eusebius/Jerome, *Chronica* 2016 BC.
13 From Epirus, in Thrace (Greece).
14 A classic example of the Dominican fondness for categorisation, numbering, and parallel structure (prologue n. 7). Jacopo's ability to accept and celebrate three different civic founders all named Janus also reflects medieval scholars' understanding of Creation as a reflection of God's divine plan: Beneš (2011a), pp. 75–8.
15 Janus and Saturn appear in Eusebius/Jerome (*Chronica* 1179 BC), as well as Paul the Deacon, *Historia romana* 1.1, p. 5: Beneš (2011a), pp. 70–1. The addition of Nimrod is unusual, however; Jacopo is probably trying to incorporate his next anecdote into the better-known chronology.
16 Genesis 5.31–2, 9.18–19, 10.1–10.

very greedy and eager to dominate [others], so he told his sons to go into Italy and bring it under their dominion. According to this view, his sons and many others came to Italy in boats and ships, and—according to what we read in a certain chronicle—they built there a certain city that they called Ravenna.[17] In the name of this city there are three syllables, each of which stands for an idea. The first syllable—that is, *Ra*—stands for 'boats' (*rates*); the second—that is, *Ve*—stands for 'they came' (*venerunt*); the last—that is, *Na*—stands for 'ships' (*naves*). All of which is to say: Those who built this city, which is called Ravenna, came in boats and ships.

The second prince who came from the East into Italy was Janus, who came into Italy in the time of Moses and reigned there first of all—although some histories seem to say that this Janus reigned in the time of Abraham.[18] Eventually arriving in these parts, he built the Genoese city, which he called Janicula after his own name. Solinus makes this point clearly in his book *On the wonders of the world*, where he says: *Who does not know that Janicula was founded and named by Janus, and Saturnia by Saturn?*[19] See how Solinus not only asserts this fact, but also states that no one should be ignorant of the fact that Janus built Janicula and named it after himself. Also, he called it not Janua but Janicula, using the diminutive on account of its small size—just as Rome, at the time of its first construction, when it was still small, was called Romula; and afterward, when it grew, it was called Roma.[20] Similarly, our own city was very small when it was first built, so it was called Janicula; and afterward when it grew, it was called Janua. And if by chance some people will try to argue that Solinus speaks of a different Janicula built by Janus, king of Italy, and not of our own city—this claim cannot stand, because in all of Italy no other city or land is to be found which

---

17 Jacopo does not specify the source of this unusual anecdote: Mannucci (1904), p. 41, suggests Papias or Eutropius; while the works of both are now lost, Jacopo cites them in the *GL*.

18 That is, much earlier than Moses.

19 Solinus, *De mirabilibus mundi* 2.5. Since Solinus's text reads *Janiculum*, Jacopo must have misread or misquoted the text as *Janiculam*, a Latin form of *Janicula*. Maintaining a distinction between *Janicula* (now Genoa) and *Janiculum* (a hill in Rome) is fundamental to Jacopo's argument.

20 While ancient authors agreed that Rome was named after Romulus, Jacopo appears to have applied logic and the principles of Latin grammar to invent the idea that Rome (*Roma*) was originally founded in the diminutive as *Romula*, thus echoing his idea for the early name of Genoa. Jacopo draws numerous parallels between medieval Genoa and ancient Rome, a benchmark of urban prosperity and magnificence: Beneš (2011a), pp. 13–36.

PART ONE: ON THE FOUNDATION OF GENOA   49

is called Janua or Janicula, and thus the reference must be understood to refer to our own land. It is true that in Rome there was a certain temple called the Janiculum, which the Romans built in honour of their god Janus, as Saint Isidore says and as will be discussed below.[21] On the other hand, if others try to claim that this Janiculum is the same Janicula of which Solinus speaks, which Janus the king of Italy built, that claim cannot stand either, because Janus the king of Italy lived six hundred years and more before Rome was built—as is attested clearly in the chronicles—and thus it is impossible that he could have built this temple. Besides, Solinus does not say that Janus built Janiculum, but Janicula. Janiculum refers to the temple, while Janicula refers to the city.

The third prince who came from the lands of the East was Saturn. This Saturn reigned first in Crete and on other neighbouring islands.[22] He had three sons—namely Jove [Jupiter], Neptune, and Pluto—among whom he divided his kingdom.[23] Thus he gave Jove Mount Olympus and the area around it, so after his death Jove was called the god of Olympus. To his second son Neptune, he gave the oceans, so after his death Neptune was called the god of the waters. To his third son Pluto, he gave all the forests; so that after his death Pluto was called the god of the underworld.

Now, the first son—that is, Jupiter—was afraid that his father Saturn would beget other sons, so he made him a eunuch; later he even tried to kill him, so Saturn fled that place, came into Italy, and lived secretly in the areas of Tuscany near Sutri.[24] For this reason that part of Italy took on the name of Latium, from 'lying hidden' (*latendus*).[25] Afterward, Saturn reigned in Italy after the death of Janus. This Saturn was the first to teach men to build themselves houses, to cultivate fields, and to plant vines, since he had ordered brought from Greece seeds for growing wheat and vines for planting. Before this men had lived in

---

21 Isidore, *Etymologies* 15.1.50.
22 The ancient Roman god of calendars, seasons, and time.
23 This genealogy aligns Saturn with the Greek god Cronos: Macrobius, *Saturnalia* 1.8.6–10.
24 A city about fifty kilometres northwest of Rome.
25 Isidore, *Etymologies* 14.4.18 and Landolfus Sagax, *Historia romana* 1.1, p. 3, both of which ultimately derive from Virgil, *Aeneid* 8.319–23. Much of Jacopo's material for the primeval history of Italy derives from the fourth-century historian Eutropius, whose *Breviarium historiae romanae* was updated in the eighth century by Paul the Deacon and in the tenth by Landolfus Sagax. As it is impossible to know what Jacopo's immediate source was, I have provided citations to Landolfus here.

caves and in huts made of branches, and they ate nuts and roots in the manner of beasts. This Saturn first taught men in Italy how to make money, ships, sails, and shields; for this reason after his death the pagans made him into a god, and they dedicated divine cults to him as a god.[26]

Chapter three: How Janus, a citizen of Troy, improved Genoa.
The second Janus was a certain citizen of Troy who came into Italy after Troy's destruction. For as the ancient histories relate, and as the poet also attests, there was a certain man in Troy by the name of Paris, who was the son of Priam, king of Troy.[27] When Paris' mother Hecuba was carrying him in her womb, she saw in a dream flames coming out of her womb, which set afire the entire city of Troy.[28] When she told this to the priest in the temple he responded that she would bear a son through whom Troy would be destroyed. Thus when Paris was born, his parents were very afraid of this and they sent him into the forest to be brought up among shepherds. When he had grown up, he became a very capable young man who used to beat all the boys his own age in all the games.

At that time Peleus, the father of Achilles, took Thetis as his wife, as Ovid tells; and to his nuptials he invited Jove, Neptune, Apollo, and Mercury, who were called gods, and three very beautiful girls, that is, Juno, Pallas [Minerva], and Venus, who were called goddesses.[29] But he refused to invite the goddess of strife and discord [Eris]; and indignant, she created a golden apple on which she wrote, 'To be given to the most beautiful'.[30] And she threw this apple into the midst of those women, whereupon each claimed it was intended for herself. Jupiter decided that they should go to the wise Paris, who was with the shepherds, and Paris himself should pronounce a fair judgment among them. Thus when they arrived, Juno, who was the daughter of Saturn, promised Paris that if he judged in her favour she would give him the kingdom

---

26 Macrobius, *Saturnalia* 1.7.19–25, Isidore, *Etymologies* 16.18.3, and Landolfus Sagax, *Historia romana* 1.1, pp. 3–4.
27 Virgil, in the *Aeneid* (*c.* 20 BC).
28 The story of Hecuba's dream, which appears in Homer's *Iliad*, survived in the west in late antique sources such as the sixth-century *Excidium Troiae* (pp. xliii, 4); also *Vatican mythographers*, p. 187.
29 Ovid, *Metamorphoses* 11.221–65; recapitulated in *Vatican mythographers*, pp. 89, 195–8.
30 *TIE* 3604; *Excidium Troiae*, pp. xix (n. 27), xlii, 3. The Latin phrase that Jacopo uses, *pulchriori detur*, does not appear in any classical source, but rather derives from one of the many medieval versions of the story; see e.g. the early fourteenth-century *volgarizzamento*, the *Istorietta trojana* (p. 382): Cornish (2011), pp. 89–98.

PART ONE: ON THE FOUNDATION OF GENOA   51

of Crete. Pallas, the goddess of wisdom, promised to give him great wisdom. Venus, the goddess of love, promised to give him Helen, the most beautiful woman [in the world], the wife and bride of Menelaus.[31] Then Paris pronounced judgment in favour of Venus. And after this the aforesaid Paris, wishing to claim Helen for himself as promised, went into Greece, stole the aforementioned Helen, and took her to Troy.[32] This same Helen was the wife of Menelaus, king of the Lacedemonians; and thus because of this, all Greece was stirred up and [the Greeks] plotted among themselves against Troy. Finally the Greeks all gathered together, armed 1,200 ships, and besieged Troy in force, remaining at that siege for ten years.

Indeed, when the aforementioned Helen was brought to Troy, the philosophers who were there went to see her. And when they caught sight of how beautiful she was, they covered their faces with their mantles, saying, 'Let us flee! Let us flee!' For they knew that the sight of beauty provokes men to unlawful acts; they also knew that the temptation of lust is better conquered by flight than by resistance.[33] For although soldiers may conquer their enemies by resisting them, there are also certain soldiers called Parthians who conquer their enemies by fleeing from them: they are very skilled in the art of archery, and when they flee from their enemies, they turn back toward them and shoot arrows at them—thus they flee while shooting and shoot while fleeing, and in this way they come out the victors.[34] In the same way temptations to other sins may be overcome by resistance, according to what the blessed James says: *Resist the devil, and he will flee from you.*[35] But the temptation of lust is better overcome by flight, according to what the Apostle says: *Flee fornication.*[36]

Thus the Greeks besieged Troy, a most famous and powerful city, with a strong army, and they captured the besieged city, and utterly destroyed the captured city. For this reason, because of the glory of this victory, the Greeks took to counting their years from the capture of Troy. Just as the Jews count their years from the liberation out of Egypt or the

31 King of Sparta (Lacedaemon), in Greek mythology.
32 Ovid, *Heroides* 17, a letter supposedly from Helen to Paris.
33 1 Corinthians 6.18.
34 The 'Parthian shot': a technique Jacopo may have known from accounts of the crusades, since western chroniclers often conflated the Turks with the ancient Parthians: Hillenbrand, *Crusades*, p. 512; Ralph of Caen, *Gesta Tancredi* 74, 86.
35 James 4.7.
36 1 Corinthians 6.18 again; see also *SD*, fol. 329r.

handing down of the law; the Romans count from the foundation of the City [i.e. Rome]; and Christians count from the Incarnation of the Lord—so the Greeks have counted from the capture of Troy.

After Troy was destroyed, many escaped and set out for diverse parts of the world. Among others who left there were three princes named Antenor, Aeneas, and Janus, who by sailing came to Italy seeking new dwelling places. They divided the area among themselves, so that Antenor went by ship to the lands of Venetia; Aeneas came to the lands of Tuscia; and Janus arrived by ship in our own lands.[37] When Antenor arrived in the lands of the Venetians, he found swampy places and did not wish to live there.[38] Rather, sailing between the islands and up a certain river called the Brenta, he found a pleasing plain, and, deciding to make his home there, built a certain city in that place which he called Padua.[39] For this reason his sepulchre is still visible in the city of Padua, where it bears the following inscription: 'Here lies Antenor, founder of the Paduan city. He was a traitor, as are those who follow him'.[40]

The second man who escaped from Troy was Aeneas.[41] Anchises begat this Aeneas by Venus, whom he knew [carnally] in the forest, so those who got out of Troy were Aeneas, his father Anchises, and his son Ascanius. They had twenty ships with which they came into Sicily, but there his father died and a man appeared to him in dreams, saying, '*Do not be afraid*, but go into Italy, because a kingdom is owed to you there. *And this [will be] a sign to you*: when you arrive there, *you will find* under

---

37 Here Jacopo adds a Trojan Janus to the arrivals in Italy of Antenor (founder of Padua) and Aeneas (founder of Alba Longa, precursor of Rome), which appear in classical sources such as Virgil, Livy, and Ovid.

38 A sly dig at Genoa's great rival. Venetian chroniclers often supplied their city with made-up classical roots to compensate for their city's late antique origin (very recent, by Italian standards): in his *Prima edificacio*, the chronicler Marco appropriates Padua's older foundation by claiming that Antenor founded Venice before sailing up the river to found Padua. Here Jacopo repudiates such claims by asserting Antenor's particular dislike for 'swampy places'—i.e. the Venetian lagoon.

39 Virgil, *Aeneid* 1.242–4, 247–9; Livy, *Ab urbe condita* 1.1, and numerous medieval versions: Beneš (2011a), pp. 44–55.

40 The sarcophagus (still extant) dates to 1283–84, but Jacopo's (mis)quotation is actually a contemporary anti-Paduan insult: Beneš (2011a), pp. 46–60.

41 The main source for Aeneas' journey to Italy is Virgil's *Aeneid*, but Jacopo's narrative reflects later versions of the Troy legend, such as Landolfus Sagax, *Historia romana* 1.1, p. 4, or the twelfth-century romance *Eneas*, pp. 55–118. These later accounts downplay (or as here, ignore) Aeneas' encounter with Dido in favour of emphasising events after Aeneas' arrival in Italy, that is, his victory over Turnus and marriage to Lavinia: see nn. 43 and 45 below.

PART ONE: ON THE FOUNDATION OF GENOA 53

a certain tree a white sow with thirty white piglets'.[42] So when Aeneas arrived there and found the white piglets, he built a city in that place for his son. At that time Turnus reigned in Italy, which certain Turnus had taken as his wife the daughter of Latinus, who had reigned there before him.[43] This Latinus established the Latin language and it began to be called Latin after his name. For his mother, a woman by the name of Carmenta, invented Latin letters; before her, the Latins used Greek letters.[44] So Aeneas met Turnus, the king of Italy, in battle and overcame him in all things.[45] And once Turnus was dead, Aeneas took his wife, who was the daughter of Latinus, as his own wife. And the son of Aeneas, as the story goes, built the city of Albano.[46] So then from this all the kings born from the line of Aeneas are called the Alban kings. Afterward they were called the Silvan kings from a certain king who was said to have been born in the forest.[47] And after that they were called the Roman kings after Romulus, who built the City.

The third man who came out of Troy was Janus, who when he arrived in his ship in the Genoese lands, had always a prosperous wind and always sailed prosperously.[48] But when he came to a certain place which is called Albarium,[49] the wind entirely ceased, and a great fresh breeze sprang up. Thus that place Albarium took its name from the breeze (*albasia*[50]). Through this Janus understood that God wished that he

42 Virgil, *Aeneid* 3.374–409, 692–713; also 8.26–85. In quoting Luke 2.10–12, Jacopo parallels the spirit's appearance to Aeneas with the angel's announcement of Christ's birth to the shepherds.
43 Latinus' daughter is Lavinia; in *Aeneid* 7.59–81, Turnus is merely her suitor, not her husband.
44 Isidore, *Etymologies* 1.4.1, 9.1.6; Landolfus Sagax, *Historia romana* 1.1, p. 4. Here the medieval tradition conflates Latinus with Evander, king of Arcadia and Carmenta's son (*Aeneid* 8.334–6).
45 A summary of the last four books of the *Aeneid* (books 9–12), which ends with the death of Turnus. In the *Aeneid*, all later events such as Aeneas' marriage (1.257–79) and Ascanius' founding of Alba Longa (8.26–85) occur only in prophecy.
46 One of several cities in the Alban hills outside Rome that claimed to be the site of Ascanius' legendary Alba Longa. *Alba* ('white') comes from the white sow of the prophecy; cf. Isidore, *Etymologies* 15.1.53.
47 Aeneas and Lavinia's son Silvius Postumus. The claim that he was born in the forest (*silva*) is a reverse-etymology to explain the name Silvius: Landolfus Sagax, *Historia romana* 1.2, p. 5.
48 Jacopo's maritime-minded audience would have considered it only appropriate for their founder to be a prosperous sailor.
49 The hill of Albaro, on the east side of modern Genoa.
50 From *arbaxïa*, a Genoese dialect word.

should not leave these parts, but that he should make a home for himself there. So when he had gone a little further, looking carefully for a site on the land, a great many pleased him, and thus he ordered his sails pulled down. For this reason that place is called Calvignano,[51] which comes from the fact that Janus loosened his sails there. So he brought [his ship] in to land and in that place which is called Sarzano, rejoicing and happy and dancing, he descended to the earth. Thus this place is named Sarzano—that is, Janus's dance.[52] There Janus encountered Janicula, [which was] still very small. And so, wishing to enlarge and improve it, he built a fortress in the place that is now called Castello.[53] And he gave it towers and fortifications in the place which is now the archepiscopal palace, and he reinforced all with the strongest walls.[54] After this many inhabitants came here and built houses round about it, and slowly Janicula began to grow.

And these things we say about this Janus, citizen of Troy, we know through his great public and ancient renown.[55] For we sons have learned it from our fathers, and our fathers learned similarly from their fathers; and thus one generation has made it all known to another generation, and one nation to another nation, so that we can say with the prophet: *These things the Lord commanded our fathers to make known to their sons, so that another generation will know them; sons yet to be born will arise and tell them to their sons.*[56] And Moses also says: *Ask your father, and he will*

51 Jacopo derives Calvignano from *calavit Ianus* ('Janus loosened his sails'): today this is the hill of Carignano on the southeast end of the city centre. Until the expansion of the port in the nineteenth century, this area used to include a small bay called *Seno di Giano* (Janus's cove).

52 Jacopo's derivation for Sarzano (*saltus Iani*: 'Janus's dance') is also given by Jacopo Doria (*DGA*, p. 4). Sarzano is another hill in southeastern Genoa (modern Piazza Sarzano). Here Jacopo uses local topography to create verisimilitude in his narrative: Janus arrived by sailing up the coast from the south, encountering these three hills in succession as he neared the future site of Genoa.

53 The name Castello (from *castrum*: fort or castle) may come from an early medieval fortification whose foundations have been found near the monastery of San Silvestro. This hill was probably one of the earliest-settled parts of the city, with archaeological remains dating to the pre-Roman period: Melli (1996), pp. 33–7, 166–9.

54 Genoa was the only city in medieval Italy in which the episcopal palace was not in the immediate area of the cathedral: Miller (2000), p. 66.

55 Jacopo had no ancient sources to cite for his claims about Janus of Troy, so he uses biblical quotations to argue for the authority and reliability of oral tradition. This parallels Jacopo Doria's recourse to 'popular opinion' on the same subject: *DGA*, p. 4, and Beneš (2011a), p. 73.

56 Psalm 77.5–6.

tell you; [ask] your elders, and they will speak to you.[57] Thus these things, even though they are not found in any other ancient history, are proved to be true by common and ancient repute.[58] Where authority is lacking, celebrity will finish the job through fame—fame which does not arise from trivialities but from serious matters, which is not localised but general, which is not recent but ancient. To this extent such fame does not merely present an assumption, does not merely create probability; rather, it presents and creates proof.

Chapter four: How Janus, an ancient god and idol of the Romans, was worshipped in Genoa. The third Janus was a certain man whom the Romans venerated as a god, whom the Genoese too once venerated when they were also still pagans and heathens. And who this Janus was, and whence he came, and how the Romans worshipped him as a god, Saint Isidore shows in his book *On the stars*.[59] For he says that a certain man by the name of Janus was king of the Epirotes; he was reviled by all, and unjustly exiled from his kingdom and from his land. He then came to Rome, finding it besieged by many barbarians. And he said to the Romans that if they were willing to worship him as a god after his death, he could liberate the city from the blockade by its enemies. When they had agreed to these things, he ordered them to bring him eleven strips of linen, to immerse them in liquid wax, and afterward to smear them with grease and soak them in oily water. When these things were done, he commanded that the eleven cloths thus prepared should be wrapped around him and that they should give him two fiery swords for his hands. After this they lifted him, so wrapped, above the walls of the city and they set fire to him. And indeed when he cried out very loudly to the besieging army that he was a god, and he shook the fiery swords at them, then the armed Romans with a great clamour advanced toward the enemy and thus they gained the victory. So when all these events had happened, the barbarians, seeing such a great fire raised upon the wall, emitting human voices and shaking fiery swords at them, and hearing this apparition proclaim itself a god,

---

57 Deuteronomy 32.7.

58 An echo of the preface to Bede's *Historia ecclesiastica*: '[I have written] such things as I could gather from common report for the instruction of posterity'; trans. Colgrave/Mynors (1993), p. 9.

59 *De astris* probably refers to Isidore's *De natura rerum* (c. 612), but the anecdote actually comes from Pseudo-Bede, *De divisionibus temporum* 15 (PL 90.659–60).

for all these reasons they were terrified and made to tremble, and they turned to flee at once. For they knew that other peoples venerated fire as a god, and they also knew that the Romans had many gods; thus, seeing such a terrible fire speaking to them, they believed it to be a god of fire who would fight on behalf of the Romans. Then the Romans pursued their fleeing enemies, killed many, and gained a great victory. But Janus was completely burned up and killed.

Then Isidore tells that the Romans, wishing to keep their promise to this Janus, built a great temple with one hundred doors for the honour of the people and called this temple Janiculum.[60] Then they made an enormous statue of bronze having two faces, one in front and one behind, so that men could worship one face and women the other. They also consecrated the month of January to the same god Janus, depicting the month similarly, with two faces: one of these is in front (with which he sees into the future) and the other is behind (with which he looks back into the past).[61]

Thus the Genoese, at the time when they were subject to the Romans, wishing to please the Romans and gain their favour, took this Janus, who was a god of the Romans, as their own god, and worshipped him for a long time. As Hugo states plainly in his book of *Derivations*, the Genoese accordingly made a great bronze statue of this Janus featuring two faces, and men worshipped one of these and women the other. And a demon came into the statue, and when asked questions he often responded through it.[62]

---

60 Isidore, *Etymologies* 15.1.50. As some medieval sources knew, the temple of Janus is in the Roman forum rather than on the Janiculan hill; *Mirabilia urbis Romae* 23–4, 31; trans. Nichols/Gardiner (1986), 3.7–10, pp. 39–41.
61 Isidore, *Etymologies* 5.33.3.
62 Huguccio, *Derivationes* I 13.9–12 (p. 593). Huguccio (d. 1210) may have been a canon lawyer and/or bishop of Ferrara: Müller (1994), pp. 35–66. On demonically possessed statues, see also part 4.1, below.

PART TWO: ON THE EARLY HISTORY OF GENOA

Here follows part two, which deals with the era of the construction of the city of Genoa. This part has three chapters: the first discusses the era in which the city was founded; the second details the era in which it was expanded, and the third discusses how Genoa was destroyed by the Carthaginians or Africans but rebuilt by the Romans, and in what era that occurred.

Chapter one: The era in which Genoa was constructed. Because it is clear that many are ignorant of when the city of Genoa was constructed, and how long ago that was, we consider it necessary to describe the era of its construction and to demonstrate its antiquity insofar as we have been able to discover it. For it was built eight hundred years before Rome was founded.[1] Furthermore, it was built 1,546 years before Christ was born into the world, and also, it was built in the third age of the world.[2]

But it does little good to say these things unless we are able to prove what we say. In fact, it is clear that the above statements are true from the words of Solinus, who in his book *On the wonders of the world* says that Janus, first king of Italy, built our Janicula.[3] And it is also clear from authentic chronicles that the aforesaid Janus reigned in the time of Moses, namely at the time in which Moses held the leadership of God's people in the desert—although other chronicles say that this same Janus reigned at the time of Abraham.[4] It is also clear from all the authentic chronicles that Rome was built in the time of Ahaz, king of the Jews.[5] When we add these dates together, we find in the chronicles

---

1 As Rome was the standard medieval benchmark for urban success, Jacopo attempts to increase Genoa's prestige by proving that its foundation predated that of Rome: Beneš (2011a), chap. 1, esp. pp. 15–22.

2 The 'third age' refers to the historical periodisation proposed in the fifth century by Augustine, which divided world history from Creation to Revelation into six 'ages'; the third age extended from Abraham to King David.

3 A diminutive form of *Janua*; Solinus, *De mirabilibus mundi* 2.5.

4 According to Eusebius/Jerome, 1511–1472 BC.

5 According to Eusebius/Jerome, Ahaz ruled 757–742 BC. See 2 Kings 16, 2 Chronicles 28, and Isaiah 7.

that 807 years passed from Moses to Ahaz.[6] Therefore if Janus reigned at the time of Moses, as the chronicles say, and he founded Janicula, as Solinus says, and Rome was built at the time of Ahaz, king of the Jews, as the chronicles say, we will find that Genoa was built 707 years before Rome, for that many years went by from Moses up to Ahaz. Similarly, if we calculate time from Moses—in whose time Janus founded Genoa—up to the advent of Christ, we find that 1,546 years passed. (We make this computation according to the calculation of the blessed Jerome, who uses a smaller number. For Bede and Methodius the martyr give a larger number and say that more years went by.[7]) From this, therefore, an absolutely accurate and indisputable computation shows manifestly that from the first establishment of the city of Genoa up to the present time—which in the years of the Lord runs 1,295—2,841 years have passed.

Furthermore, Genoa was constructed in the third age of the world.[8] For the sacred doctors recognise six ages of the world: the first was from Adam to Noah, and this age encompassed 2,242 years according to the calculation of Bede and Eusebius. The second age ran from Noah to Abraham; this lasted 942 years according to the calculation of Bede and Eusebius. The third age lasted from Abraham to David; this age had 940 years, and in it lived Moses. The fourth age lasted from David up to the exile of the Jewish people into Babylon; this age had 485 years. The fifth age was from the Babylonian exile up to the birth of the Lord; this age had 590 years. And thus from the beginning of the world up to the advent of Christ 5,199 years passed; this number is generally agreed upon by the Church. The sixth age is from the advent of Christ up to the end of the world; this age presently has 1,295 years,

---

6 The manuscripts of Jacopo's *Chronicle* are internally inconsistent in the year ranges given here: Monleone's base manuscript (A), for example, gives first 800, then 807, then 707 as the number of years between the founding of Genoa and the founding of Rome, all in this paragraph. Yet both Eusebius/Jerome and Bede—whom Jacopo mentions as his sources—state clearly that Rome was founded 753 years before the birth of Christ, which suggests a span of 793 years between the founding of Genoa and that of Rome. The other computation in this paragraph—adding spans of years between the founding of Genoa and the birth of Christ (1,546), and from there to Jacopo's own day (1,295), for a total of 2,841—is valid as written.

7 Bede, *De temporum ratione*, and Pseudo-Methodius' *Revelationes*, an anonymous apocalyptic work attributed to Bishop Methodius of Olympus (d. 311) but probably of seventh-century Syriac origin, which circulated in several Latin versions in the medieval west.

8 Augustine, *De catechizandis rudibus* 39 (*CCSL* 46.163–4).

and how many years it will have in the end, only God knows.⁹ Thus if Genoa was built in the time of Moses and Moses lived during the third age of the world, it is obvious that this Genoa was also built in the third age.

Chapter two: The era in which Genoa was expanded. We may easily learn of the time in which Genoa was expanded if we recall to memory certain things which were mentioned above. For we said earlier that when Troy was destroyed, three princes left that place and came into Italy, namely: Antenor, who founded the city of Padua; Aeneas, who founded the city of Alba; and Janus, who expanded the city of Genoa, which at that time was small and humble.¹⁰ So according to this, Janus' expansion and development of Genoa occurred during the period in which Troy was destroyed. We know from the chronicles that Troy was destroyed in the time of Samson, a very strong man; therefore Genoa was expanded during his time.¹¹ And if we calculate the years according to the chronicles, we will find that 420 years passed from Samson to the foundation of Rome, and 1,019 years passed from Samson to Christ.¹² This therefore demonstrates that 420 years before Rome and 1,019 years before the advent of Christ, Genoa was not founded by Janus the Trojan—because it had already been founded by another Janus—but was expanded and improved by him. Nonetheless, this is why some say that Janus the citizen of Troy founded the city, because he made it much larger out of its smallness.

Chapter three: How the city of Genoa was destroyed by the Carthaginians, or Africans, but rebuilt by the Romans, and in what time this occurred. During the time when the Romans dominated the entire world with their power, they were merciful to their defeated enemies, forcefully suppressed rebels, cherished their allies as brothers, and kept faith with both friends and enemies. In his book *On the city of God*, Augustine says that the Romans preferred to forgive the injuries

---

9 Jacopo's use of the past tense here (*novit*, 'has known'), emphasises God's omniscience and foreknowledge.

10 See part 1.3, above.

11 Eusebius/Jerome, *Chronica*, dates the sack of Troy to 1182 BC and the reign of Samson to 1176–57 BC.

12 The number 1019 here is probably a scribal error: 420 years before 753 BC is not 1019 but 1173, and 1173 BC falls within the customary dates for the reign of Samson (see previous note).

they received than to avenge them; indeed, he says in the same book that the verse of the poet, *to spare the lowly and to subdue the proud*, was said in praise of the Romans.[13] In these times the Genoese were allied with the Romans, and lived untroubled in their shadow.[14]

But the Carthaginians and Africans rebelled against the Romans, and often caused them many losses and damages.[15] And at that time in Carthage there were two brave and famous men, namely Hannibal, who was king of the Carthaginians, and his brother Mago.[16] These two gathered a large army against the Romans by both sea and land; while Mago led the naval troops, Hannibal led the mounted ones. Then Mago came into Italy with thirty warships in addition to many other supply ships, carrying two thousand cavalry and twelve thousand infantry.[17] And when the aforesaid Mago heard that the Genoese were allied with the Romans, and friends of theirs, he quickly descended upon the land of the unsuspecting Genoese and assailed their city with arms out of hatred for the Romans. He killed many and captured the city, almost entirely destroying it.

Titus Livy, who was greatly distinguished among Latin historians, attests to the time at which this occurred, saying that it was in the 534th year from the founding of the City.[18] *With thirty beaked warships*

13 Augustine, *City of God*, 1.pr, which cites James 4.6 and 1 Peter 5.5 as well as Virgil, *Aeneid* 6.853. It also echoes Luke 1.51-2, which medieval Christians would have been familiar with as the *Magnificat*, a prayer that formed part of the daily office. The passage shows the richness of quotation common to educated churchmen of the period: Jacopo is simultaneously quoting Augustine, the Bible, and Virgil.

14 In the Bible, the shadow of a bird's wing and the shade of a tree (both rendered as Latin *umbra*) are common metaphors for protection: cf. Judges 9.15, Job 40.16-17, Psalms 16.8, *Song of songs* 2.3.

15 The characterisation of the Punic Wars as a Carthaginian 'rebellion' is inaccurate, as at that time Carthage (near modern Tunis) was an independent rival of the expanding Roman empire. Jacopo appears to have copied much of the following account from the *GA* of Jacopo Doria (*DGA*, pp. 4-5), whose narrative incorporates numerous quotations from the third decade (books 21-30) of Livy's *Ab urba condita*.

16 Hannibal (247-183/182 BC) was not king of Carthage but a Carthaginian general during the Second Punic War, best known for the invasion of Italy in 218 BC during which he marched his entire army (including war elephants) over the Alps. His younger brother Mago (243-203 BC) was a commander under Hannibal during the latter's campaigns in Italy, and later under their third brother Hasdrubal in Iberia (Spain). In 205 BC Mago led a naval invasion of Italy, from which he was called back to resist the Roman counter-invasion of Africa in 203 BC, but he died at sea before reaching Carthage.

17 *DGA*, p. 5; Livy, *Ab urbe condita* 28.46.7-8.

18 Livy's words are 'in the fourteenth year of the Punic War' (*Ab urbe condita* 28.38.12), that is, 205 BC or 548 AUC. (548 AUC means 548 years *ab urbe condita*, or 'from the

and many supply-ships holding twelve thousand infantry and about two thousand cavalry, Mago came to Genoa and took it in an unexpected attack while it was entirely unguarded and nearly destroyed it: this is what Titus Livy says, that this capture and destruction occurred in the 534th year from the founding of the City. Following the chronicles, this may be calculated to have occurred 230 years before the advent of Christ. If therefore some should disbelieve the antiquity of the city of Genoa for which we have argued above, at least they may not deny the following truth that may be gleaned from the words of Titus Livy: that Genoa was constructed and built at a minimum 230 years before the advent of Christ.

And indeed, when it became known in Rome that Mago had taken and destroyed Genoa in this way, the senate and the entire people of Rome lamented greatly, not only because the Genoese were their friends and subjects but also because the city of Genoa was in some measure a Roman port. For when the Romans wished to send a navy into Africa or Spain they assembled at the port of Genoa. For this reason the same Titus Livy, in his second part[19] where he discusses the Second Punic War between the Romans and the Carthaginians, says this: *in the 534th year from the founding of the City, Publius Cornelius Scipio was at Marseilles with his ships, and when he heard that Hannibal was setting off for Italy he sent his brother Scipio into Spain against Hasdrubal with a large part of his troops. Then he took his own ships to sea and went to Genoa with his best troops so that he could cross Hannibal's path as he was coming over the Alps.*[20] From this it is clear that Genoa was to some extent a Roman port, to which the Romans sent warships when they wished to set out for Spain.

Afterward, the Romans sent the noble man Lucretius to rebuild Genoa and restore it to a pristine state.[21] The aforementioned Titus Livy explains this near the beginning of the tenth book [of this decade], saying: *when Cornelius Servilius was consul in the sixteenth year of the Punic War, 545*

---

founding of the city'—the Roman method of calculating dates). The date 534 AUC (= 218 BC) is miscopied from Doria, who refers earlier in the paragraph (*DGA*, p. 4) to the beginning of the Second Punic War in that year. Jacopo is also wrong, however, in identifying 534 AUC as 230 BC, an error which cannot be explained by reference to *DGA*.

19 A reference to the third decade of Livy (books 21–30): since the second decade was (and remains) lost, the 'first part' would have been books 1–10, and 'the second part' books 21–30.

20 Publius Cornelius Scipio (d. 211 BC), father of the more famous P. Cornelius Scipio Africanus, and his brother Gnaeus Cornelius Scipio (d. 211 BC). *DGA*, p. 4; Livy, *Ab urbe condita* 21.32.5.

21 Spurius Lucretius: Livy, *Ab urbe condita* 30.1.9–10.

years from the founding of the City, Lucretius was given the authority to rebuild the town of Genoa [Lat. *Genua*], *which had been nearly demolished by Mago*.[22] From these words of Titus Livy, therefore, it is evident that the city of Genoa had lain devastated for as long as eleven years. For if it was destroyed by Mago in the 534th year from the founding of the City and rebuilt by Lucretius in the 545th year from the founding of the City, it is clear that it had stood thus ruined into an eleventh year.[23] And the aforementioned Lucretius came to Genoa, repaired it, and restored it to a pristine state.

Then Hannibal, who had a mounted army, came to Rome and overcame the Romans to such an degree that he besieged the City itself.[24] But Scipio Romanus (who was afterward called Africanus) prepared a navy while Hannibal was besieging Rome, set out for Africa, and destroyed everything by iron and fire.[25] When Hannibal learned of this, he abandoned the siege and returned to Africa to rescue his compatriots.[26]

Eventually the Romans captured Carthage and all of Africa and subjugated it under their dominion. As a result, as Saint Augustine says in his book *On the city of God*, counsel was taken in the senate on what should be done with Carthage.[27] Then Cato spoke out, saying that he judged it necessary to the republic that Carthage should be utterly destroyed.[28] 'For', he said, 'when the whole world is obedient to us and Carthage stands so often in rebellion, if Carthage is destroyed the whole

---

22 *DGA*, p. 5; Livy, *Ab urbe condita* 30.1.10. Another indication that Jacopo is working from the *GA*: first in *GA* and then here, the three separate officials mentioned in this section of Livy (29.38.3-4, 30.1.1) are conflated into a single consul called Cornelius Servilius.

23 The manuscripts read 'Cornelius' here and in the next sentence, but Livy (*Ab urbe condita* 30.1.10) and Jacopo Doria are quite clear that the rebuilding was done by Lucretius (n. 21, above). Similarly, the timespan referred to is not eleven years but only two or three: 548-545 AUC, or 205-202 BC.

24 Untrue: although historians have speculated as to his reasons (especially after his massive victory at Cannae in 216 BC), Hannibal never made a direct attack on Rome.

25 Publius Cornelius Scipio Africanus (d. 183 BC), son of the P. Cornelius Scipio mentioned above (n. 20). 'By iron and fire' (*ferro et igne*) is a common classical formulation for military devastation.

26 Livy, *Ab urbe condita*, book 30.

27 The next three paragraphs are a paraphrase of Augustine, *City of God* 1.30-1; cf. *SD*, fol. 384r.

28 Cato the Elder (Marcus Porcius Cato, 234-149 BC), who reputedly ended all his speeches in the Senate in this period with 'and furthermore, it is my opinion that Carthage should be destroyed' (*Carthago delenda est*): e.g. Pliny the Elder, *Natural history* 15.20.

PART TWO: ON THE EARLY HISTORY OF GENOA   63

world will enjoy the comfort of peace'. But after this Scipio spoke, saying, 'The advice of Cato does not please me. I think it useful to the republic to keep some of our enemies, because this will keep us afraid and fear will keep us united. For if we do not have external enemies, internal ones will appear among us; if we have no external war from any side, we will without doubt have an internal war because that very security and leisure will be the cause of many evils for us'.[29]

Yet Cato held to his own opinion. Therefore the Romans ordered the Carthaginians to surrender all their ships, and when they had been handed over, the Romans ordered that they should give up all their arms as well. When these had been handed over, they ordered everyone—men and women, great and small—to abandon the city. When the Carthaginians heard this, they gave themselves over to despair, saying that they wished to defend the city or else to perish there together. But all their weapons and iron had been handed over to the Romans, so they made weapons out of gold and silver and resisted the Romans, killing all the Romans who were then in Carthage. In the end, the Romans besieged Carthage again, and after some skirmishes here and there the Carthaginians saw that they could not defend themselves and petitioned the Romans to take them as their slaves. So the Romans ordered that their lives should be preserved and they should all leave the city, and when they had left, Carthage was thoroughly destroyed.

The experience of later times, however, proves how much truth was in the words Scipio spoke above. For with all their wars won, domestic unrest and civil war were born in Rome that brought that City to oblivion. Saint Augustine speaks of this in his book *On the city of God*: *This proves how truly Scipio spoke. For with Carthage destroyed—which had been a source of great terror to the Romans—all evils followed, namely sedition, civil war, greed, and lust for power.* And the same Augustine continues: *Scipio did not wish the city destroyed, so that lust would be vanquished by fear; under pressure, lust would not turn to decadence; and thus restrained, decadence would not grow.*

---

29 The censor Publius Cornelius Scipio Nasica (d. 141 BC), a distant cousin and son-in-law of Scipio Africanus.

PART THREE: ON THE NAME OF GENOA

Here follows part three, which discusses how Genoa (Janua[1]) came to be called by that name. This part has four chapters: the first chapter presents the opinion of those who say that it was named Janua firstly after the Janus who built it, and secondly after the Janus who enlarged it. The second chapter gives the opinion of those who say that Janua is named after Janus, an idol of the Romans who was once venerated in Genoa. The third chapter gives the opinion of those who say that it is named Janua because from it one enters into Lombardy. The fourth chapter explains why it bears the name of Genua in all the books of the ancients.

Chapter one: The opinion of those who say that Janua was named after the Janus who built it, and also after the Janus who enlarged it. The name of our city, that is, Janua, is a name sweet to consider, delightful to utter, pleasing to hear, and renowned in reputation. The word is also honey on the lips, a song in the ear, and a joy in the heart.[2] Different people have different opinions, however, about how our city came to be dignified with such a name.

The first group claims that a certain Janus, who built the city, gave it this name; then another Janus who expanded it confirmed that gift. This is the opinion or judgment of Solinus in his book *On the wonders of the world:* namely that Janua or Janicula ('little Janua') was named after Janus, first king of Italy, who built it.[3] For ancient cities were often called by the names of those who built them: thus Ninus who built Nineveh, and Cres who built Crete, and Romulus who built Rome, and the queen Mathys who built Mantua, all called them by their own names.[4] In the same way Janus called Janua by his own name. For the

---

1 *Janua* is the medieval form of the classical *Genua*: see prologue n. 8, above, and part 3.4, below.
2 Bernard of Clairvaux, discussing the name of Jesus in sermon 15 on the *Song of songs* (*Opera* 1.86); trans. Walsh (1981), p. 110.
3 Solinus, *De mirabilibus mundi* 2.5.
4 Augustine, *City of God* 16.3 (Ninus); Isidore, *Etymologies* 14.6.14 (Cres), 15.1.55 (Romulus). The founder of Mantua is usually cited as Manto, daughter of Tiresias: Isidore, *Etymologies* 15.1.59, deriving from Virgil, *Aeneid* 10.198–200; cf. Dante, *Inferno* 20.55.

PART THREE: ON THE NAME OF GENOA

ancients desired that their names should be perpetuated and their memory be propagated through the ages. Accordingly, they built cities and imposed their names upon them, so that—although they themselves could not be immortal—they could still be immortal in the cities they built and which they called by their own names. Indeed, if Romulus had not built Rome or if he had not called it by his own name, no one today would know who Romulus was. In the same way, if Janus had not built Janua and called it by his own name, no one today would know who Janus was. Of these things the prophet says *they have called the lands after their own names.*[5]

But it does little good to impose one's name upon the earth if it is erased from the Book of Life, and if it is not written among the names of the just. Of these things the prophet says, *let them be erased from the book of the living, and not be inscribed among the righteous.*[6] For what good does it do Romulus to have a name celebrated throughout the world if his soul is tortured in hell? And how does it hurt any of those saintly men whose names are not recorded among the lands, but are written in the heavens in the sight of God? Of these matters the Lord says in the Gospel: *rejoice, for your names are written in heaven.*[7] This is why, when he was speaking in the Gospel of the splendidly attired rich man and the pauper covered in sores, the Lord chose not to give the name of the rich man but said instead, *there was a certain rich man who arrayed himself in purple,* etc. But he did give the name of the poor man, saying, *and there was a certain beggar, by the name of Lazarus.*[8] His point is that the names of the sinful are erased from the Book of Life, while the names of the virtuous are inscribed therein. It is therefore more advantageous that our names be inscribed in the Book of Life than that they be memorialised in some city; for the former is blessedness, but the latter is a kind of vanity.[9]

---

5 Psalm 48.12.

6 Psalm 68.29; but see also the many references to the 'book of life' (*liber vitae*) in Revelation 3.5, 13.8, 20.15, among others.

7 Luke 10.20.

8 Luke 16.20: *Et erat quidam mendicus, nomine Lazarus, qui iacebat ad ianuam eius* ('And there was a certain poor man named Lazarus, who lay at [the rich man's] gate'). This is a bit of playfulness: while Jacopo does not directly quote the part of the verse containing the word *ianua* (gate), he would have expected some of his readers to recognise the pun given its appearance in a discussion of the etymology of *ianua.* Cf. *SD*, fols. 169r, 208v, 212r.

9 A comparison fundamental to Augustine's *City of God* (2.18, 19.19, 20.3, et al.): heavenly glory is blessed while earthly glory is vanity.

Chapter two: The opinion of those who claim that Janua is named after Janus, an idol of the Romans who was once venerated in Genoa. Others say that the name of Janua comes from Janus, an idol of the Romans who was venerated in Genoa in antiquity; this is the opinion and judgment of Huguccio in his book of *Derivations*. Now, it is no disgrace to our city if we say that it worshipped idols. Indeed, with the exception of the Jewish people—who venerated the one true God—the entire rest of the world worshipped idols before the advent of Christ. Some worshipped the stars, others the elements, others images or statues. Indeed, many regions worshipped the stars: the Saracens worshipped Venus; the area of Italy around Rome worshipped Saturn; and another part of Italy worshipped Mercury.[10] Many peoples also worshipped the elements. In fact, the first person to worship the elements was Nimrod, who worshipped fire and forced others to worship it as well. It is said in the *Scholastic history* that this Nimrod lived until the time of Abraham, and when Abraham refused to worship fire Nimrod threw him into the fire, but God preserved him unharmed.[11] Thus the Lord said to Abraham, as it is written in Genesis: *I am the Lord your God, who led you out of Ur, that is, out of the Chaldean fire.*[12]

Therefore, following the teaching of this Nimrod the Chaldeans worshipped fire as a god; conversely, the Egyptians venerated statues. This is why the *Scholastic history* says that the god of the Chaldeans, namely fire, consumed and dissolved all other gods (that is, all idols). For once an Egyptian priest had a great earthen vessel made, full of holes, and he closed the holes up with wax. Then he filled the jar with water, and had it placed on the head of a statue like a crown. Then the Egyptians and Chaldeans assembled, and ordered that the gods of each should be set up together, and whichever god prevailed, those people should have victory over their enemies. So the Egyptians produced their statue and the Chaldeans lit their fire around it, but the fire melted the wax and the holes opened up, so the water gushed forth and put out the fire, and thus the Egyptians gained the victory.

---

10 On Venus: Bede, *Expositio Actuum apostolorum* for Acts 7.43, p. 36; Scarfe Beckett (2008), pp. 125–38. On Saturn: Landolfus Sagax, *Historia romana* 1.1, p. 3. On Mercury: this probably refers to Cisalpine Gaul (northern Italy), since classical texts regularly characterise Gauls as Mercury-worshippers (e.g. Caesar, *Gallic war* 6.17).

11 Peter Comestor, *Historia scholastica*, discussed in part 1.1. Jacopo is probably thinking of *Historia scholastica* 1.41 (*PL* 198.1091), in which the citizens of Ur throw Abraham into the fire—but some versions of the story attribute that act to Nimrod.

12 An amalgamation of Genesis 15.7, Genesis 28.13, and Nehemiah 9.7.

PART THREE: ON THE NAME OF GENOA

There were also many other peoples who venerated graven images. As it is stated in the *Scholastic history*, these images had their origin under Ninus, king of Assyria. For this Ninus was so grieved by the death of his father, a man by the name of Bellus, that as solace for his sorrow he ordered a statue made in the likeness of his father, and he held it in such reverence that if runaway slaves or other criminals ever took refuge at that statue, he totally pardoned all their offences.[13] The men who attained such benefits by the grace of this image then placed it on a pedestal and rendered it divine honours, and other men, seeking to please King Ninus, rendered similar sacrifices in the same way. Thus by this example others in places nearby had golden statues created in honour of their forebears, and had them worshipped similarly by their own people, and in this way the cult of idolatry grew.

Beyond this, others worshipped animals, as is stated in the book of Wisdom: *they worship also the vilest creatures*.[14] Even the Romans worshipped a golden goose, as we read in the histories of the Romans, as Augustine discusses in his book *On the city of God*, and so does Orosius in one part.[15] Attracted by the sweetness of the wine, a hundred thousand Teutons from the areas around Swabia and a hundred thousand Gauls from the regions of the Senones came into Italy and built Milan, Pavia, Bergamo, Brescia, and Verona. These cities were built 350 years before the advent of Christ in the fifth age of the world, around the time of King Ahasuerus and Queen Esther, as far as can be clearly understood from the ancient histories and chronicles.[16] And afterward these aforesaid Swabians and Senones went to Rome and besieged it even up to the Capitoline. From there, the Romans shot arrows into their army. And when they ran out of cord, they cut off the tails of their horses and made strings for their bows out of the hair. When these ran out, the women cut off their hair and made strings out of their own hair, which they gave to their husbands.[17]

---

13 *Historia scholastica* 1.40 (*PL* 198.1090).

14 Wisdom 15.18.

15 Augustine, *City of God* 2.22, referring to the Gauls' siege of Rome in Livy, *Ab urbe condita* 5.47. The episode does not appear in Orosius' *Against the pagans*.

16 Eusebius/Jerome, *Chronica*, gives the reign of Ahasuerus as 406–366 BC. This account derives from Justinus' epitome of Pompeius Trogus's *Historiae philippicae*, 20.5.8, which was transmitted through John of Salisbury (*Policraticus* 6.17) and was much cited in medieval Italy: cf. e.g. Benzo d'Alessandria, *Chronicon* 14.136, p. 146. Jacopo's text here, however, comes from the anonymous *Memoriale temporum*, pp. 98–102, 193–4.

17 Vegetius, *De re militari* 4.9 (discussing catapults rather than bows).

Then one night when the watchmen were asleep, their enemies scaled the walls with ladders. But there was a great flock of geese there, which heard the approaching enemy and began to squawk all at once in loud voices. Thus the watchmen were roused by their noise and put the enemy to flight. Afterward the Romans said that while all the other gods of the Romans slept, the only god vigilant was a goose who saved Rome from its enemies.[18] Accordingly the Romans created a goose out of gold, and for many years they worshipped it as a god and burned incense to it.

The Romans also worshipped the gods of other peoples and other regions, cities, and places, building altars and creating statues to them. The Romans had two special gods or particular patrons, however: namely Romulus, who built their City, and Janus, who freed it from its enemies.[19] They always rendered the greatest reverence to these two, and it pleased them greatly and generated much good will when any province or city accepted one of these two as its god and offered sacrifices to it. Thus at a time when they greatly needed the good will of the Romans, the Genoese took Janus as their god and venerated him for a long time.

Therefore, as was stated above, Janua is named after this Janus because of its worship of this idol Janus, and also because of a particular representation of this idol. For the pagans (*gentiles*) depicted this idol Janus with two faces, one in front and one behind. Because they attributed to him the beginnings and endings of all things, they gave him two faces—one in front, with which he oversaw beginnings, and the other behind, with which he oversaw endings. For this reason, when the Romans wished to begin some work, they sacrificed to the face of Janus which was on the front part [of the statue] so that he would look favourably on their undertaking. And when they finished, they sacrificed to the face that was on the back because he had looked favourably on their conclusion.[20]

Janua is named for its similarity to this image, since the city has two faces: one in front with which it beholds the sea, and another behind with which it beholds the land. In this way Janua seemed similar to this Janus with respect to these two faces. So the Genoese worshipped Janus before the advent of Christ, and they made a great statue to him which had two faces, one in front and one behind; men worshipped the

---

18 Cf. Augustine, *City of God* 2.22, itself based on Livy, *Ab urbe condita* 5.47.
19 Recounted in part 1.4, above.
20 Isidore, *Etymologies* 5.33.3; cf. Dante, *Paradiso* 6.81.

face that was in front, and women worshipped the one that was in back. And because they attributed the beginnings and endings of things to this god Janus, when the Genoese wished to begin some work, they offered a sacrifice to Janus of animals or birds on the part that faced front, so that this Janus would look favourably on their beginning. And when they finished the same work according to his will, they sacrificed to Janus on the part that faced back, because he had looked favourably on their finishing.

Chapter three: The opinion of those who say that Janua is named after the fact that it is the entrance into Lombardy. Others say that Janua is so called because it is the entrance into Lombardy, Tuscany, and Provence.[21] It is important, however, to note here the difference between a portal (*porta*), a front door (*foris*), a door (*valva*), a gate (*ianua*), and a doorway (*ostium*). For a portal (*porta*) is called after the act of carrying (*portandus*), and it is properly a thing of cities.[22] For when the ancients wished to build some city, they traced the whole circuit with a plough. And when the wind blew through the place where the gate of the city ought to be put, they picked up the plough and carried it over that spot, and from this carrying (*portandus*) it was called a portal (*porta*). Front doors (*fores*) are portals which open to the outside (*foris*). And doors (*valv[a]e*) are portals which open to the inside. They are called *valve* either from 'turning' (*volvendus*), because they turn on hinges, or from 'veiling' (*velandus*), because they veil those inside who are hidden from us. A gate (*ianua*) is a portal with a grill of holes through which one can see both in and out, something that was generally done with chisels. And finally, a doorway (*ostium*) is common to all these things previously mentioned. And it is called *ostium* from opposing (*o[b]standus*), because it obstructs the way so that no one enters unless he should do so.

Thus our city is not called after *porta*, *fores*, *valve*, or *ostium*, but after *ianua*, because it is the gate or grill by which we see both in and out. For by it we enter into Lombardy, just like going into a house, and by it we exit to the sea, just like going out of a house. This is the reason it was called Janua: because it is the entrance into Lombardy, says Huguccio in the book of *Derivations*.[23] For he says that it is called Janua not so

---

21 Anonimo genovese, *Poesie*, p. 566; also Giovanni Balbi, *Catholicon* on *Ianua*, fol. v2r.
22 Cf. Isidore, *Etymologies* 15.7.4, and Huguccio, *Derivationes*, I 13.12–16 (pp. 593–4), the latter expanding on Varro, *On agriculture* 2.1.9–10.
23 See Huguccio, *Derivationes*, I 13.31 (p. 596); also Giovanni Balbi, *Catholicon* on *Ianua*, fol. v2r.

much because of the cult of the god Janus there, but rather because it is the entrance to Lombardy. It must also be noted that a portal (*ianua*) in a house is both decorative and functional, because without it nothing would be able to be brought into or taken out of the house. It is also healthy, because if a house had no doors or windows by which air could enter, the house would reek with the stench it gave off.

In this way the city of Genoa is the ornament and glory (*decor et decus*) not only of Lombardy but even of all Italy. It is of the greatest service to Italians because its citizens transport goods from lands beyond the sea which they share with other cities. It is also extremely healthy for its own inhabitants.[24] In many other cities there are fetid swamps that give off fumes which pollute the air; in summer, western winds and winds with pestilential heat blow, opening the pores and corrupting the human body. But in our city there are no swampy places, only pleasant orchards; no miasmas, only fresh breezes.[25] And although the south winds often blow in the summer, they do not cross over sulphurous, swampy, or desert places but over the sea. Thus these winds are purified by the sea and imbued with coolness, so the people there are not afflicted by any noxious heat but delighted by welcome coolness.

Chapter four: The reason why the city of Genoa (*Janua*) is called *Genua* in many books.[26] We must not, however, pass over in silence the fact that in almost all the ancient books our city is not called Janua but Genua. It took this name from the knees (*genua*), which are the meeting point of the thighs and the lower legs, and according to the ancients the knees were dedicated to mercy.[27] Indeed, the philosophers recount that the pagans dedicated all of the parts of the body to various deities: the ears were consecrated to memory, the face to intellect, and the knees to mercy. For when we wish to incline someone to mercy, we

---

24 Different winds were believed to affect the balance of the bodily humours: see Isidore, *Etymologies* 4.5, 4.6.17, 13.11.

25 'Swampy places' (*loca paludosa*) is the same phrase Jacopo uses for Antenor's criticism of the Venetian lagoon in part 1.3, above (at n. 38); this is therefore a snide comparison of Genoa's climate versus Venice's (and perhaps even Rome's, which was notorious for the unhealthiness of its surrounding marshes).

26 The classical form *Genua* had been replaced by the medieval form *Janua* around the tenth century: see prologue n. 8, above. In the century after Jacopo, Boccaccio (*Genealogy of the pagan gods* 7.41) and the Genoese annalist Giorgio Stella (*Annales genuenses*, pp. 10–11) reverted to using the classical term *Genua*, replacing Genoa's Janus myths with that of a founder called Genuinus to account for it: *CMG*, p. 210 (Beneš).

27 Isidore, *Etymologies* 11.1.108–9; *DGA*, pp. 7–8.

bend our knees; and when someone turns his eyes or cheeks to his knees, his eyes are naturally bathed in tears. This makes sense because a child in its mother's womb sits naturally curved this way, holding its cheeks to its knees. This is why the cheeks (*genae*) are named after the knees (*genua*). And thus when someone lowers his cheeks or his eyes to his knees he naturally weeps, because his nature is mindful of his lowliness and the lowly state he was in while in his mother's womb. Similarly, therefore, mercy is designated by the knees because the knees are dedicated to mercy, because we bend the knees when we wish to incline someone to mercy, because when we bend our cheeks and eyes to our knees we provoke weeping and compassion. Our city is therefore rightly called Genua—that is, mercy—because it exhibits mercy in all its deeds. For there the hungry are fed; there the thirsty are quenched; there the naked are clothed; there travellers receive shelter; there the infirm are visited and restored; there the imprisoned are revived with good works and alms.[28]

Alternatively, one might say that the knees are necessary for the body to move: just as the feet are necessary for the body to stand up, so the knees are necessary for its perambulation. It should be noted that it is one thing to go backward, another to stand, and another to walk forward—and knees are intended not for going backward or standing but for walking. There are certain cities which have regressed because they were once great but are now small. This is apparent in Rome, Babylon, Constantinople, Ravenna, Aquileia, and many other cities.[29] These cannot be called Genua because they have regressed. There are others which persist in their smallness or the size in which they were begun: these cannot be called Genua either because they persist in a single constant state. The city of Genoa, on the other hand, has neither regressed nor persisted in its small size; instead, it has always moved forward, because from smallness it became large and from largeness it became great. And because it has thus moved forward—that is, it has progressed—thus it has deserved to be called Genua.

28 The corporal works of mercy commanded by Jesus in Matthew 25.34–40. Jacopo may also be referring to the charity shown by the Genoese during the famine of 1276: *GA* 4.175–6.

29 The idea of *translatio imperii* (relocation of empire), in which the mantle of greatness passes from ancient cities—most commonly Rome—to various successors. Jacopo is challenging the claims not only of other post-Roman 'imperial' cities (Milan, Ravenna, Aquileia), but also more recent foundations such as Florence and Venice, whose inhabitants were also trying to posit themselves as heirs of the Roman legacy during this period: Beneš (2011a), pp. 13–36.

PART FOUR: ON THE CHRISTIANISATION OF GENOA

Here follows part four, which describes the time in which the city of Genoa was converted to the faith of Christ. This part has three chapters: the first chapter explains how the entire world was enslaved to the cult of idolatry. The second chapter explains how Genoa was the first city, or one of the first cities in Italy, to be converted to the faith of Christ. The third chapter supports this same assertion through reason.

Chapter one: How the entire world was enslaved to the cult of idolatry before the advent of Christ. Before the advent of Christ the human race was blinded by the shadows of sin, so much that nearly all of them abandoned the true God and venerated many false idols; they made statues of gold and silver, offering divine honours and sacrifices to them. Then demons entered into these images, and through them seemed to predict many unknown and future things to men. For Saint Isidore says that demons can know the unknown and the future in three ways: first, through the subtlety of their senses: for we see that when a man is very subtle, when he has a sharp wit and a subtle intellect, he will by the subtlety of his intellect and his sharp reasoning understand how to predict many things which will eventually happen in reality.[1] For just as watchmen sometimes see something far off with the eyes of the body, so wise and holy men sometimes see the unknown and the yet to come with the eyes of the mind. Because of this it is said in Ecclesiasticus: *the soul of a holy man sometimes discovers more truth than seven watchmen sitting on high to keep watch.*[2] Therefore, since demons have a very subtle nature and a very sharp intellect, by the subtlety of their nature they can predict many hidden and future things which afterward come to pass.

Secondly, as Saint Isidore says, demons are able to see hidden and future things by their experience of time. For we see that when men are ancient and long-lived, when they have seen many things and experienced more,

---

1 Most of the material for this chapter comes from Isidore, *Etymologies* 8.11.1–16, but see also Augustine, *De Genesi ad litteram* 2.17 and Isidore, *Sententiae* 1.10.17.

2 Sirach 37.18.

it is certain that they know many things and can assess future events that are similar to past ones. For this reason it is said in Ecclesiasticus: *a man that has much experience will think of many things, and he that has learned much will display his understanding.*[3] Someone who is not experienced will recognise little, but demons are very ancient because they were created more than six thousand years ago. So they are experienced in many, nearly infinite things, and from past events they can make inferences about similar things in the future.

Thirdly, demons are able to know the future, as that same Isidore says, by the revelation of heavenly spirits. For when God wishes to uncover some secret, he sometimes reveals it by his angels and demons, so that as the justiciars of God they may do his ministry and show him obedience. This is explained in the book of Kings, which relates that when God desired that Ahab, king of Israel, should fall in battle and be killed for his sins, he conjured a certain evil spirit and ordered him to deceive Ahab by advising him to attack so that he would perish—and this is what happened.[4]

So the demons secretly entered into these images and predicted future events that they were able to know by the subtlety of their nature, or by their experience and great age, or by angelic revelation. And in this way nearly the whole world was blinded, so that all men believed these idols to be so many gods. There were four causes of the deception of the whole world into the worship of these idols and images, of which three are given in the book of Wisdom. The first cause was misguided love. For a father who loved his son misguidedly and too much said to himself after his son had died that he had been taken up among the gods, so he made a golden statue to his son and offered sacrifices to it. Thus it is said in the book of Wisdom: *for a father who was afflicted with bitter grief made an image of his son who had been taken from him; thus he began to worship the one who died as a god, and established rites and sacrifices among his servants.*[5]

The second cause was false worship. For men who wished to flatter their kings and princes made images of them and offered incense and sacrifices to them, so that they could venerate and worship those whom they were not able to have present. For this reason it is said in the same book of Wisdom: *and they made a physical reproduction of the king they*

---

3 Sirach 34.9.
4 Husband of Jezebel, r. *c.* 871–852 BC: 1 Kings 16–22, especially 22.20–35.
5 Wisdom 14.15 (paraphrased).

wished to honour, so that by their diligence they could venerate one who was absent as if he were present.[6]

The third cause was excessive greed. For craftsmen and painters and silversmiths made these extremely beautiful gilded images and pictures, and they claimed they were gods. In this way they deceived simple souls by the great beauty of these images, and made a great deal of money out of them. For this reason it is said in the same book of Wisdom: *and the extraordinary diligence of the craftsman also led to the worship of these things.*[7] For multitudes were deceived by the splendour of their work, believing that men who before then had only been honoured as men were now in fact gods.

The fourth cause was the treacherous deception of demons. For demons entered into these images and responded to enquiries, so simple men believed the images to be gods.[8] But Christ sent the apostles throughout the world to preach the true faith, eradicate the cult of idols, and teach the faith of Christ. Christ did not wish to accomplish this through kings lest the world seem to believe out of fear and worldly power, nor through rich men lest the world seem to believe due to the distribution of an abundance of riches. Rather, he accomplished this through illiterate fishermen and beggars who had neither worldly power, nor human wisdom, nor an abundance of worldly goods. Thus through fishermen he converted emperors; through illiterates he converted philosophers; through beggars he converted rich men—all so it would be understood that the world did not adopt the faith of Christ deceived by human wisdom or seduced by the giving of presents, but rather moved by the inspiration of God, enlightened by the wisdom of God, and called forth by miraculous signs.

Chapter two: How the city of Genoa was the first city in Italy, or one of the first, to receive the faith of Christ. After the glorious ascension of Christ and the sending of the Holy Spirit, the apostles met together to proclaim collectively the faith of Christ and to divide up amongst themselves provinces for preaching.[9] In proclaiming the faith

---

6 Wisdom 14.17.

7 Wisdom 14.18.

8 The belief that pagan statues were inhabited by demons was common among the church fathers, e.g. Tertullian, *De idololatria* 3.2–4 (*CCSL* 2.1102–3).

9 Acts 1–2 (Ascension and Pentecost); Matthew 28.16–20 (the Great Commission); and Mark 16.14–20 (Dispersion of the Apostles). In the Middle Ages, the Dispersion was celebrated on 15 July: William Durandus, *Rationale divinorum officium* 7.15.1.

of Christ, therefore, they composed a creed (*symbolus*) in which they placed twelve articles of the faith.[10] For a creed is so-called from *sym-*, which is 'at the same time', and *-bolus*, because each apostle placed into it his favourite bit (*bolus*[11]), that is, his own article. In this way doctors and theologians both ancient and modern have affirmed in their writings and recorded in their *summae* that the apostle Peter chose the first article, saying, *I believe in God the father almighty, creator of heaven and earth.*[12] John then chose the second, saying, *and in Jesus Christ his only son our Lord.* James son of Zebedee chose the third, saying, *who was conceived by the Holy Spirit and born of the Virgin Mary.* Andrew chose the fourth, saying, *who suffered under Pontius Pilate; was crucified, died, and was buried.* Thomas chose the fifth, saying, *he descended into hell.* Bartholomew chose the sixth, saying, *on the third day, he rose again from the dead.* Philip chose the seventh, saying, *he ascended into heaven, and sits at the right hand of God the father almighty.* Matthew chose the eighth, saying, *whence he will come again to judge the living and the dead.* James the son of Alphaeus chose the ninth, saying, *I believe in the Holy Spirit.* Simon chose the tenth, saying, *and in the holy catholic church.* Thaddeus chose the eleventh, saying, *and in the communion of saints and the remission of sins.* Matthias chose the twelfth, saying, *and the resurrection of the body, and life everlasting.*[13] And then all the apostles responded, *Amen.* [The apostle] Paul, however, did not contribute an article, because at this time he was not yet converted to the faith.

Since they had been granted the grace of preaching, once they had done these things the apostles divided up the regions of the world to which each one would go, just as the Lord had commanded them, saying, *go out into the whole world preaching the gospel to every creature.*[14] And in this division of provinces Peter took the preaching in Judea; Andrew, Greece; James the son of Zebedee, Spain; John, Asia; Thomas, India; Matthew, Ethiopia; Bartholomew, Armenia; Simon and Thaddeus, Persia; Philip, Asia, the city of Hierapolis, and Syria; and Matthias, Judea along with

---

10 The belief that each apostle contributed a section to the Apostles' Creed goes back at least to the fourth-century Synod of Milan (*PL* 17.671). Cf. *SS*, fols. 455r, 458r–v; also *SD*, fols. 360r–363r.

11 As Bertini Guidetti notes (*CCG*, p. 115), Latin *bolus* denotes a throw of the dice or a cast of the net, meaning one turn in a sequence.

12 A *summa* ('totality' or 'summary') was a form of encyclopaedic scholarship common to the medieval universities, the most famous being Aquinas' *Summa theologiae*.

13 Matthias was chosen in Acts 1.21–6 to replace Judas among the apostles.

14 Mark 16.15.

Peter.[15] The Lord's brother James remained in Jerusalem because he had been ordained bishop there by the apostles.[16] Other disciples were also sent to different provinces, and of these, some travelled to Italy. Barnabas came, preaching the faith of Christ first in Rome and later in Milan.[17] Saint Mark the evangelist also came: he composed his gospel at Rome and Aquileia.[18] Finally, the princes of the apostles Peter and Paul came, sending various disciples around Italy to eradicate the cult of idolatry, banish diabolical illusions, and plant the true faith of Christ.[19] Some of these came to Genoa and preached the word of faith there—and so great was the grace which the Lord worked there that the city of Genoa broke its idol of Janus in pieces and received the saving faith of Christ.[20] Thus it was the first city in all of Italy, or one of the first, which publicly received and publicly confessed the faith of Christ.[21]

We intend to prove this point both through authorities and through reason. By 'authorities' here, we mean histories and legends of the saints: for a certain history that deals with the cities of Italy mentions Genoa among other cities, asserting that it was the first city of Italy, or one of the first, in which the faith of Christ was publicly preached and publicly received, or in which the sacrifices of the Lord were first celebrated.[22] Indeed, while we believe that the faith of Christ was preached earlier at Rome and perhaps elsewhere, it was not done so publicly but rather secretly. Nor did they confess Christ publicly but rather secretly; nor were the sacrifices of the Lord celebrated there publicly but rather secretly. Because anyone who did any of these three things in a public place would soon have been slain by some means: if anyone preached

---

15 Rufinus/Eusebius, *Historia ecclesiastica* 3.1–2.

16 Eusebius/Jerome, *Chronica* 32; also Rufinus/Eusebius, *Historia ecclesiastica* 2.23.1.

17 *GL*, p. 321; also Cambiaso (1917), pp. 169–71; Di Fabio/Besta (1998), p. 32.

18 *GL*, p. 243.

19 The title 'princes of the apostles' for saints Peter and Paul dates at least to the late classical period, but it became more common after the eighth century as a statement of Roman primacy—appearing, for example, in the *Donation of Constantine*, 19. By Jacopo's time it was a common epithet for Peter and Paul.

20 On the idol, see parts 1.4 and 3.2 above.

21 Notable here is Jacopo's framing of the Genoese as agents in their own conversion and Christian faith, even as he acknowledges the contributions of local saints and martyrs. The story of Saint Nazarius that follows is characteristic both for Jacopo's insistence that the Genoese must already have been Christian before Nazarius' arrival, and for his contrast of Nazarius' welcome by the pious Genoese v. the saint's martyrdom by the still-pagan Milanese.

22 The fifteenth-century annalist Giorgio Stella was unable to identify this history, and lamented that Jacopo did not name it more explicitly (*Annales genuenses*, p. 14).

PART FOUR: ON THE CHRISTIANISATION OF GENOA

Christ publicly, or confessed the faith of Christ publicly, or celebrated the sacrifices of Christ, they would quickly have been killed without any hearing. Thus the city of Genoa is said to have been the first city in which the faith of Christ was preached publicly, in which everyone confessed Christ publicly, and in which the divine sacrifices were performed publicly.

Moreover, in the legend of the saints Nazarius and Celsus we read that Emperor Nero ordered the blessed Nazarius and Celsus, who were preaching the faith of Christ, to be put on a ship and drowned in the depths of the sea.[23] But just when they had been tossed overboard, an angel of God came to them and a massive tempest arose around the ship. Afraid of the danger, the ship's sailors asked the holy men to climb back into the ship and pray for them, promising that they would receive the faith of Christ. And so it was that when the holy men had done this and tranquillity had returned, they came unharmed to Genoa.

The same legend continues word for word as follows: 'Then as they wished, they were led to the city of Genoa by the will of God'. And indeed, when Nazarius and the boy Celsus had entered the city of Genoa, they did not cease day and night to preach the word of God, announcing the remission of sins through the baptism of salvation in the name of our Lord Jesus Christ, and they baptised those who believed. And in another legend of Saint Nazarius we read thus: 'Then they buried Saints Nazarius and Celsus in a place almost six hundred paces from the city of Genoa, where through their merits those who prayed were heard and their vows were fulfilled. This place was called "to the holy pilgrims" (*ad sanctos peregrinos*)'. We believe this place to be where the church of San Nazario in Albaro is today.[24]

After they had come to the city of Genoa and preached there for a little while, they went next to Milan. Now, presented with this very same legend of Saint Nazarius, one must acknowledge one of two facts: either—the option we believe more likely—that the city of Genoa was

---

23 *GL*, pp. 406–7; *DGA*, p. 5. Nazarius and Celsus are usually considered Milanese saints, as their relics were among those claimed to be have been discovered by Ambrose of Milan in 395: McLynn (1994), pp. 363–4. There is nonetheless much disagreement in the sources: Gregory of Tours, *Gloria martyrum* 46, 60 (pp. 69–70, 79). On their cult in Genoa: Cambiaso (1917), pp. 200–1.

24 The church of Santi Nazario e Celso is attested in a document of 987, which describes it as 'the basilica of Saint Nazarius which was founded along the seashore in the place called Albaro known as "to the holy pilgrims"'; *Cartario genovese*, p. 27. The church was demolished for the construction of Corso Italia after World War I.

already of the faith before Nazarius preached there, so that Nazarius confirmed in the faith those Genoese who had already converted and gave new birth in the sacred font to those who had not already been baptised; or that Saint Nazarius converted the entire city of Genoa to the faith of Christ at that time. For if neither of these two things was true, the Genoese would not have allowed the blessed Nazarius to preach publicly in Genoa for so many days. Instead, they would have expelled him with blows or slain him with assorted punishments as the Milanese did. For when Nazarius had gone from Genoa to Milan and preached Christ there, both he and the blessed Celsus were beheaded by the Milanese, who were then still unbelievers (*infideles*). Just as the Milanese killed Nazarius for preaching the faith of Christ because they were still unbelievers, so the Genoese would have murdered the aforesaid Nazarius for preaching the faith of Christ in Genoa if they had not already been believers.

Thus if someone asks when Genoa was converted to the faith of Christ, we say: if it received the faith of Christ at the same time as Nazarius was preaching there, it will be correct to say that the city of Genoa received the faith of Christ in the thirty-fifth year of the years following the Passion of Christ. We can explain and prove our reasoning in this way: it is agreed among the authentic chronicles that Emperor Nero was killed in the thirty-sixth year after the Passion of Christ, and, as the blessed Jerome says in his book *On famous men*, this Nero murdered the holy apostles Peter and Paul in the last year of his reign.[25] Saint Nazarius was also killed in that year, so we conclude that Nazarius was crowned martyr in the thirty-sixth year after the Passion of Christ.[26] For he preached in Genoa at least a year before his death and thus it is manifestly clear that Nazarius preached the faith of Christ in Genoa in the thirty-fifth year after the Passion of Christ and converted that same city to the faith of Christ. According to this reasoning, therefore, the city of Genoa was converted to the faith of Christ in the sixty-eighth year from the birth of the Lord, which is the thirty-fifth year from the Passion of the Lord. And if we affirm that which is even more likely—that Genoa had been converted to the faith of Christ even before Nazarius preached there—then we must conclude that the city of Genoa was converted to the faith even fewer than thirty-five years after the Passion of Christ.

---

25 Jerome, *De viris illustribus* 1, 5.

26 That is, AD 68. (Following Eusebius/Jerome, Jacopo's calculations usually date the Passion to AD 32.)

PART FOUR: ON THE CHRISTIANISATION OF GENOA

Therefore, from the things which have been stated above and from the fact that the city of Genoa came to the faith of Christ so quickly after the Passion of Christ, what we have previously claimed as true ought to be obvious to all: namely, that the city of Genoa was the first city, or one of the first cities, in Italy in which the faith of Christ was publicly preached and publicly recived, and in which the sacrifices of God were celebrated publicly.

Chapter three: Here it is demonstrated through reasoning that the city of Genoa was the first in Italy, or one of the first, which received the faith of Christ. Now that we have proved via authorities that our city of Genoa was the first in all of Italy, or one of the first, to receive the faith of Christ, we should nonetheless demonstrate the same thing again through reasoning.[27] For it is agreed by all the chronicles and authentic histories that Nero was the first emperor to inflict persecution upon Christians. The second was Domitian, the third Trajan, the fourth Hadrian, the fifth Antoninus Verus, and the sixth Aurelius Commodus.[28] In fact, nearly all the other emperors up to the time of Constantine cruelly persecuted the faith of Christ. And according to the chronicles, from Emperor Nero up to the time of Constantine 252 years passed, between when Nero took the throne in the year of the Lord 57, and Constantine in the year of the Lord 309.[29] Throughout this whole period, the emperors sent an edict through the whole world that Christians everywhere should be investigated (*inquirerentur*).[30] Furthermore, in these same years during which the persecution of Christians lasted, many thousands of Christians were killed—as many in Syria as in Greece and also Italy, and most especially in Rome, Milan, Ravenna, and in other parts of Italy. And in all of these years there was not one Christian killed in Genoa. Hence it appears that Genoa was converted to the faith of Christ in the time of Emperor Nero, under

---

27 In seeking to increase the credibility of his claim about the precocity of Christianity among the Genoese, here too Jacopo demonstrates scholastic methods of argumentation: after having appealed to 'authorities' (that is, reliable and authoritative sources), he anticipates and rebuts possible challenges to his argument using logic.

28 The last two are known today as Marcus Aurelius and Commodus. The confusion comes from books 4 and 5 of Eusebius' *Historia ecclesiastica*, which mixes up the extremely similar official names of the Antonine emperors.

29 Nero actually took the throne in AD 54, and Constantine was proclaimed emperor in 306, so Jacopo's dates are three years off.

30 The verb *inquirere* implies official investigation, being the root of both 'inquest' and 'inquisition'. (Like the Dominican order, the papal inquisition had been founded in the early thirteenth century to combat heresy.)

whom the first persecution of Christians occurred. For if its people had been unbelievers, it is certain that they would have killed many Christians just as other cities did.

Perhaps someone will argue that the Genoese did not kill Christians because Christians did not travel through Genoa—but this argument cannot stand. For it is agreed that the faith of the Christians had its origin in Syria, in Palestine, because all of the apostles and early Christians are known to have been from the Kingdom of Jerusalem. From there the faith of Christ came out of Palestinian Syria into Greece, and from Greece it came into Italy. In particular, the faith of Christ was preached by the blessed Peter the apostle at Rome, where that same blessed Peter held the pontifical throne for twenty-five years.[31] Indeed, who does not know that in those twenty-five years in which Saint Peter lived in Rome, many Christians came to Italy—as many from Syria as from Greece—to seek out Saint Peter and visit him, who was the vicar of Christ? Who does not know that during the 252 years during which the persecution lasted, many thousands of Christians, as many from Syria as from Greece, came to Italy, and from Italy set out again for Greece or Syria? And since the Genoese have always had ships with which they have sought out lands beyond the sea, including Greece, there can be no doubt whatever that many Christians came through Genoa during this time, be they those who wished to go from Italy into Syria or Greece, or those who desired to come to Italy from Syria or Greece.[32] And yet, as has been said, not one Christian was killed there at any time. From this it is manifestly clear that the Genoese were at that time catholic and faithful Christians.

But perhaps others will say: on account of the excellent reasoning given above, we cannot deny that many Christians passed through Genoa—but they will have passed secretly so that they remained unknown. This argument does not have the semblance of truth, however. For how likely is it that so many thousands of Christians should pass through Genoa over the span of 252 years, and not even some of them were recognised as such? At that time the emperors were still ordering that Christians should be diligently sought out and killed in all lands. If they were still unbelievers, the Genoese would have pursued that investigation, and if they had investigated it is certain that they would have found many

---

31 GL, p. 342.

32 An aside reinforcing the idea that the Genoese were naturally inclined toward maritime activity.

PART FOUR: ON THE CHRISTIANISATION OF GENOA

whom they ought to have killed. But no Christian was ever killed there, and from this it is obvious—as was affirmed above—that from that time the Genoese were themselves faithful Christians, so they did not persecute believers. It is just as Saint Augustine says: the good do not persecute the good, nor the bad the bad, but rather the good the bad, and the bad the good.[33] So, after having become Christians, the Genoese did not persecute other Christians because the good do not persecute the good. Furthermore, while they were still given to idolatry, the Genoese did not persecute other idolators because the bad do not persecute the bad. But having become Christians the Genoese persecuted heretics because the good persecute the bad. And the heretics likewise persecuted catholics because the bad persecute the good.

In fact, this faith of Christ to which the city of Genoa held—which it adopted so quickly after the Passion of Christ—it served so wholly, so undiminished, that no heretic was ever able to spread the seed of any error there, nor was any heresy ever able to sprout forth there. For although many cities of Lombardy (which are very close to the city of Genoa) were corrupted by heretical depravity, the city of Genoa has held undiminished to the purity of the faith and protected it honourably.[34] No contagion of error was ever able to be introduced there; rather, the city has held always to the foundations of the catholic truth. For from the beginning it has been unheard of that anyone of the Genoese homeland should be corrupted by heretical depravity; in fact, if it ever happens that other heretics from Lombardy or elsewhere come to Genoa, they are taken and burnt in fires as soon as they are discovered. And because the Genoese were so opportunely united and founded in the faith of Christ, they are today constant and steadfast in the sacraments of the faith, assiduous in ecclesiastical office, and devoted to hearing the word of God.

---

33 A sentiment recurring numerous times in the works of Augustine, e.g. letter 93 to Vincentius, para. 8.

34 A pointed contrast between Genoese orthodoxy and heresies such as that of the Patarenes, which were known to have flourished in Lombardy, particularly in Milan; see Taylor (2016); in 1216, for example, Jacques de Vitry called Milan a 'den of heretics' (*fovea hereticorum*; letter 1, p. 72).

PART FIVE: ON THE GROWTH OF THE CITY

Here follows part five, which addresses the three different states in which the city of Genoa has existed according to the vagaries of time. This part has three chapters: the first discusses the city's nature and size (qualis et quanta) *at the time of its founding; the second discusses its nature and size during the time of its growth, and the third discusses its nature and size as it was and is now at the time of its perfection.*

Chapter one: The nature and size of the city of Genoa at the time of its founding. Since no one arrives at a summit all of a sudden, all great matters begin as small ones, and the highest things start from the lowest ones—thus the city of Genoa began from small things. From small things it progressed to great things, and from great things to the greatest ones. For it went through three phases, namely the states of creation, development, and perfection. At the time of its creation it was very small. At the time of its development it was fairly large. And at the time of its perfection, it was—and is now—very great and powerful. For this is the manner and process of development, namely to begin from small things, to proceed to great things, and eventually to arrive at the greatest things.

We see examples of this in natural, corporeal, and spiritual things.[1] In natural things we have the example that daylight does not spread itself out in its fullness all at once, but with the modest light of dawn; afterward it proceeds to a greater light, and finally *grows into perfect day*. This is what the very wise Solomon says: *the path of the just, like a shining light, increases and finally develops into perfect day.*[2] We also see an example of this in corporeal things, because when a person is born, he is never born perfected in body or age, but from childhood he comes to youth and from youth to the stage of adulthood. Finally, we see an example of this in spiritual things because no one acquires perfection in grace immediately; rather, from the beginnings of grace one advances to a proficient grace; and from a proficient grace one reaches a state of

---

1 Bertini Guidetti (*CCG*, p. 124), notes Augustinian echoes here.
2 Proverbs 4.18, paraphrased; cf. *SS*, fol. 424v.

PART FIVE: ON THE GROWTH OF THE CITY 83

confirmed and perfect grace. Thus the city of Genoa at the time of its establishment was like the dawn, that is, a modest light; at the time of its development it was like a fairly strong light, and at the time of its perfection it was and is like full (*perfecta*) day. Similarly, at the time of its establishment it was like a child; at the time of its development it was like a steady youth; and at the time of its perfection it was and is at the stage of robust adulthood. Similarly, at the time of its establishment it had the initial grace by which one begins wisely; at the time of its development it had the proficient grace by which one proceeds laudably; and now in the time of its perfection it has achieved that perfect grace through which one acquires power and glory.

The nature and size of the city of Genoa at the time of its foundation, or how that foundation occurred—these things have not been handed down for our knowledge. Nonetheless, certain facts may be read regarding this matter which demonstrate the city's small size in the beginning. Solinus does not call it Janua, but Janicula ('little Janua'), wishing by this to imply its smallness.[3] Titus Livy does not call it a city (*civitas*), but a town (*oppidum*).[4] For a town is a kind of fortified settlement (*castrum*), so-called either from the opposition (*oppositio*) of its walls or from the wealth (*ops*)—that is, the riches—which are stored there for safekeeping in time of war.[5] On this subject Titus Livy says that a certain African named Mago suddenly seized and destroyed Genoa: if it had been large and well-fortified, he would not have been able to capture the city so quickly.[6] Similarly, we read in the register of the archiepiscopal palace in Genoa as well as in the legend of Saint Romulus that the Saracens came often to our lands in galleys and ships and perpetuated terrible slaughters.[7] Further, in the ancient histories nothing but occasional mention is made of Genoa, and we believe this is so for two reasons: one is that the city was so small that historians did not care to discuss it. The other reason is that because of its small size it was not well known except in places nearby, and so the historians had no knowledge of it. All these things which we have put forward suggest that the city

---

3 Solinus, *De mirabilibus mundi* 2.5, discussed at greater length in parts 1.2 and 3.1 above.
4 Livy, *Ab urbe condita* 30.1.10.
5 Isidore, *Etymologies* 15.2.5.
6 During the Second Punic War; see part 2.3 above.
7 *RC* 2.424—the archiepiscopal register, maintained by Jacopo's own chancery (*CMG*, pp. 32–3)—and *Vita beati Romuli episcopi*. On the Fatimid sack of 934–35, see n. 19, below.

of Genoa was small in the beginning. But let us examine how these things which originally suggested smallness have recently been turned into very great things, and now suggest its great dignity. For what was called Janicula can not only be called *Janua*, that is, 'gate', but also *Janitrix*, that is, 'gatekeeper', because she is the *janitrix* or gatekeeper of the sea: if she closes this gate, no one can open it, and if she opens it, no one can close it.[8] That is, if she closes the sea, there is no one—from as far as Syria and Greece to the furthest coast of Spain—who could venture to navigate it safely. If, however, she opens the sea and watches over it, everyone may navigate it safely.

Indeed, where once Genoa was called a town or fortress, now it can only be called a realm or even an empire.[9] Where once the city was captured and destroyed by the Africans, now it would be the easiest thing for Genoa to capture and destroy all of Africa, rather than Africa destroy Genoa. Where once she was invaded by Saracens, now she assaults the cities of the Saracens forcefully, invades them daringly, and captures them triumphantly. Where once, because of her small size, she was not named in any of the ancient histories, now due to her superiority she is called a realm and empire throughout the whole world. Where once her name was not well known except in nearby places, now it is spread even *to all the ends of the earth*.[10] Behold, then, how the city of Genoa began from small things, from small things proceeded to great things, and from great things achieved the greatest.

Chapter two: The nature and size of the city of Genoa during the time of its development. Now that we have explored the era of the foundation of our city, when it was quite small in size, let us explore the era of its development, when it was quite large in size. For after it had begun to grow, the city of Genoa reached a large size and accomplished many great, magnificent, and victorious deeds. If we wished to enumerate every one of these magnificent and victorious deeds that it achieved after it had begun to grow—which are included in a certain chronicle of the commune of Genoa—the task would be very laborious for us and we would need to write a very large book.[11] Accordingly we

---

8 Revelation 3.7.
9 Compare the similar words of Jacopo Doria: *DGA*, 5.172–5.
10 Psalm 71.8.
11 The *Genoese annals* (*GA*), which were so closely supervised by the commune that the work has survived in only three copies, the original consulted by Jacopo being now Paris, Bibliothèque Nationale MS lat. 10136: *CMG*, pp. 37–8 (Macchiavello/Rovere). For reasons that remain unknown, the annals ended in 1293 with Jacopo Doria (*DGA*).

PART FIVE: ON THE GROWTH OF THE CITY

will recount here only four of the magnificent and victorious deeds which are recorded in the chronicle of the city of Genoa.

Every city has responsibilities to God, to itself, to its friends, and to its enemies; for it is bound to show honour to God; to establish the common good for itself; to support its friends, and to love its enemies according to the law of the Gospel. Unfortunately, the men of this world desire more to have victory over their enemies than to bestow laborious charity upon them. And therefore we are recording in this present work one great victory which the city of Genoa achieved during the time of its development, which was to the honour of God; a second, which was of great benefit to the city itself; a third, which was of great consolation to its friends and fellow Christians; and a fourth, which was a great victory and an exaltation of the city.

First, therefore, we include the victorious deed which was to the great honour of God. When the enemies of the cross of Christ—that is, the Saracens—held Jerusalem and were worshipping Mohammed in the place where Christ was crucified, that land which was consecrated with the blood of Christ was defiled with the foul works of the sons of the devil. The tomb in which the precious body of Christ lay was given into the hands of pigs and dogs.[12] For this reason, the Genoese were inspired to avenge this great injury to Christ and to reclaim the tomb of Christ from the hands of the Saracens. They valiantly armed forty galleys, took Jerusalem, and made Godfrey of Bouillon king.[13] They then took Acre and Gibelet, as well as *Cersona*, Arsuf, and Tartus.[14] Jerusalem was captured in the year of the Lord 1099, and when they came to the tomb of the Lord, they asked Christ to send them a light from heaven as he was accustomed to do at certain times. After they had prayed thusly, they clearly saw a light descend from heaven, the sixteen lamps which were hanging there were put out and relit by that

---

12 Crusading rhetoric relied heavily on tropes of pollution or uncleanness: Akbari (2012), pp. 235–7; Morton (2017), pp. 213–14. 'Pigs and dogs', as many Christian authors knew, were particularly opprobrious insults to Muslims.

13 Perhaps one of the shortest and most biased descriptions of the First Crusade ever written. For further details, see *LCO*.

14 Acre (*Acharon*) and Gibelet (*Gibellum minor*; also known as Byblos; now Jubayl) fell to the crusaders in spring 1104; Tartus (*Tortosa*) in 1102: *CGA*, p. 14. (Tartus should not be confused with Tortosa, Spain—also known as *Tortosa* in Latin—which the Genoese captured in 1147–48.) For Arsuf (*Arzotum*), which the crusaders took in May 1101, see *CGA*, p. 9. *Cersona* is unclear: Monleone (*JVC* 2.85 n. 1) and Bertini Guidetti (*CCG*, p. 128) both suggest a misspelling of the biblical *Secrona* (Joshua 15.11), but disagree as to what city that might be; given the context, it may also be a miscopying of Ascalon (*Scalona*) or Caesarea (*Cesaria*). For all places mentioned in the text, see fig. 1.

divine fire, and they all gave thanks to God.[15] Caffaro—who was the first chronicler of the deeds of the commune of Genoa—says that he was present at the aforementioned capture of Jerusalem, and that he saw the aforementioned light descend from heaven, and the lamps being lit.[16] In the following year [1100] they armed twenty-six galleys and six ships and went to Syria, and upon the death of Godfrey, king of Jerusalem, they made Baldwin (duke of Lotharingia and that same Godfrey's brother) king in his place. They also took in battle Caesarea and many other cities of the Saracens, and erected the churches of Christ in them.[17] In the year of the Lord 1106 the Genoese armed forty galleys, went to Syria, took Tripoli and Jableh, and filled those cities with the churches of Christ.[18]

The city of Genoa accomplished another victorious deed during the time of its growth, which gave great benefit to the city itself. Around the year 933, when the aforementioned Genoese were on their way somewhere with their armed galleys: behold! many galleys of Saracens came from Africa and entered the city of Genoa as enemies, overrunning the city by force of arms and creating a great slaughter of men. They stole the treasures and riches of the city and took many children and women captive, carrying them off to their own land.[19] When the Genoese galleys returned and landed, they heard this sad and painful story, and with hearts aflame they immediately pursued the enemy as fiercely as lions. Now, the Saracens had stopped on a certain Sardinian island of the *Buxinarii*, which is called Insclamontor, to divide up the spoils and amuse themselves in feasting.[20] The Genoese bravely attacked the enemy

15 The miracle of the Holy Fire, believed by Orthodox Christians to occur annually at the Holy Sepulchre on Holy Saturday (the day preceding Easter).

16 *CGA*, pp. 8–9 (Jacopo embroiders here, since Caffaro simply says that 'the lamps came to light'). On Caffaro, see *JD*; *HP*, pp. 2–6; *CMG*, pp. 323–5 (Petti Balbi).

17 Despite Jacopo's descriptions, Godfrey was never king of Jerusalem (see part 11.17) and Baldwin was count of Boulogne, not duke of Lotharingia. The crusaders took Caesarea in May 1101: *CGA*, pp. 9–12; *LCO*, pp. 112–13.

18 Tripoli and Jableh (*Gibellum maior*) were both conquered in 1109: *CGA*, p. 14.

19 The Fatimid sack of Genoa in 934–35, described by Liudprand of Cremona in *Antapodosis* 4.5, trans. Squatriti (2007), p. 142; discussed in *CMG*, pp. 86–7 (Balzaretti), which notes that while Liudprand describes the attackers as 'Phoenician' (i.e. African), they probably came from a Muslim base on Sardinia or the coast of Provence. While based on Liudprand, Jacopo's account comes from *DGA* (pp. 6–7) via Sigebert of Gembloux's *Chronica* (p. 347). In the earlier sources, however, the bloody fountain portends (that is, occurs before) the sack, while Jacopo's words imply that the miracle occurred afterward.

20 Monleone (*JVC* 2.87–8 n. 1) connects this to the Isola di Mortorio, off northeastern Sardinia.

PART FIVE: ON THE GROWTH OF THE CITY 87

and put every one of them to the sword, and to this day—say those who have seen it—a heap of the bones of those killed is displayed there in witness to the immense slaughter that occurred there. Then the Genoese returned to Genoa with great joy, having rescued their wives and sons and treasure. But since the Saracens made such a great massacre of men in Genoa, the water in a certain Genoese fountain changed to blood, which it gave off copiously for a single day in the place that is today called Fontanella, as is explained later in the chapter about Theodulf, the ninth bishop.

The city of Genoa accomplished another victorious deed during the time of its development that brought great consolation to Christians. Since the city of Antioch had been captured by the Saracens and taken away from the Christians [in 1084], the church and all of Christianity were beset by immense sadness, equally because it was a noble city, and because the name of Christianity had its first beginning there, and because the blessed apostle Peter held the first episcopal seat there (which he occupied for seven years), and because the clerics' crown or tonsure first began there.[21] Accordingly the highest pontiff (*pontifex maximus*, i.e. pope) requested the Genoese to send an army of ships to recover the city—and in obedience to him the Genoese sent out to Syria forty galleys strongly armed as stated above. Thus in the year of the Lord 1099, with a great army of Franks (*Gallici*) and other pilgrims under Duke Godfrey of Bouillon, they came to Antioch and took it by force, giving great thanks to God.[22] Then the Saracens gathered up a great army and returned to Antioch, wishing to retake it—but the Genoese, together with the other Christians, put them entirely to flight, and thus the Genoese returned home with a great victory and much rejoicing.

Finally, during this time of its development, the city of Genoa accomplished another magnificent deed that brought it great victory over its enemies. For around the year of the Lord 1125 the Genoese strongly armed eighty galleys along with many ships and other boats against the Pisans.[23] They sailed up the Arno River, disembarked, planted their standard and banners into the earth, and put to flight the army of the Pisans—so that the terrified Pisans settled with them, promising to do whatever the Genoese wanted of them. And because the Pisans held

---

21 Acts 11.26; *GL*, pp. 163–6.
22 The siege of Antioch (1097–98), related in *LCO*, p. 109.
23 *CGA*, pp. 16–17 (actually 1120, as Jacopo records elsewhere in the *Chronicle*).

many Genoese imprisoned, the Genoese went and freed them from that place—and having thus achieved everything that they wanted according to their desires, they returned to Genoa in great glory.

Chapter three: The nature and size of the city of Genoa as it was and is now at the time of its perfection. Now that we have seen Genoa's nature and size during the eras of its establishment and development, it remains only to examine its nature and size as it was and is now at the time of its perfection. In this period it has been and is still at its greatest and most powerful. We believe that this period began about the time the city was raised to the honour of an archbishopric, which occurred in the year of the Lord 1133: at that time the city of Genoa began to expand enormously, and its fame began to spread everywhere throughout many lands. Indeed, it was fitting that it began to be raised up at the same time as it merited to be exalted with the honour of an archbishopric—so that, as its spiritual authority began to grow, so too its secular power increased, so that it began to be more glorious in riches and power, and these were made more sublime by the dignity of the archbishopric. Thus from then on it increased greatly in riches and glory, and expanded its dominion.[24] It grew so much, in fact, that its magnificence has challenged the power of kings, the Saracen people, the city of the Venetians, and even the city of the Pisans.

Let us demonstrate this fact by a few examples which we find in the chronicle of the commune of Genoa, which we believe to be true due to the manner of its recording.[25] For if we wished to include here everything which is written on this topic there, a too-great prolixity would oppress the souls of our listeners. Let us therefore demonstrate simply how the magnificence of the city of Genoa challenges even imperial authority. For whenever kings, princes, or emperors have chosen to speak against the church, the Genoese have always supported the church—remaining unshaken in their faith and diligent in their piety, without fearing the power of kings, without being intimidated by the wrath of princes, and giving little thought to the threats and warnings of emperors. In the year of the Lord 1155 Emperor Frederick ordered Genoa to send solemn ambassadors into his presence with full authority

---

24 The word 'dominion' (*dominio*) here has both generic and specific meanings, since the Genoese referred to their numerous overseas holdings as 'the Dominion': *CMG*, chap. 18 (Origone).

25 See n. 11, above.

PART FIVE: ON THE GROWTH OF THE CITY 89

to do whatever he told them.[26] The ambassadors were therefore sent—but without holding full authority as he had wished. When they arrived, the emperor sought to make the Genoese do homage to him, to swear fealty, to surrender pledges, and to pay tribute; he also demanded many other oppressive things. So when the ambassadors heard this from their ungracious host they returned to Genoa and reported everything in council, and it was determined in council that they would refuse everything that the emperor demanded, and instead offer him only their loyalty. When the emperor heard this he was roused to the greatest anger and fury, and threatened to come in force to the city and subdue it to his authority. The Genoese therefore prepared to defend themselves manfully, encircling the city with a wall and raising other fortifications.[27] But when the emperor heard of their great steadfastness, he abandoned this behaviour and contented himself just with their loyalty.

Also, in the year of the Lord 1162 when Alexander III was canonically elected pope, Emperor Frederick tyrannically arranged for four others in succession to be made highest pontiff, opposing the aforesaid Alexander with all his resources.[28] Those others who were so inappropriately elected, however, were destroyed by death, for those who have come by evil also go by evil. This was the cause of a schism between the pope and the emperor that lasted for a long time.[29] But when Alexander was unable to remain in the City [Rome] out of fear of the emperor, he sent to the Genoese to rescue him *out of the hand of Pharaoh* and bring him to Genoa.[30] The Genoese accordingly armed their galleys and carried Pope Alexander off to Genoa, caring little for the threats of the emperor since they were serving the church. Afterward they took him into France. The Genoese similarly resisted Frederick I, Otto, Conrad, and Frederick

26 Frederick I 'Barbarossa' (emperor 1155–90); the term 'solemn ambassadors' indicates formal representatives authorised to negotiate for the commune. Although Jacopo only mentions 1155, this paragraph summarises events of 1154–58: *CGA*, pp. 42, 50–4; Freed (2016), pp. 234–42.

27 Recounted more fully in part 12.1, below (nn. 23–4).

28 As Caffaro reports (*CGA*, pp. 55–9), Alexander was consecrated on 20 September 1159. The four antipopes supported by Frederick were Victor IV (1159–64), Paschal III (1164–68), Calixtus III (1168–78) and Innocent III (1179–80); see Freed (2016), chaps. 10, 12.

29 1160–77; Frederick recognised Alexander as pope after being defeated at Legnano in 1176, but the schism continued until 1180, with some of the Roman nobility supporting antipopes Calixtus III and Innocent III.

30 Early 1162: *CGA*, p. 63. The reference to Deuteronomy 7.8 and/or 2 Kings 17.7 analogises Genoa as the Promised Land.

II with all their might in favour of the church when those emperors had been excommunicated and declared schismatic by the church—but these events have found sufficient expression in all the chronicles and histories.[31]

Also, in the year of the Lord 1244, when the other Emperor Frederick [II] was holding the lord pope Innocent IV besieged at Sutri, the Genoese armed twenty-four galleys, collected the pope from Civitavecchia, and took him to Genoa.[32] This displeased the emperor greatly, particularly when he learned that Innocent was going to Lyons intending to convene a council against him and depose him as emperor—as indeed he went and did so depose him.[33] But the Genoese did not much care about Frederick's humiliation.

Furthermore, the race of the Saracens often felt the might of the Genoese. For the Genoese besieged and captured many famous cities of theirs, namely Almería and Tortosa, which they took in the year of the Lord 1148 with a great fleet of galleys.[34] For in the capture of Almería the Genoese had sixty-four galleys and many other ships.[35] In taking the aforesaid city, they captured 20,000 men, not including those who were slain in the battle. Proceeding to Tortosa in the following year, they took it by force.[36] In the year of the Lord 1232, they also took Ceuta, a famous and populous city of the Saracens, by force; at this battle there were seventy great ships and thirty smaller ones, as well as twenty galleys and many other armed boats.[37] Then in the year of the Lord 1220 they took Damietta by force with the help of the French (*Franci*).[38]

The city of the Pisans has also often experienced the power of Genoa. For the Genoese often went into Porto Pisano and razed its towers to

31 'Conrad' here may be either Conrad II, duke of Swabia (fourth son of Frederick I), or Conrad IV, king of the Romans (1237–54), the second son of Frederick II.

32 Sutri is about 50 km north of Rome, while Civitavecchia is west of it on the coast. Innocent (the Genoese Sinibaldo Fieschi, 1243–54) arrived in Genoa on 7 July 1244: *GA* 3.151–6.

33 The First Council of Lyons (June–July 1245), at which Innocent officially deposed Frederick.

34 A three-phase expedition to Spain extending over 1146–48, narrated in Caffaro's *Ystoria captionis Almarie et Turtuose* (*YCAT*); see *HP*, pp. 37–40. Caffaro was one of the consuls in charge of the initial 1146 expedition.

35 1 August–17 October 1147.

36 1 July–30 December 1148.

37 The Genoese campaign against Ceuta (on the African coast) lasted 1231–35: *GA* 3.56, 68, 72–6.

38 The Fifth Crusade (1217–21): *GA* 2.159–61. The capture of Damietta was its only success: see part 12.4 n. 107, below.

PART FIVE: ON THE GROWTH OF THE CITY 91

the foundations.[39] They also thoroughly destroyed Piombino, bringing its women and children back to Genoa.[40] What more, then? If we tried to describe all the victories which the Genoese have had over the Pisans at different times, we would exhaust ourselves; furthermore, we would incite disgust in our readers and oppress the ears of our listeners. Therefore anyone who wishes to know such things may read the chronicles of the city of Genoa, where he will find all these things diligently inscribed.

But there is one other victorious deed of our own time that we do not wish to pass over in silence. In the year of the Lord 1283 [actually 1284] the Pisans armed seventy-two galleys and many other ships, intending to sail up the coast of Genoa and inflict much damage. Against them, the Genoese manfully armed eighty-six galleys, of which the lord Oberto Doria—who was then the *capitano* of the commune of Genoa—was made admiral.[41] Thirty-six further galleys had been already been fitted out many days earlier; the lord Benedetto [Zaccaria] had been made admiral of these and advanced against the Pisans in Sardinia. And behold! when he arrived with his fleet and joined it to the fleet of the lord *capitano*, and when the galleys of the Genoese encountered the galleys of the Pisans at Porto Pisano, they attacked them so powerfully that they took thirty-three galleys and sank many others into the sea.[42] So great was the slaughter there and the massacre of men among the Pisans that recollection must inspire compassion and hearing inspire astonishment: it is said that the number of those killed or taken captive rose to ten thousand and more. Yet the Genoese displayed no ostentation or arrogance on account of this victory; rather, they praised the mighty works of God, who alone creates great wonders.[43]

Regarding the city of the Venetians, it should be said that these Venetians once inflicted many losses on the Genoese.[44] The reason for this was

---

39 Pisa is upstream from the mouth of the Arno, so the Pisans built a fortified seaport at the river's mouth known as Porto Pisano in the mid-twelfth century. It was finally destroyed by the Genoese in 1290: *DGA*, pp. 119–20.

40 The promontory of Piombino—on the coast approximately 100 km south of Pisa—was the Pisans' other major medieval seaport: *CGA*, pp. 22–3.

41 On the office of *capitano*, see part 6.1 n. 4, below.

42 The battle of Meloria (5–6 August 1284): *DGA*, pp. 51–7; *CMG*, pp. 464–6 (Kirk).

43 Psalm 135.4. The pious humility of the victorious Genoese contrasts vividly with the unmerited arrogance of the Venetians in the next section.

44 Since the *GA* ends in 1293, the rest of this chapter is entirely original, serving as the source of later accounts such as the Stella brothers' *Annales genuenses* (pp. 34–5). It is generally considered one of the best sections of the *Chronicle*, since Jacopo was not only an eyewitness but also a major player in the negotiations.

that our citizens, who at that time were paying little attention to the potential consequences, had placed in their galleys the people of Lombardy, who were unfamiliar with the nautical art and inexperienced in naval warfare.[45] They were just as ignorant of rowing as they were useless in fighting, being rough and inexperienced in all things. Such people know better how to till the earth than to plough through the watery waves, better how to pull wagons than to handle seagoing ships. People beset by stomach upset and headache prefer to groan piteously than to attack an enemy with force; they prefer to collapse prostrate on the ground rather than to support their wounded bodies while holding back their tears. Accordingly such men should occupy themselves with land wars without ever getting involved in naval battles. For every man performs better in that work in which he has more experience, for which reason our present citizens follow better counsel: they do not place Lombards or any other foreigners on their galleys and ships but only their own people and those of their own region. And thus they have subsequently had many victories over the Venetians and Pisans and their galleys.

Indeed, we will relate here one victorious deed which we know to have occurred recently. In the year of the Lord 1294, while certain merchants from Genoa were sailing into the regions of Romania [Byzantium], they learned that some Venetian galleys had captured three Genoese ships laden with costly goods and inflicted many other injuries on the Genoese in various places. The Venetian galleys were twenty-eight in number, with four more ships carrying eighty rowers. The galleys of the Genoese merchants were eighteen in number, with two ships of eighty rowers. So, driven by patriotic zeal these merchants of Genoa left their cargo at Pera; they elected as their admiral the noble man, lord Nicolino Spinola, who had been named solemn ambassador to the emperor of the Greeks by the commune of Genoa, and they went to assist their brothers.[46] First, however, they sent two Friars Minor [Franciscans] to the captain of the Venetian galleys, asking him to make peace between them and to free their brothers whom he had captured, together with their ships and their goods. The Venetians responded with great arrogance, being very confident of their numbers, and rushed to destroy the Genoese galleys with all their strength. The

---

45 The sardonic tone of this explanation for why 'the people of Lombardy' make bad sailors is characteristically Genoese.

46 Spinola appears in *DGA*, p. 23, as the admiral of a fleet against Pisa in 1282. Pera was the Genoese quarter in Constantinople.

Genoese therefore tried to avoid battle, especially because the Venetians were far greater in number. But when they had gone with their galleys into the port of Laiazzo, and they saw the fleet of galleys the Venetians were preparing against them, they came out of that port and prepared to defend themselves manfully. And behold, an incredible victory occurred—something unheard of in our times and, as we believe, ordained in Heaven—because, fighting bravely against such a multitude of Venetian galleys, these few Genoese galleys defeated them all and successfully captured twenty-five of them, all laden with precious goods, while the rest escaped the field of battle in flight.[47]

In this deed are fulfilled the words of Judas Maccabeus as they are written in the book of Maccabees: for when those on the side of the Judeans were very few and their enemies were many, Judas, wishing to encourage them, said to them: *it is easy for many to be captured by the hands of a few: and there is no difference in the sight of God in heaven to effect rescue with many or with a few, since victory in battle does not come from the great size of the army; rather, strength comes from heaven. They come against us with a proud and insolent multitude to destroy us, but we will fight for our souls, and the Lord himself will destroy them in front of our faces.*[48] These words which were spoken of that ancient battle can all be said appropriately of this recent battle. They were many, while we were few. They approached with insolence and pride; we stood for justice. They came to ruin and plunder us; we stood fast to defend ourselves. And thus it was easy for God to capture the many in the hands of a few, because there is no difference in the sight of God in heaven between freeing many and freeing a few.

The rest of the Venetians were so humiliated by this slaughter that they were filled with great grief and embarrassment, and they attempted to conceal their immense shame by words and deeds, and to whitewash it with certain colourful fictions.[49] First, they tried to conceal it with words: they are said to have written to various provinces both near and far that they did not now wish to clash with the Genoese in the regions

---

47 28 May 1294: Laiazzo (now Yumurtalık, Turkey) was a key port city of the Armenian kingdom of Cilicia in the northeastern Mediterranean.

48 1 Maccabees 3.18–22, slightly abridged, narrating the Maccabean Revolt against the Persian/Seleucid empire in 167–160 BC. As Bertini Guidetti (*CCG*, p. 139) points out, in his effort to remind the Genoese of their Christian mission Jacopo never loses sight of the connection between biblical events (the past), earthly events (the present), and God's universal plan (the future).

49 A moralising comment noting how the Venetians compounded their initial shame with further dishonourable behaviour.

of Armenia or Syria, but rather that they intended to encroach powerfully on their borders, to enter their gates by force, and to vanquish them triumphantly. Second, they attempted concealment with deeds, because they ordered that no Venetians should go to sea, but rather all should prepare themselves for battle with the Genoese. They also offered bribes and promises to the Catalans and Sicilians to become their allies against the Genoese, and they further began to recruit to their side the people of Treviso, Padua, Ferrara, Cremona, and others living along the banks of the Po, and to hire sailors and soldiers in those places. Finally, they began to build many new galleys, as well as to prepare arms and other supplies. You would then have seen the entire city of the Venetians occupied with nautical affairs, filled with commotion, and resounding with cries: here the din of craftsmen, there the clash of arms, there the clamour of irrational peoples.

For their part, upon hearing this din, the Genoese girded themselves bravely, built galleys, readied arms, and supplied all things necessary for war with diligent effort, not caring to form alliances with any others, nor to hire soldiers or sailors from anywhere else, nor to beg help from any others, knowing that they in themselves were sufficient to resist their enemies and indeed to triumph nobly over them. They did, however, enact a ruling that no one should go to sea, and they decreed that all Genoese, wherever they were, should return to Genoa (although few enough are reported to have returned).[50] Then in the month of January in the year of the Lord 1295, they made the noble man, lord Oberto Doria, chief admiral, and they assigned him full authority over the Council of the Credenza to organise and carry out all preparations for this undertaking.[51] And although the commune and various citizens owned many galleys, the aforesaid lord admiral of the Council of the Credenza ordered the building of many more brand-new galleys, so that in total they had a fleet of more than two hundred galleys.

While these things were happening, behold! notorious rumour carried to the ears of the highest pontiff lord Boniface VIII the news that the Genoese and the Venetians were making great preparations to engage each other at sea, to test their relative strengths and contend in combat with each other. And the highest pontiff saw that great discord between

---

50 A similar ban had been announced in 1282 at the outbreak of war with Pisa: *DGA*, p. 25.

51 Doria, a hero of the battle of Meloria (discussed earlier), served as *capitano del popolo* from 1270 to 1285. The Council of the Credenza was formed in 1282 (*DGA*, p. 25) to oversee military preparations, making it one of the earliest examples of an 'office of the admiralty'.

PART FIVE: ON THE GROWTH OF THE CITY 95

these two cities would bring losses to all of Christianity, and would especially pose an obstacle to business in the Holy Land.[52] Wishing to avoid these perils, he therefore sent official legates to each city, ordering them by apostolic letters to send official ambassadors bearing full [negotiating] authority into his presence without delay.[53] He sent the bishop of Messina to Genoa, and he ordered the archbishop of Reggio [Calabria] to go to the Venetians. These arrived in the cities to which they had been sent at the beginning of March. At the same time, Boniface ordered me to hasten into his presence for the same reason; and that highest pontiff kept the bishop of the Venetians, who had gone to the curia regarding another matter, there on account of this matter as well.[54] Then through his legates he declared truces between the cities, which he ordered observed until the coming feast of Saint John the Baptist [24 June 1295] under pain of excommunication, which he ordered applied immediately to any who transgressed.

Then two noble men were elected ambassadors—namely, the lord Luchetto Gattilusio and the lord Porchetto Salvago—along with two legal scholars, namely, the lord Manuel Osbergerius and the lord Pietro di Ugolino.[55] And when we had arrived in the presence of the highest pontiff, a treaty of peace or truce was considered at length by both sides. But we encountered a delay of one hundred days and more there, first because the highest pontiff was occupied in brokering a peace between the illustrious king of Sicily [Charles of Anjou] and the Sicilians, and then because two of the Venetian ambassadors returned to Venice, and only returned to the curia long after they were expected.[56] Now

52 A paraphrase of Boniface's first encyclical of 24 January 1295 (*Gloriosus et mirabilis*, p. 142; Potthast (1874), no. 24021, p. 1924), in which Boniface advocated for a general peace in Europe and attempted to rally Europe's Christians for a new crusade.
53 Boniface VIII, 'Breve ai Veneziani' (13 February 1295).
54 One of Jacopo's rare insertions of himself into the narrative: subtle, since he just says 'ordered me' (*michi mandavit*) instead of mentioning his office as archbishop. Although this chapter downplays his participation, he was in fact closely involved in these negotiations.
55 Luchetto Gattilusio (fl. 1266–1301) held numerous civic and ambassadorial posts (*DBI* 52.617–20); Porchetto Salvago, however, cannot be definitively identified (see 'Porchetus Salvaticus', *DBI* 85.26–7). Similarly, while Manuel and Pietro come from families known for their notaries and legal experts, they cannot be identified precisely.
56 Charles II of Anjou, king of Naples 1285–1309. Sicily and other Neapolitan dominions had been occupied by the Aragonese since 1282. Boniface succeeded in brokering the Treaty of Anagni, which was signed on 20 June 1295 by the kings of Aragon, Naples, France, and Majorca, but it was rejected by the Sicilians and Frederick of Aragon (King James' brother), who had himself crowned king of Sicily shortly thereafter.

these ambassadors knew that the force the Genoese were reputed to be preparing was so glorious, noble, and powerful that by various covert and clandestine methods they worked with all their might to induce the highest pontiff to totally ban these preparations, whether by influencing him to warn both Venetians and Genoese to abandon their arrangements under penalty of excommunication, and to call off their plans to engage their galleys against one another, or by persuading the highest pontiff that by apostolic authority he should extend the truce that had already ended up to the feast of Saint Michael [29 September 1295], to prevent the Genoese from completing their plans.[57]

But because Solomon says that *the net is spread in vain before the eyes of the birds*, so the Genoese ambassadors—both eyed and feathered, that is, both wise and cautious—detected their subterfuges and brought their efforts to naught.[58] But seeing their business at the Roman curia so greatly prolonged with nothing achieved, and considering that the term of the truce set by the highest pontiff had already elapsed, the Genoese bravely proceeded to complete and perfect their preparations: assigning commissions, distributing banners, raising their standard, and having pennants made, so that eight thousand pennants of silk and gold are said to have been prepared in a brief time.[59] Then you would have seen the entire city of Genoa filled with immense jubilation, and the entire Riviera moved to joy and delight. For some walked about adorned with silken flowers, others decorated with golden and silk insignia, and still others adorned with gleaming arms—and all were filled with great exultation. Thus all eagerly anticipated this battle, whether they were looking forward to dividing the spoils, seeking to discover treasures, or rushing into marriage. Many who could have remained offered themselves voluntarily or went of their own free will; indeed, they could not be held back. For just as men are usually forced to go into battle, so it was necessary that these should be somehow forced to remain, needing more to be reined in from battle than to be urged on with spurs. Also astounding was the fact that the son was not held back by his father, nor the father by his son, nor brother by

---

57 Here Jacopo reveals that he and the Genoese embassy remained at the papal court past the truce's original end-date of 24 June.

58 Proverbs 1.17; another ironic comment stressing the righteousness of the Genoese in the dispute.

59 The Genoese battle standard was that of Saint George: first attested in the twelfth century, it was kept between campaigns in the church of San Giorgio; see *CMG*, pp. 204–5 (Beneš). 'Pennants' (*supersigna*), by contrast, refers to personal banners.

PART FIVE: ON THE GROWTH OF THE CITY 97

brother, but instead the son followed the father, the father the son, and the brother the brother, all with wondrous eagerness. The entire nobility of the city joined this renowned fleet or force: all the *flower of its youth*, all the magistrates of its people, all the strength of the Riviera.[60] Thus just as we were prompt to avenge the wrongs done to Christ, so we are prompt to avenge those wrongs done us. Would that so glorious a force were turned to the recovery of the Holy Land, because all the enemies of the Christian faith who spied such a magnificent fleet would lose their courage, flee in terror, and bow their necks! But I hope in the Lord that in the future we will do those things for Christ which we have already been seen to do for the world.[61]

Why delay further? Between the fifteenth day of July and the fifteenth day of August [1295], two hundred galleys were fitted out with great glory, delight, and triumph. It then pleased the lord admiral and wise men that they should reduce the number to 165 galleys, and it was commonly said that this was done so that there was no galley which had fewer than 220 armed men; however, some are said to have had 250 and others 300. And all the nobles who were able to recruit men from the city or the Riviera to their galleys did not spare costs or expenses. Thus it is reported that there were 45,000 fighting men in this magnificent navy. But also, so many men remained in the city and along the Riviera that if it were necessary they could have nobly manned up to forty more galleys, with sufficient guards left behind in the city and along the Riviera.

And indeed, because the Genoese understood that the Venetians had been spewing out many bombastic words full of lies, and had written to various regions both near and far claiming that they would sail with a large fleet of galleys right up to the harbour of Genoa itself to both demonstrate their power and assert their rights, letters were sent on the behalf of the podestà, the *capitano*, and the wise men of the Credenza to the doge of the Venetians.[62] These stated among other things that it would seem indecent if the Genoese allowed a so large a fleet of Venetian galleys to traverse the marine waterways, to furrow so great

---

60 Livy, *Ab urbe condita* 8.8.6, 37.12.7.
61 Here Jacopo recalls the reader's attention to the broader Christian purpose of Genoa's good fortune and military success.
62 'The harbour of Genoa' (*portum Ianue*), while perfectly good Latin, is also a pun on *portus* (port) and *porta* (gate), given the equivalency Jacopo has previously established between *porta* and *Ianua*; see part 3.3, above.

an expanse of watery waves, or to expend such efforts in navigating that that they should come sailing even up to the harbour of Genoa itself. Accordingly, they made it known to the Venetians that the lord admiral Oberto Doria was planning to meet them with his fleet of galleys in the area of Sicily, either to seek them out if they were already present, or await them if they were absent. Then the Venetians might present their claims, and the Genoese would produce theirs likewise, and God—who knows all secrets and assesses all men most wisely—would in his judgment weigh the claims of both parties on his scale, and the law would give to each his rights insofar as He should see fit and as justice should demand. Once these letters were sent off, the lord admiral and his fleet departed from the environs of Genoa to seek out Sicilian parts, taking with him the salvation-bringing sign of our well-being and triumph: that is, the banner of the True Cross. Meanwhile, we returned from the curia with our business there unfinished and found the entire fleet of galleys already gone from Genoa and its borders.[63]

When the lord admiral arrived in the regions of Sicily, however, he and his entire company grieved exceedingly that they did not find the Venetians there. Accordingly he waited for them for eighteen days, sometimes in the port of Messina and sometimes elsewhere—to the admiration and stupefaction of all the Sicilians, who had never seen a fleet of galleys so magnificent, so glorious, or so powerful. But they might have had to wait for a very long time because there was neither news nor rumour of the Venetian fleet. For those who had once boasted that they would sail right up to the furthest confines of Genoa did not wish to come even as far as the much nearer areas of Sicily, and the same ones who had claimed they would force their way into the port of Genoa meekly shut themselves inside their own harbours. At this stage the Genoese would have advanced further and gone into the Gulf of Venice but the season was now autumn, and the change in the season usually taking place around that time would have made the voyage long and dangerous.[64] For that reason the lord admiral returned home with his fleet in great glory, and was received gloriously by the whole people and clergy and by ourselves, preceded by the salvific banner of the Cross in immense joy and triumph.

---

63 If the fleet had already sailed, Jacopo must have returned to Genoa after 15 August, making his stay at the papal court nearly six months long.

64 Probably not the modern Gulf of Venice but a broader reference to the Adriatic Sea.

PART FIVE: ON THE GROWTH OF THE CITY 99

Therefore regarding these Venetians the very wise words of Solomon seem appropriate: *Like clouds and winds which do not bring rain, so is the boastful man who does not fulfill his promises.*[65] For often we see that clouds emitting great claps of thunder threaten great rains, yet often do not bring what they portend. And often certain winds threaten their desire to bring the rains, and yet often they do not do so. Just so are the many arrogant people who produce magnificent words but do no deeds. It is said accurately of such people that like clouds and winds which do not bring rain, so the boastful man (*gloriosus*)—that is, the arrogant man (*vanagloriosus*)—does not fulfill his promises. And we see this confirmed in all the deeds of these Venetians: they have produced much thunder (that is, their threatening words); they have blown out winds (that is, their windy words); and they have made grand promises—but they have not produced any rain, because they have not done any powerful deeds. And thus it is well said of them that, *like clouds and winds when the rain does not follow, so is the boasting man—that is, the arrogant man—who does not fulfill his promises.*[66]

[Due to Jacopo's own death early in 1298, this section ends with the conflict between the Genoese and Venetians unresolved, before the great Genoese victory at Curzola on 8 September 1298. Feeling the lack of resolution, however, the anonymous scribe of one of the manuscripts of the *Chronicle* appended a passage to this chapter detailing these events: this has been translated in the appendix.]

---

65 Proverbs 25.14.
66 A clear statement of the attitude of the Genoese toward the Venetians shortly before the great Genoese victory at Curzola (8 September 1298). Bertini Guidetti (*CCG*, p. 146) stresses the rhetorical power of this last section—parallel structure, repetition, the use of proverbs and exempla—as revealing its emotional weight both for Jacopo as author and for his Genoese audience as readers and hearers.

PART SIX: ON GOVERNMENT

Here follows part six, which discusses the secular government of the city of Genoa. This part has three chapters: the first recounts how the city of Genoa has been governed by a variety of regimes. The second explains that it is safer to be ruled by one than by the many, unless that many is united for good. The third details the danger that arises from a bad government, and the advantages that accrue from a good one.

Chapter one: How the city of Genoa has been governed by a variety of regimes. Depending on the vicissitudes of time, the Genoese city has had many different types of rulers. First, consuls ruled the city: these were elected annually from within the city itself, and they accomplished many virtuous deeds in their time. The rule of consuls lasted up to the year of the Lord 1190, after which the city was ruled alternately by consuls and podestà, and this was true up to the year of the Lord 1216.[1] From that time on there were no more consuls from within the commune, but instead there were always podestà from outside [the city]; afterward the city was ruled by podestà, the first of which was Manegold, citizen of Brescia.[2] Additionally, every year, eight nobles were elected to assist the podestà, and the podestà conducted himself according to their counsel.[3] Podestarial rule lasted up to the year of the Lord 1270, but it would take far too long to record here the names of all the consuls and podestà, so he who wishes to know them may seek them in the chronicle of the commune. After that, *capitani* were elected, starting with the noble men lord Oberto Spinola and lord Oberto Doria.[4] Also elected were an abbot (*abbas*) and elders

---

1 On medieval Genoa's erratic political history, see *CMG*, chap. 4 (Filangieri), and Epstein (1996), pp. 325–8.

2 Foreign, non-citizen podestà were preferred, being professional magistrates with legal training, who could theoretically judge civic disputes with greater impartiality. The first was Manegold, appointed in 1190: *GA* 2.37.

3 The Council of Eight Nobles: *CMG*, pp. 109–10 (Filangieri).

4 *Capitano del popolo*: a citizen magistracy that replaced foreign podestà in the second half of the thirteenth century. The *popolo* was a political association of non-nobles, and the *capitano* served as its voice in government: *CMG*, p. xx. (I use the Italian

PART SIX: ON GOVERNMENT   101

(*antiani*).[5] And although a different podestà was elected every year, both criminal and civil authority (*merum et mixtum imperium*[6]) resided in the hands of the *capitani*. The rule of the *capitani* lasted up to the year of the Lord 1291, at which time rule returned to the podestà. Now, however, the *capitano* is elected from outside the city; the abbot and the elders continue their role in the regime, and so this kind of government continues for now. Whether the regime will change again, we do not know; but if it must be changed at some point, we ask God that it should always be exchanged for something better.

But there is no objection to the rule of consuls or podestà or *capitani* or abbots as long as the commonwealth (*res publica*) is ruled well.[7] On this subject we may cite the following example, which Saint Augustine discusses at one point.[8] Say a man has three keys to certain doors or gates (*porte sive ianue*[9]), the first of which is gold, the second silver, and the third wooden. With regard to the costliness of their material, the gold and silver keys will be worth more than the wooden one; but if the wooden one opens the door best, the wooden one will be worth more than the gold and silver with regard to the task of opening [the door]. Therefore let us imagine three men, one of whom is very powerful; he is like the gold key. The next is wealthy or wise; he is like the silver key. And the third is poor and of low condition; he is like the wooden key. It is certain that in the judgment of the world, the powerful and the wealthy are valued higher and regarded as better than the poor. But if a poor man rules a commonwealth better and more justly than the rich and powerful, he ought to be viewed as better with regard to the task of ruling.

---

capitano [*del popolo*] because the Anglicised 'captain of the people' sounds inaccurately democratic and/or populist.) Curiously, this summary of Genoese politics omits the regime of the first *capitano* Guglielmo Boccanegra (1257–62). 1270, by contrast, marked the first of several double captaincies (also discussed in parts 5.3 and 12.6).

5 The *abate del popolo* (abbot of the people)—not an ecclesiastical office despite its name—is poorly understood but seems to have replaced the *capitano* as the representative of the *popolo* in government once the office of *capitano* had been co-opted by the nobility; see *CMG*, p. xx. The *anziani* (elders) formed another advisory council.

6 While this was a common phrase inherited from the Roman legal tradition, medieval jurists disagreed on the distinction between *merum* ('full') and *mixtum* ('mixed') authority: Maiolo (2007), pp. 153–6.

7 *Res publica* does not carry the same political implications as the modern term 'republic', being used here in its literal sense of 'the public thing': matters pertaining to the public. 'Commonwealth' is the closest English equivalent.

8 *On Christian doctrine* 4.26 (*CCSL* 32.134–5).

9 Another pun on Genoa/Janua/*ianua*.

We have an example of this in the Old Testament.¹⁰ There were two men: one, a rich and powerful king named Saul who was like the gold key; the other, a poor shepherd named David who was like the wooden key. God saw that Saul was not ruling the commonwealth well, and he knew that the poor shepherd David would rule the commonwealth better, so he removed King Saul and placed the poor man David in power. By this we are given to understand that there is no objection to any ruler—of whatever status he might be—while he governs the commonwealth justly and commendably. In the same way, we say that there is no barrier to whoever rules our city, as long as it is ruled well and justly. For if it is ruled better by consuls than by podestà, then the consuls are better. But if instead it is ruled better by podestà than by consuls, then the podestà are more worthwhile. And again, if it is ruled better and more justly by *capitani* and abbots, then these are more worthwhile than the others. For he who is found to be most capable of governing should always be put in charge of governing. The status of a person should not be considered in [choosing] a ruler: rather, the uprightness of his character, the evenhandedness of his justice, the mature discernment of his heart, and the greatness of his soul.

Chapter two: That it is more prudent to be ruled by one than by the many, unless the many are united in doing good. Rulers and magistrates are useful and necessary for the governing of a commonwealth.¹¹ For as the blessed Peter the apostle says, they are placed by God *for the punishment of evildoers and the praise of the good.*¹² Further, it is more prudent to be ruled by one than by the many, because many rulers often generate discord, and discord between rulers produces the greatest disorder among their subjects. Just as the sea is agitated by contrary winds, so a people is destroyed by quarreling rulers. Thus the Lord laments through the prophet, saying: *Many shepherds have destroyed my vineyard.*¹³ Therefore the rule of one is more prudent than that of the many. In this way the Lord promised his people a great reward through the prophet, saying that *a head will be placed over them* and *a prince will be in the midst of them.*¹⁴

10 1 Kings 15–16.
11 Part 6, chaps. 2–3, are heavily dependent on Aquinas, *De regimine principum* 1.3–4, although Jacopo has reworked Aquinas' ideas into his own logical sequence.
12 1 Peter 2.14.
13 Jeremiah 12.10.
14 Hosea 1.11; Ezekiel 46.10.

PART SIX: ON GOVERNMENT

We can provide many examples of this in nature. One example, in fact, is the world itself, because the entire world is ruled by one Creator. Just as God alone created all things, so he alone governs and rules all things. We also have an example of this in the human body, because all parts of the body are ruled by a single head. If there were two heads on a single body, then there would be great schism and division among its members. We also have an example of this in the soul (*anima*), because all the forces and powers of the soul are ruled by one reason (*ratio*). For reason assembles all thoughts, intentions, and desires, then organises and executes them, just like a king. We also have an example of this in bees, which are ruled by a king. They are all obedient to the one king: they go out when he goes out, they return when he returns, and they rest when he is still. We have a final example in numbers, for all numbers are derived from [the number] one. Since, therefore, we find in that natural matters all things are organised based on the number one, so it ought to be among men that all should be ruled by one, because art ought to imitate nature as much as possible.

However, it is also true that when there are many rulers in harmony who are united for justice and desirous of preserving the commonwealth—by such as these, even though they are many, the commonwealth may be governed well. Therefore it is desirable that when there are many rulers, they should always be in harmony with one another; unless by chance they should be inclined to injustice, for in that case it would instead be desirable that they should be at odds with one another. Just as the good are stronger when united, so are the bad weaker when divided. For we see that when many men are hauling a ship or other heavy object, they are stronger in their pulling if their strengths are united; likewise, they are weaker if their strengths are divided. In the same way it must be said that wherever there are many good rulers, they are stronger in their preservation of the commonwealth if they are united; but if they are bad and they are divided, they are weaker in their exercising of injustice. And thus, as was stated above, just as it is preferable that good rulers should be united, so it is desirable that bad rulers should be divided. Among good rulers and other good men, harmony is good and discord is bad. Among bad ones, it is the reverse: harmony is bad and discord is good.[15]

Furthermore, we may corroborate this principle which we have just affirmed with the testimony of Sacred Scripture, for it is stated in

---

15 Isidore, *Sententiae* 3.31.2.

Ecclesiasticus that harmony among the good is good: *With three things my spirit is well pleased, which are commended by God and men: harmony between brothers, the love of neighbours, and a man and a woman that agree well together.*[16] It is pleasing to God and men when others maintain harmony outwardly in their deeds and love inwardly in their hearts—and thus it says *harmony between brothers and love of neighbours.* Similarly, when in domestic matters people cooperate well in peaceful discourse, in this way expressing *and a man and a woman that agree well together.* And indeed, it is affirmed that discord between good people is bad in the words of the Apostle in the letter to the Corinthians, where he reprimands his disciples for some argument that they were having amongst themselves on the subject of baptism.[17] Some were saying that their baptism was better because they had been baptised by Peter, while others were saying that theirs was better because they had been baptised by Paul, and still others were saying that theirs was better because they had been baptised by Apollo. The Apostle rebuked them for this dispute, explaining that Peter and Paul were able to cleanse them on the outside, but Christ alone baptises them on the inside when he forgives their faults and fills them with grace. Thus the Apostle reproached them for their argument, saying: *it has been revealed to me regarding you, my brothers, that there are arguments among you. For I say this, that each of you says, 'Indeed, I am for Paul, and I am for Apollo, and I am for Cephas—that is, Peter'. But was Paul crucified for you? Or are you baptised in the name of Paul?* In this way discord is greatly displeasing to God when it occurs among good people. In the same way in Ecclesiasticus it is said that *God hates anyone who foments discord among brothers.*[18] For this is the work of the devil, who *sows tares in the midst of the wheat* when he introduces divisions and scandals among good people.[19]

Moreover, concord among bad people is bad. For it is bad when thieves agree amongst themselves about thieving, looters about looting, and murderers about murdering. The prophet reviles such concord and peace, saying, *I was jealous of the wicked, seeing the peace of sinners.*[20] But discord among the wicked is good, as is evident from the book of the Acts of the Apostles which explains that there were two sects among the Jews:

---

16 Sirach 25.1–2.
17 1 Corinthians 1.11–13.
18 Not Sirach but Proverbs 6.14, 19.
19 Matthew 13.25.
20 Psalm 72.3.

the Pharisees, who acknowledged the resurrection, and the Sadducees, who denied the resurrection.[21] And although these two were divided on that matter, they were nonetheless united in their persecution of Paul. So together they captured Paul, intending to kill him. But Paul worked to incite quarrels between them so that he could escape them, and said in a loud voice that he believed in the resurrection, and that he had been arrested for this belief. When the Pharisees, who believed in the resurrection, heard this, they said that they did not wish Paul to suffer any harm. The Sadducees, on the other hand, said that he should die. A great dispute thus arose between them, and so Paul escaped from their clutches. This conflict was good because unless Paul had divided them in this way they would have killed him. It is therefore useful when evil rulers are divided, because then they impede one another in doing evil; they contradict one another, and by this contradiction many evil deeds are prevented which would have been accomplished if they had been united in their wickedness.

Chapter three: That great danger arises from a bad government, and great advantage from a good one. He who always strives after his own benefit, who does not seek the common good of the people and does not attend to the commonwealth, must be said to be a tyrant and not a ruler. He will torment the people subject to him according to the diverse passions of the vices to which he is subject. For if he hungers with the jaws of greed, he will seize the goods of his subjects.[22] As Solomon says, *a just king nourishes the land, but a greedy man destroys it.*[23] If he burns with the fires of wrath, he will shed innocent blood for no reason. Thus the Lord says in Ezekiel, *her princes [are] in the midst of her like wolves tearing at their prey to shed blood.*[24] If he is tortured by the bruising of envy, he will be jealous of the virtues of his subjects, for tyrants do not suffer those under them to be virtuous because they suspect that all excellence or virtue in their subjects might lead to their overthrow. Therefore virtuous men conceal their virtues lest tyrants become wickedly suspicious of them, as Solomon has said: *when the impious rise up, men will hide themselves.*[25] Thus virtuous men hide their virtues lest they should be held in suspicion. Such tyrants are not rulers,

---

21 Acts 23.6–10.
22 Greed, wrath, and envy are three of the seven deadly sins.
23 Proverbs 29.4.
24 Ezekiel 22.27.
25 Proverbs 28.28.

but wild beasts; for a beast (*bestia*) is said to be monstrous (*vastia*) from the act of devastation (*vastandum*).[26] Hence such rulers are beasts—that is, monsters—because they ravage their subjects. They destroy them in repute by dishonouring their reputations; they destroy them in material goods by seizing all their property; they destroy them in their persons by frequently oppressing them physically, wounding and killing them. Of the cruelty of such beasts, Solomon says: *like a roaring lion and a ravenous bear, so is an impious prince over his unfortunate people.*[27]

Therefore, lest a ruler turn to pride and tyranny, he ought to remember that he is a mortal man whose great punishment will be proportionate to his cruelty in inflicting injustice, as is said in the book of Wisdom: *greater punishment awaits the mightier, and the powerful will suffer powerful torments.*[28] Contemplation of these things will hold a ruler in fear and preserve him in humility. In this way, when any of the Romans' consuls returned victorious, the Romans did three things to honour them and three things to preserve them in humility. As Tullius[29] reports, the first honour was that the entire Roman people ran to meet him with great joy. The second was that all the prisoners whom the victor had captured followed after his chariot with their hands bound behind their backs. The third was that they dressed the victor in the tunic of Jupiter (*tunica Iovis*), and four white horses pulled his chariot all the way up to the Capitoline. Yet lest he become too puffed up in himself on account of the victory he had gained and the honours extended to him, they tempered his victory and his honours in three ways. First, a man of low condition wearing a short tunic was placed with him in his chariot, so that anyone of any status, however low, might hope to be given such an honour if his virtue should deserve it. Second, this man gave a blow to the victor himself, saying, 'Know yourself, and remember that you are mortal'. Third, on that day anyone could insult him however they wished, so that humiliation would prevent him from becoming arrogant.

---

26 Peter Comestor, *Historia scholastica* 1.8 (*PL* 198.1062), an etymology cited by Thomas Aquinas and Bonaventure among others.
27 Proverbs 28.15; cf. *SD*, fols. 157v, 355r.
28 A conflation of Wisdom 6.9 and 6.7.
29 Marcus Tullius Cicero, the Roman orator—although this description does not appear in his works. Some of the details derive from Sicard of Cremona's liturgical treatise *Mitrale* 2.6 (*PL* 213.13–434, at col. 82); cf. also *TIE* 4126. Bertini Guidetti (*CCG*, p. 155) notes the medieval popularity of the Platonic dictum 'know thyself'; cf. *SD*, fol. 85r–v.

PART SIX: ON GOVERNMENT 107

Great utility also results from the governance of a good ruler. For good rulers cherish justice, advance the commonwealth, neglect their own interests, and always seek the common good. Such a ruler may reasonably be compared with the stomach.[30] For the stomach, having received and digested nourishment, does not keep it for itself but distributes it to the limbs so that they may be reinvigorated. In the same way, a good ruler does not arrogate any potential benefits to himself but rather turns them to the common benefit of his subjects.

It must be noted that if the stomach is in good order, then it digests well the food it has received and distributes the digested food to the individual limbs for reinvigoration; thus the entire mass of the body is reinvigorated and governed. But if the stomach is weak, then it neither digests the food it has received nor distributes it to the limbs, and the entire body becomes weak and collapses. In the same way, if a magistrate and his advisers are well-ordered, they digest everything that they do—that is, they investigate it with conscientious discussion—and then they distribute what they have digested and discussed to their subjects for their protection. In this way the entire commonwealth is preserved and governed in stability. But if those same rectors are weak, resolute in their vices and intent only on their own benefit, then they do not consider any of those things that should be done for the common good, nor do they act on any of the things that they have considered; rather, they neglect and ignore those things common to all.[31]

And thus the entire commonwealth is destroyed when it is not sustained by its rulers, because these rulers of cities may be understood as the stomach or belly and their subjects as the limbs—as Titus Livy demonstrates in his first book.[32] He relates how a great disagreement arose between the Roman people and the fathers of the City, meaning the senators. The people said that they endured the burden and heat of the day, that they were exposed to sufferings and dangers, that they travelled the world to fight and defend the commonwealth—while the fathers remained in their peaceful houses, were exposed to no sufferings, spent

---

30 John of Salisbury, *Policraticus* 6.24. This extended metaphor comparing government with the stomach relies on the double meaning of the Latin *digere* ('to digest' both food and ideas—a concept echoed in Revelation 10.8–11). The metaphor also appears in Ptolemy of Lucca, *On the government of rulers* 2.7.7.

31 Note the irony of 'weak' rulers who are nonetheless 'resolute' and 'intent' in their pursuit of vice.

32 Actually *Ab urbe condita* 2.32.

their time in pleasure, and endured no battles. And because of this the unrest grew until the people left the City and gathered on a certain hill.[33] Then Menenius Agrippa was sent to them to seek reconciliation. The aforesaid Menenius gave a speech in which he said that once, when the limbs were talking together, they conspired against the belly.[34] For they said that all the sustenance that the limbs collected with the greatest of efforts, the belly consumed, and expended no effort in acquiring; rather, it remained always at rest, spending its time with meals and other pleasures. Accordingly, they ordered the hands not to bring any food to the mouth; they ordered the mouth not to receive any food given to it; they ordered the teeth not to chew any food. But when the body had remained without food for some days, the limbs became very weak and the entire body was on the verge of wasting away. Seeing this, the limbs revoked their edict; they understood that the stomach did not retain food for itself, but digested it and distributed it to the veins, which it brought it forth as blood; this was transmitted to the limbs, which reinvigorated them, and also to the entire body, which is how it was sustained and ruled. Then the aforesaid Menenius interpreted this parable, explaining that the senate was the belly or stomach and the people were the limbs; for the senate maturely considered the business of the commonwealth and other useful things, and arranged them in a certain way, and having considered and arranged these things it then distributed them to the people—and thus the limbs were repaid, since the food had not been diverted by the stomach. Thus the commonwealth would be totally destroyed were it not nourished by the mature counsel of the senators. And so by this metaphor the aforesaid Menenius pacified the Roman people and brought them back into the City.

---

33 The so-called first secession of the plebs, *c.* 494 BC.

34 Menenius' parable of the 'body politic' is Aesop's fable 'The belly and the feet' (Perry (1952), no. 130), which circulated independently of Livy in the Middle Ages. 1 Corinthians 12.14–23 applies the metaphor to the church.

PART SEVEN: ON RULERS

Here follows part seven, which describes how the rulers of a city ought to be. This part has four chapters: the first asserts that rulers ought to be powerful and magnanimous so that they can govern without fear; the second, that they ought to be God-fearing men; the third, that they ought to be truthful in everything; and the fourth, that they ought to hate all avarice and cupidity.

Chapter one: That rulers ought to be powerful and magnanimous so that they can govern without fear. Sacred Scripture is the queen of all the sciences: the other sciences attend upon her as servants and footmen, so every science is justified insofar as it follows in the footsteps of Sacred Scripture herself. She is also the instructor (*magistra*) of all kings, princes, and rulers, giving each particular rules to guide them in their duties. Thus she teaches the rulers of cities and peoples how they ought to behave in the work of governance. This is discussed in Exodus where Moses' kinsman [Joshua] advises him, saying: *choose powerful and God-fearing men who have truth in them, and who hate greed; and from among these appoint tribunes, centurions, sergeants, and squad leaders who can rule the people at all times.*[1] By these words we understand that rulers ought to observe four rules if they wish to govern in a fair and responsible manner: namely, they ought to be powerful, to fear God, to embrace all truth, and to hate all greed and cupidity.

First, they ought to be powerful and magnanimous so that they can govern without any sort of fear, and in their governing fear no one. Thus it is said in Ecclesiasticus: *do not desire to become a judge unless you are strong enough in virtue to root out iniquities, lest you lose courage when faced with the powerful.*[2] And in the same book it is said of a certain great judge of God: *in his day he feared no prince, and no power conquered*

---

1 A conflation of Exodus 17.9 and 18.21. In the Roman army, tribunes were officers of whole legions (1,000–3,000 men), centurions led centuries (100 men); *quinquagenarii* (here 'sergeants') led divisions of fifty men, and *decani* (here 'squad leaders') led squads of ten.

2 Sirach 7.6.

him.³ This is different from many timid and fearful judges and rulers, who dare neither to govern nor to punish the rich and powerful, but only the poor and simple. Thus the Lord says in John: *do not judge according to appearance, but adjudge a just judgment (iustum iudicium iudicate)*.⁴ Someone judges according to appearance when he judges not with regard to the merits of a case but rather with regard to a person's appearance. The prophet condemns such behaviour, saying: *you favour the faces of sinners*.⁵ Against such people, Solomon says: *weight and weight is an abomination before God*.⁶ For such timid and unjust rulers and judges have [one] *weight and* [another] *weight*, that is, a light sentence and a heavy one: they pronounce the light sentence against the rich and powerful, who are more guilty, and the heavier sentence against the poor, who are less guilty. On this subject, Valerius [Maximus] says that the philosopher Anacharsis compared the laws and statutes of men to the webs of spiders:⁷ just as small animals were captured and killed in those webs, much larger animals broke the webs and went through freely; thus the poor are caught and punished by human laws at the same time as the rich and powerful are not constrained by the same laws, although both great and small ought equally to be subject to the laws. Thus it is said in Ecclesiasticus: *Act justly to great and small alike*; and in the book of Wisdom it is said of the universal Judge: *Because He himself made the small and the great, and his care is for all equally*.⁸ Therefore rulers ought to be magnanimous, not soft or cowardly, in punishing vice. This is so, as Solomon says, because *he who is lax and careless in his work is the brother of someone who destroys* his own work.⁹ The difference is between softness and hardness: the soft man is one who yields too quickly while the hard man is one who never yields. Certain rulers are too weak because they quickly abandon the righteousness of justice at the first harsh word. Others are too harsh because they are unwilling to be swayed by any kind of compassion. A ruler may sin in either direction, then, by being too weak or too harsh; therefore he ought to

---

3 Sirach 48.13, referring to the prophet Elias.
4 John 7.24: the alliterative repetition provides emphasis.
5 Psalm 81.2.
6 Proverbs 20.23. 'Weight and weight' refers to unequal (and therefore false) weights and balances.
7 Valerius Maximus, *Factorum et dictorum* 7.2.ext.14, quoting Plutarch's *Life of Solon*, 5.
8 Sirach 5.18; Wisdom 6.8.
9 Proverbs 18.9.

be neither weak nor harsh but temperate in moderation. He who is too lenient is weak; he who is too severe is harsh; but he who mixes the strictness of justice with the sweetness of mercy is temperate in moderation. For this reason, when Solomon was about to be anointed king his father David did not have him seated upon a horse or a donkey, but upon a mule.[10] For a horse signifies ferocity and a donkey signifies gentleness, but a mule combines a donkey's gentleness with equine ferocity. By this we are given to understand that a ruler ought to have neither too much ferocity nor too much gentleness; rather, he ought to mix the severity of justice with the gentleness of mercy.

For virtues are turned into vices when they stray into extremes, and justice has two extremes: one is by way of excess—namely, too much severity—and the other is by way of weakness—namely, too much forgiveness. So when justice (*iustitia*) strays either into too much severity or too much forgiveness, it is a vice, but when it keeps to the middle path it is a virtue. In the same way, prudence (*prudentia*) has two extremes: one is by way of excess—that is, deceit—and the other by way of weakness—that is, gullibility. So when prudence strays either into deceit or gullibility, then it is a vice; but when it keeps to the middle path it is a virtue. In the same way, temperance (*temperantia*) or self-control has two extremes: one is by way of excess—that is, gluttony; and the other by way of restraint—that is, too great self-denial. Thus when temperance or self-control strays either into gluttony or into too-great self-denial, it is a vice; but when it keeps to the middle path it is a virtue. In the same way, bravery (*fortitudo*) has two extremes: one is by way of excess—that is, cruelty—and the other by way of weakness—that is, cowardice. Thus when courage strays either into cruelty or into cowardice, it is a vice; but when it keeps to the middle path, it is a virtue.[11]

Chapter two: That rulers ought to be God-fearing men. It is right that a ruler or judge should be attentive to the fear of God so that he will judge rightly and justly. For if he does not have the fear of God [in him], he will often fall into injustice. For this reason it is written in the book of Paralipomenon [Chronicles] that the holy king Josaphat

---

10 1 Kings 1.33, 38.
11 Jacopo here covers the four cardinal virtues of prudence, justice, temperance, and fortitude; they had been adopted from the works of Plato and Cicero by the church fathers, especially Saint Augustine, as well as (more recently) Thomas Aquinas.

created judges in every place throughout the land, instructing them and saying: Be careful what you do, for you enact the judgment not of man, but of God, and whatever you judge, it will reflect upon you. Let the fear of the Lord be in you and do all things with diligence: for there is no iniquity in our Lord, neither manipulation of persons nor greed for gifts.[12] See how well this holy king exhorted his judges: specifically, that in all the judgments they make they should always attend to the fear of God. For the fear of God is a kind of shackle by which the judges of the lands of the world are bound lest they should be led astray into something illicit. And therefore he who does not have this shackle rushes headlong into everything that is prohibited.

Now, if a judge or ruler wishes to judge cases justly and appropriately, at the beginning of a case he must have great perspicacity in his investigation; in the middle of the case he should have mature discretion in his deliberations; and at the end of the case he should have great constancy in pronouncing sentence. The fear of the Lord should direct him in all these things. At the beginning of a case, a judge ought to have great perspicacity in his enquiries, because he should examine and enquire into all offences wisely in order to discover the truth—as the prophet Daniel did when he wisely examined the malicious elders who had slandered Susannah.[13] And because [their stories] disagreed on various points, he wisely convicted them. It is the fear of the Lord that directs this wisdom: as Solomon says, *the fear of the Lord is the beginning of wisdom.*[14] One who had such wisdom in investigation was the holy Job, who said: *The case that I did not know, I investigated most diligently.*[15] He who *investigates most diligently* is someone who enquires solicitously and neither neglects nor omits anything. The fear of God creates such conscientiousness as this because, as is said in Ecclesiastes, *he who fears the Lord neglects nothing.*[16]

Furthermore, in the middle of a case a judge ought to exercise mature discretion in his deliberations. After he has investigated and discovered crimes, he ought to weigh them on the scales of his discretion and judgment to see which are more serious and which are more trivial. The more serious [crimes] he ought to punish seriously, and the more trivial ones, more lightly, as the prophet says: *the sons of men are liars*

---

12 2 Chronicles 19.5–7.
13 Daniel 13.
14 Proverbs 9.10 (an inversion of Proverbs 1.7).
15 Job 29.16.
16 Ecclesiastes 7.19.

on the scales, so that they deceive by vanity itself.[17] Those judges are *liars on the scales* who do not consider their judgments with fairness. But the fear of the Lord oversees each side of the scales, and then the scale will weigh lightly or heavily, as it should. Because where there is greater weight—that is, greater offence—[the scale will hang] more heavily; where there is less weight, it will weigh more lightly. Thus it is said in Ecclesiasticus: *the fear of the Lord oversees all things.*[18] For when the fear of God does not oversee such scales, then the scales become treacherous. Regarding this, Solomon says: *a false balance is an abomination to the Lord, a just weight his desire.*[19] The scale is deceitful when it measures as heavy those things which are light or measures as light those things which are heavy, but the measuring is fair when its weight is right and just. The fear of the Lord keeps us from this evil and deceitful weighing, which is why Solomon says: *By the fear of the Lord every man departs from evil.*[20]

Finally, at the end of his case a judge ought to have great constancy in sentencing: he must not hesitate for fear of others, but rather pronounce his sentence and oversee its implementation. The fear of God creates such constancy, as Solomon says: *The just man, like a bold lion, will be without fear.*[21] For however much a judge has investigated wisely and considered maturely, if he is still timid in pronouncing sentence everything that went before will be for nothing—and thus, if the fear of God is not present, his whole judgment will be subverted. For this reason it is said in Ecclesiasticus: *Unless you hold yourself insistently in the fear of the Lord, your house*—that is, all your works—*will quickly be overthrown.*[22]

If, therefore, a ruler or judge proves himself to be without the fear of God by failing to investigate wisely, deliberate maturely, or pass sentence resolutely, he subverts his own judgment, absolving the guilty and punishing the innocent. The holy words of the prophet Isaiah pronounce a curse upon such as these, saying: *Woe to you who forgive the wicked in return for bribes, and snatch justice from the just man.*[23] For such men who forgive the wicked and condemn the just ought not to be called judges

---

17 Psalm 61.10; cf. *SQ*, p. 257.
18 Sirach 25.14.
19 Proverbs 11.1.
20 Proverbs 16.6.
21 Proverbs 28.1; cf. *SS*, fol. 6r.
22 Sirach 27.4.
23 Isaiah 5.23.

or rulers, but rather tyrants and savages. As the blessed Augustine says in his book *On the city of God*: *When justice is removed, what are kingdoms but great acts of robbery?*[24] And he gives the example of a certain pirate called Dionides who was captured and brought before the emperor Alexander. Alexander said to him: 'What do you mean by taking hostile possession of the sea?' And Dionides responded: 'What do you mean by taking hostile possession of the whole world? When I do it in a small boat I am called a thief, but when you do the same thing with a great navy, you are called emperor. My poverty makes me a thief, but your arrogance and insatiable greed do the same'. This was as if to say: 'You and I are both similar and dissimilar. We are similar in that I am a thief and you are a thief, but we are dissimilar in that I am a petty thief and you are a great one: I prey on the sea and you, on the entire world. I do with a small boat the same thing that you do with an enormous navy. My lack of wealth has made me a brigand, but your pride and greed have made you the same'. Delighted with this response, Alexander had him enrolled in the army, and ordered a sufficient salary allotted to him so that in future he would have no occasion or cause for piracy. Thus bad rulers do not have the credibility to punish evildoers. This is why, when the judges of Athens ordered a certain thief led away to be hanged, the philosopher Xenocrates said, 'Great thieves are punishing a small thief'.[25]

Chapter three: That judges and rulers ought to embrace all truth. Wise and learned men have identified and distinguished three truths, namely the truths of justice, of doctrine, and of life. And this truest of trifectas is of such virtue and authority that it must not be abandoned despite any temptation. For if someone should object to the fact that I judge rightly and I render judgment rightly, he offends against the truth of justice. And if someone else should be vexed that I preach the truth of faith and teach those things which lead to true salvation, he offends against the truth of doctrine. And if another should object to the fact that I lead a just life and obey the commandments of God, he offends against the truth of life. Such truths—whether of justice or doctrine or life—must not be abandoned or relinquished even if others

---

24 *TIE* 113, from Augustine, *City of God* 4.4. The pirate is not named in Augustine; Jacopo was probably recalling the story as told in John of Salisbury, *Policraticus* 3.14; see discussion in Cary (1956), pp. 95–8. The story also appears in Ptolemy of Lucca's near-contemporaneous *On the government of rulers* 3.5.4.

25 See *SD*, fol. 355v.

PART SEVEN: ON RULERS

seem offended by them. For this reason, one time when the Lord was preaching about a certain truth of doctrine, *the disciples said to him, 'Do you know that the Pharisees were offended when they heard your word?'* But the Lord responded, *'Every plant that my heavenly father has not planted will be uprooted. Leave them alone: they are blind leaders of blind men'.*[26] Furthermore, [such men] are known to pervert this threefold truth. For bad advocates who pervert the truth of justice by their greed and avarice corrupt the truth of justice. Against these the Apostle says: *they have changed the truth of God into a lie, and they have served the creature more than the Creator.*[27] He who falsifies the truth of judgment because he has been corrupted by material greed changes the truth of God into a lie. He who forsakes God for money serves the creature more than the Creator. Heretics who sow many errors contrary to the truth of faith falsify the truth of doctrine, regarding which the Apostle says: *In the last days some will depart from the faith, following spirits of error and the doctrines of demons, speaking lies out of hypocrisy, forbidding [people] to marry and commanding them to abstain from foods which God has created.*[28] Hypocrites who mimic a holy life while maintaining an iniquitous spirit falsify the truth of life: they pretend to be sheep to conceal the minds of wolves.

Also, Saint John Chrysostom says that truth can be falsified in three ways: either by selling it, by silencing it, or by failing to defend it.[29] First, truth is falsified by selling it, as greedy judges do. Regarding this Saint Augustine says: *Even so far has the evil of greed sprung up now that laws are customarily sold, oaths are broken, sentences are for sale, and no case can be pursued without personal benefit.*[30] Secondly, truth is falsified by remaining silent about it, as the timid and cowardly do—regarding which Saint Isidore says: *He who conceals the truth out of fear of the mighty provokes the wrath of the truth upon himself, because he fears man more than he fears the divine majesty.*[31] Thirdly, the truth is falsified by he who fails to defend it, as unjust rulers do—for example, it is said in Ecclesiasticus:

---

26 Matthew 15.12–14.
27 Romans 1.25. For these two paragraphs, compare *SD*, fol. 373r.
28 1 Timothy 4.1–3.
29 From a homily on Matthew 10.28 traditionally attributed to John Chrysostom (*PG* 56.762).
30 Augustine (attributed), sermon 82 on Luke 3.12–14 (*PL* 39.1905). English idiom fails to convey the neat repetition of *nulla iam causa possit esse sine causa* (literally, 'there can be no case without a case [cause]').
31 Isidore, *Sententiae* 3.55.7.

Strive for justice for your soul, and fight for justice even to death.[32] In order to judge according to truth, a judge or ruler should keep in mind and observe three words which we find in Daniel: as Belshazzar the king was resting in his room, behold! a hand came down from heaven and wrote these three words on the wall of his bedchamber: *Numeravit, appendit,* and *divisit* (he has counted, weighed, and apportioned).[33] By these three words judges and rulers are instructed how to behave if they wish to *adjudge a just judgment.*[34] For they must enumerate the crimes of culprits and malefactors: that is, they must investigate them one by one so that none shall pass unexamined. After that, they must weigh these enumerated crimes—that is, these enquiries made one by one—on the scale of their own judgment, so they know which crimes are trivial, which moderate, and which serious. And finally they must apportion them: that is, they must punish [each crime] separately. For they must not punish all crimes equally, but rather they should punish trivial crimes lightly, moderate crimes moderately, and serious crimes severely.

Unfortunately, there are many who—however much they are condemned and punished according to this truth of justice—still hate it. This is because, as Tullius says, flattery begets friends but truth begets hate.[35] For so it is of the truth just as it is of light, taste, and smell. For light is painful to sore eyes, sweet tastes seem bitter to a weak and insipid palate, and odors are hateful to serpents.[36] The sore [eyes] are the proud, for pride is a soreness of the soul which prevents one from recognising the light of divine truth. Thus truth is odious to the proud as light is painful to sore eyes because they refuse to be criticised for their own vanities. The weak palate represents weak and self-indulgent men, for all spiritual goods, however sweet, seem foolish to the weak, since they understand only carnal things: as the Apostle says, *carnal man does not perceive those things which are of the spirit of God.*[37] The truth of justice is hateful to such as these just as taste is bitter to the weak palate, because they refuse to be criticised for their debauchery. Finally, the snakelike men are the greedy, who devour the earth in the manner

---

32 Sirach 4.33; cf. *SD*, fol. 373r.
33 Daniel 5, especially verses 25–8; cf. *SQ*, p. 257.
34 John 7.24 (cf. n. 4, above).
35 Cicero, *Laelius de amicitia* 89, quoting Terence, *Andria* 1.1.68.
36 Also in *SD*, fol. 120r; *SQ*, p. 346; *Mariale* 29/C8 (*cypressus*).
37 1 Corinthians 2.14.

of serpents because they always covet material things. To these, the truth of justice is hateful just as smell is hateful to snakes, because they refuse to be judged for their lust, plundering, and avarice. But however much the truth of justice may be hateful to such people, judges and rulers must constantly call them to account, as the Apostle says to a certain ruler he had appointed: *Rebuke with all [your] authority.*[38]

But there are many negligent and feeble rulers and prelates who neither dare nor care to rebuke or accuse the sore-eyed men, that is, the proud; nor the tasteless men, that is, the self-indulgent; nor the snakelike men, that is, the avaricious. According to this, the Lord says in the Gospel: *Because iniquity has abounded, the charity of many will grow cold.*[39] For today iniquity abounds among subordinates and charity grows cold among their superiors. And the Lord has said accurately that they grow cold (*refrigescet*). For many rulers and prelates are extremely hot-blooded (*calidi*) at the beginning of their term of office; in the middle they are tepid (*tepidi*); and at the end they actually become chilly (*frigidi*).[40] In other words, there are many who at the beginning of their terms of office are bold and steadfast in punishing vice. In the middle of their terms they are lukewarm and careless, so that they ignore many evils and allow them to pass unpunished. And at the end of their terms they are basically cold and care nothing for their responsibilities.

Such people cannot be called rulers and prelates but chimeras. According to philosophers and poets a chimera is not a real animal but an imaginary one. For philosophers and poets have imagined this animal: its front part resembles a lion; its middle resembles a goat, and its hindquarters resemble a snake: this beast they have named a 'chimera'.[41] Now, a lion is a hot animal, a goat is a temperate animal, and a snake is a cold animal. Therefore such rulers and prelates are chimeras who at the beginning of their rule are like lions, meaning enthusiastic and bold. In the middle, like goats, they prove temperate, meaning lukewarm and negligent. And at the end, like snakes, they prove cold and they care for nothing. On this subject the Lord speaks in the Apocalypse of a certain prelate who had previously been very fervent, but afterward

---

38 Titus 2.15.
39 Matthew 24.12.
40 'Prelates' (*prelati*) also appears as 'superiors' in the previous sentence, but there the implication was inferiors v. superiors, whereas here it it is secular v. ecclesiastical officials. Jacopo applies the same metaphor to personal piety in *SD*, fol. 177r–v.
41 Isidore, *Etymologies* 1.40.4; *Vatican mythographers*, pp. 41–2, 161–2.

had become very tepid and lax: *I have*, says the Lord, *taken somewhat against you because you have abandoned your earlier charity. Be mindful, therefore, of how far you have fallen, and do penitence, and return to your first practices.*[42]

Chapter four: That judges and rulers ought to hate all avarice and cupidity. As the Apostle says, *greed is the root of all evils*.[43] We know this especially from our experience of judges and rulers of lands, in whom such greed is the root of three particular evils. For greedy rulers and judges pervert judgments; they steal away what belongs to others; and they do not take care of the commonwealth. Let us look at these three things a little more closely. First: whenever judges and rulers are greedy and willingly accept gifts, they pervert their judgments. As it is said in Ecclesiasticus, *presents and gifts blind the eyes of judges, so that they turn aside from correction as if mute*.[44] Regarding this verse the commentator says that a 'mute' (*mutus*) is a small frog (*ranuncula*), which is called mute because of its effect: when it is placed in the mouth of a barking dog it immediately renders him mute.[45] Presents and gifts are therefore like these frogs, because when they are tossed into the mouth of a greedy judge or ruler, they immediately stop him barking against evils; he will not dare to criticise evildoers further. Good judges and rulers, however, are like the dogs of God (*canes Dei*) who bark at wolves—that is, against impious and unjust men—and therefore are very necessary to God's flock.[46]

The great doctor Peter Manducator [Comestor] reports that while Philip, king of Macedon—who was the father of the great Alexander—was besieging Athens, certain intermediaries attempted to mediate between them.[47] King Philip said to the Athenians, 'The whole cause of discord

---

42 Revelation 2.4–5.

43 1 Timothy 6.10.

44 Sirach 20.31.

45 Vincent of Beauvais, *Speculum naturale* 19.19.6; also Apuleius, *Metamorphoses* 9.34.

46 A common metaphor framed God as shepherd (Latin *pastor*) of his flock, with preachers as his sheepdogs. Saint Dominic, the founder of Jacopo's own order, was often associated with dogs for this reason: in the *GL* (pp. 430–1), Dominic's mother has a vision of him as a dog while pregnant with him. Regrettably, the pun of etymologising Dominicans as *Domini canes* ('dogs of the Lord') is a much later invention: Mandonnet (1948).

47 Bertini Guidetti (*CCG*, pp. 171–2) notes that this episode is not in the *Historia scholastica*, although it is in Isidore, *Etymologies* 1.40.7. Cf. also *SD*, fol. 261v, and Jacques de Vitry, *Exempla*, no. 45, pp. 17–18.

between me and you is your judges and lawyers. If you wish me to withdraw from your [city], give me six of the wisest judges and lawyers among you, whom I will choose; I will take them with me as hostages and leave you in peace'. When Demosthenes, that wisest of orators, had heard this he spoke to the people, saying, 'There was great conflict for a long time between the wolves and the shepherds. Then the wolves said to the shepherds: "The whole cause of discord between us and you is those dogs. Just give us the dogs, and we will leave you in peace". The shepherds were naïve and gave them the dogs, and the wolves killed them at once. Then while the shepherds were sleeping and there were no dogs, the wolves came among the flock and killed the sheep. This is what Philip wishes to do to us, for he knows that the wise men of Athens rule the land by their wisdom; they care for the people, prosecuting and punishing crimes. But if he can remove these wise men from Athens, then he will return—and in the absence of the advice of our council of wise men, he will subjugate us entirely to himself'. Then the people unanimously cried out, 'Let us totally reject King Philip's request so that these wise men can in no way be removed from Athens'. By this it is shown that good judges are extremely useful and necessary, because they are like the good dogs of God, who by the barking of their tongues accuse the wolves, meaning wicked men, and protect the sheep, meaning the simple and innocent.[48]

Greedy judges and rulers are also similar to Judas Iscariot, since Judas sold Christ out of greed. But Christ was the truth, as he himself said: *I am the way, the truth, and the life.*[49] So by selling Christ Judas sold the truth. In the same way evil judges and rulers sell the truth of their judgment out of greed, and thus it is not incorrect to call them Judas. On this subject the blessed Jerome says: *Do you wish to know how dangerous is the love of possessing money? For out of this Judas sold even the Savior.*[50] When we hear of his crime, we are all horrified; we condemn this wicked disciple and we stab him with our own blades. Yet after this Jerome adds: *O, how many Judases damn Judas!* For all are Judases who sell the truth of justice; yet while these same Judases condemn the traitor Judas with their words, they imitate him in their deeds.

---

48 See n. 46, above.
49 John 14.6.
50 From a letter attributed to Saint Jerome (Letter 32.5–6, *PL* 30.241); Rees, however, suggests authorship by Pelagius or one of his followers (*Pelagius*, pp. 320–5).

For greedy judges and rulers do not refrain from stealing the goods of others. Regarding this, Valerius reports that once a Roman consul had to be sent from Rome into Spain.[51] When two such were proposed, Scipio—who knew that one of them was greedy and the other poor—said in the public assembly, 'Neither pleases me: one because he has nothing, the other because he is satisfied with nothing'. This is like saying, 'The poor man would not act except to steal according to his own need, and the greedy man would not act except to steal according to his insatiable avarice'—and thus neither was sent.

For this reason such greedy judges and rulers may be called worse than demons, which can be shown by the following explanation. Every man has three things, namely, temporal goods, a body, and a soul. The devil does not care about temporal goods because he has no earthly possessions, nor does he care about the body, because the body is worth nothing without the soul; rather, all his concern is for the soul, to lead it into sin. For this reason Saint Gregory says that the devil believes that he has accomplished nothing except when he wounds a soul.[52] Now, it is true that the devil sometimes takes away someone's worldly goods, or harms someone else's body—as is shown by reference to the holy Job, all of whose worldly possessions the devil took away while also gravely wounding Job's body.[53] But the devil does not do this except for the sake of the soul: namely, so that by these acts of property theft and bodily injury he can seduce the soul to impatience, blasphemy, and despair.[54] However, although the devil might not care for goods or for the body, but only for the soul, greedy judges and rulers care about all these things. For they steal worldly goods from their inferiors, and they injure their bodies by oppressing them, so that by that oppression they can extort money out of them. Furthermore, by their bad example they corrupt those souls and force them into despair, and thus they are worse than demons.

Moreover, greedy judges and rulers do not care for the commonwealth but only for themselves. Roman judges and consuls, by contrast, were zealous more for the commonwealth than for themselves, and therefore they made it splendid, regarding which Augustine says that Roman

---

51 *TIE* 841, from Valerius Maximus, *Factorum et dictorum* 6.4.2; cf. *SD*, fol. 356r.
52 Gregory the Great, *Moralia in Job* 11.28, 14.15, and elsewhere; cf. *SD*, fols. 155v–156r.
53 Job 1–2.
54 See *SD*, fol. 156r.

consuls maintained an extremely opulent state but an impoverished domestic life.⁵⁵ For when the Romans were elevated to the consulship, they refused to be found richer after the consulship than before it. In fact, the same Augustine reports in his book *On the city of God* that a certain consul was expelled from the senate by its members because he was found to have ten pounds of silver more than he had had before the consulship. Also, the Romans had this virtue [*magnanimitas*]: they thought it more important that their commonwealth should be ennobled by dominating men who had gold than that they should possess gold themselves. On this subject Vegetius reports in his book *On military matters* that ambassadors from the Epirotes came to Rome with a great weight of gold and silver to purchase their liberty, and one evening, when they appeared before Fabricius, the consul of the Romans, they found him eating at a rustic table with wooden dishes.⁵⁶ And when they had offered him their great weights of gold and silver, he responded: 'Go, and take your gold and silver with you, because Romans prefer to exercise authority over men who have gold than over gold itself. And know that Fabricius cannot be conquered by either gold or enemies'.

Therefore, because greedy judges and rulers pervert justice, because they steal what belongs to others, and because they do not care for the commonwealth, thus they will all be submerged together in the torments of hell. Indeed, a certain philosopher records that Emperor Nero, who was very cruel and greedy, was seen after his death boiling in liquid gold in the baths of hell, and when he saw a great crowd of judges and lawyers, he said to them, 'Come to me, you venal race of men, and bathe here with me, because I have saved the best spot for you'.⁵⁷ Beyond this, Orosius records that greedy judges and rulers will fulfil the words of another [philosopher]: there was a certain man who always thirsted for gold and could not be satisfied. Then he was captured by his enemies, and they poured boiling liquid gold into his mouth, saying, 'You thirsted

---

55 Augustine, *City of God* 5.18.
56 G. Fabricius Luscinus was a Roman consul and general of the third century BC. While Augustine mentions this anecdote in *City of God* 5.18, it derives not from Vegetius but the *Stratagems* of Frontinus—probably through Aulus Gellius (*Noctes atticae* 1.14) or Valerius Maximus (*Factorum et dictorum* 4.3.6). It was clearly well known in Jacopo's time: cf. Dante, *Purgatorio* 20.25–7, and Ptolemy of Lucca, *On the government of rulers* 3.15.4 (which also incorrectly credits Vegetius). Cf. *SD*, fol. 355v.
57 *TIE* 2505: cf. Jacques de Vitry, *Exempla* no. 36, p. 14; Jacques cites 'a tragedy of Seneca', but this seems to be a common misattribution. Cf. *SD*, fol. 328v; *SQ*, p. 143.

for gold; drink gold'.[58] So demons might say to a greedy man, 'You thirsted for gold; drink gold'. And thus it is shown that greedy judges and rulers will bathe in boiling liquid gold and they will drink boiling liquid gold. And finally, Saint Ambrose tells of a certain greedy king by the name of Midas, who prayed to his god Apollo that whatever he touched might turn into gold.[59] His prayer was fulfilled, so everything he touched was immediately turned to gold. Accordingly, when he came to the table, bread and other edibles turned to gold when he touched them, and were no longer good to eat. So he ordered his servants to pick up the food for him and place it in his mouth, but when the food touched his lips it immediately turned to gold—and so he died of hunger. For because he lusted too ardently after gold he lost both his gold and his life. In the same way greedy men who too ardently lust after gold lose thereby both their gold and their eternal life.

---

58 *TIE* 5039: as Bertini Guidetti (*CCG*, p. 175) notes, classical sources generally associate this story with Crassus after his defeat by the Parthians at Carrhae in 53 BC: Cassius Dio, *Roman history* 40.27, evoked in Dante, *Purgatorio* 20.116–17. Jacopo may be remembering Orosius' similar story of the Persian king Cyrus: *Against the pagans* 2.7.6.

59 Ambrose, *Expositio in Lucam* 6.88 (*CCSL* 14.206), probably working from Ovid, *Metamorphoses* 11.103, but see also *Vatican mythographers*, pp. 155–6. Repeated in Jacopo, *SQ*, p. 75.

PART EIGHT: ON CITIZENSHIP

Here follows part eight, which addresses how the citizens and inhabitants of the city ought to act. This part has three chapters: the first chapter demonstrates that the citizens ought to be thoughtful and mature in making decisions; the second, that they ought not to be subject to vice but disciplined in virtue; and the third, that they ought to exhibit the greatest zeal for the commonwealth.

Chapter one: That the counsellors (*consiliarii*[1]) of cities ought to be wise and mature. It is written in the book of Tobit, *always seek counsel from wise men.*[2] And conversely, we read in Ecclesiasticus: *Do not take advice from fools, for they cannot appreciate anything but those things which please them.*[3] Therefore counsellors must be both prudent and mature: they must not be boys, nor decrepit old men, nor adolescents, but men of maturity and seniority. This is logical because—as Saint Isidore says—hot blood is the source of sharp (*acuta*[4]) knowledge, tepid blood is the source of little knowledge, and cold blood is the source of foolish senility, while temperate blood is the source of mature knowledge.[5] Hence boys do not yet know anything because the blood has not yet heated in them, and the elderly grow senile because the blood has grown cold in them. Youths know sharply because the blood is heating in them, and elders have mature knowledge because their blood is neither hot nor cold but temperate. Therefore counsellors must not be boys, because boys do not yet have wisdom and they are not able to judge well, nor

---

1 Latin *consiliarii* encompasses both 'counsellors' (givers of advice) and 'councillors' (members of council); Jacopo sees membership in civic councils as being a form of official advice-giving. While I have used the spelling 'counsellors' throughout, the two meanings function interchangeably here.

2 Tobit 4.19.

3 Sirach 8.20.

4 While I have translated *acutus* literally as 'sharp' throughout this passage, Jacopo clearly does not mean this as a compliment. A modern equivalent might be 'half-cocked', implying that while young people (*iuvenes*) hold very strong opinions, they see things in black and white rather than appreciating the complexities of a problem.

5 Isidore, *Etymologies* 11.1.123, 11.2.127. Deriving from Hippocrates and Galen, these ideas about the nature of blood are elaborated in Avicenna's *Canon of medicine* 1.1.3.51–62 (a standard medieval reference). Cf. *SD*, fol. 126r–v.

to discern, nor to see or understand what must be done. Nor should they be senile old men, because these grow increasingly foolish and demented. Nor should they be youths, because youths have too excited a spirit and too sharp a heart. Rather, they should be older, senior men, because these are mature in sense and temperate of soul.

Nonetheless, while it is said in Job, *wisdom is in the ancients, and prudence in great experience*, some young men may be found who have grey-haired sense and mature spirits; regarding them it is said in the book of Wisdom, *grey hairs lie in the understanding of a man, and old age in a spotless life.*[6] Such young men, I argue, are extremely suitable for consultation, and should be counted among one's advisors on all subjects. Such a one was Daniel, who even though he was young in body was nonetheless mature and venerable in his understanding; for this reason the judges of Israel said to him, *come and sit among us, because God has given you the honour of old age.*[7] Therefore counsellors must be both wise and mature. They are mature who are neither precipitous nor hasty; not reckless but circumspect; not hot-tempered but tranquil of mind; not wanton in their habits but distinguished in their manner of life; who do not value cruelty but love fairness. Such as these—who may be called mature—are fit to be chosen as counsellors.

But let us expand on these points in greater detail. First, counsellors ought to be neither precipitous nor hasty; rather, they should be extremely deliberate in the matters on which they must advise. This is because, as Solomon says, *he who is hasty with his feet will offend*, and in Ecclesiasticus it is said: *The words of the wise will be weighed on a balance.*[8] For wise men weigh their words on the balance of their own judgment, and examine them before they offer them. This is the difference between the wise and the foolish: the wise man keeps his mouth in his heart because he examines his words within himself before he says them, but the foolish man keeps his heart in his mouth because whatever he feels in his heart immediately appears in his mouth. Thus Ecclesiasticus says, *the hearts of fools are in their mouths and the mouths of the wise are in their hearts.*[9] Furthermore, when people are over-hasty in giving advice they are often found to be in error in that advice. As Socrates

---

6 Job 12.12; Wisdom 4.8–9.
7 Daniel 13.50.
8 Proverbs 19.2; Sirach 21.28.
9 Sirach 21.29.

said, *repentance—that is, regret—follows hasty advice.*[10] In the same way we read in the book *On the Twelve Caesars* that Augustus Caesar used to say that *haste and recklessness were ill-suited to a leader*; he then added to this, saying, *whatever is done well is done quickly enough.*[11] Similarly, the philosopher Varro said that *wanting to do very difficult things quickly is a sign of inexperience.*[12]

Second, counsellors must not be reckless but extremely circumspect, because they must not only consider the beginnings of issues and processes, but also their ends and those things that ought to happen at the end. God demonstrates this in the Gospel through two examples. The first example is that *if anyone wants to build a tower, he ought not to begin building it immediately; instead, he ought first to look and consider if he has the resources to be able to bring the tower to completion—lest he begin it and then find himself unable to finish it, so that everyone laughs at him and says, 'This man began to build something but was unable to finish it'*.[13]

The other example is that *if a king wishes to do battle with another king, he ought not to begin the battle immediately; instead, he ought first to see if he has sufficient arms and soldiers with which he can achieve victory.*[14] We read that a certain philosopher went and stood in the piazza of a certain city, announcing that he would sell to anyone the explanation they needed.[15] So when a certain prince heard this, he sent a messenger with gold and silver to buy an explanation for him. The philosopher wrote on a slip: 'In everything you plan to do, always consider what might happen to you', and when the prince received the slip, he had these words inscribed above his palace doors in golden letters. Shortly thereafter, some of the prince's enemies conspired with his barber to cut the prince's throat with the razor while shaving him. The next time the barber came to shave the prince, he somehow learned of the letters, looked up, and read them. But having read them, he began to think about what might happen to him—and then he began to tremble and

---

10 A proverb attributed to Socrates in Sedulius Scottus' ninth-century *Collectaneum miscellaneum* 80.6.6. This reference and the next two all appear in *SQ*, pp. 404–5.
11 Suetonius, *Augustus* 25.
12 Not M. Terentius Varro (d. 29 BC) but a later work attributed to him: Pseudo-Varro, *Sententiae* 111.1.
13 Luke 14.28–30, paraphrased.
14 Luke 14.31–2, paraphrased.
15 This anecdote also appears in *SD*, fol. 203r-v, but its source is unknown.

grow fearful, and the colour of his complexion turned pale. When the prince saw this, he had him seized and extracted the truth from him: he had mercy on the barber, but executed the instigators of the crime. From this we may clearly deduce that we ought not only to examine the beginnings of things, but to consider them fully to their end and fulfillment.

Thirdly, counsellors must not be hot-tempered, but tranquil in mind. For sound advice cannot emanate from a heart that is full of wrath because anger so inhibits the soul that it is unable to perceive correctly. This is why Chrysostom says, *someone whose heart is agitated cannot speak peaceably.*[16] On the same topic Socrates says, *there are two things most contrary to the giving of advice, namely haste and anger.*[17] But it must be noted that there is some anger which is evil, called hatred; some anger which is good, such as the anger a man feels against vice and sin; and some that is neither good nor evil, namely the sudden impulse to anger, without which the present life cannot be led. The first type of anger is contrary to the giving of advice because it so obscures the intellect that it is unable to recognise good advice. But the other two types of anger are not contrary to the giving of advice because they do not obscure the intellect. Indeed, Saint Augustine asks in his book *On the city of God* whether the souls of the wise are free of anger and confusion, and notes on this subject that Stoics have concluded one thing, Peripatetics another, and Christians still another.[18] For Stoic philosophers said that anger and confusion do not arise in the wise man because he maintains a firm and steadfast spirit in all adversities, and thus is unaffected by mental turmoil. Peripatetic philosophers, on the other hand, say that wise men are sometimes moved to wrath and confusion, but they nonetheless keep their anger and confusion subject to reason, moderated by the bridle of discretion. Christian philosophers, meanwhile, do not ask whether men become angry or not, but whether they become angry with or without cause. For the Lord says in the Gospel: *everyone who is angry with his brother shall be in danger of judgment,*

---

16 From a homily on Matthew 23.27 traditionally attributed to John Chrysostom (*PG* 56.886, no. 45).

17 Sedulius Scottus, *Collectaneum miscellaneum* 80.6.18, who attributes it to the Athenian statesman Phocion (d. *c.* 318 BC).

18 Augustine, *City of God* 9.4; cf. *SD*, fol. 251v. Stoic and Peripatetic denote two major schools of philosophy in ancient Greece: Peripatetics, following Aristotle, emphasised experience and the natural world as a path to knowledge; while Stoics, following Socrates and Zeno, emphasised personal virtue.

but other books say there: *everyone who is angry with his brother without cause, etc.*[19] For if someone is angry with the his brother's wickedness, his anger has cause: it is good and should occur in a wise man. But if someone is angry with his brother for a reason other than his brother's wickedness, his anger is without cause: it is evil and should not occur in a wise man.[20]

Fourth, these counsellors ought not to be wanton in their habits, but virtuous in their manner of life. On this subject Saint Ambrose says in his book *On duties*: *we stress that in seeking advice, we attach a great deal to probity of life, preeminence of virtue, and the habit of benevolence.*[21] Also, after this he adds: *For who looks for a spring in the mud? Who tries to drink from muddy water? Where there is luxury, there is excess. Where vices are mingled, what will someone imagine he could drink there? Why would he consider useful to the matter of his soul someone whom he considers useless in his own life? How is it possible to judge as superior in counsel someone who seems to be inferior in his habits? Someone to whom I am ready to entrust myself should be better than I am. Can I really think someone suitable who would give me advice he does not give to himself, and will I believe I can trust someone who is not himself someone he can trust?* It is the same in these matters: The man to whom we entrust our well-being (*salus*[22]) should be both just and intelligent: he should act justly so that there is no fear of fraud, and he should be intelligent so that there is no suspicion of error. That said, we entrust ourselves more readily to a just man than to an intelligent one, because the advice of a just man often prevails over the cleverness of a very wise man.

Fifth, counsellors ought to hate cruelty and love fairness. For it often happens that those who advise the cruel meet with divine judgment because of it, as is read in the book of Esther.[23] For Prince Haman once had a very high tree prepared so that he could have the Jew Mordecai hanged from it, and he persuaded King Ahasuerus that it was appropriate to punish and hang the said Mordecai as a criminal. But when the king had examined the matter he found Mordecai innocent and

---

19 Matthew 5.22. Jerome and Augustine both discuss how some pre-Vulgate texts of Matthew's gospel—here 'other books'—included the phrase *sine causa* ('without cause'): Mattison (2007), esp. pp. 841–3.
20 Cf. *SD*, fols. 251v–252r.
21 *De officiis ministrorum* 2.12.60–62; cf. *SD*, fol. 203v.
22 Latin *salus* signifies both physical health and spiritual salvation.
23 Esther 5–7.

praiseworthy; furthermore, he found Haman to be a criminal deserving of punishment, so he had Haman hanged from the same tree that Haman had prepared for Mordecai. As Solomon says, *he who digs a pit will fall into it.*[24] Furthermore, the great historian Orosius records that when a certain tyrant by the name of Phalaris was very cruelly torturing prisoners, a metalsmith by the name of Perilus wished to please him by assisting him in his cruelty.[25] He made a bronze bull, in the side of which he placed a door by which those to be punished could be shut in. Then he presented it to the tyrant, telling him to have those whom he hated shut into it and fires laid underneath, so that the groans they gave out in their torment would seem not the groans of men but rather those of a bull. The tyrant disliked this creation, however, and told him that he should be the first to enter, so that he could hear his own bellowing. Thus he had Perilus forcibly shut up in the bull, and he himself was the first to experience the horrible death that he had invented for others. In this way were fulfilled the words of Ecclesiasticus: *Malicious counsel will be returned to him who gave it, and he will not know whence it comes to him.*[26] This is also shown by Caiaphas, who advised the Jews that Christ should be killed so that the Romans would not come and destroy the place and its people.[27] But this advice, malicious as it was, redounded upon their own heads—because after the Jews killed Christ, the Roman princes Titus and Vespasian destroyed that place, and dispersed and killed its people.[28]

Chapter two: That citizens ought not to to be subject to vice but disciplined in virtue. Noble and renowned citizens ought not to be subject to vice but disciplined in virtue, for those who are subject to vice cannot be characterised as rational but rather bestial. They are not free men but slaves; they are not manly but effeminate and weak. To the first point: they are not rational but bestial, which is why the

---

24 Proverbs 26.27.
25 Phalaris of Agrigento (r. *c.* 570–554 BC): *TIE* 811 and Orosius, *Against the pagans* 1.20. Cf. *SD*, fol. 204r.
26 Sirach 27.30.
27 John 18.14. Caiaphas was the Jewish high priest at the time of Jesus' death.
28 Referring to the First Roman-Jewish War: following riots in Jerusalem in AD 66, Vespasian (emperor 69–79) and his son Titus (emperor 79–81) were sent to put down the Jewish rebellion. The war culminated with Titus' sack of Jerusalem in 70, a victory commemorated by the famous Arch of Titus in the Roman Forum. Among other accounts: Orosius, *Against the pagans* 7.4, 7.9. Cf. *SD*, fol. 276v.

PART EIGHT: ON CITIZENSHIP

prophet says: *But man, despite being honoured, did not understand; he is compared to senseless beasts and he becomes like them.*[29] For a man is similar to a range of beasts according to his range of vices. How this is, Boethius shows elegantly in the book *On Consolation*, saying: *It happens that when you see a man transformed by vice, you may no longer consider him a man: someone who burns with greed and violently despoils others' possessions, you might call a wolf; an aggressive and unsettled man who exerts his tongue in litigation, you could compare to a dog; a secret ambusher who rejoices in having stolen things through fraud becomes a young fox. He who clamours with unrestrained rage can be said to harbour the soul of a lion; the terrified fugitive who dreads what need not be feared is similar to a deer. Someone stupid and slothful who lounges lethargically lives like an ass; someone superficial and inconstant whose interests change constantly is no different from the birds; while he who wallows in fetid and unclean lusts keeps the sordid pleasures of a sow. So it happens that he who has abandoned honour ceases to be a man: since he cannot become a god, he becomes a beast.*[30]

Men subject to such vices are not free men but slaves. As the Lord says in the Gospel, *everyone who commits a sin is a slave to sin.*[31] Similarly, the blessed Peter the apostle says: *Indeed, whatever has mastered someone: to that he has become a slave.*[32] And also as Augustine says, a sinner is a slave to *as many masters as he has vices.*[33] The philosopher Diogenes demonstrates this in a conversation with Alexander.[34] This philosopher did not wish to interact with men, but lived in a glade in the wilderness; in the summer he turned his bottom to the sun so he always had shade, and in the winter he turned his face to the sun so he always had sun. Then the emperor Alexander came to visit him in wintertime, and as he stood before him cast a shadow upon him. Alexander said to the philosopher that he would grant him a wish if he liked, but Diogenes

---

29 Psalm 48.13.
30 Boethius (d. 524), *Consolation of philosophy* 4P3.16–25.
31 John 8.34; cf. *SD*, fol. 363v.
32 2 Peter 2.19.
33 Augustine, *City of God* 4.3; cf. *SD*, fol. 305v.
34 *TIE* 1673: Seneca, *De beneficiis* 5.4.4 and Valerius Maximus, *Factorum et dictorum* 4.3.ext.4; probably taken from John of Salisbury, *Policraticus* 5.17. Cf. *SD*, fol. 305v and *SQ*, pp. 94–5. This is only one of numerous stories about Diogenes and Alexander that circulated in the Middle Ages, mostly exempla on the theme of Diogenes' contempt for Alexander's wealth and power: Cary (1956), pp. 83–91, 146–9, 275–8. Plutarch (*Life of Alexander* 14.1–5) reports merely that they met once—including the anecdote about Diogenes' request for sunshine—and died on the same day in 323 BC.

responded: 'I wish you would not take from me that which you cannot give'. When Alexander had moved to one side, he asked the philosopher if he recognised him, and the philosopher replied: 'I recognise you because you are the servant of my servants'. When Alexander asked him the meaning of this statement, he said, 'Pride (*superbia*) is your master because she leads you wherever she likes, but she is my servant because I have used her as necessary. Extravagance (*luxuria*) is your master because you allow yourself to be led by her, but she is my servant because I have subjugated her profoundly. Anger (*ira*) and greed (*avaritia*) are your masters because they lead you as they wish, but they are my servants because I lead them where I wish and trample them under my feet. Thus you are the servant of my servants and my maidservants'. Then, when Alexander told him that he was surprised that Diogenes did not seem to fear his authority, since he was speaking so boldly to him, Diogenes responded: 'I do not fear your authority, because either it was in the past and so no longer exists, or else it is in the future and thus it is doubtful and uncertain; or else it is in the present, and thus it is brief and fleeting'. Alexander's soldiers became indignant at these words; they wished to attack the philosopher and beat him severely, but Alexander stopped them, saying, 'Beware lest you hurt him in any way: for he is truly a servant of God and all the things he says and to which he testifies are true'.

Thirdly, those subject to vice are not manly but effeminate and weak. The effeminate are those who adorn themselves in the manner of women with gold ornaments and costly soft garments. Against these the poet says: *let them be far from us, these young men dressed as women.*[35] It is read in the histories of the Romans that Tullus Hostilius, the third Roman king and the first Roman accustomed to wear purple clothing, was burnt up in a fire along with his entire household; this is also testified by Saint Augustine in his book *On the city of God*.[36] Indeed, human vanity has been much increased by vanity with regard to clothing. For the material of the earliest clothes was very cheap because it was made of simple wool—as we read in Genesis that when Adam and Eve were naked *God made them tunics of animal pelts.*[37] Then came wool striped with different colours; then came silk, out of which came purple. After that came silk and gold together, which is how gilded fabrics are made.

---

35 Ovid, *Heroides* 4.75 (Phaedra to Hippolytus).
36 Augustine, *City of God* 3.16 and Livy, *Ab urbe condita* 1.31.8; see also *SD*, fol. 212v.
37 Genesis 3.21; f. *SD*, fol. 17v.

Then all this progressed to embellishments of gold and precious stones.[38] Behold! *Vanity of vanities, and all is vanity.*[39] Those subject to carnal delights and pleasures are also effeminate, for such men care for nothing except gratifying their own desires and pleasures. Long ago, in fact, certain people did not dare to appear in military camps (*castra*) unless they were chaste (*casta*). Thus camps are called after the chaste. On this topic, Valerius recounts that when Cornelius Scipio was sent to Spain with a large army, he ordered all sources of pleasure and incentives to lust completely removed from the army.[40] Hence the prostitutes had to retreat two miles away. For this diligent man knew that pleasure feminises manly minds, while diminishing and sapping strengths of iron. So, for example, once when Alexander was still a young man he was singing to his lyre, but his tutor Antigonus took it from him and broke it in anger, saying, 'at your age it is now fitting for you to reign, so it is shameful for the heart of a king to be ruled by pleasure and dissipation'.[41] Indeed, although Alexander was certainly a generous and virtuous man he was still full of vices. It is said in *Policraticus* that although Alexander conquered the world, he was nonetheless himself conquered by anger, violence, and lust.[42]

For more than anything else, carnal desire makes a man effeminate and weak. When a certain effeminate man said to the philosopher Pythagoras that he would more willingly stand with the women than with the philosophers, Pythagoras responded: 'And pigs lie more willingly in swill than in pure water'.[43] For lust enervates the strongest men, the wisest

38 See *SD*, fol. 212v. Late thirteenth-century Italy was a nexus of the international cloth trade, both wool from northern Europe and silks from the East. Elaborate damasks and brocades—visible in the works of Cimabue, Giotto, and others—were therefore a major target of preachers denouncing conspicuous consumption.

39 Ecclesiastes 1.2.

40 Valerius Maximus, *Factorum et dictorum* 2.2.

41 John of Salisbury, *Policraticus* 3.14.

42 See the episode of Alexander and Dionides in book 7.2 (n. 24). Also see *SD*, fols. 89v, 305v (on which see also n. 33 above), 355v.

43 An analogue of 2 Peter 2.22 and the proverb *sus magis in ceno gaudet quam fonte sereno* ('a pig rejoices more in mud than in a clear fountain': Walther/Schmidt, *Proverbia* 30909, 30911), framed in an anecdote about the Greek philosopher Pythagoras (d. *c.* 495 BC) and variously attributed in the Middle Ages to Saints Jerome and Gregory the Great. Hanna/Lawler (*Jankyn's book*, p. 40 n. 86) call it 'a "philosophical" apothegm of fairly wide late medieval distribution'. Cf. *SD*, fols. 40v, 120r. While Jacopo repeats numerous misogynistic aphorisms against women generally, in accordance with long medieval tradition, these are balanced by anecdotes commending noble and/or virtuous behaviour in particular women; see the discussion in Epstein (2016), pp. 158–9, 211–26.

men, and—what is most deplorable—even the most virtuous men. Who is stronger than Samson? who wiser than Solomon? who more virtuous than David? Yet all of these were made weaker by women. We read in the book of Ezra that this question was posed to certain wise men in the presence of the powerful king Ahasuerus: what is the strongest thing in the world?[44] One said that wine is the strongest, because wine takes away men's sense and reason, dissolves all their debts, and renders them safe amidst enemies. Another said that the king or the emperor is the strongest, because all are obedient to his word, all tremble at his authority, and all are killed as he commands, or live and are preserved as he pleases. A third said that women are the strongest, because they soften, feminise, and weaken minds of iron and virility—and he gave the example of this Ahasuerus himself, who had a certain mistress who so weakened and softened him that if she was angry with the king about something and slapped him in the face, he still smiled at her. Also, when she seemed angry, the king too pretended to be angry; when she seemed happy, the king too displayed happiness; if she seemed troubled, the king soothed her with blandishments. Ultimately, this philosopher was judged to have spoken the best. From these examples it is manifestly clear that carnal desire softens minds of iron, feminises manly spirits, and enervates strong men. Men who are effeminate in this way are not fit for military concerns and should not be enrolled in the army; nor should they be called men, but rather womanly. Indeed, it is read in the *Proverbs of the philosophers* that once when a man smelled very strongly of fragrance, the philosopher Democritus said: 'From which of these men is a woman giving off such a scent?' And when he identified him, he said: 'It offends me that you are called a man, since I know that to be false by your scent'.[45]

Finally, citizens ought not to be subject to wantonness, but practised in virtuous and warlike deeds. For the art of war is learned better through experience than through knowledge, better through habit than through art. It is read in the book of Judges that the Lord decided to send certain enemies to the sons of Israel so that they could learn the art of fighting and be practised in such matters. As it is said there:

---

44 Apocryphal: 3 Esdras 3.5–4.42, referring to Darius, not Ahasuerus. (3 Esdras is known as 1 Esdras in most English translations.)

45 Numerous and varied *florilegia* (collections of quotations) circulated by this name during the Middle Ages; see e.g. Rouse/Rouse (1979), pp. 148–50. Democritus (d. c. 370 BC) was often associated with discussions of the senses and sensation because of his famous theory of atoms.

PART EIGHT: ON CITIZENSHIP

These are the peoples whom the Lord left, so that by them he could instruct Israel and all who did not know the wars of the Canaanites, so that their sons would afterward learn to battle with their enemies and be used to fighting.[46] Therefore those who wish to triumph over their enemies should exert themselves boldly rather than comporting themselves wantonly, weakly, or feebly. On this point we read in the book of Judges about the time the Lord wished to rescue his people out of the hand of the Midianites. Gideon was the leader of the Lord's people, and although he had a large army God did not wish that so great a multitude should accompany him.[47] So God told Gideon to lead his people to a river, and there he would show them who should accompany him into battle. Then God set a great thirst among the people so that when they came to the water, some of them lay down on the ground to drink but others remained standing and brought the water to their mouths. And the Lord did not wish that those who drank lying down but only those who stood up to bring the water to their mouths should go to war, by which is signified that those who abandon themselves to ease and pleasure are not to be enrolled in the army nor included in military matters, but only those who exert themselves by very bold and virtuous deeds.

For this is how the Romans triumphed so many times: because they always exerted themselves to virtuous and bold deeds. Regarding this it is said in *Policraticus* that three things made the Romans victorious, namely effort, honour, and knowledge.[48] First, effort made the Romans victorious, for they exerted themselves with warlike arms and virtuous deeds, and therefore they rejoiced in victory. Vegetius notes in his book *On military matters* that a small number of trained men are more likely to claim victory than a large multitude of untrained and ignorant ones.[49] Also, Saint Augustine says in his book *On the city of God*—when he examines how the empire of the Romans came to be so far-reaching—that the Romans first exerted themselves with virtuous deeds to preserve their liberty, so that they would be subjugated to no people but could rule themselves freely, since many cities and kings sought to subdue them. Then after they had assured themselves of liberty by many battles, they began to exert themselves by virtuous deeds and military arms to expand their glory, and thus they spread their glory and their name

---

46 Judges 3.1.
47 Judges 7.4–7 (paraphrased).
48 John of Salisbury, *Policraticus* 6.2; see also *SD*, fols. 377v–378r.
49 Vegetius, *De re militari* 1.1; the sentiment is also voiced by Sallust (see next note).

throughout the whole world. Thus, although in the beginning these Romans only controlled an area up to the fifth milestone—that is, the fifth mile [from the city], as the same Augustine says—afterward they spread their dominion so far so that they dominated the whole world.[50] But afterward they began to practise envy and greed, and from these beginnings came civil wars among them by which they mutually destroyed themselves.[51]

Secondly, honour (*fides*) made the Romans victorious, for they treated not only their friends but also their enemies with honour, so everyone trusted them.[52] On this topic we read in the *Deeds of the Romans* that when Hannibal captured a certain Roman citizen, he sent him to Rome under oath to collect the price of his own ransom.[53] He was unable to collect the necessary sum but he did not wish to return, so the senate had him bound and sent back to Hannibal. They did not wish to break a promise which he had made himself under oath, because they believed honour should be preserved even with enemies.

Finally, knowledge also made the Romans victorious. For this reason Romulus, and after him Numa Pompilius, appointed one hundred wise men from among the people, and the commonwealth was ruled by this council, whose members were called senators and conscript fathers.[54] They were called senators for their experience of life and their maturity of age, as in 'seniors'; they were also called 'fathers' on account of their solicitude, because just like fathers they were supposed to care for and succour the commonwealth, to nourish and defend it. They were called

---

50 Augustine, *City of God* 5.12, citing Sallust, *Catilinarian conspiracy* 6–7, 53–4; cf. *SD*, fol. 355r–v. While the ancient *ager Romanus* was held to end at the fifth or sixth milestone on roads leaving the city (cf. Ovid, *Fasti* 2.639–84), I have not found any reference to this fact in the works of Augustine.

51 Sallust, *Catilinarian conspiracy* 10–13.

52 See *TIE* 4127.

53 *Contra* Bertini Guidetti (*CCG*, pp. 191–2 n. 238), this is not the story of Marcus Atilius Regulus, but rather one dealing with a Roman captive who dishonourably planned to break his parole after being unable to raise the sum of his ransom. While Jacopo credits the *Gesta Romanorum*—and there were several large collections of *exempla* circulating under that title—the anecdote ultimately derives from Cicero, *De officiis* 1.40. Cf. also Valerius Maximus, *Factorum et dictorum* 4.8.1.

54 Most of this paragraph comes from Livy, *Ab urbe condita* 1.8.7, and Isidore, *Etymologies* 9.4.8–12. The detail about the mitres, however, is unusual: while some medieval authors extrapolated the *Donation of Constantine* (which attested the transfer of Roman authority from Emperor Constantine to the pope) to align the new college of cardinals with the ancient Roman senate, the claim that senators wore mitres—as the putative origin of papal and episcopal mitres—is unique.

'conscript fathers' on account of their rank, because they all wore mitres and each one's mitre had his name written on it. Later, Emperor Constantine gave his mitre to the lord pope, and he also bestowed the senators' mitres on the cardinals, so that just as the senators used to process in mitres, the cardinals now process in theirs. Alternatively, the senators may be called conscript fathers because their names and deeds were noted down in the public annals.

Furthermore, Pompeius Trogus demonstrates how knowledge is necessary in battle against one's enemies; he relates how, when Alexander was marching toward a particularly dangerous battle, he did not choose the strongest soldiers but veterans who had fought with his father. And so it occurred that, aided by their advice and wisdom, he triumphed over his enemies.[55] For just as Solomon says, a wise and learned man is stronger than a brave one,[56] because when a battle is begun on good advice, there will be safety where there is much counsel.

Chapter three: That citizens ought to be zealous on behalf of the commonwealth. Citizens ought to be zealous on behalf of the commonwealth to such an extent that they ought to place its own good first; they ought to endanger themselves sometimes even to death to preserve it; and they should take up arms even father against son and son against father to defend it.[57] We can demonstrate this by means of three examples. Augustine discusses our point that the particular good of the commonwealth itself must be placed first in his book *On the city of God*, as does Tullius in his book *On duties*.[58] They relate that when Marcus Regulus, a great Roman consul, was captured by the Carthaginians at the same time as the Romans seized many young Carthaginian men, this Regulus was sent to Rome to arrange an exchange of prisoners, agreeing under oath to return if the proposed exchange was not approved. Yet when he arrived in Rome he made a speech in the senate that such an exchange would in no way lead to the benefit of the commonwealth, since he himself was worn out with age and would soon die, but the Carthaginian youths were strong in war and capable of inflicting great damage on the Romans in future. Therefore he advised against such an exchange taking place. He also said that he did not wish broken the

---

55 *TIE* 95: Justinus, epitome of Pompeius Trogus's *Historia philippicae*, 11.6.4–5.
56 Proverbs 24.5.
57 See *SD*, fol. 377v, which cites several of the same examples.
58 Cicero, *De officiis* 3.99–115; Augustine, *City of God* 1.15, 5.18, etc.; see also Bertini Guidetti, *CCG*, p. 191 n. 238. Cf. *SD*, fol. 378r.

Romans' decree—which had been ordained and signed—that any Roman who fled from battle should suffer capital punishment, and whoever allowed himself to be captured alive and armed in battle should remain unransomed. And therefore since he had been captured alive, he should not be ransomed. Furthermore, when his friends begged him not to return to Carthage, he nonetheless chose to return according to his promise and was then very cruelly murdered by the Carthaginians. See how he subordinated his individual good to that of the common good![59] It would certainly have benefited him to be ransomed and freed from prison, but it would have damaged the commonwealth because the Carthaginian youths who were sent home would have inflicted great injuries on the Romans. Thus Tullius says in his book *On duties* that Plato issued two precepts for preserving the commonwealth.[60] The first was that all should be intent on the common good and blind to their own benefit; the second was that they should care for the whole body of the commonwealth, lest they favour one part and neglect others.

That a man ought to endanger himself sometimes even to death to preserve the commonwealth, Augustine demonstrates in his book *On the city of God*, as does Valerius Maximus.[61] For they say that when war had begun between the Athenians and the Peloponnesians, the [Peloponnesians] received a message from the gods that the victorious side would be the one whose king was killed in battle.[62] Hearing this, Codrus, the king of the Athenians, went over to the enemy dressed like a poor man, carrying branches on his shoulder and a sickle in his belt. So when he threatened one of the enemy soldiers with his sickle, the soldier rose up against him and immediately killed him. But when these enemies learned that the body was that of King Codrus and they remembered the response that the gods had given, they fled in terror and thus the Athenians had the victory. In the same way Tullius asks in his book *On duties*: *If two wise men, having suffered a shipwreck, cling to a single plank that is unable to support both of them together, what should they do?*[63] And he responds that the less wise man ought to yield to the wiser man since that the latter is more useful to the commonwealth.

---

59 Ptolemy of Lucca makes the same point: *On the government of rulers* 3.4.5.

60 Cicero, *De officiis* 1.85.

61 *TIE* 1136: Augustine, *City of God* 18.19; Valerius Maximus, *Factorum et dictorum* 5.6.ext.1; *Vatican mythographers*, pp. 73, 184. See also *SD*, fol. 377v.

62 Referring to the Dorian invasion of Athens in 1068 BC.

63 Cicero, *De officiis* 3.90. Monleone (*JVC* 2.173 n. 1) notes that Ambrose considers the same question but disagrees with Cicero: *De officiis ministrorum* 3.4.

Furthermore, we read in the histories of the Romans—and Augustine mentions it in *On the city of God* as well—that there was once a great pestilence in Rome that lasted two years. Eventually the earth itself opened up in the middle of the City, and a deep chasm was formed that somehow revealed the infernal regions below. And when all feared that the City would collapse, behold! a voice sounded out of the chasm, saying that if the Romans wished to heal their city, the gods ordered that some Roman nobleman should be offered to them in that chasm. Therefore it was ordered in the senate that whoever would throw himself headlong into the pit on behalf of the City would have a bronze statue in the Forum. And when no one else could be found [to volunteer], behold! a very noble soldier by the name of Mercurius put on his best armor, mounted his horse, and rode headlong into the pit.[64] At once the chasm closed and the pestilence ceased completely. See how both of these men gave themselves up to death for the well-being of their fatherland (*patria*)!

Furthermore, that it is lawful for a father to take up arms against his son and a son against his father in defence of the commonwealth, Tullius asserts in his book *On duties* where he asks whether a son should be silent if a father tries to divide a country or negotiate with its enemies.[65] Tullius responds that the son ought first to ask his father to stop, and if his entreaties have no effect he ought to add threats, namely, that he will denounce him to the authorities; but if neither entreaties nor threats cause his father to decide to abandon [his behaviour], the son ought to oppose himself to his father, and take up arms against him in defence of the fatherland.

This zeal which citizens ought to feel for the commonwealth, however, ought to be thoughtful, so that they do nothing for the commonwealth that might be unjust or dishonest, however useful it might seem. For a great question was once posed among certain wise men and philosophers, namely: should the useful be preferred to the honest, or the honest preferred to the useful? And they decided that the honest must always be preferred to the useful, and on this subject they adduced four examples. The first is related by Ambrose in his book *On duties*, where he says: *once when the Macedonians had sent out a great fleet of ships against the*

---

[64] Not Mercurius but Marcus Curtius: *TIE* 2745; Livy, *Ab urbe condita* 7.5; Valerius Maximus, *Factorum et dictorum* 5.6.2; Augustine, *City of God* 5.18. See also *SS*, fol. 422r–v (where Jacopo correctly attributes the act to Curtius).

[65] Cicero, *De officiis* 3.90; cf. *SD*, fol. 377v.

Athenians, a certain messenger from their army came to the Athenians saying that they should send two wise men with him, and he would show them something that would be very useful to them.[66] *When the wise men were chosen, he told them that the Macedonians had placed their fleet of ships in a particular place, and if they went there secretly by night they could burn the entire fleet of ships. Then the two wise men returned to the waiting assembly, saying, 'The thing which this man has told us is certainly useful, but it is not honest. If you wish to win usefully, you should do what he has suggested; but if you wish to win honestly, you should not do it'. And at once they all cried out with one voice, saying, 'Let us win honestly; let us win honestly'.* And thus they refused that victory because it would not have been acquired honourably, and Ambrose adds: *for they preferred to be less successful by doing something honestly than to be more successful by doing it shamefully.*

The same Ambrose provides a second example in this same book, one also related by Annetus Florus in the *Histories of the Romans*.[67] They say that when the king Pyrrhus and the Roman consul Fabricius assembled large armies to do battle with each other, king Pyrrhus's doctor came to Fabricius and offered to give the king poisoned medicine, so that with the king dead Fabricius would gain the victory. Upon hearing this, Fabricius was repulsed at the idea of such a victory, because it would not be gained honestly but treacherously. Accordingly, he had the aforesaid doctor—who had been such a traitor to his lord—bound and sent back to his lord. And Ambrose continues, indeed, it is noble that he who had undertaken a contest of virtue did not wish to win through fraud. When the king heard this story, he killed the doctor and said, 'That is Fabricius: just as the sun cannot go backward on its path, so he [cannot go back] on his law-abiding nature'—and so he came voluntarily to an agreement with Fabricius.

The third example is about Regulus, greatest consul of the Romans, who had sworn to return to prison, as stated [earlier] in the present chapter. It would have been useful to him not to return to prison, but it would not have been honest, given his oath.

Valerius [Maximus] provides our fourth example, of the Roman leader Camillus, who was besieging a certain city when a certain master of

---

66 Ambrose, *De officiis ministrorum* 3.14.87, based on Cicero, *De officiis* 3.49; perhaps via Valerius Maximus, *Factorum et dictorum* 6.5.ext.2. See also *SD*, fol. 378r.

67 *TIE* 3761: Ambrose, *De officiis ministrorum* 3.15.91, based on Cicero, *De officiis* 3.86–7; see also *SD*, fol. 378r–v. Florus refers only in passing to this episode (*Epitome* 1.13.20–2).

the art of grammar, who taught the children of the nobility, left the city with the excuse of taking a walk and fell into the hands of the enemy.[68] And when Camillus heard this, he denounced his capture, saying, 'We Romans seek to conquer by virtue and arms, and we serve the law as much in war as in peace; we take up arms not against boyish youth—which is spared even in captured cities—but against rebels'. Therefore he ordered the man bound, reunited with his students, and then led back to their parents. So when the [parents] heard this story, they opened their gates to the Romans and negotiated with them.

Thus this commonwealth was extended, improved, and governed by the uprightness of its morals and the honour of its virtues as much as by the quantity of its riches, the multitude of its peoples, or its abundance of horses or arms. Cato shows this elegantly and eloquently. (Not the Cato who wrote the primer for boys but the more famous Cato [the Younger], who may claim [the title of] prince of Latin philosophers.[69]) This Cato favoured the party of Pompey against Caesar since he believed Caesar to be an enemy of the commonwealth. Thus when he heard that the aforesaid Caesar had gained victory over Pompey, so great was his honour that he sought out poison and his sword: having taken the poison, he stuck his sword into himself and inflicted a [fatal] wound lest he see his enemy Caesar ruling the commonwealth. Speaking on behalf of the commonwealth, this Cato spoke thusly, and the blessed Augustine repeated his words in his book *On the city of God*: *Do not*, says Cato, *imagine that our ancestors created a great commonwealth out of very little by arms. Indeed, if it had been thus, we would still have a very small one. Indeed, we have a greater number of allies and citizens, as well as arms and horses, than they did. But there were other things which they themselves did brilliantly but which we no longer have, namely: diligence at home, just governance abroad, and minds impartial in deliberation, guilty neither of crime nor of lust.*[70] These words of Cato which are very true teach us by their experience what the chief of all truths is. For it is a fact that our modern citizens are more abundant in arms, horses, people, and riches than the ancients were; yet our ancient citizens often governed

---

68 Valerius Maximus, *Factorum et dictorum* 6.5.1.

69 Confusion between Marcus Porcius Cato the Elder (Cato the Censor, 234–179 BC) and his great-grandson Cato the Younger (Cato of Utica, 95–46 BC) was fairly common in Jacopo's time. Cf. the similar case of Pliny in part 10.2 n. 18. The 'primer for boys' is the *Distichs of Cato*, which was often attributed to Cato the Elder despite having been written by Dionysius Cato in the third or fourth century.

70 Augustine, *City of God* 5.12, citing Sallust, *Catilinarian conspiracy* 52.21.

better than do our modern ones, who have so much more wealth.[71] For a commonwealth often falls into danger between too much wealth and an overabundance of possessions. Regarding this Augustine says: *Those who pay close attention will grieve more at the demise of Roman poverty than Roman wealth. For in poverty the integrity of morals was preserved; but in opulence terrible wickedness—that worst enemy of all—corrupted not only the walls of the city but the minds of its men.*[72] And also the poet: *No offence, outrage, or wantonness was absent, and thus Roman poverty perished.*[73] Thus it is obvious from the words of Cato that these four things—an abundance of arms, horses, people, and riches—are not the sources of a well-run commonwealth; rather, there are another four things which he lists further on.

The first is that its citizens are industrious with regard to domestic affairs so that they understand how to arrange and supervise their households well. As the Apostle says, *he who does not take care for his own possessions and especially his own household denies the faith and is worse than an unbeliever.*[74] Also, it often happens that when a master of a house is himself disorganised, he keeps his whole family in a state of disorder. For this reason it is said in Ecclesiasticus: *A people and their officials are like their judge, and the inhabitants of a city resemble its ruler.*[75] For he who cannot manage his own household cannot manage others. On this topic Saint Jerome tells of the great philosopher Gorgias, who had a disgraceful wife and a very beautiful maidservant.[76] And although he was entirely faithful, his wife was nonetheless jealous of him; she suspected him of dallying with the maid and so hounded him daily with accusations that he could not find peace in his own house. Now, the aforesaid Gorgias wrote a very beautiful book about how the Greeks (who quarreled amongst themselves) should be able to establish peace between themselves. But when he presented his book to the other philosophers and wise men, one of his servants said, 'This man wishes to bring peace to all of Greece, but he cannot pacify his own home! When there are three

---

71 A sentiment common to many late republican Roman authors such as Sallust and Cicero, which clearly resonated with Jacopo and his fellow Genoese.

72 Augustine, letter 138 to Marcellinus, para. 16 (*CCSL* 31B.287), citing Juvenal, *Satires* 6.287–95. see also *SD*, fol. 355v.

73 Juvenal, *Satires* 6.294–5.

74 1 Timothy 5.8.

75 Sirach 10.2.

76 Jerome, *Adversus Jovinianum* 1.48; cited by Vincent of Beauvais, *Speculum doctrinale* 6.6.1.

PART EIGHT: ON CITIZENSHIP 141

in one house—namely master, wife, and maidservant—they cannot establish peace between themselves'.

The second point is that [citizens] ought to possess and to preserve justice toward all others. Now, justice is a virtue which gives to each his own: therefore a man is just when he gives respect to a superior, peace to an equal, instruction and discipline to an inferior, good will to friends, patience to enemies, and helpful compassion to the unhappy and unfortunate. The third point is that they ought not to be subject to vices, for it would hardly be useful to the commonwealth if its buildings remained standing but its morals collapsed. For this reason Augustine says that Scipio did not consider a commonwealth happy if it had intact walls but ruined morals.[77]

The fourth point is that [citizens] ought to be impartial in deliberation, because they ought to speak freely and support the truth. But there are many who remain silent regarding the truth either out of timidity or because of they have accepted bribes. Elinandus, who was a very learned man, tells us that king Philip of Macedon inflicted many damages and troubles upon the Athenians, which became a great quarrel between them; at last by common agreement it was decided that each side should choose an advocate.[78] So as their advocate the Athenians chose Demosthenes, who was a very wise and eloquent man: all the lawyers and judges dreaded his oratory. And when King Philip heard this, he was very afraid that Demosthenes' eloquence would cause his man to lose the case—on account of which he sent a large weight of silver to Demosthenes, asking that he should act neither for him nor for the Athenians, but should merely be silent. And indeed, Demosthenes was perverted by greed: he accepted the silver and promised to stay silent. Thus as the appointment approached the Athenians sent word to Demosthenes that he should hasten to the place assigned and defend their cause, but when he heard this he feigned illness: he threw himself on his bed and began to exclaim loudly that he suffered from angina. Then one of the Athenians' messengers, who had heard of his acceptance of the silver, replied to him, saying, 'See, Demosthenes, you do not suffer from angina, but from silverness (*argentinas*)'. In this way he was perverted by the desire for money into remaining silent regarding the

---

77 Augustine, *City of God* 1.33.
78 Helinand of Froidmont (d. *c.* 1237), *Chronica*, book 8 (?). While less than half of Helinand's *Chronicle* has survived (*PL* 212.771–1082), it was a major source for Vincent of Beauvais' *Speculum historiale*, which may be how Jacopo knew it. *Speculum historiale* 30.128 contains a related story about Demosthenes.

truth of justice. The same Elinandus says that if the tongue of a judge is bound with silver cords, he is immediately rendered mute. But just as it is a sin to speak a lie, so it is also a sin to remain silent regarding the truth. For this reason the blessed Augustine says: *Both he who conceals the truth and he who lies are sinners before God. The first because he chooses not to do good, the latter because he seeks to do harm.*[79]

---

[79] Attributed to Augustine by Gratian (*Decretum* 2, case 11, question 3, canon 80) and Thomas Aquinas (*Summa theologiae* 2.2, question 70, article 1, s.c.), but not found in Augustine's works; see *SD*, fol. 373r.

PART NINE: ON DOMESTIC LIFE

Here follows part nine, which deals with familial and domestic matters. This part has six chapters: the first addresses how a wife should be guided, and how one may know if she is good or not; the second, how she should be looked after. The third posits that both spouses ought to love one another; the fourth, that they ought to live in peace. The fifth discusses how parents ought to behave toward their children, and children toward their parents, and the sixth, how masters ought to behave toward their servants (famuli) *or slaves* (servi), *and servants toward their masters.*

Chapter one: How a wife should be guided, and how one may know if she is good or not.[1] Citizens ought to keep not only their commonwealth in order, but also their familial and domestic lives.[2] These are orderly when spouses maintain order between themselves while also keeping their family in order. Now, order in familial and domestic matters depends much upon a good and wise wife, regarding whom Solomon says: *a wise woman builds up her house, but a foolish one destroys it with her own hands.*[3] Thus a man ought to work hard so that he can have a good and wise wife. And although a wise wife is given by God—because, as Solomon says, one receives a house and riches from one's parents, but a prudent wife from God himself—nonetheless, a man about to take a wife ought to enquire diligently regarding her morals and situation.[4] Saint John Chrysostom demonstrates how this ought to be done, saying that he who wishes to take a wife ought to consider if the girl he wishes to marry has both good parents, or both bad, or one good and the other bad.[5] If both parents are good, he may

---

1 Much of this chapter also appears in *SD*, fols. 43r–45r.

2 Classical political thought imagined close ties between different levels of sovereignty, paralleling the responsibilities of a ruler with those of a male head of household: Aristotle, *Politics* 1.1–2; Cicero, *De officiis* 1.53–4.

3 Proverbs 14.1. See also *SS*, fol. 317v; *SD*, fol. 43v; *Mariale* 25/C4 (*cedrus*), 35/C14 (*contrivit*), 146/T5 (*thesauraria*), 152/V4 (*venter*).

4 Proverbs 19.14.

5 From a homily on Matthew 23.27 traditionally attributed to John Chrysostom (*PG* 56.888, no. 45); cf. *SD*, fol. 44r.

safely marry her because a good tree bears good fruit. If both are bad, he should give her up entirely because a bad tree cannot bear good fruit. But if one is good and the other is bad, he should be cautious and watch diligently [to see] what he ought to do. If her father is bad and her mother good, he may be less wary of marrying her, but if, on the contrary, her father is good and her mother bad, he should be more wary of marrying her. This makes sense because girls interact more with their mothers than with their fathers, so they are more inclined to imitate the habits of their mothers than of their fathers.[6]

Hence a man taking a wife ought not to dwell on her wealth as greedy men do, nor her beauty as lascivious youths do, but rather the uprightness of her character, as wise and discerning men do. For a man ought not to consider her wealth, as Saint John Chrysostom says: *young man, when you seek to take a wife do not ask about her wealth but her good character, because those of good character always acquire riches but the wealthy do not acquire good morals, and the poverty of the faithful is more glorious than the riches of sinners.*[7] A philosopher by the name of Aureolus Theophrastus asks whether a man ought to take a rich or a poor wife, and affirms that he who takes a rich wife brings a tempest into his house because a rich wife wishes to be master (*domina*[8]) of her husband: she will harass him day and night with arguments and hold her riches over him.[9] Regarding this, Solomon says *it is better to sit on a corner of the roof than to share a home with a quarrelsome woman.*[10] The roof is the covering of a house, where sparrows and swallows are accustomed to build their nests; Solomon wishes to say that it is better to live on the roof of a house with sparrows and swallows than inside the house with a quarrelsome woman, because a woman's nagging is worse than a swallow's twittering. Therefore a man ought not to look to wealth in his wife, and a wife should ideally have more fortitude, character, and wisdom than wealth. Regarding this, someone once asked the philosopher

---

6 An idea developed in the first of Chrysostom's *Sermons on Anna* (*PG* 54.633–4).

7 From the homily on Matthew 23.27 cited in n. 5, above (*PG* 56.888).

8 It seemed preferable to lose the gender of *domina* than to adopt the anachronistic implications of its English equivalents ('lady' or 'mistress').

9 Theophrastus, Aristotle's successor among the Peripatetics, argued in his treatise *On marriages* that marriage and scholarship were incompatible. While Theophrastus' full work is lost, a long fragment is preserved in Jerome's *Adversus Jovinianum*: Hanna/Lawler, *Jankyn's book*, pp. 149–55. From Jerome it was incorporated into John of Salisbury's *Policraticus* and Vincent of Beauvais' *Speculum historiale*, both texts much consulted by Jacopo.

10 Proverbs 21.9; see *SD*, fol. 43v.

PART NINE: ON DOMESTIC LIFE   145

Themistocles whether he would more willingly give his daughter in marriage to a poor man of distinguished character or to a rich but less worthy man, to which he responded, 'I would prefer to give my daughter to a man in need of money than to money in need of a man'.[11]

Also, a man about to take a wife ought not to dwell on her beauty as lascivious youths do because beauty in a woman is dangerous both to behold and to possess. To behold, because often it cheats the man who beholds it. As Solomon says, *charm is deceitful and beauty is hollow. A God-fearing woman will be praised for herself*.[12] It is also dangerous for a woman to possess, because as Solomon says, *a beautiful and foolish woman is a golden ring in a pig's snout*.[13] When a woman is both foolish and ugly there is no danger because no one bothers her, and when she is beautiful and wise, similarly there is no danger because she comports herself wisely. But when she is beautiful and foolish, then there is danger, because—just like a sow with a gold ring in its snout or around its neck digs itself into the muck along with its gold—the beautiful but foolish woman immerses her beauty along with [the rest of] herself into the muck of her foul habits. Indeed, the aforementioned philosopher Aureolus [Theophrastus] asks if a man ought to take a beautiful or a repulsive wife, and he answers that a beautiful one will be coveted by all while a repulsive one will be despised by all, but it is difficult to guard a beautiful one whom everyone desires to possess, and tiresome to keep a repulsive one whom no one wishes to look at.[14] Therefore he who has a beautiful wife will always be afraid but he who has a repulsive wife will always be depressed. For this reason he should pursue a middle path, so that his wife is afflicted neither with too much beauty nor with too much ugliness: then her beauty will not cause him too much anxiety, nor her loathsomeness cause him too much misery.

Therefore he ought not to pay attention to riches or beauty, but to the uprightness of her character; namely, a woman should be peaceful and respectable rather than raucous and quarrelsome—because, as Solomon says, *a quarrelsome woman is like a leaky roof on a cold day*.[15] When a man is in bed and it is very cold, it will be a great nuisance to him if the

11 *TIE* 1444: Cicero, *De officiis* 2.71 and Valerius Maximus, *Factorum et dictorum* 7.2.ext.9, the latter repeated in Vincent of Beauvais, *Speculum doctrinale* 6.4.2. Cf. *SD*, fol. 43v.
12 Proverbs 31.30. Cf. *SD*, fol. 350r; *SS*, fol. 438r.
13 Proverbs 11.22. Cf. *SD*, fol. 43r, 350r; *SQ*, p. 397; *SS*, fol. 438r.
14 Theophrastus via Jerome, *Adversus Jovinianum* 1.47; cf. *SD*, fol. 43v.
15 Proverbs 19.13, 27.15. Cf. *SD*, fol. 167v.

roof leaks and drops are falling on him; Solomon wishes to convey that a quarrelsome woman is like the raindrops falling from the roof on a cold day that disturb the man lying in bed. Saint Jerome and Seneca recount that the philosopher Socrates—despite being a very wise man—was nonetheless ugly and loathsome in appearance.[16] He had two wives who were very jealous of him, and one day when he reprimanded them for their vile and overweening jealousy, they became indignant and attacked him, dragging him to the ground by his hair and hammering him with blows. And another day, when one of them was thundering away at him and he did not want to respond to her, he left the house and took a seat on a certain beam sticking out of the wall of the house. Then she took a bucket full of water and poured all of the water on his head—and Socrates, wiping his head and looking up at her, said, 'I know well that rain follows thunder'. But when his friends advised him to banish these wives who so afflicted him, he said, 'I will never do that because they serve a great purpose for me. They make me patient—and I learn patience in my house so that I may exhibit it in the forum'.

Chapter two: How men ought to look after their wives. Because woman is weaker than man, she requires more looking after than a man. As Saint John Chrysostom says, women are more easily misled because they are more unguarded than men.[17] Because they are weaker, they are more easily persuaded either to good or to evil. Because they are more fragile, they are sooner overcome. And because of these facts, when the devil sought to lead our first parents astray he did not approach the man but the woman, knowing that the woman would be more easily misled than the man: hence she is the less cautious sex and more easily influenced; hence she is the weaker sex and more easily overcome; and hence it says in the book *On the ten strings* that there should be four restraints placed upon a woman, of which a man is only one.[18] The first restraint is the fear of God, which should keep her from sin because, as Solomon says: *Out of fear of the Lord every man retreats from evil*.[19] The second is the restraint of her husband, because a man ought to

---

16 Seneca the Younger, *De constantia sapientis* 18.6, quoted in Jerome, *Adversus Jovinianum* 1.48. Cf. Vincent of Beauvais, *Speculum doctrinale* 6.3.2, and *SD*, fol. 39v.

17 From a homily on Matthew 23 attributed to John Chrysostom (*PG* 56.880, no. 44). Cf. *SD*, fol. 324r.

18 Augustine, sermon 9 ('De decem chordis'), chaps. 9–12 (*CCSL* 41.124–32). Cf. also *SD*, fols. 350v–351r; *SQ*, pp. 261–2, 399.

19 Proverbs 16.6, also cited earlier in part 7.2.

PART NINE: ON DOMESTIC LIFE 147

restrain his wife, as is said in Ecclesiasticus: *If a wife does not walk at your hand, she will confound you in the sight of your enemies.*[20] The third is the rebuke of the world, because great shame and confusion devolve upon a woman who is caught in adultery. As Solomon says, *a diligent woman is a crown to her husband, but she who does things worthy of disgrace is like decay in his bones.*[21] The fourth is fear of the public laws, which condemn adulterous wives. Thus the Jews said to Christ, *'Master, here is a woman recently discovered in adultery; in the law Moses ordered us to stone such people'.*[22]

By contrast, a man has only one restraint upon him, namely the fear of God, which should keep him from sin.[23] For he does not have his wife as a restraint, because he should not allow her to control him, nor does he fear the rebuke of the world—indeed, in some cases he boasts of it. As Augustine says, *so great is the perversity of the human race that anyone should ever fear embarrassment for seeming chaste among the unchaste.*[24] Finally, he does not fear the punishment of the law because laws do not condemn fornicating men as they do fornicating women.

Now, the aforementioned philosopher Aureolus also asks whether a woman ought to be controlled by a man. His answer is that there is no point to a man's attempting to control a woman because either a wife is good or she is bad. If she is good she ought not to be controlled; if she is bad he will not be able to control her.[25] Although this is the philosopher's opinion, we nonetheless say that there are some wives who are worthy, some who are of dubious character, and some who are in between.[26] Those who are worthy should not be restrained but set free at their liberty in all things. Saint Jerome records in his book *Against Jovinian* that a certain great Roman consul by the name of Duilius had taken a noble young girl as his wife.[27] But he had very bad breath, and once, after he was already an old man, he was reproached [with the fact] that he had terrible breath. Upon returning home, he

---

20 Sirach 25.35; cf. *SD*, fol. 220v.
21 Proverbs 12.4; cf. *SS*, fol. 432r.
22 John 8.4–5.
23 Augustine, sermon 9 ('De decem chordis'), chap. 12 (*CCSL* 41.131).
24 Ibid.
25 Theophrastus via Jerome, *Adversus Jovinianum* 1.48. Cf. also *SD*, fol. 44r.
26 Cf. *SD*, fol. 220r–v.
27 Jerome, *Adversus Jovinianum* 1.46. Cf. also Vincent of Beauvais, *Speculum doctrinale* 6.3.2, and *SD*, fol. 44r–v.

rebuked his wife, asking why she had never alerted him to this fact so that he could have taken a cure or medicines. To this she responded: 'I would have done so, lord, but I believed that all men had such a smell'. Thus she who is worthy should not be controlled.

Others are of doubtful character: these should be restrained and compelled to the law. And although their actions cannot be entirely controlled, they may still often be prevented from committing many evil acts. As the Lord says via the prophet Hosea regarding a fornicating woman: *behold, I will close off her paths with thorns so she cannot find her way; she will pursue her lovers, but she will not overtake them.*[28] In this way a man restricts the paths of an immodest woman with thorns when he places many restrictions and restraints upon her. Finally, some wives are in between [these two extremes], being neither very virtuous nor entirely suspect. These should be neither restrained too much nor given too much freedom; rather, they should be tested first. For if a friend should be tested before a man confides in him, so much more should a wife. As it is said in Ecclesiasticus: *If you wish to gain a friend, take him on trial: that is, test him, and do not believe him too easily.*[29]

Chapter three: That husbands and wives ought to love one another. Mutual love is necessary between man and wife. For a man ought to love his wife, as the Apostle says in the letter to the Ephesians: *men, love your wives as Christ [loves] the church.*[30] Indeed, a man ought not to fear his wife as a master (*domina*) nor subjugate her to himself as a servant, but love her as a sister and partner. For this reason the first woman was not made from man's head because she was not intended as his master, nor from his foot because she was not intended as his servant, but rather from man's side because she was intended to be his partner and equal. Similarly, a wife ought to love her husband; as it is said in Tobit of parents who advised their daughter to honour her in-laws, love her husband, rule her family, and manage her household.[31] This love ought to be sensible on the part of the husband, perfect on the part of the wife, and heartfelt on the part of both.

First, marital love ought to be sensible on the part of the man because a man ought to love his wife sensibly and appropriately—unlike many

---

28 Hosea 2.6–7 (paraphrased); cf. *SD*, fol. 44v.
29 Sirach 6.7. Cf. *SD*, fol. 220v.
30 Ephesians 5.25. Cf. *SD*, fols. 40r, 220v.
31 Tobit 10.12–13.

PART NINE: ON DOMESTIC LIFE   149

who love their wives too ardently and inappropriately. Criticising such men, Seneca says that *love of a woman's appearance is the oblivion of reason, akin to insanity; it throws off advice; it breaks high and generous spirits; it retreats from great thoughts to humiliations. While the origin of this love is respectable, its excess is disgraceful.*[32] And the philosopher Sixtus says thus: *An overly ardent lover of his own wife is an adulterer.*[33] A man loves his wife appropriately when he knows to abstain from the conjugal act at the right times, and also knows to beware of mortal sin there. For according to Chrysostom there are four times when one must abstain from the conjugal act: the first is during his wife's menstrual period, since during that time children may be generated who are blind, lame, and leprous, as Saint Jerome says, and this is a rule.[34] The second time one must abstain is during pregnancy and childbirth; the third, in times of solemnity [such as Advent or Lent]; the fourth, during times of fasting—but all these things we do not believe to be rules, merely advice.[35] Someone who loves his wife appropriately also knows how to avoid mortal sin in the conjugal act. For conjugal intercourse sometimes involves no sin, sometimes venial sin, sometimes mortal sin, and sometimes the worst mortal sin. Now, it involves no sin when it is done with the intent of producing children, as Saint Gregory says: *Spouses are without sin in intercourse when they copulate to produce offspring.*[36] [The act] involves venial sin when it is done to satisfy desire, when the satisfaction of that desire is subject to the reason that it will not be satisfied except with one's own wife. For this reason a particular gloss on the letter of Saint Paul to the Corinthians says: *Conjugal intimacy for the sake of begetting offspring has no sin; but when it is done with one's own wife for the purpose of satisfying desire, it carries venial sin.*[37] Nonetheless, it is also possible to commit mortal sin, which occurs when this desire is immoderate: that is, when it is satisfied with any woman whatsoever, whether one's own wife or another. On this topic, Augustine says in his

---

32 Seneca the Younger, *De matrimonio*, preserved in Jerome, *Adversus Jovinianum* 1.49. Cf. Vincent of Beauvais, *Speculum doctrinale* 6.3.7, and *SD*, fol. 44r.

33 Jerome, *Adversus Jovinianum* 1.49, referring to the *Sentences* of Sextus (often attributed to the third-century pope Sixtus II). Cf. Vincent of Beauvais, *Speculum doctrinale* 6.7.1; *SD*, fols. 44r, 195v.

34 Jerome, *Commentariorum in Hiezechielem* 6.18.5–9 (*CCSL* 75.235).

35 Cf. *SD*, fol. 220v.

36 Gregory the Great (AD 590–604), *Pastoral rule* 3.27. The line also appears in the pseudo-Gregorian *Expositio in septem psalmis poenitentialis* (*PL* 79.549–660); Stegmüller (1950), no. 2649.

37 Augustine, *De bono coniugali* 6, discussing 1 Corinthians 7. Cf. *SD*, fol. 351r.

book *Against Julian: What is someone who is intemperate in his marriage except an adulterer?*[38] And finally, [sex] involves the worst mortal sin when a man abuses his wife, as Augustine says in his book *On the good of marriage: That practice which is contrary to nature is detestable when done to a prostitute, but even more detestable when done to a wife.*[39]

Second, marital love on the part of the wife should be perfect because a wife ought to love her husband with a perfect love. John Chrysostom demonstrates this in the following way, saying, *if a man has a wife, his wife's full love may be known in this way: she ought to think no one wiser than her husband, and if another be wiser, she ought not to recognise it. A wife ought to think no one braver than her husband, and if another be stronger, she ought not to recognise him as stronger. A wife ought to think no one more handsome than her husband, and if another be more handsome, he ought not to seem so to her; for perfect hate and perfect love do not recognise the absolute qualities of things. If you despise someone utterly, all things to do with him will seem awful to you, whatever they are; but if you love someone perfectly, all things to do with him are pleasing to you: whatever he says, whatever he does. For even if they are evil, they nonetheless seem good to you.*[40]

Thirdly, marital love ought to be heartfelt on the part of both spouses, namely both man and woman. For the woman is made from the flesh of the man near his heart, meaning that the man ought to love his wife with a heartfelt (*praecordialis*, literally 'close to the heart') love, and a man marries a woman by placing a ring on her fourth finger, where the vein is which goes from the heart all the way to that finger, meaning that the wife ought to love her husband from her innermost heart.[41]

Chapter four: That a man and a woman ought to live peacefully, and abide in concord. It is very pleasing to God when a man and his wife live peacefully and in concord. For as the holy one says often in Ecclesiasticus: *My spirit is pleased with three things approved before God and men: concord between brothers, the love of neighbours, and a husband and wife agreeing well together.*[42] Similarly, Saint Augustine on the Psalms

---

38 Augustine, *Contra Julianum* 2.7.20 (*PL* 44.687); cf. *SD*, fol. 351r.

39 Augustine, *De bono coniugali* 12; cf. also *SD*, fol. 351r. By 'abuse' Jacopo means not domestic abuse in the modern sense, but anal or oral sex: see Walsh's notes on the Augustine passage, pp. 25–8.

40 From a homily on Matthew 22 traditionally attributed to John Chrysostom (*PG* 56.873–4, no. 42). See also *SD*, fol. 221v.

41 See *SD*, fols. 28r, 42r, 166r.

42 Sirach 25.1–2; cf. *SD*, fols. 41v, 221r.

says that when a man and wife disagree with one another, there is much disturbance in their household.⁴³ Also, when a man is subjugated and his wife dominates him, then a perverse peace is in the household, but when a man dominates and his wife is subject to him, then a righteous peace is in the household. Finally, we may add a fourth point: when a man and a woman get along well, it is pleasing to men because the peace of God is present. But when a man and a woman get along badly, this is sometimes the fault of the man, sometimes the fault of the woman, and sometimes the fault of both. It is the fault of the man when the man is too severe with his wife, as the Apostle says: *Men, love your wives and do not be too harsh with them*.⁴⁴ It is the fault of the woman when she is too quarrelsome and too jealous. As Saint Jerome recounts in his book *Against Jovinian*, a certain noble Roman had a wife who was publicly gracious but privately very quarrelsome with and jealous of her husband, so he disavowed her and cast her out.⁴⁵ And when he was reproached by his neighbours for having disavowed such a gracious woman, he put out his foot, saying, 'You see here my shoe: it is very beautiful on the outside but it pinches me on the inside. You see the exterior beauty of these shoes, but you do not see my internal pain. So it is also with my wife, who outwardly seems very gracious to you, but privately was very troublesome to me'. Finally, sometimes this disturbance is caused by both of the two together, namely, when the man is too severe and the woman is too quarrelsome—and then there is great unrest in the household. Now, this point we have just made we may demonstrate by perceptible example: for if someone wishes to weld iron and join it to another [piece of] iron, he must soften both pieces by heating them in the fire.⁴⁶ If he should leave both hard, or one of the two, then the conjunction or union to be made will not hold. In the same way it must be said that when a man and a woman are both inflexible, when the man is severe and the woman compliant, or conversely when the woman is demanding and the man compliant, then they cannot live together [peaceably]. Rather, it is necessary that both should be flexible, namely, that the man should be benevolent and the woman compliant, and then what the Scripture says is accomplished, because a man and a woman who agree well together are very pleasing to God.

43 *Enarrationes in Psalmos* 143.6 (*CCSL* 40.2077). Cf. *SD*, fol. 350v; *SQ*, pp. 431–2.
44 Colossians 3.19.
45 Jerome, *Adversus Jovinianum* 1.48. Cf. *SD*, fol. 39v.
46 See *SD*, fols. 184r, 222r–v.

There is one instance, however, in which a wife is permitted to bring a quarrel against her husband, namely when she knows her husband to be a fornicator [adulterer]. Then she ought to draw him back from such crimes by four methods, as Saint Augustine says in his book of fifty sermons.[47] First, by admonishing him sweetly and lovingly, explaining the peril into which he is so thoughtlessly placing his soul, body, and possessions. For if his wife were to remain silent, then she would seem to consent; regarding this Augustine says in the same place, *above all else I admonish you, I command you, I urge you, even as Christ urges in me: do not allow your husbands to fornicate.* Secondly, she ought to draw him back by reproaching him gravely, because if loving admonitions do not work, she should make grave reproaches. In other things that a man does, a wife ought to exercise patience, as Augustine says in the same place: *Has your husband sold your jewelry? Bear it patiently, woman. Wish only for him to be chaste; argue only for chastity. Let your house collapse, but do not let his soul perish because of your silence.* Thirdly, she ought to draw him back by involving the church, that is, the bishop; because, if warnings have failed, if reproaches have failed, and the deed is nonetheless public and notorious, a wife ought to resort to the bishop of her city to frighten her husband and curb him by his authority. As Augustine says in the same place: *Respectable women, do not permit your husbands to fornicate. Alert the church against them—that is, the bishop and the prelates of the church, whose task it is to coerce publicly fornicating husbands by a sentence of excommunication.* Fourthly, she ought to draw him back by resorting to God, because if all of the above fail to work then she ought to pour out her prayers to God on his behalf. And she ought to consult with spiritual men, so that they may pour out prayers to God on behalf of her husband.[48] As Augustine says in the same place: *I do not say that you should set against your fornicating husbands public judges or a proconsul or a count or an emperor, but rather God the Father, Jesus Christ his son, and the Holy Spirit.* And although other wives may say, 'because my husband does not keep faith with me in this act, neither I will keep faith with him', Saint Augustine continues: *Chaste women, do not imitate your shameless husbands; either let them live with you or perish without you. A woman does not owe her modesty to a shameless husband, but to Christ; [preserve your modesty] not on account of your husband, who does not deserve it, but on account of Christ.*

---

47 Augustine, sermon 392 ('To spouses'), chap. 4 (*PL* 39.1711–12).
48 Ibid.; see also *SD*, fols. 39v–40r.

Chapter five: How parents ought to act toward their children, and children toward their parents.[49] Because domestic matters are best managed when the head of the family (*pater familias*) keeps his family in order, he ought to begin with his children, and inculcate good habits in them. Truly, parents ought to love their children; they ought to inculcate good habits in them in their childhood and correct them when they err. First, then: they ought to love them wisely. One must note, however, that [parental] love is sometimes good and worthy, other times bad, and other times indifferent. It is good and worthy when a father loves his son who is good and just, or so that he will become good and just, for then he does not love his son so much because he is his son, as because he loves God in his son. This act thus recalls the precept *love your neighbour as yourself.*[50] But sometimes this love is bad: for example, when parents commit usury or appropriate the possessions of others out of love for their children, so that later they become a reason for the children's damnation. Such children might indeed wish their father in hell, as is said in Ecclesiasticus: *The children will complain of an ungodly father, since because of him they are in disgrace.*[51] Also, sometimes [parental] love can be indifferent, meaning neither good and worthy nor bad: namely, when a father gives no thought to the evil in his son if he is bad, nor to the good in his son if he is good, but only to his nature—that is, he loves his son because he is his son. That love is called natural because it is also common to beasts, as Augustine says in his book of fifty sermons: *Since snakes and wolves love their offspring, he who loves his children is not praiseworthy, but he who does not love them is detestable. If you love your children, you are comparable to snakes; if you do not love your children, you are worse than snakes.*[52]

Another point: this natural love is greater in parents with respect to their children than in a child with respect to his parents. The reason is that by their nature parents have given their bodies to their children, but children have given nothing to their parents in return. Accordingly parents love their children as their own possession, their own body, their own limb. For we see that the sap of a tree flows from the roots to the branches, not from the branches to the roots. The root is the

---

49 Much of this chapter also appears in *SD*, fols. 322v–325r.
50 Matthew 19.19 and 22.39; Mark 12.31; Romans 13.9; Galatians 5.14; James 2.8.
51 Sirach 41.10; cf. *SD*, fol. 222r.
52 Augustine, sermon 385 ('On brotherly love'), chap. 2 (*PL* 39.1691); cf. *SD*, fols. 336v–337r.

father; the branch is the son. Thus the love of a father, who is the root, flows more to the son, who is the branch, than from the son to the father. Furthermore, this natural love for children is greater in mothers than it is in fathers: first, because we love things more when we know we have greater control over them. For although the son contains as much of his father as he does of his mother with respect to the body, nonetheless his mother puts into him more of her essence than the man does, as the Philosopher says, and thus she has more influence over the body of her son than her husband does.[53] The second reason is that we love things more when we have worked harder for them, and the mother works harder for her children than the father does, as much in carrying them [in pregnancy] and giving birth to them as in nourishing them. The third reason is that we love things more when we know with certainty that they are our own. A mother knows with certainty that she bore a particular son herself; but although a man may believe so, he can nonetheless never be certain that his son was generated from his own seed.[54]

The love of a father and a mother differ, however, with regard to a son, because a mother laments more at her son's adversity while a father rejoices more in his son's prosperity. For a woman naturally suffers more and has more compassion than a man, since she has a softer spirit; this is why 'woman' (*mulier*) resembles 'softer' (*mollier*).[55] According to the Philosopher in his book *On animals*, females are weaker than males in every type of animal except the bear and the leopard.[56] Thus when a woman (*mulier*) is severe and harsh she cannot be called a lady (*femina*) but rather a she-bear or leopardess. For women are naturally cold and wet [in their humours] so they are more susceptible to emotion, while men are naturally hot and dry, so they do not suffer or feel compassion as easily.[57] Therefore on the death of a son his mother grieves more than his father, because men have bolder hearts; they desire and love greater and more lofty things. Solomon demonstrates this clearly, saying *a wise son makes his father rejoice; but a foolish son is the sorrow of his*

---

53 Aristotle, *Generation of animals* 2.4.

54 Jacopo reuses these reasons in *SQ*, p. 315, and *SS*, fol. 57r, along with the sermon in *SD* just mentioned (n. 52).

55 Here Jacopo returns to etymology to confirm the innateness of women's frailty and inferiority. Cf. *SD*, fol. 322v; *SQ*, p. 314.

56 Aristotle, *History of animals* 9.1.

57 Humoral theory associated cold and wetness with the bodily fluid phlegm, and therefore with passivity: Isidore of Seville, *Etymologies* 4.5.3, and Vincent of Beauvais, *Speculum naturale* 31.5. Cf. part 8.1 n. 5.

PART NINE: ON DOMESTIC LIFE   155

mother.[58] See how clearly he says that the father of a wise son is joyful, but the mother of a foolish son is sorrowful. For this reason parents ought to inculcate good habits to their children from childhood. For the character they assume in childhood they will always retain even in old age. As Solomon said, *a young man will not depart from his own way even when he grows old.*[59] Boys are as soft as wax in being easily led toward virtue, and the prophet says regarding them: *My heart is made like liquid wax in the middle of my stomach.*[60] They are like fresh clay, because they always preserve a sweet smell, just as a pot will forever taste of whatever was infused into it when it was fresh clay.[61] Also, they are like flexible twigs because they bend easily toward virtue, as the prophet says, *whose sons are as new plants in their youth.*[62]

Thirdly, parents ought to correct their children when they err, remembering the priest Eli; because he did not chastise his sons, he and his sons perished by an evil death.[63] Now, there are good and obedient sons; these should progress from good to better, for they are a great consolation to their father and a delight to his heart. Regarding these, Solomon says: *Instruct your son, and he will refresh you and bring delights to your soul.*[64] Otherwise are those sons who sometimes offend, but when they do, they immediately correct themselves according to the gentle admonishment of their father and submit themselves to him. Such sons should not be severely scolded but lovingly admonished. The Apostle says in the letter to the Ephesians: *You, fathers, do not provoke your sons to wrath, but instruct them in discipline and the correction of the Lord.*[65] Such sons should not be provoked, but rather educated in discipline, that is, in honourable morals. Still other sons are hard and proud and disobedient to their parents. These should be beaten with whips, as Solomon says: *He who spares the rod hates his son, but he who loves his son corrects him assiduously.*[66] Likewise, in Ecclesiasticus it is said that *he who loves his son makes regular use of the whip.*[67]

58 Proverbs 10.1.
59 Proverbs 22.6.
60 Psalm 21.15; see also *SD*, fol. 141r; also *Mariale* 12/A12 (*arcus coelestis*), 23/C2 (*candelae*).
61 Horace, *Epistles* 1.2, ll. 69–70 (paraphrased).
62 Psalm 143.12; cf. *SD*, fol. 141r.
63 1 Samuel 2.12–36, 4.13–22 (summarised).
64 Proverbs 29.17.
65 Ephesians 6.4.
66 Proverbs 13.24.
67 Sirach 30.1.

Next, sons ought to behave humbly toward their parents. They ought to honour them, serve them, and look after them; and to this end they should be led by precept, duty, and the instinct of nature. First by precept, because the teaching of God says *honour your father and your mother, so that you may be long-lived on the earth, and he who curses his father or his mother will die the death.*[68] In no other commandment of the Decalogue do we find the promise of serving or the condemnation of failing to do so except in the commandment regarding parents—meaning that it is greatly pleasing to God when parents are honoured and it is greatly displeasing to him when they are not. And this honour is understood to involve not only confronting evils, but also serving [one's parents] and looking after them.

Secondly, children ought to be taught to serve their parents by duty. For they receive three things from their parents, namely being, nourishment, and education, and for having received [these things] they owe them great reverence. As it is said in Ecclesiasticus: *honour your father and do not ignore the groans of your mother; remember that but for them you would never have been born.*[69] Similarly, because they received nourishment from them, they owe them diligent assistance, so that they in turn nourish their parents in old age just as their parents nourished them in youth. As it is said in Ecclesiasticus: *Sons, support the old age of your father.*[70] Finally, because they received education from [their parents], they owe them strict obedience. As the Apostle says: *Children, obey your parents in the Lord, for this is just.*[71]

Thirdly, children should be taught to care for their parents by the instinct of nature. For nature teaches and instructs us all that children ought to assist their parents when they are in need, when they have reached old age, and when they are dead. To demonstrate these three points Valerius Maximus gives three examples. To demonstrate that children ought to assist their parents when they are in need, he relates how a certain noble and powerful man who had become old committed a certain crime. Out of respect for his ancestors, the judge did not wish to punish him with a public death, but shut him in prison instead so that he would die there of hunger. His married daughter visited him every day in prison: this occurred with the judge's permission, but he had her searched carefully

---

68 A conflation of Exodus 20.12 and 21.17. Cf. *SQ*, pp. 225–6; *Mariale* 13/A13 (*assumpta*).
69 Sirach 7.29–30.
70 Sirach 3.14.
71 Ephesians 6.1.

PART NINE: ON DOMESTIC LIFE   157

before [each visit] lest she bring her father anything edible. Yet every day she would take out her breast and nourish her father with her own milk. When the judge marveled that [the man] was still alive after a long time, he ordered the guards to watch through the cracks in the door while the daughter was with her father. They saw that she was giving her father milk to drink, and reported this to the judge; moved by pity, he pardoned the father for the sake of the daughter.[72]

Also, to demonstrate that children ought to assist their parents when they have reached old age, the same Valerius gives the example of the stork, saying that when storks grow old, their offspring place their parents in a nest and, just like infants, they keep them close to their breasts, warm them, and feed them. Meanwhile vultures allow their parents to die of hunger.[73]

Finally, to demonstrate that sons ought to care for their parents in death and arrange proper burial for them, the aforesaid Valerius gives the example of the Scythians. He reports that when King Darius invaded the Scythians' borders and threatened to overrun the tombs of their ancestors, the Scythians sent [a message] to him that they could bear the destruction of their fields and vines with equanimity, but if he should lay hands on the tombs of their ancestors, then he would feel the Scythians' power and force because they were prepared to die in their [ancestors'] defence. When he heard this, Darius did not dare to invade or destroy their ancestral tombs.[74]

Chapter six: How masters ought to act toward their servants or slaves, and servants toward their masters. After the head of the family has organised domestic matters with regard to his wife and children, he ought also to do these things with regard to his servants. For the scholars say that there are four types of servants. First there are those born to a maidservant and those taken in battle—because, as

72 *TIE* 3969: Valerius Maximus recounts two such stories (*Factorum et dictorum* 5.4.7, 5.4.ext.1); in one the prisoner is the woman's mother, while in the other it is her father. Cf. also Solinus, *De mirabilibus mundi* 1.124–5, and Jacques de Vitry, *Exempla*, no. 238, pp. 232–3. Filial breastfeeding was often cited as the height of Roman duty or *pietas*: Sperling (2016), esp. pp. 240–8.

73 Not actually from Valerius Maximus: for storks (cf. *SD*, fol. 236v), see Isidore, *Etymologies* 12.7.17, following Pliny the Elder, *Natural history* 10.32. The contrasting claim about the vulture may be from Vincent of Beauvais, *Speculum naturale* 16.7.1. Cf. *SD*, fols. 236v, 324v–325r.

74 Valerius Maximus, *Factorum et dictorum* 5.4.ext. 5–6. All three examples appear essentially verbatim in *SD*, fols. 324v–325r. Cf. also *SQ*, pp. 140, 227.

the blessed Peter says: *Whenever a man is defeated by someone, he becomes that person's slave.*[75] People such as these are said to be slaves (*servi*) from 'saving' (*servare*), because they were saved by their enemies instead of being killed by them. Others are hired servants, who are employed for an annual salary; others are purchased servants, who are bought with money. Paul instructs all these [four types of] servants in the letter to the Ephesians, saying: *Servants, obey your masters in the flesh with fear and trembling, in the simplicity of your heart, serving not to the eye, as if pleasing men, but just as the servants of Christ, doing the will of God from the soul.*[76]

We must note, however, that some servants are intelligent, some lazy and idle, and others malicious. Intelligent servants are much to be cherished, as is said in Ecclesiasticus: *An intelligent servant should be cherished just like one's own soul.*[77] Also, Solomon says of such servants, *a wise servant will rule over foolish sons, and will divide an inheritance among brothers.*[78] Yet lazy and idle servants must be supervised with continual tasks. As is said in Ecclesiasticus: *He works under discipline, and he seeks to rest: his hands are idle, and he seeks liberty. A yoke and a whip bend a stiff neck, and continual labours bow a slave down. Put him to work lest he be idle, for idleness has taught much evil.*[79] Finally, malevolent and malicious servants must be compelled with harsh fasts, shackles, and beatings, since it is said in Ecclesiasticus that they should be mortified with abstinence. Ecclesiasticus also says: *Fodder, a switch, and a load for an ass; bread, discipline, and work for a slave.*[80] It is said in the same place that they should be restrained with shackles: *Torture and shackles [are] for a malicious slave.*[81] And indeed, it is said in the same book that they should be beaten with whips: *Do not be ashamed*—meaning, do not be timid or afraid—*to bleed the side of a bad slave*—meaning, to beat him until he bleeds.[82]

Now, although servants—by whatever name they are reckoned, and whether born of a slave, acquired in battle, hired, or purchased—should be the inferiors of their masters, they are nonetheless their equals in five things. The first equality pertains to the earliest part [of life],

---

75 2 Peter 2.19, also cited in part 8.2, above.
76 Ephesians 6.5–6.
77 Sirach 7.23.
78 Proverbs 17.2.
79 Sirach 33.26–9.
80 Sirach 33.25.
81 Sirach 33.28.
82 Sirach 42.1–5.

because all—free men and slaves alike—were created naked from the earth and born crying. As it is said in the book of Wisdom: *I myself am a mortal man like all others, of the race of the one who was first made out of the earth; in my mother's womb I was fashioned into flesh, and like all others I uttered my first noise by crying. For no king had any other beginning at his birth.*[83] The second equality pertains to the middle part [of life], because all—free men and slaves alike—have the same home, namely: the same world, the same earth, the same air. As it is said in the same book of Wisdom: *And having been born I drew in the common air and fell out onto the earth, made all the same.*[84] The third equality pertains to the end [of life], because all—free men and slaves alike—die, are turned to ashes, and decay. As it is said in that same book of Wisdom: *Thus for everyone there is a single entrance into life and a like exit.*[85] Regarding this, Saint Cyprian says, *to you, the lord, and to your slave are the same fate of being born, the situation of dying, the same bodily prison, the reason common to all souls; with the same decrees and the same laws you come into this world and afterward depart from the world.*[86] The fourth equality pertains to the question of lordship, because all—free men and slaves alike—have a single Lord. As the Apostle says in the letter to the Ephesians, *and you, lords: refrain from threatening your servants, knowing because your Lord and theirs is in the heavens, and favouritism of persons is not with God.*[87] The holy Job says thus: *The small and the great are there*—namely under the dominion of God—*and the slave is free from his master.*[88] The fifth equality pertains to the question of the Last Judgment, because all—free men and slaves alike—will arrive at the judgment of God and render an account for all their deeds, and will there receive glory or punishment. As the Apostle says in the letter to the Corinthians: *It is certain that all of us will be manifested before the tribunal of our Lord Jesus Christ, so that each may receive the appropriate things of the body according to how he has conducted himself, whether well or ill.*[89] And in the letter to the Ephesians the same Apostle says: *Each man who does a good thing will receive the same from the Lord, whether slave or free.*[90]

---

83 Wisdom 7.1–5.
84 Wisdom 7.3.
85 Wisdom 7.6.
86 Cyprian, *Ad Demetrianum* 8 (*CCSL* 3A.39).
87 Ephesians 6.9 (paraphrased).
88 Job 3.19.
89 2 Corinthians 5.10.
90 Ephesians 6.8.

PART TEN: ON THE GENOESE CHURCH

Here follows part ten, which deals with the spiritual governance of the city of Genoa. This part has two chapters: the first explains the time in which the city was awarded the honour of a bishopric, while the second explains the time in which it was raised to the dignity of an archbishopric.

Chapter one: When and in what era the city of the Genoese was awarded the honour of a bishopric. Although we do not find written in any history the era when the city of Genoa became worthy of being a bishopric, we nonetheless believe that it was deemed worthy to be awarded the dignity of a bishopric while the princes of the apostles, Peter and Paul, presided at Rome. The reasoning which leads us to believe this is as follows: it is well known that the apostles customarily assigned bishops to certain cities or inhabitants of those cities when they came to the faith of Christ. Hence the blessed Peter promptly gave Saint Apollinaris as bishop to those who converted in the city of Ravenna, and the evangelist Mark named Saint Hermagoras as bishop for those who converted in Aquileia. Likewise, he assigned Saint Anianus as bishop for those who converted in Alexandria.[1] Saint Paul the apostle named bishops for all the cities which he converted, by which he made Timothy bishop at Ephesus and Titus [bishop] in Crete.

Furthermore, we demonstrated above [in part 4] via authorities and logic that the city of Genoa was the first city of Italy, or one of the first, in which the faith of Christ was publicly adopted and in which the sacrifices of God were first publicly celebrated, for it was converted to the faith of Christ—as stated above—about thirty-five years of the Lord after the Passion of Christ. At that time the princes of the apostles, Peter and Paul, were still living in the flesh at Rome. And thus it must be reasonably likely that the blessed Peter, who was pope when he heard that the city of Genoa had converted to the faith of Christ, sent a bishop to that city. For if the apostles sent bishops to more remote converted

---

1 Paul the Deacon, *Liber de episcopis Mettensibus*, p. 261.

cities, it is both likely and probable that these princes of the apostles, living at Rome, would have sent a bishop to the city of Genoa when it converted to the faith, since it was so nearby.[2]

Furthermore, this hypothesis is supported and corroborated by another rationale. It is well known that all the ancient historians who wrote before the advent of Christ did not call Genoa a city (*civitas*) when they wished to refer to it; rather, they called it a town (*oppidum*)—as, for example, in Titus Livy.[3] But after it was converted, the city was referred to as we see in the legend of Saint Nazarius, in which it is called 'city': *urbs* or *civitas*.[4] Nazarius preached in Genoa in about the thirty-fifth year after the Passion of Christ; so either he converted that city to the faith of Christ then, or he confirmed its previous conversion to the faith, as was demonstrated previously. From then on it was called a city, and thus it seems that from that time onward it was distinguished with the honour of a bishopric. For when speaking [of an urban settlement], the term 'city' (*civitas*) is not used unless it has been adorned with the episcopal honour.[5]

Unfortunately, the names of the earliest bishops are not found recorded. The first bishop whose name is given was Saint Valentine, whom we believe lived around the year of the Lord 540, as will be discussed below [in part 11]. We nonetheless believe that there were other bishops before Valentine. It is said in the legend of Saint Valentine that Valentine was elected to the episcopate upon the death of the bishop of Genoa—from which it is obvious that there was already an episcopate in Genoa before Valentine.[6] How many of these bishops there were, or who came before Valentine, we do not know because we have not been able to find these facts recorded anywhere.

Chapter two: When and in what time the city of Genoa was raised to the dignity of an archbishopric. A change was made at the right hand of the Most High when the bishopric of Genoa was found worthy to be converted into an archbishopric, an act that was appropriate to its dignity, consonant with law, and consistent with reason. For just as

---

2 See part 11.1 n. 1.

3 Part 5.1, above.

4 Jacopo's life of Nazarius uses *urbs* to describe Genoa: *LA*, p. 441.

5 An idea popularised by the church fathers, e.g. Tertullian, *Apologeticum* 20.

6 On the early bishops of Genoa, see *CMG*, pp. 35–6 (Macchiavello/Rovere) and pp. 72–92 (Balzaretti); also Polonio (2002a), pp. 32–72.

the city of Genoa rules over many cities, commands many peoples, and is subject to no one—except God in all things and the emperor in a few—thus it was also fitting that its archbishop should be suffragan to no primate, subject to no one except the highest pontiff, but rather that he himself should exercise his jurisdiction over other bishops, extend his authority, and preside over many prelates. Let us consider, then, in what time and for what reason the city of Genoa merited being raised to the archiepiscopal dignity.

When Innocent II, a man revered by all, was canonically elected to the highest pontificate, a certain group of cardinals schismatically elected against him a certain Roman by the name of Peter Leone, whom they called Anacletus; to this Anacletus the Roman people also devoted its favour and assistance.[7] This Anacletus pillaged the entire treasury of the church and distributed it to his supporters, and on account of his influence the aforesaid Innocent was unable to stay in the City, so he was rowed in Genoese galleys to Genoa in the year of the Lord 1130. Now, this Pope Innocent had among other cardinals a certain cardinal named Siro [Syrus], of great prudence and uprightness of life. So when the bishop's seat in Genoa was left vacant, he named him bishop of the Genoese church. It should not seem implausible that a cardinal should be made bishop of Genoa, because we read of many cardinals in other cases who were similarly appointed. For at that time the cardinals were not perceived [to be] of such lofty rank as today; rather, any bishop would take precedence over a cardinal priest or deacon.[8]

Then, after the aforesaid pope Innocent had spent some time in Genoa, the Genoese armed their galleys and rowed him as far as France, where, he stayed for the space of about two years before returning to Genoa.[9] And in the year of the Lord 1132, at the request of this same pope, the Genoese armed a fleet of galleys and carried the pope to Rome, where by the favour and assistance of Emperor Lothar they captured towers and fortifications in the City, wholly expelled the usurper Anacletus

---

7 Innocent II (1130–43) and Pietro Pierleone, the antipope Anacletus II (1130–8): *CGA*, p. 25. Technically neither candidate was canonically elected: Robinson (1990), pp. 69–78.

8 Cardinals were originally the chief clergy of Rome and its surroundings, but as the church grew from a local into a universal institution, the group came to be defined by rank and influence at the papal court: Robinson (1990), pp. 33–120.

9 *CGA*, p. 26; Doran/Smith (2016), pp. 105–21 (Duggan, Montaubin).

from the City as a tyrant, and restored Innocent to his seat.[10] Upon seeing this, the Romans returned humbly to the command of the lord pope, and the Genoese returned triumphantly with their fleet of galleys to Genoa.

Then, because at that time there was great discord and conflict between the Genoese and the Pisans, the aforesaid pope went to Corneto, where he ordered the Genoese and the Pisans to send him official ambassadors with full negotiating power. And when the ambassadors came to Corneto, the pope reconciled them one to another.[11] He also sent [a message] to Siro, the bishop of Genoa, summoning him into his presence at Corneto, intending to honour him and the city of Genoa in many ways for the many great services and favours which he had received from the Genoese. So when bishop Siro had arrived at Corneto, in the year of the Lord 1133 the lord pope bestowed an archbishopric [upon Genoa], presenting the aforementioned Siro with the cross and pallium.[12] In addition, he gave half of the entire island of Corsica in fief to the commune of Genoa in return for the payment of one pound of gold every year to the Roman church. Pope Lucius afterward remitted this tax to the commune of Genoa as a special grace, however.[13] Innocent also gave three bishoprics to the archbishop of Genoa as suffragans, sees in Corsica which were previously suffragans of the archbishop of Pisa: the bishopric of Mariana, the bishopric of Nebbio, and the bishopric of Accia.[14] In addition, he gave the archbishop of Genoa other suffragans, namely the bishopric

---

10 Actually 1133: *CGA*, pp. 26–7. The struggle pitted Lothar III and Innocent II against Conrad III Hohenstaufen and Anacletus II: see *HP*, p. 13; Doran/Smith (2016), especially pp. 27–68 (Robinson). Lothar sought to establish Innocent in Rome so he could receive imperial coronation, but they both left immediately afterward.

11 *CGA*, p. 26. The agreement of 20 March 1130 also negotiated the assistance of both Pisans and Genoese in the pope's attempted return to Rome. Corneto, now Tarquinia, is a city 90 km north of Rome.

12 The broader papal–imperial struggle had grave repercussions for the archbishopric of Milan, since Archbishop Anselm V (*DBI* 3.415–17), was excommunicated and deposed shortly after he crowned Conrad king of Italy in 1128: Robinson, *Papal reform*, p. 73. Milan's disgrace was thus linked to Genoa's rise: with Genoa's elevation to an archbishopric, its rivals Milan and Pisa lost three and two suffragan bishoprics respectively: Doran/Smith (2016), pp. 319–21 (Schoenig).

13 Lucius II (March 1144–May 1145).

14 Nebbio, Mariana, and Accia: small bishoprics in northern Corsica; all three were eventually incorporated into the diocese of Ajaccio.

of Bobbio and the bishopric of Brugnato.[15] Later Alexander III made the bishop of Albenga a suffragan of the bishop of Genoa as well, on account of the many services he had received from the Genoese, while Innocent IV converted Noli to a city and gave it a bishop, and named its bishop also a suffragan of the Genoese archbishop.[16]

Thus from that time forward it was called the province of Genoa (*provincia Ianuensis*). Once, as it is claimed in the *History of the Lombards*, Genoa had been part of the province called the Cottian Alps, for there was a certain king by the name of Cottius who reigned in those parts, and from that king the whole province of the Cottian Alps took its name.[17] Pliny (*Plinius Secundus*), conversely, says that Genoa was in the province of Liguria.[18] This Pliny was a great orator and historian living at the time of the emperor Trajan, who ruled in the year of the Lord 100. When Pliny was governor of a certain province, he killed many Christians because they honoured Christ and refused to worship idols. But seeing their innocence, he wrote Trajan a letter in which he absolved the Christians and argued for their innocence. In response to this letter, Trajan wrote back to him that Christians should not be sought out, but that if they presented themselves they should be punished.[19] Now, this Pliny says that the province of Liguria extends along the sea coast from Ventimiglia and the river Merula as far as Sestri Levante and the river Magra, and he says that in this province of Liguria are Genoa and the

---

15 Bobbio: a city in the Apennines about 75 km from Genoa, which grew up around the abbey founded by Columbanus; the city became a bishopric in 1014, but the monastery and the bishopric remained separate entities: Destefanis/Guglielmotti (2015). Brugnato is in the Ligurian interior about 15 km northwest of La Spezia; it had grown up around a dependency of Bobbio and had not previously been a bishopric. Innocent II's bull of 20 March 1133 is *Codice diplomatico* 1.77–80 (doc. 65); cf. *CGA*, pp. 25–7.

16 For Alexander's bull of 25 March 1162: *Codice diplomatico* 1.387–91 (doc. 305); *CGA*, p. 66; also *GA* 2.129–30. The donation attributed to Innocent IV actually took place under Gregory IX in 1239 (*GA* 3.94).

17 Paul the Deacon, *Historia Langobardorum* 2.15–16, pp. 96–7. Paul also asserts that the term 'Liguria' comes from the beans (*legumines*) which grow there. Interestingly, his definition of Liguria extends into the Po Valley (including Milan and Pavia). The Cottian Alps are the southwestern section of the Alps between France and Italy (Hautes-Alpes, Savoy, and Piedmont).

18 Pliny the Elder, *Natural history* 3.7–8; fig. 2. As was usual in the Middle Ages, Jacopo conflates the two classical authors called Plinius Secundus—the letter-writer Pliny the Younger (*c*. 61–113), governor of Bithynia, and his uncle Pliny the Elder (23–79), author of the *Natural history*. Only twenty years after Jacopo's death did Giovanni Mansionario of Verona disentangle them in his *Brevis adnotatio*.

19 Pliny the Younger, *Correspondence with Trajan from Bithynia*.

river Polcevera [see map 2].²⁰ He also mentions there the noble port of the city of Luni, which today is called Portovenere but then was called the port of Luni.²¹ He makes no mention, however, of Portofino or the port of Vado. He does not mention Savona, either, because we believe that at that time it had not yet been built, but instead was constructed after the destruction of Vado.²² Thus the city of Genoa, which was once part of the province of the Cottian Alps or the province of Liguria, was afterward found worthy to have its own archbishopric, and to exist as part of no province.²³ Instead, it was made a province in itself with its own dioceses, suffragans, and territory (*districtus*), and it was called the province of Genoa.

---

20 Pliny the Elder, *Natural history* 3.7–8.
21 The *Luna* praised by Strabo (*Geographia* 5.2.5) refers to the entire Gulf of La Spezia, on which Portovenere is located, but medieval Portovenere had assumed the defensive and port functions of the ancient city of Luni.
22 While Savona's origins are certainly pre-Roman, assigning it a more recent origin suited the purpose of the Genoese as they attempted to dominate Liguria.
23 'Liguria' as a concept continued to evolve in shape and significance through the centuries; on its extent and classification in this period: Pavoni (1992), pp. 18–36; *CMG*, pp. 49–71 (Guglielmotti).

PART ELEVEN: THE HISTORY OF GENOA UNDER THE BISHOPS

Part eleven describes the dates, names, and orders of all the bishops who are recorded as having existed in the city of Genoa. This part has as many chapters [nineteen] as the names of the bishops who are included here.

Regarding the time in which the city of Genoa first received a bishopric, we expressed our opinion in the preceding part—specifically, that the city of Genoa merited being awarded the honour of an episcopate while the princes of the apostles, Peter and Paul, presided at Rome. Yet the names of its earliest bishops who preceded Valentine have not come down to our knowledge in any way.[1] Setting these aside, therefore, we will discuss only those bishops whose names the writings of earlier fathers have passed down to us.

We must not omit to note, however, that for all the bishops between Valentine and Theodulf, we have their names, but we have been unable to find their dates. That said, we know for certain that Saint Syrus, who was the third bishop [after Valentine], lived before the time of the pope Saint Gregory because this Gregory explicitly mentions the church of Saint Syrus, bishop of Genoa, in his book of *Dialogues*.[2] While Gregory flourished around the year of the Lord 600, it is unknown by how much time Syrus preceded Gregory. We may suppose, however, that he preceded him by a space of twenty years, in which case it will be reasonable to estimate that Valentine, who was the first bishop among those whose names we have been able to find, took office around the year of the Lord 540; and Felix, who was the second bishop, took office around the year of the Lord 560; and Syrus, who was the third bishop, took office around the year of the Lord 580; and Romulus, who was the fourth

---

1 There is evidence for a Christian community in the area of Genoa from the mid-fourth century, with a bishop Diogenes attested *c.* 381. Little else can be said with certainty about the early Genoese church: to demonstrate 'the extreme uncertainty of the tradition' (p. 45), Angeli Bertinelli (1999) offers six contradictory proposed lists of early bishops from Diogenes to Romulus.

2 Pope Gregory I (590–604), *Dialogues* 4.53, referring to the Genoese church of San Siro.

bishop, took office around the year of the Lord 600.³ According to this calculation Gregory and Romulus flourished at the same time: the first in Rome, the second in Genoa.

Just as we have spoken of the predecessors of Saint Romulus, so we must also speak of his successors, because from Saint Romulus up to Theodulf the dates of each bishop are not recorded precisely. Theodulf took office around the year of the Lord 930, so between Romulus—whom we have estimated to have taken office around the year of the Lord 600—and Theodulf—who became bishop around the year of the Lord 930—we see that 330 years passed, and from Romulus to Theodulf again only five bishops are recorded. If we divide that 330 years equally between the five bishops, we must assign a reign of 66 years to each. But it is not remotely credible that each of these bishops should have been bishop for so many years, so we must conclude either that many bishops between Romulus and Theodulf are missing because their names were not recorded out of some negligence, or that the Genoese church was vacant for many years at various times and the years of the vacancies were not noted down, or perhaps that both of these explanations are true.⁴ But whether the first possibility or the second or both together are true, the fact nonetheless remains that 330 years went by between Romulus and Theodulf according to the calculation made above. Hence it is necessary that these years should be divided between those five bishops, and 66 years must be allotted to each one. Beginning from Saint Valentine, therefore, we will describe the subsequent bishops in order.

Chapter one: Regarding Saint Valentine, the first bishop. Valentine was the first bishop of those whose names are recorded. He took office around the year of the Lord 540, a date we arrive at by supposing that Syrus preceded Gregory by twenty years. If Syrus preceded Gregory by more years than the stated twenty, then Valentine will have been older than we describe him here. Indeed, Valentine lived to the age of 75 years; this is written in his legend along with other facts, such as: once when a certain man was eating something, a bone from some meat stuck in his throat so that he could neither swallow it nor spit it out.⁵

---

3 As Jacopo freely acknowledges, these are totally arbitrary choices of date (see n. 1, above).
4 On the early bishopric: Polonio (1999, 2002b); also Balzaretti (2013), pp. 90–121.
5 The *Sermo* of Saint Valentine: *AASS* 14 (2 May, vol. 1), pp. 278–9.

Fearing the threat of death, he turned with complete devotion to Saint Valentine and made an internal vow: immediately the bone flew out of him and he made a full recovery. Likewise, a certain girl who was lame and unable to walk dedicated herself to Saint Valentine with the greatest devotion. And look! Saint Valentine appeared to her in the night: he consoled her, comforted her, raised her up, and restored her to full health.

Around the same time, two brothers became famous in Gaul, namely Saints Medardus and Gildardus: twins who were born the same day, consecrated as bishops (*pontifices*) on the same day, died on the same day, and were taken up to Christ on the same day.[6] These things must not be attributed to fate or the stars; rather, they must be ascribed to divine ordinance.[7] For the stars or constellations cannot impose necessity on human beings because many inconsistencies would follow if they could, as Saint Gregory of Nyssa says.[8] For then laws would be superfluous; judgments would be superfluous; praise and reproach would be nonsensical; speeches would be foolish and superfluous; divine providence would be eliminated and free will removed.[9] From this would follow that God is not good, or that he is impotent or unjust. For if the stars can compel people to either theft or adultery, and if God can remove this terrible power of theirs but he will not, then he is not good; if he wishes to but cannot, then he is not omnipotent; and if he punishes people for something which they are forced to do of necessity, then he is unjust.

In Valentine's time there was a man called Theophilus who was the vicar of a certain bishop in the region of Sicily.[10] He was deposed from his office and fell into such desperation that he swore homage to the devil, wrote a copy of his oath in his own hand, and gave it to the devil. In return the devil promised him that he would restore him to his office and cause him to prosper with many good things: and all these things were achieved to his satisfaction. But with the passing of time the aforementioned Theophilus returned to his own heart; grieving and

---

6 Sigebert of Gembloux, *Chronica* 535, p. 316; cf. *GL*, p. 753. Many of the *GL* references in part 11 come from the synopsis of Paul the Deacon's *Historia Langobardorum* inserted into the life of Pope Saint Pelagius (*GL*, pp. 753–70).

7 Cf. *SS*, fols. 76v–77r.

8 *Against fate* 40.2 (*PG* 45.145–73).

9 Cf. *Mariale* 78/L5 (*liberum arbitrium*); also Dante, *Purgatorio* 16.67–72.

10 *TIE* 3572; Sigebert of Gembloux, *Chronica* 537, p. 316. See also *GL*, p. 543; *Mariale* 17/A17 (*augusta*).

mourning, he took refuge in the Queen of Heaven. And the blessed Virgin granted his plea and his prayer, making the devil return the copy of the oath to Theophilus so that he could no longer harass him. Sad and doleful, the devil himself appeared to Theophilus and gave back his copy of the oath: thus Theophilus' prayer and plea were both fulfilled.

Around the same time, a certain Jewish boy received the Eucharist with other Christians, upon which his outraged father threw his son into a hot oven.[11] The Christians were very much disturbed when they heard this, and looked into the oven: and there they saw the boy whole, uninjured, and happy. So they pulled him out and asked him who had preserved him uninjured, and he responded that the lady whose image is in the church, holding a boy in her arms, held back the flames with her mantle and saved him. Then the Christians threw his father into the oven, where he was immediately burnt up.

Also around the same time, Theodoric, king of Italy, was corrupted by the Arian heresy, and sent the philosopher Boethius, a consul and patrician, into exile at Pavia when he defended the commonwealth against Theoderic; it is reported that he wrote the book *On Consolation* there.[12] This Boethius had a wife by the name of Elpes who composed a hymn in honour of the apostles Peter and Paul, which begins: *Happy over all crossroads of the world, O Rome, etc.* She also composed an epitaph to be inscribed upon her own tomb, saying, *I was called Elpes, a child of the region of Sicily; love of my husband caused me to fall ill far from my own country. Now I rest quietly at the sacred doors as a pilgrim, a witness to the throne of eternal judgment.* And as time passed the aforesaid Theodoric had the aforesaid Boethius killed.[13] This Theodoric also put Pope John in prison and allowed him to die of hunger.[14] In fact, Gregory reports in the book of *Dialogues* that when Theodoric died, a certain hermit saw Pope John throw him naked, shoeless, and shackled into the pit of Vulcan.[15]

And in the same period Clovis, king of the Franks, was still a pagan, although his very Christian wife, who was called Clotilde, often preached

11 GL, pp. 473–4, based on Gregory of Tours, *Gloria martyrum* 9, p. 44. See Rubin (1999), pp. 8–11.
12 The Ostrogoth Theodoric, king of Italy 493–526.
13 See *GL*, p. 760; *MO* 22.455.
14 Pope John I (523–6): Sigebert of Gembloux, *Chronica* 523, p. 315.
15 Gregory, *Dialogues* 4.30; cf. *GL*, p. 760.

the faith of Christ to him, although he did not wish to listen to her.[16] But it happened that he got into a serious war with the Alamanni, and when he was losing a battle he vowed a vow, saying, 'God of my wife, help me and I will worship you as God'. As soon as he had made this vow, he regained his powers against the enemy and achieved victory, and so afterward he underwent holy baptism. By this what the apostle says is confirmed: *And a faithless* (infidelis) *man will be saved by a faithful woman.*[17] Following this, the entire Frankish people was converted to the faith of Christ.

Also about the same time, Mohammed was suffering from the falling sickness [epilepsy]. And when he fell, he said that the Angel Gabriel had appeared to him and instructed him in laws which he gave to the people, but he fell on his face because he was unable to bear the splendour.[18]

Chapter two: Regarding Saint Felix, second bishop. Felix, the second bishop, took office around the year of the Lord 560. According to his legend, Felix lived 77 years, and was the teacher of Saint Syrus.[19] Indeed, one time when he was celebrating mass with Syrus as his assistant, Syrus saw a flame of fire descend upon Felix's head; more than that, he saw the right hand of God shining in the flame. That flame was the Holy Spirit, who had descended upon Felix in the form of fire just as it once descended upon the apostles.[20] Also, the right hand of God signifies the virtue and power of God, who by a heavenly benediction consecrated the host with which Felix was celebrating mass.

Around this time points of fire could be seen in heaven, which represented war with the Lombards and blood that would be spilled in Italy, as Gregory says in the *Homilies*.[21] For Albuin, who was king of the Lombards, had killed a certain king of the Gelibalds while he was in Pannonia, and had ordered a cup made for himself from this king's skull, enclosed in gold and silver. He also took the king's daughter Rosamund as his

---

16 Clovis, king of the Franks 481–511, married the Burgundian princess Clotilde in 496 and converted from Arianism to catholic Christianity in 508: Gregory of Tours, *Historia Francorum* 2.29–31. Cf. *GL*, p. 86.
17 1 Corinthians 7.14.
18 See *GL*, pp. 766–7; *MO* 22.457.
19 Now lost.
20 Acts 2.2–4.
21 Gregory the Great, *Homiliae in evangelii* 1 (*PL* 76.1077–81, at 1078).

wife. And after he had seized nearly all Italy, he was celebrating a feast near Verona and he made his wife drink out of this cup. But when she found out that she was drinking out of her father's head, she was roused to a feminine furor, and arranged for the king to be murdered by one of his armsmen while he was lying in bed one afternoon. Thus the wrath of a woman is very dangerous. As it is said in Ecclesiasticus: *There is no head worse than the head of a serpent, and there is no anger above the anger of a woman.*[22] Just as the characteristic vice of man is pride, so the characteristic vice of woman is anger. Indeed, women are very easily roused to anger; they are very difficult to bring to reconciliation, and they are very cruel in encouraging punishment.[23] We speak of those women who have cast away the fear of the Lord and the respect of the world. This Rosamund lies at Ravenna, and on her tomb the verse is inscribed: 'Here in this tomb lies Rosamund, an impure rose (*Rosimunda, non rosa munda*)'.[24]

Around the same time, as it is read in the *Deeds of the Lombards*, when Albuin had taken Milan and other cities in Lombardy, Honoratus, archbishop of Milan, fled to Genoa seeking safety from the arrival of the Lombards, who at that time were still pagans.[25] For within a short space of time the Lombards had taken five provinces: the first of these was called Venetia, which today is called the march of Treviso, and its capital was Aquileia.[26] The second province was called Flaminea, which today is called Romagnola, and its capital was Ravenna. The third was called Liguria, whose capital was Milan. The fourth was called Emilia, and its capital was Ticinum or Pavia. The fifth was called the Cottian Alps, which were named after a certain king named Cottius; this province included all of Piedmont and the city of Genoa with its entire Riviera.[27] The Lombards had taken all five of these provinces and murdered their inhabitants, except in the coastal areas, namely Genoa and its Riviera. They did not dare to go that far because so many Christians had come to Genoa for safety there, fleeing the presence of the Lombards, who were then still pagans.

---

22 Sirach 25.22.

23 See *SD*, fols. 42r, 167r.

24 Paul the Deacon, *Historia Langobardorum* 2.28; cf. *GL*, pp. 754–5. The compound *Rosa munda* can mean either 'rose of the world' or 'pure rose'.

25 *DGA*, p. 6, relying on Paul the Deacon, *Historia Langobardorum* 2.25. Albuin, king of the Lombards *c.* 560–72, led the Lombard invasion of Italy in 568.

26 Paul the Deacon, *Historia Langobardorum* 2.14–19.

27 See part 10.2, above.

Of these Lombards, it should be known that they originally lived first on the island of Scandinavia (*Scandinaria*), which is in the regions of Dacia. But they went into Pannonia because that land was unable to contain them. Next they came to Italy and seized nearly all of Italy except the lands along the coast. They were previously known as *Vinuli*, but afterward they were called Longobards (*Longobardi*) from 'long beards' (*longae barbae*) because they wore their beards long.[28] Nowadays, however, a syllable has been dropped in the middle [of the word], so they are called Lombards (*Lombardi*). They came into Italy around the year of the Lord 560 under their king Albuin. All the Italians (*Ytalici*) were Christians and these Longobards were pagans, so they killed all the Christians except those who lived in the coastal areas. These Lombards remained pagans for forty years after they came into Lombardy, until the time of Theodelinda, daughter of the duke of Bavaria and a most Christian woman; after being taken as wife by Agilulf, king of the Longobards, she converted her husband to the faith of Christ and in this way the entire people adopted the faith of Christ.[29]

See how many good things follow from a good woman! For a woman—a queen by the name of Clotilde—caused the conversion of the entire race of Franks (*Franci*) to the faith of Christ, as was recounted in the preceding chapter. These Gauls (*Gallici*) were converted to the faith of Christ around the year 540. Likewise, another woman—the queen Galla—caused the conversion of the entire race of the Hungarians, as is explained below in the chapter about John, the twelfth bishop.[30] These Hungarians were converted to the faith of Christ around the year of the Lord 1015. And another woman—the queen Theodelinda—caused the conversion of the whole race of the Lombards, as was just narrated above. The Lombards were converted to the faith of Christ around the year of the Lord 600. Another woman by the name of Isis who lived in the time of Abraham invented Greek and Egyptian letters. And another woman named Carmenta—a queen who was the mother of Latinus, king of Italy—invented Latin letters. See how there were once wise and pious women who converted peoples to the faith of Christ and invented Latin, Greek, and Egyptian letters![31] Yet women of our own time busy

---

28 Paul the Deacon, *Historia Langobardorum* 1.1–10; cf. *GL*, p. 753.

29 Paul the Deacon, *Historia Langobardorum* 3.35; cf. *GL*, p. 755. Agilulf, king of the Lombards 590–616, married his predecessor's widow Theodelinda and converted to catholic Christianity about 603.

30 Part 11.12 below (n. 110).

31 Isidore, *Etymologies* 1.3.5 (Isis), 1.4.1 (Carmenta).

themselves more with the vanities of the world than those things that honour God or educate people.

Chapter three: Regarding Saint Syrus, third bishop. Syrus, the third bishop, took office around the year of the Lord 580. He was born in Molassana, and a noble church has been constructed in the place of his birth.[32] He began to live a holy life in his youth, which is demonstrated by a small bird that he revived; during his youth and the rest of his life he lived ever more holily, which is demonstrated by the basilisk he killed.[33] He finished most holily in his death, which is demonstrated by the cloth soaked with his blood by which he healed many sick people. By his merits, he acquired for the church of Genoa the lands of Saint Romulus [Sanremo] and Ceriana, with all their appurtenances and income.[34] He also acquired the tithe of the Bisagno [valley] up to the river Sturla and from the road down to the sea; the tithe of Carignano, both demesnes and other places; and the tithe of Ravecca from the river to the sea along the road which goes from Bisagno before San Martino and the hospital of Santo Stefano up to the gate of the city.[35]

His body was placed in the basilica of the twelve apostles, which today is called the monastery of San Siro [Saint Syrus], because that is believed to have been his episcopal seat, and his body remained there up to the time of Landulf, eleventh bishop. When the episcopal seat was moved to the church of San Lorenzo, the aforesaid bishop desired that Saint Syrus' body should be transferred there as well, and reburied in the choir where the entry to the chancel now is; this translation was done around the year of the Lord 985.[36] But with the passing of time, when the [new] church of San Lorenzo was going to be consecrated by Pope Gelasius [II], Otto the eighteenth bishop took the body of Saint Syrus from its place in the chancel and placed it reverently under the altar of that same martyr; this translation was done around the year of the

---

32 Molassana is a village in the Apennine foothills just north of Genoa.

33 Jacopo, *LSS*, pp. 370–1; *Vita Sancti Syri*, *AASS* 27 (29 June, vol. 7), pp. 440–2. The basilisk is traditionally interpreted as the Arian heresy: Angeli Bertinelli (1999), p. 44.

34 Cities in the far western Ligurian Riviera. (The name Sanremo probably derives from 'San Romolo' via contraction in the local dialect, i.e. 'San Rœmu'.) The Genoese church gained these properties not via Saint Syrus but the first Archbishop Siro, in 1143: *RC*, pp. 119–23; Liva (1981), pp. 56–62.

35 See *RC*, pp. 444–5.

36 See n. 100, below.

Lord 1018.³⁷ Again with the passing of time, Bonifacio the third archbishop took the body of Saint Syrus from under the altar and reverently relocated it to a marble coffer upon the altar of San Lorenzo; this translation was done around the year of the Lord 1188. Finally, to remove all ambiguity, we ourselves opened this coffer in the presence of a provincial council and found there all the bones of Saint Syrus, as will be recounted below in our own chapter [part 12.8]; this discovery was made in the year of the Lord 1293 in the month of June.³⁸ Furthermore, by diligent study we have compiled a legend for Syrus in which many miracles are recorded which we have accepted as worthy of faith but which are not written in the older legend.³⁹

Around the time of Saint Syrus an old man appeared in Antioch garbed in a white robe; he held a handkerchief in his hand, which he shook over the centre of the city. Immediately the entire centre of the city fell into ruin together with its houses and inhabitants.⁴⁰ But he had two colleagues, who quickly asked him to spare the rest of the city. They gained this concession from him with great difficulty, and immediately afterward he disappeared and was never seen again. Who this man was is unknown, but we believe that it was an angel of God, either good or bad. Because God sometimes punishes bad men with good angels, as he punished Sodom; sometimes he punishes bad men with bad angels; and sometimes he punishes good men with bad angels—as he punished the holy Job, so that he would acquire greater glory through patience, and as he punished the apostle Paul, to whom the angel of Satan was assigned to guard his humility by boxing his ears, that is, physically assaulting him.⁴¹ But I do not recall having read that God punishes good men with good angels.

Around the same time Liuvigild, a king of the Goths polluted with Arian filth, shut up his son Ermengild in prison because he had been converted to the catholic faith by his wife; Liuvigild even killed him with an axe on Easter Eve because he was unwilling to affirm the Arian heresy.⁴²

---

37 Actually 1118 (at the time of San Lorenzo's consecration as cathedral).
38 Listed in a 1451 act by notary Andrea de Cairo: *JVC* 2.248 n. 1.
39 The eighth- or ninth-century 'older legend' is *AASS* 27 (29 June, vol. 7), pp. 438–42; Jacopo's 'new legend' is *LSS*.
40 Probably the earthquake of 526: *MO*, p. 455.
41 Job 1–2; 2 Corinthians 12.7.
42 Liuvigild was an Arian king of Visigothic Spain (r. 568–86) whose son Ermengild married a Frankish princess, abjured his Arian beliefs, and was executed in 585: Gregory I, *Dialogues* 3.31.

PART ELEVEN: GENOA UNDER THE BISHOPS 175

But if anyone wishes to know those praiseworthy things which Saint Syrus did during his episcopate and the miracles which the Lord worked through him, let him look in Syrus' legend and there he will find everything fully recorded.

Chapter four: Regarding Saint Romulus, fourth bishop. Romulus, the fourth bishop, took office around the year of the Lord 600.[43] He was a man of great sanctity toward God, great integrity toward himself, and great piety toward the poor. At that time there was a certain village along the coast called Matuciana, which had been given to Saint Syrus with full privileges. Once when Saint Romulus came to this place, he fell ill and reached his blessed end. His body was reverently entombed there, and numerous miracles have occurred before his sepulchre. The blind have received their sight; the lame, mobility; the leprous, cleansing; and other invalids, cure—and for this reason the region's inhabitants named the village San Romolo [Sanremo].[44] But after many years the African Saracens invaded these coastal areas and totally destroyed the village [part 11.9]. Its inhabitants accordingly retreated into the mountains for safety from their enemies and built a fortress which is now called San Romolo, but the opportunity never arose of building a church for Saint Romulus and translating his body—so his body remained there in Matuciana until it was transferred to the church of Genoa by Bishop Sabatinus.[45]

Around that same time, when Sigebert, infant son of King Dagobert, was being baptised by Saint Amandus, the infant miraculously responded 'amen' when those standing around the bishop failed to respond.[46]

Around that same time, Saint Columbanus came from Francia. He built the monastery at Bobbio and gathered many monks there; he led a holy and praiseworthy life and God worked many miracles through him.[47]

---

43 *AASS* 54 (13 October, vol. 6), pp. 204–11. Cf. *RC*, pp. 305–6; *Liber privilegiorum*, doc. 8, pp. 22–3.
44 See n. 34, above.
45 See n. 52, below.
46 *TIE* 197: *GL*, p. 158. Saint Amandus evangelised Francia under Dagobert (r. 623–34); Dagobert's son was Sigebert III (c. 630–56), later canonised.
47 The Irish missionary Columbanus (543–615) founded numerous monasteries, of which the most famous are Luxeuil and Bobbio. He established the latter in 614 on a tract high in the Ligurian Apennines that he had been granted by the Lombard king Agilulf, recently converted from Arianism.

Around that same time Pope Boniface [IV] obtained the temple of the Pantheon from the emperor Phocas; he consecrated it in honour of blessed Mary and all martyrs, since the feasts of the confessors were not yet celebrated by the church.[48] After this, another pope by the name of Gregory [IV] decreed that the aforesaid feast in honour of all saints should be solemnly celebrated by the whole world every year on the first of November: since we cannot create an individual feast for every saint, we may at least honour all of them together.[49] For it would be impossible to create a feast for every saint because the time available would be insufficient: setting aside the confessors, whose numbers are nearly infinite, even the martyrs are so many that—as Saint Jerome says—there is not a single day in the year on which fewer than five thousand martyrs were killed for the faith of Christ, with the exception of January first.[50] This was because the Romans ordered that no one should be killed on the first of January; instead, that day should be spent in celebration both because it was the first day of the year and because it was dedicated to Janus, who was the greatest and favourite idol of the Romans.[51]

Chapter five: Regarding Sabatinus, fifth bishop. The fifth bishop, Sabatinus, took office around the year of the Lord 666. He translated the body of Saint Romulus from Villa Matuciana to the church of Genoa.[52] After the Saracens destroyed the village, this Bishop Sabatinus went there and honourably transferred the body of Saint Romulus to Genoa, placing it in a marble coffer under the altar of San Lorenzo. Indeed, it was not inappropriate that Saint Romulus should repose in his own city, where three of his predecessors—Saints Valentinus, Felix, and Syrus—all reposed, so that he too should repose with them. These four holy men are the four-horsed chariot (*quadriga*) of God by whom the city of Genoa was moistened by examples, rained upon by teachings, and watered with virtues. These four are the winds of heaven who

---

48 Phocas' donation dates to 609–10: *Life of Boniface IV* in *Liber pontificalis*, p. 62; Sigebert of Gembloux, *Chronica* 609, p. 321; *MO*, pp. 422, 457; *GL*, p. 756.

49 Gregory IV (827–44); cf. *GL*, p. 659.

50 Preface to the *Martyrology of Jerome*: *AASS* 63 (November, vol. 2.1), p. lxxxii; also Augustine, sermon 252, chap. 8 (*PL* 38.1178).

51 Parts 1.4 and 3.2, above.

52 Sabatinus was bishop 865–89. Romulus' *translatio* is attested in a 980 diploma of Bishop Theodulf (part 11.9) and a contemporary written account: Balzaretti (2013), pp. 101–2.

protect us on the sea of this world, navigating by tides; they defend us from unexpected obstacles and lead us up to the gate of eternal rest. These four are the gemstones of God assembled in the crown of the Genoese church: one shines to the front to provide foresight for the future; another shines out from the back to resolve past events with justice; the third shines on the right to maintain temperance among the prosperous; while the fourth shines on the left to give great steadfastness during challenging and difficult times.[53]

About that time, Bede flourished in England—an exceptional doctor, perfect monk, and renowned preacher of homilies.[54] Indeed, it would have been fitting if he had been named a saint, but instead he is called 'venerable': there are two reasons for this. One is that after his eyes had clouded over, he was preaching in a valley full of stones because his companions had told him—as a source of humour and depravity—that a great multitude of people was awaiting his preaching there. But when he had finished his preaching, saying, 'through all ages of ages' (*per omnia secula seculorum*), by divine command angels and the stones themselves responded, 'Amen, venerable father'. For this reason he was afterward called 'venerable', and thus he is called Venerable by the church.[55] The other reason is that after his death a certain cleric devoted to him wished to create a verse to be carved on his tomb, beginning this way: 'Here in this grave are' (*Hac sunt in fossa*) and ending this way, 'the bones of the holy Bede' (*Bede sancti ossa*), but the harmony of the verses did not permit this. The following day he went to the tomb out of devotion, and there he found the verse resolved as follows, carved by angelic hands: 'Here in this grave are the bones of the Venerable Bede' (*Hac sunt in fossa Bede venerabilis ossa*). After a long time his body and those venerable bones were transferred to Genoa and venerably entombed in the monastery of San Benigno di Capodifaro, where his feast is solemnly celebrated and many hold him in devotion.[56]

---

53 See Jacopo, *LSS*, p. 364.
54 The Northumbrian monk Bede the Venerable (*c.* 673–735), a scholar best known for his *Historia ecclesiastica gentis Anglorum*; cf. *GL*, p. 761.
55 *TIE* 542.
56 *GL*, p. 761. The Genoese Bede (Bede the Lesser) was a ninth-century monk whose name and tomb were later ascribed to the better-known English Bede: *AASS* 10 (10 April, vol. 1), pp. 856–64. The relics of Bede the Lesser came to San Benigno in 1225 and remained there through the nineteenth century; around 1880 the skull was taken to Australia by a missionary and presented to Saint John's College (now part of the University of Sydney), which still owns it.

Chapter six: Regarding Viator, sixth bishop. The sixth bishop, Viator, took office around the year of the Lord 732.[57] In his time, the bones of blessed bishop Augustine were transferred from Sardinia to Genoa, prompted by the king of the Lombards, a most Christian man by the name of Liudprand.[58] When the king heard this, he came to Genoa from Pavia, but when he wished to have the bones moved to Pavia they weighed so much that they could not be lifted by the porters in any way. Then the king swore an oath to the blessed Augustine that if he permitted himself to be lifted and taken to Pavia, the king would order a church built in his honour at the place where he had been hosted in Genoa. As soon as the vow was made, those who were carrying the body immediately lifted it easily and the king carried out his oath faithfully. Where this church might be, however, is not known today. Some say that it is the church of San Thoma, others San Teodoro; others say that it is the archbishop's palace near San Silvestro, where the aforementioned king was staying; that this is why the palace was built there, and why the chapel of Sant'Agostino—which still exists today—was constructed in the same place.[59]

Around the same time, Emperor Leo ordered images of Christ, the blessed Virgin, and other saints to be burned and broken everywhere, saying that worshipping images is idolatry.[60] In response, the then-pope Gregory admonished him that he should not do this, and excommunicated him when he did not desist—and when he still persisted in his obstinacy, deposed him.[61] For Emperor Leo ordered these impieties foolishly when he burned the images of Christ and the saints. It was not idolatry, as he claimed, because we do not believe that there is any divinity in such images, as the Gentiles believe of their idols. Rather, we create images

---

57 Possibly a corruption of Victor: *JVC* 2.257 n. 2. While there is early medieval evidence for Viator's predecessors, and the episcopal register (*RC*) contains documents from Rampert (part 11.10) onward, the next three chapters are our earliest evidence for Viator and his two successors.

58 The bones of Saint Augustine (d. 430) were supposedly moved from Hippo (in Africa) to Sardinia in the sixth century, then to Pavia in the eighth: Paul the Deacon, *Historia Langobardorum* 6.48; Stone (2002), esp. pp. 32–5. Genoa appears on the route in the *GL* (p. 514) as well as in *MO*, pp. 459–60: Di Fabio (1978).

59 Genoa was one of the only cities in Italy where the (arch)bishop's residence was not adjacent to the cathedral: Miller (2000), pp. 65–7; *CMG*, pp. 222–3 (Gorse). The Augustinian convent of Sant'Agostino was founded next to the palace in 1257: Poleggi/Grossi Bianchi (1980), pp. 118, 124–6.

60 The 726 and 728 edicts of the Byzantine emperor Leo III (r. 716–41) against icon-worship: see Noble (2009) on its reception in western Europe.

61 Pope Gregory II (715–31): Noble (2009), pp. 54–6.

only so that through them we may be inspired to commemorate those whose images they are. Also, we do not offer the honour we devote to images to those objects on which the images are depicted in their various colours; rather, we offer it to those whom the images represent. It is true that there is no image of God in the Old Testament because God was then invisible, so an image of him would have been impossible to make. But while first invisible in his divine nature, God was later made visible in his human nature, and thus we can represent in images those things which Christ did in his human flesh—such as his birth, passion, resurrection, ascension, and the other miracles which he accomplished. Similarly, while Christ's actions were written down for our information and instruction, there are many who do not know letters, so the holy fathers ordered that the deeds of Christ and other saints should be represented by images so that such laypeople may be instructed by these images as though by a book.

Furthermore, the image of Christ and the blessed Virgin ought to be depicted as they are taught by the holy doctors. For John of Damascus says that Christ was monobrowed (*consuperciliatus*)—meaning, he had joined eyebrows—that he had good eyesight and a long face, and that he was stooped, which was a sign of his humility and maturity.[62] Likewise Saint Epiphanius says that Christ's body was six feet in stature, that he had long golden hair and pronounced black eyebrows, along with shining, joyful eyes; that he had a long nose and a golden beard the colour of grain; and that he did not have a proud neck but more of a bent and ruddy one.[63] The same Epiphanius says of His mother that she was of medium height with golden hair the colour of grain, good eyes, black eyebrows, and an oblong nose and oblong hands, with long fingers and a long face. Thus it is manifestly clear from these things that are said of Christ and His mother that the son was very similar to His mother.

At that time in the fields of Italy grain, barley, and legumes came down from heaven like rain, as it is read in the chronicles.[64] And around the same time the university (*studium generale*) was moved to Paris; for at one time a university flourished in Greece, but from Greece was it was

---

62 Pseudo-John of Damascus, 'Letter to Theophilus' 3e, pp. 148–9.

63 Not the canonised fourth-century bishop of Salamis, but the eighth-century monk Epiphanius, author of a *Sermo de vita sanctissime Deiparae* (*PG* 120.185–214, at cols. 194, 203).

64 Sigebert of Gembloux, *Chronica* 722, p. 330.

transferred to Rome; and then Alcuin, the schoolmaster of Charles [the Great], a man learned in every science, transferred it to Paris where it flourishes even today.[65]

Around this same time in Syria the Jews pierced a certain image of Christ in its side with a lance, and from this wound blood gushed most copiously. Accordingly the stupefied Jews held a bowl underneath it which was immediately filled with this blood. The blood was dispersed and divided among many churches, and even today it is preserved and displayed in many churches. From that time on churches began to be built in honour of Saint Savior. Furthermore, a great amount of this blood was transferred to Rome, where the church of San Salvatore was built and consecrated, and an ampule full of that blood is kept there. Thus these Jews were converted to the catholic faith upon seeing such a great miracle.[66]

Chapter seven: Regarding Dionysius, seventh bishop. The seventh bishop, Dionysius, took office around the year 798. In the time of this bishop Emperor Charles celebrated a synod in the city of Genoa, as can be read in the *Deeds* of that emperor.[67] For at that time Desiderius, king of the Lombards, was harassing the empire, and African Saracens were devastating Genoa and the coastal lands badly, so the aforementioned emperor divided his army into two parts.[68] One part he gave to his uncle Bernard to advance against Desiderius, who was in the regions of Lombardy. Accordingly Bernard went: he put this Desiderius to flight and pursued him as far as Pavia, where he captured him and exiled him to Lyons with his wife and children. Then King Charles sent the remaining part of the army to Genoa to defend the lands of the coast from the Saracens.

---

65 Ibid. 790, p. 335; *MO*, p. 426. The principle of *translatio studii* (transfer of studies) derived from that of *translatio imperii* (transfer of empire), arguing that the medieval University of Paris was the heir of Plato's Academy via ancient Rome: Gabriel (1988), pp. 605–12.

66 *GL*, pp. 556–7, regarding the city of Berith, Syria, in 750; Aron-Beller (2017), esp. pp. 218–20.

67 Probably a miscopied reference to the 773 Synod of Geneva: Mansi/Labbe (1901), 12.857. The transposition of Geneva to Genoa both here and in the *DGA* suggests either that Jacopo da Varagine adopted this detail from Jacopo Doria, or that the two Jacopos were working from the same (miscopied) source.

68 Annalista Saxo 773, p. 19.

Around this time Pope Leo, a man outstanding in sanctity and distinguished in knowledge, occupied the Roman seat.[69] But the Romans were upset by his election; egged on by a diabolical madness, they put out his eyes and cut out his tongue while he was going through the major litanies.[70] But God miraculously restored his vision and his tongue. He then fled to Charles and told him what the Romans had done, so Charles came to Rome, avenged him, and restored him to his seat.[71]

At that same time, when both the Romans and the Greeks held the empire, it was divided between them so that the Greeks kept their emperor while the Latins made Charles emperor by the authority of the church.[72] And this Emperor Charles arranged that the Ambrosian office which was then sung in all churches should be abandoned, and the Gregorian office should be adopted by all churches.[73] But since it is difficult to give up a habit there was a great uproar about this through the entire church, with some wishing to retain the Ambrosian office and others wishing to adopt the Gregorian. So the holy fathers took the Ambrosian and Gregorian missals and placed them together on the altar, asking God to show them by some sign which office was more pleasing to him. They left this offering locked up [overnight], and when they returned the next morning they found the Ambrosian missal open on the altar, while the Gregorian missal had been totally pulled apart and dispersed here and there about the church. By this sign they understood that the Ambrosian office should be sung only in his [Ambrose's] church, while the Gregorian should be spread throughout the whole world.[74] In fact, Ambrose originally instituted the singing of the office in Italy and also first invented hymns, as Saint Augustine says in the book of the *Confessions*.[75] He says that the empress Justina, who

---

69 Pope Leo III (793–816), who crowned Charlemagne emperor in Saint Peter's, Rome, on Christmas Day, 800: *NCMH* 2.330–1 (Brown).

70 25 April 799. The major litanies are a series of prayers performed annually in procession in Rome on the feast of Saint Mark (25 April): *GL*, pp. 285–8.

71 Annalista Saxo 799, pp. 36–7; the *Life of Leo III* in *Liber pontificalis*, pp. 184–8; also *MO*, p. 459. Leo was attacked by supporters of his predecessor Adrian I: Noble (1984), pp. 199–202, 291–3.

72 Annalista Saxo 800, pp. 38–9; Noble (1984), pp. 291–9.

73 E.g. Charlemagne, *Admonitio generalis*; Hiley (1993), pp. 514–18. Cf. also *GL*, p. 763.

74 Landulf Senior, *Historia Mediolanensis* 2.10–12, pp. 49–50; Hiley (1993), p. 540. See also *GL*, pp. 182–3.

75 *Confessions* 9.7.

was a supporter of the Arians, locked Ambrose and the catholics inside a church and would not permit them to leave. For this reason Ambrose composed hymns to be chanted in the church lest the people pine away from boredom and grief.[76] Then, because the Ambrosian office was seen as too prolix, after a long while Gregory abbreviated it, organised it better, and restored it to a better harmony.[77] However, it was granted that the Milanese church was still allowed to use the Ambrosian office.

About the same time near Constantinople a marble arch was found under the earth where an elderly man lay facing upward, and on the arch were found [inscribed] these letters: 'Christ will be born of the Virgin and I believe in Him; O Sun, you will see me again'.[78] From this it is clear that this man died and was buried before the birth of Christ, and that he prophesied the birth of that same Christ. However, we do not know who he was.

Chapter eight: Regarding Sigebert, eighth bishop. The eighth bishop Sigebert took office around the year of the Lord 864. Around the time of this bishop, there was a certain woman gifted with great knowledge and distinguished in eloquence, who went in men's clothing to the Roman curia. As she spent time there she gained office because of her probity and great wisdom; she was made a cardinal and afterward elected pope, and seemed worthy in the sight of all.[79] But before she assumed the papacy, it is said, she had secretly taken a husband; and from him, at that earlier time, she had conceived. Because of this, one day while she was going in procession about Rome with the cardinals, clergy, and people, the pains of childbirth suddenly came over her. They carried her into a small house located in that street; she gave birth, died of her pains in childbirth, and was buried there. Thus even today a custom has developed in the Roman curia that the pope never walks through that street, but avoids it by walking around. Also, there is a marble image in that place declaring this fact.

---

76 Empress Justina (*c.* 340–88) was a staunch Arian who encouraged the persecution of catholic Christians such as Ambrose: Augustine, *Confessions* 9.7; McLynn (1994), pp. 158–219. See also *GL*, p. 763; *SS*, fol. 188r–v.

77 *GL*, p. 180; *SS*, fols. 130r, 451r–v, 453v.

78 Sigebert of Gembloux, *Chronica* 782, p. 335; *MO*, p. 461.

79 *TIE* 2813 and *MO*, p. 428: this is the famous legend of Pope Joan, who supposedly reigned between Leo IV and Benedict III (that is, 854–5). The tale was popularised by Dominican preachers in the mid-thirteenth century: Noble (2013).

PART ELEVEN: GENOA UNDER THE BISHOPS

This woman began presumptuously, continued deceitfully and foolishly, and ended ignominiously, for this is the nature of woman: in doing some task, at the beginning she displays presumption and impudence; in the middle, she shows foolishness; and at the end she incurs shame. A woman who begins presumptuously and impudently does not see the end or those things which the end entails; rather, she believes she has accomplished great things. A woman who has managed to begin something well does not understand wisely how to continue what she has begun after she has begun and reached the middle [of the project]; this is due to her lack of discernment. And thus it is right that she finishes with shame and ignominy what she began with presumption and audacity, and continued with foolishness. And thus it is clear that a woman begins presumptuously, proceeds futilely, and ends ignominiously.

Also around this time, a certain cardinal called 'Pig's Mouth' (*Os Porchi*) was elected pope, but he changed his name so that he was called Sergius.[80] From that time on it was ordered that all popes should change their given names, so that they could be distinguished with an honourable name if by chance they were blemished by some dishonourable name. In this [policy] they also followed the example of Christ, who changed Simon's name and called him Peter when he named him prince and shepherd of the others. By this we are given to understand that as they are changed in name, so they ought to be changed in the perfection of their life.

Also around this time, Theodulf, bishop of Orleans, was falsely accused before the emperor and imprisoned in a certain tower, where he composed those verses which are sung on Palm Sunday: *All glory, laud, and honour be to you*, etc.[81] One day when a procession went past with the emperor, he sang these verses and sent them [wafting] down onto the people in the procession. They were so pleasing to the emperor and everyone in the procession that the emperor himself released him from prison and restored him to his seat. And because these verses had been chanted in a tower with the doors locked, now it is the custom elsewhere for boys to ascend a tower and chant the verses from there, and then the entire

---

80 Jacopo is confusing Sergius II (844–47) with Sergius IV, formerly Pietro Bocca di Porco ('Pig's Mouth', 1009–12); cf. *GL*, p. 765.

81 *MGH Poetae* 1, pp. 558–9. Theodulf, bishop of Orléans, was imprisoned in 818 on suspicion of conspiracy against Louis the Pious: although he probably wrote this hymn during that time, he died in prison in 821 without being restored to his see. Cf. *GL*, p. 764.

clergy responds. And in places where there is no tower to ascend, [the verse] is chanted with the doors of the church closed.

Also around the same time, near Brescia, it is said that blood rained from heaven for three days and nights, as is recorded in many chronicles.[82]

Chapter nine: Regarding Theodulf, ninth bishop. The ninth bishop was Theodulf. From this bishop up to our own time we have the years and ages for the reigns of all the bishops and archbishops. We find these partly in the chronicles of the commune of Genoa and partly in the register which is kept in our palace. The aforesaid bishop [Theodulf] took office around the year of the Lord 930 and completed 38 years in the episcopate.[83] But in the third year of his episcopate—namely, the year of the Lord 933—a terrible portent and a tragic misfortune occurred in the city of Genoa. For, as Filibert [i.e. Sigebert] tells in his chronicle as well as Vincent in his, a fountain of blood gushed forth copiously in the city of Genoa, presaging the future slaughter and simultaneous ruin of that city.[84] For in that same year the city was taken by the African Saracens, despoiled of all of its treasures, and bespattered with the blood of the massacred.[85] For everyone was killed except for women, children, and those who retreated into the mountains, and their children and wives were taken away into slavery. This fountain of blood gushed forth in the place which is now called 'Little Fountain', for the place has taken its name, Fontanella, from that same fountain of blood.[86] But how the Genoese later retrieved their wives, children, and treasure is stated above in part 5, chapter 2.

Around the same time, when Louis, who was of Frankish origin, held the empire but did not assist the church against the Lombards, the right of empire was transferred from the Franks (*Franci*) to the Germans (*Theutonici*).[87] For first the right of empire lay with the Romans, then

---

82 Sigebert of Gembloux, *Chronica* 874, p. 341; cf. *MO*, p. 463; *GL*, p. 765.

83 930–68, although the accepted dates are 945–81: Balzaretti (2013), pp. 78–80. See Monleone on Jacopo's use of the archiepiscopal register (*RC*): *JVC* 2.273 n. 1.

84 Sigebert of Gembloux, *Chronica* 935, p. 347, whence Vincent of Beauvais, *Speculum historiale* 24.66.

85 The sack of 934–35: see part 5.2, above, and *DGA*, pp. 6–7.

86 Based on Liudprand of Cremona, *Antapodosis* 4.5.

87 Probably Louis III 'the Blind', emperor 901–5; the long conflict that included his reign ended with the establishment of the Ottonian dynasty.

it was transferred to the Greeks, then to the Gauls (*Gallici*, i.e. the Franks), and then to the Germans.[88]

Around the same time Pope Sergius, who was discussed above, was deposed [from the papacy] by a certain man named Formosus who was elected [in his place].[89] When Sergius regained the papacy upon Formosus' death, he had Formosus disinterred, dressed pontifically on the papal seat, and beheaded; then his corpse was thrown into the Tiber. Nonetheless, it was found by fishermen and entombed in the church of Saint Peter. Then certain images of the saints were seen to venerate this Formosus and to greet him reverently, for it is believed that this Formosus repented greatly on his death that he had deposed Sergius, and pardon followed. Furthermore, the harsh revenge which the aforementioned Sergius later inflicted on him was greatly displeasing to God and to all men. This Sergius should have been wary lest God should be equally severe with him—as the blessed James says, *judgment without mercy will come to him who does not act with mercy.*[90]

Chapter ten: Regarding Rampert, tenth bishop. The tenth bishop, Rampert, took office around the year of the Lord 968 and completed seventeen years in the episcopate.[91] Around this time there was a pope by the name of Sylvester; when he was still a youth and clothed in the habit of a layman, he conjured the devil through the art of magic and did him homage, and the devil promised to bestow many great honours upon him.[92] In this way he became archbishop first of Reims, then of

---

88 Transfer of empire (*translatio imperii*) is the influential medieval idea that the mantle of supreme earthly power passes from one group to the next according to divine decree: Goez (1958); cf. n. 65, above.

89 *TIE* 2147: after a contentious papacy, the body of Pope Formosus (891–96) was disinterred, tried, and condemned in 897 by Pope Stephen VI (896–97) during the famous 'Cadaver Synod'. Jacopo's attribution of the episode to Sergius III (904–11) comes from Liudprand of Cremona: *Antapodosis* 1.30 (*CCCM* 156.23). Cf. Sigebert of Gembloux, *Chronica* 907, p. 345; Vincent of Beauvais, *Speculum historiale* 24.58; *MO*, p. 430.

90 James 2.13.

91 968–85. Bertini Guidetti (*CCG*, p. 257) excludes Rampert from the accepted list of bishops, but Balzaretti (2013), p. 104, includes him.

92 Gerbert of Aurillac, Pope Sylvester II (999–1003), a renowned scientist and the childhood tutor of Emperor Otto III. After an unsettled papacy, numerous stories connecting him with sorcery circulated among the polemics of the Investiture Contest: e.g. Beno, *Gesta Romanae ecclesiae* 2.4–5, p. 377, and William of Malmesbury, *Gesta regum Anglorum* 2.172. See also Riché (1987), pp. 10–12.

Ravenna, and after that he was raised to the highest pontificate. Next, he asked the devil how long he would live in this world, and the devil replied that he would live until he had celebrated mass in Jerusalem. He was utterly delighted with this response, and hoped that death was far distant for him since he had no intention of going on pilgrimage. But there is a certain church in the city of Rome called 'in Jerusalem', and during Lent he was celebrating [mass] in it when the devil revealed himself, and he knew he was near death.[93] But when he complained that the devil had not kept his promise, the devil replied that of course he was keeping his promise because he would not die until he had celebrated [mass] in Jerusalem—and thus when he had said mass 'in Jerusalem', it was certainly time for him to die.

Then, although [Pope Sylvester] was a very wicked man, nonetheless he did not despair of God's mercy and confessed his sin before all. And as he was finishing the words written in the book of Wisdom—*by what things a man sins, by these also is he tormented*—he ordered cut from him all the limbs with which he had done obedience to the devil, decreeing that afterward his body should be torn limb from limb, then placed on a cart and buried in whatever place the animals stopped.[94] He ordered the same of his severed feet with which he had gone to consult with the devil, the tongue with which he had summoned the devil, the hands with which he had done homage to the devil, and also his plucked-out eyes, because they had provided the vision for these deeds. Then his mutilated body was placed on a cart pulled by animals, which suddenly stopped next to the church of the Lateran—and so they buried [the pope] in that church with due honour.[95]

From this it is clear that there is no one so wicked that he cannot obtain mercy from God if he is willing to turn to God in his heart. For pardon and mercy are natural and proper to God, while punishment is alien to him and contrary to his nature. Moreover, we do freely and easily those things which accord with our nature, but we do reluctantly and slowly those things which are contrary to our nature. So God pardons

---

93 Santa Croce in Gerusalemme (the Basilica of the Holy Cross in Jerusalem), Rome. According to tradition, the basilica was founded *c.* 325 to house relics of Christ's Passion, with a floor covered in earth from Jerusalem.

94 Wisdom 11.17; cf. *SD*, fol. 213v.

95 *TIE* 3586 and 906; Annalista Saxo 999, pp. 269–70; *MO*, p. 432. Unlike many authors, Jacopo emphasises the mercy shown Sylvester upon repentance rather than dwelling on his crime.

freely and punishes reluctantly; he is quick to give mercy, and slow to punish. For this reason, as we read in Genesis, although Adam sinned at midday God only moved to punish him in the afternoon, to give him time to repent.[96] Likewise as we read in the Evangelist, when the prodigal son returned to his father, his father ran to him and kissed him.[97] That he ran demonstrates that God pardons quickly and readily; that he kissed him demonstrates that He pardons freely.[98]

Chapter eleven: Regarding Landulf, eleventh bishop. Landulf, the eleventh bishop, took office in about the year of the Lord 985 and completed thirty years in the episcopate.[99] He transferred the body of Saint Syrus from the basilica of the Twelve Apostles—which is today called the monastery of San Siro [Saint Syrus]—to the cathedral church of San Lorenzo, where the body was reburied in the church choir in the place which is now the entry of the chancel.[100] He wished to transfer Syrus' body for two reasons: first, because this precious body could be kept more safely in the church of San Lorenzo, since the monastery of San Siro was then outside the city walls and the African Saracens often came in their galleys and despoiled the churches.[101] For the same reason the entire treasury was moved to the church of San Lorenzo because it would be more secure there. The second reason is that since Saint Syrus was bishop of Genoa, it was more fitting and appropriate that he should repose in the episcopal church than in a monastic church.

Around this time there was a certain king of the Franks named Robert, very much devoted to God and illustrious in wisdom and [manner of] life.[102] He composed many sequences and responsories in honour of the

96 Genesis 3.8 (paraphrased).
97 Luke 15.20 (paraphrased).
98 See *SD*, fol. 202v; *SQ*, pp. 181–2.
99 985–1015, although the accepted dates are 1019–35: *RC*, pp. 488–90.
100 The basilica of San Siro (already extant *c.* 600, per n. 2 above, and outside the Carolingian walls of the city) served as Genoa's first cathedral, but by 1007 the bishop's seat had been transferred inside the walls to San Lorenzo: *CMG*, p. 346 (Rosser); Filangieri (2006), pp. 28–9. The translation of Syrus' relics probably occurred around 1020, but the reliability of Jacopo's account may be compromised, since while writing the *Chronicle* he was engaged in a long struggle with the monks of San Siro over Syrus' relics: Macchiavello (1997), pp. 30–1, esp. n. 28.
101 Another reference to the sack of 934–35 (part 5.2, above).
102 The second Capetian king of France, Robert the Pious (r. 996–1031) was a noted musician and composer; see Helgaud of Fleury's *Vie du roi Robert* (*c.* 1035), but also Hamilton (1997).

saints: as some say, he created a sequence which begins *The grace of the Holy Spirit be upon us*. This king was so pious that he often wore a silken cape (*capa*[103]) in the choir and directed the choir. In fact, once when he was besieging a certain fortress (*castrum*) which had rebelled against him and a certain major feast was approaching, he dismissed his army, went to church, and piously completed the office, asking God to allow him to recover his fortress in peace. And when he said the 'Lamb of God' (*Agnus Dei*) clothed in his silken cape, speaking in a loud voice, and bending his knees three times, as soon as he said 'grant us peace', the walls of the fortress toppled completely, and thus the fortress was recovered in peace without the shedding of blood.[104]

From this is it clear that the prayers of holy men are often worth more than the arms of soldiers in achieving victory over one's enemies. On this topic, we read of Moses that when a certain people called Amalekites were fighting against the people of Israel, Moses raised his hands to heaven and began to pray for his people of Israel. And when Moses raised his hands to heaven, the people of Israel gained the advantage, but when he lowered his hands in fatigue, their enemies would start winning. Seeing this, two strong men held up Moses' hands and arms and thus they gained victory over their enemies.[105] It is also read of Joshua, Moses' disciple, that when he was besieging a certain city called Jericho, he ordered the priests to blow their trumpets and call out to God. At this clamour the walls of the city were overthrown and they captured the city.[106]

Also, although we mentioned above that Robert, king of the Franks, created the sequence *The grace of the Holy Spirit be upon us*, some say instead that the German, Herman the Lame, composed it.[107] This Herman was lame and much devoted to the blessed Virgin, so the blessed Virgin appeared to him, saying that he could choose whichever of two things was most pleasing to him: either the health of his body or the grace of inventing pious songs in honour of God; and he chose the latter. Then he had himself taken to all the churches, and he composed antiphons,

---

103 A cloak worn by priests and monks.
104 Helgaud of Fleury, *Vie du roi Robert*; MO, p. 432; GL, p. 764.
105 Exodus 17.10–13.
106 Joshua 6.20.
107 Herman of Reichenau (1013–54), known as *Hermannus contractus* ('the lame'), was a noted composer and scholar, as well as author of a *Chronicon*. See GL, p. 764; SS, fol. 454v.

sequences, and responsories in honour of their saints, many of which are still chanted in the various churches. Among other works he also composed a very beautiful antiphon in honour of blessed Mary that begins *Sweet mother of the redeemer*, etc. (*Alma redemptoris Mater*). Also in the time of Bishop Landulf, specifically in the year of the Lord 991, the church of Santa Maria delle Vigne is said to have been built by viscount Oberto and Guido di Carmadino.[108]

Chapter twelve: Regarding John, the twelfth bishop. John, the twelfth bishop, took office around the year of the Lord 1015 and completed thirty years in the episcopate.[109] In the time of this bishop the Hungarians were converted to the faith of Christ by Galla, sister of Emperor Henry, who had been given as wife to King Stephen of Hungary.[110] This most Christian holy woman converted her husband to the faith of Christ and had him baptised, and when the other Hungarians heard that the king had converted to the faith of Christ and been baptised, they likewise flocked to the grace of baptism. This King Stephen was so full of holiness that he was canonised by the church because God worked many miracles through him; his feast is celebrated solemnly among the Hungarians and many hold him in devotion and reverence. Thus in praise of this holy woman [Galla] one might echo the words of Solomon: *who will find a valiant woman?*[111] Certainly many women are weak and have little courage, but this one was most courageous. The weak are those who succumb to temptation, or do not resist sin, or serve God only half-heartedly. The valiant are those who despise this world and its carnal delights in the name of Christ, just as the holy virgins did who suffered martyrdom for the faith of Christ; and among the valiant we may number the aforementioned holy Galla: although she did not suffer

---

108 Oberto and Guido were distantly related members of the local nobility: Epstein (1996), pp. 19–20. Jacopo is correct that Santa Maria delle Vigne probably dates from the tenth century: *CMG*, p. 35 (Macchiavello/Rovere).

109 1015–45. The currently accepted chronology puts John between Theodulf and Landulf (i.e. 984–1019): Polonio (2002a), p. 18.

110 In 996 Gisela (here Galla) of Bavaria (985–1065), sister of Emperor Henry II, married Stephen I of Hungary (king 1001–38). The couple are credited with the rapid spread of Christianity in Hungary; see *GL*, p. 766. After Stephen's death, Gisela returned to Bavaria, took holy orders, and was beatified in 1975. She also appears in part 11.2, above.

111 Proverbs 31.10. Jacopo uses this verse to begin sermons on three female saints—*SS*, fols. 12v (Lucy), 82r (Agnes), 267r (Mary Magdalen)—and two sermons on the Virgin: *Mariale* 57/F8 (*fortis mulier*), 156/V8 (*virginitas*).

martyrdom, she contributed much to the common good when she converted a whole people to Christ. Most valiant of all, however, was the blessed Virgin who conquered the unconquerable and overcame the all-powerful, specifically when by her humility and virginity she caused God to descend into her womb.

Around this time, certain bandits were crossing the thresholds of the Apostles and despoiling all the pilgrims. Pope Gregory VI excommunicated them but they refused to stop, so he took up arms himself and put them to flight, and caused many of them to be killed.[112] But when he was approaching death, the cardinals assigned him an unworthy tomb because of this slaughter, so he said: 'When I am dead, put my body in front of the doors of the church and bar the doors very carefully. If they should be opened by the will of God, bury my body within the church; otherwise, do whatever you like with it'. When this was done, the doors were suddenly opened and his body was therefore entombed honourably within. From this it is manifestly clear that he did not order these killings to be done in the bitterness of vengeance, but rather in the zeal of justice. And if it is argued that this was irregular, it must be said that a pope cannot commit irregularity, or else one must admit that irregularity often occurs without sin, as is clear from [the cases of] a bigamist or a just judge who justly condemns a thief to hanging.[113]

About that same time, Emperor Conrad was roaming through a certain forest while hunting, and after nightfall, he received hospitality in the house of a poor woman. That night the woman gave birth to a son, and behold! a voice came to the emperor saying that this boy would be his son-in-law and successor to his empire.[114] So he got up and ordered two soldiers to steal the boy away and kill him. But they were moved by pity, so they laid him at a crossroads, where a certain duke found him, had him brought up, and called him Henry. When the boy grew up, he was extremely gracious to all and the emperor made him [part] of his

---

112 Gregory VI (1044–46) was pope during a period of serious upheaval; he abdicated at the Council of Sutri in 1046 and died in 1048. Cf. *GL*, pp. 767–8; Vincent of Beauvais, *Speculum historiale* 26.22–5; *MO*, p. 433.

113 Irregularity: that which is contrary to canon law. Jacopo is referring to 'successive bigamy', the condition of having been married more than once (not a sin, but an impediment to clerical ordination).

114 Presumably the story refers to Emperor Conrad II (r. 1027–39) and his successor Henry III (r. 1046–56), although Henry was Conrad's son; see also *GL*, pp. 766–7; *MO*, pp. 466–7. The story of the baby condemned to exposure who is rescued to fulfil some illustrious destiny (*TIE* 647) is a common trope, however.

entourage; rumour said, and the general opinion was, that if the emperor should die, this one should reign in his place because the emperor did not have a son. But the emperor wrote letters [carried] by this boy to the empress, who was then at Aachen, saying that she should have him killed on the day he arrived. But while he was staying at a certain church, a priest took these letters from his bag while he slept and opened them out of curiosity; abhorring the crime [proposed], he wrote other letters to the queen in the emperor's name, saying that on the day Henry arrived, she should give her daughter to him in marriage. Carefully affixing the seal of the emperor, he placed the letters back where he had found them. Henry therefore sought out the queen, gave her the letters, and that same day took the emperor's daughter as his wife. When the emperor heard this, he was completely astonished, but he made diligent enquiries regarding the boy from the day of his birth up to that day. Recognising that it would be foolish to challenge divine providence, he therefore approved the marriage and arranged that Henry should reign after him. And indeed, after Conrad's death Henry was made emperor, and he had a noble monastery constructed in the place of his birth.

Chapter thirteen: Regarding Conrad, the thirteenth bishop. The thirteenth bishop, Conrad, took office around the year of the Lord 1045 and completed twenty years in the episcopate.[115] As is demonstrated by a public deed (*instrumentum*) preserved in the archiepiscopal palace, the noble man Conrad, count of Ventimiglia, confirmed to this bishop Conrad the fortresses of Saint Romulus [Sanremo] and Ceriana with all their appurtenances.[116]

At the time of this bishop, Alexander—a man of Milanese birth—was elected pope, but the bishops of Lombardy sought to elect the bishop of Parma as pope against him.[117] The Pisans gave substantial assistance to this presumptuous bishop of Parma, while the Genoese remained loyal to Alexander. Later this Alexander gained and held the papacy peacefully.

115 1045–65. Conrad I was bishop 1036–51: *RC*, pp. 490–3; Polonio (2002a), p. 18.
116 *RC*, p. 441 (dated 1038).
117 Schism followed the death of Pope Nicholas II in 1061: under the leadership of Hildebrand (later Gregory VII), the reform cardinals in Rome elected Alexander II (1061–73). Alexander was consecrated on 1 October, but about a month later in Basel, an assembly of anti-reform German and Lombard bishops elected Cadalus, bishop of Parma, who took the name Honorius II (now antipope). The Council of Mantua (1064) eventually declared in favour of Alexander.

Around this time lived the countess Matilda, who called herself the daughter of blessed Peter; she always supported the church against the emperor, and when she died without heirs, she placed all her possessions (*patrimonium*) on the altar of Saint Peter, for which reason even today it [the papal state] is called the patrimony of Saint Peter.[118] In this holy woman was fulfilled the statement in Ecclesiasticus that *a woman is better than a man.*[119] For although she was a woman, she had a very manly (*virilis*) spirit; she was entirely devoted to the church and refused to accept the emperor's son in marriage because the emperor was believed to be opposed to the church. Anyone who wishes to understand her ancestry should know that Sigefredus, who was a great prince in the regions of Tuscany, came into Lombardy and acquired many castles and lands there. This Sigefredus begat Atto; Atto begat Thealdus; Thealdus begat Boniface; and Boniface begat the countess Matilda.[120] But once Matilda had borne her husband a son, she did not afterward wish to couple with him due to the pains she had suffered in childbirth; accordingly, after her son died, all her line was finished. The countess held many cities in Lombardy, chiefly Mantua, Ferrara, Modena, Reggio, and Parma; and when she died without an heir, she made the church of God her heir.

Around this same time flourished Lanfranc, a native of Pavia: an extraordinary doctor (*doctor eximius*) and teacher of Anselm the distinguished doctor (*doctor precipuus*).[121] This Lanfranc used to teach in Paris, but he renounced the schools and went off secretly to a place where he could serve God in the greatest humility.[122] At that same time Berengar, a certain solemn doctor who taught theology at Paris, spread a poisonous

---

118 Matilda of Canossa, countess of Tuscany (1046–1117), ruler of a vast domain in north-central Italy as well as a key ally of the reform papacy: see Hay (2008). Jacopo's excursus on Matilda is largely condensed from Donizo of Canossa's *Vita Mathildis*.

119 Possibly a misquotation of Sirach 42.14.

120 *GL*, pp. 768–9, following Donizo, *Vita Mathildis*, pp. 360–1, 374.

121 Lanfranc of Pavia (c. 1005–89) renounced a brilliant legal career to become first prior of Bec, then archbishop of Canterbury, and was later beatified; see *GL*, p. 768. Anselm of Aosta (1033/4–1109) was Lanfranc's most famous student at Bec, succeeded him as archbishop of Canterbury, and was later canonised. 'Doctor' here signifies 'scholar': well-known scholars were often given such epithets—e.g. Thomas Aquinas, *doctor angelicus*—but not all with such epithets are official doctors of the church (Anselm is, but Lanfranc is not).

122 In 1042 Lanfranc left teaching to enter the newly founded abbey of Bec; he lived there in total seclusion until 1045, when he opened a school there under Abbot Herluin.

rumour that he dared not pronounce publicly out of fear of Lanfranc, asserting that the body of Christ does not exist on the altar in truth, but only by representation.[123] He was accordingly called before the curia and a council was convened [to pronounce] against this error. Upon learning of it, Lanfranc sought out that place disguised in a pilgrim's garb so that no one would recognise him, and when he had disputed neatly with Berengar, Berengar was stupefied and said, 'either you are the devil or you are Lanfranc'—and having been thus confounded, he abjured his heresy. After this, Lanfranc was made archbishop of Canterbury, where Anselm succeeded him in the archiepiscopate.

Also around this time, as we read in the chronicles, there was a marble statue in Apulia with ancient writing around its head that said: 'When the sun rises on the first of May, I will have a head of gold'. So one morning a Saracen astrologer ordered the place where the statue's head cast its shadow to be dug up, and found there a great treasure. Since the statue cast the shadow of its head over the gold, therefore it truly had a head of gold.[124]

Chapter fourteen: Regarding Albertus or Obertus, the fourteenth bishop. Albertus or Obertus, the fourteenth bishop, took office around the year of the Lord 1065 and completed nineteen years in the episcopate.[125]

In the time of this bishop, Hildebrand, prior of Cluny, was made cardinal and afterward sent as legate into France.[126] He was so full of zeal, especially against simoniacs, that he pursued them everywhere. And indeed, when the archbishop of Embrun had been corrupted by the vice of simony—becoming involved in simony by wishing to provide for himself—he even corrupted all his accusers by gifts of money.[127] But

---

123 Berengar of Tours (c. 999–1088), master of the cathedral school at Chartres, denied transubstantiation—the belief that the Eucharistic bread and wine are physically transformed into Christ's body and blood. Lanfranc, then prior of Bec, led the church's defence of transubstantiation although he and Berengar probably never debated the matter in person: Fichtenau (1998), pp. 285–93. On the basis of Lanfranc's arguments, set out in *De corpore et sanguine Domini* (c. 1060), transubstantiation was declared church doctrine by the Fourth Lateran Council in 1215.

124 Ourscamp continuation of Sigebert of Gembloux, *Chronica* 1039, p. 470; thence Vincent of Beauvais, *Speculum historiale* 26.17.2 and *MO*, p. 467.

125 1065–84. More recent research gives 1052–c. 1078 for Obertus: Polonio (2002a), p. 23; see also *RC*, pp. 492–6.

126 Hildebrand—later Pope Gregory VII—was never a monk of Cluny.

127 Hugh, archbishop of Embrun, was deposed in 1055 for simony (the sin of buying or selling ecclesiastical offices and privileges): Robinson, *Papal reform*, p. 200.

when the aforesaid legate [Hildebrand] investigated him due to the loud voices of rumour, he was not able to find any suitable witnesses against [the archbishop], from which we conclude that all had been corrupted by money. For this reason Hildebrand convened a council against him, and had him stand in the middle, saying to him: 'I have been unable to render human judgment on this matter, so I am resorting to the help of God. Since episcopal grace should be the gift of the Holy Spirit, I request the Holy Spirit that if you have bought that grace with money, you should be incapable of naming him. So please say that versicle which is chanted frequently in church, namely, *Glory to the Father and to the Son and to the Holy Spirit*'. The archbishop began fearlessly, pronouncing *Glory to the Father and to the Son* clearly. But when he arrived at *Holy Spirit* speech failed him: he was rendered mute and spoke by babbling. So he began a second time, but as soon as he came to *Holy Spirit* speech failed him. Realising this, he began to lament—and confessing his sin before all, he surrendered his archbishopric into the legate's hands. But since he showed great remorse, the legate said to him, 'In this matter, we may also know whether you have regained the grace of the Holy Spirit through true and unfeigned repentance, if you can name him. Therefore please recite the blessed versicle again now'. [The archbishop] began the verse with some trepidation but finished with piety and zeal, and thus everyone saw that he was truly contrite and had made full confession, and that he had regained the grace of the Holy Spirit which he had formerly lost.[128]

Indeed, the holy fathers utterly condemned simoniacs because, strictly speaking, simony is a sin committed against the Holy Spirit—since a simoniac sells or buys ecclesiastical benefices or the sacraments of the church, both of which are the gifts of the Holy Spirit. Thus, as we read in the Acts of the Apostles, when Simon Magus wished to give money to the apostles in return for the power of giving the Holy Spirit to others as the apostles gave it—namely, by placing his hand upon them—*Peter said to him, May you and your money both be damned, if you imagine that money can purchase the gift of God*.[129] Furthermore, as Saint Ambrose says, simony is a habitual evil, so it must be cut out with a very sharp knife; he also says it is a cancerous evil and therefore a

---

128 *TIE* 4380: Donizo's *Vita Mathildis*, pp. 376–88, quoted in *SD*, fol. 208v. Cf. *GL*, pp. 768–9; *MO*, pp. 467–8.

129 Acts 8.20.

red-hot iron must be used upon it.[130] For as the Decretum says, *all sins are considered as nothing in comparison with the heresy of simony.*[131] And this is said out of horror and revulsion at the offence.

Chapter fifteen: Regarding Conrad, the fifteenth bishop.

The fifteenth bishop, Conrad, took office around the year of the Lord 1084 and completed six years in the episcopate.[132] In the time of this bishop the Hildebrand discussed above was made pope and called Gregory.[133] He convened a synod and excommunicated all the clergy of the western church [who kept] wives and concubines, and totally banned their masses from being heard.[134] Such a scandal arose regarding this matter that no contemporary heresy struck the holy church with more serious schism—to the point that, with Emperor Henry [IV]'s support, the schismatics deposed Gregory and made Archbishop Wibert of Ravenna pope.[135] The Pisans supported the schismatic Wibert with all their might while the Genoese faithfully aided Gregory. The aforesaid Gregory excommunicated Emperor Henry and damned Wibert to perpetual anathema.

Around this time there was a certain rich and powerful man, who as he ate was suddenly surrounded by a great multitude of mice who began to chew and eat him. This multitude of mice always followed him wherever he went, and this happened to no one else. He accordingly boarded a ship and went to sea, but the mice threw themselves into the sea to continue their pursuit of him, and when he returned to land

---

130 Gratian (*Decretum 2*, case 1, question 1, canon 7) cites Ambrose, probably referring to any of several pseudo-Ambrosian tracts against simony that circulated broadly, such as *De dignitate sacerdotali* (*PL* 17.567–80).

131 *Decretum 2* (case 1, question 1, canon 11), citing Gregory of Nazianzus: Gilchrist (1965).

132 Polonio (2002a), pp. 22–3, gives *c.* 1080–*c.* 1087. Both Obertus and Conrad sided with Henry IV against Gregory VII: Conrad participated in the 1080 Council of Brixen (n. 135, below).

133 Pope Gregory VII (1073–85): Cowdrey (1998); Robinson, *Papal reform*.

134 Combating nicolaism—clerical marriage or concubinage—was among the aims of the eleventh-century papal reform: Parish (2010), pp. 87–122.

135 The pro-imperial Council of Brixen in 1080 deposed Gregory and elected Wibert as Clement III (r. 1080–1100, now antipope). Clement was not consecrated, however, until Henry IV's forces took Rome in 1084: Hamilton (2003); Loud (2007), pp. 134–44. On Clement's papacy see Robinson, *Papal reform*, pp. 198–200; Longo/Yawn (2012). On the conflict of empire and papacy more generally, see *NCMH* 4.1, chap. 9 (Robinson); *NCMH* 4.2, chaps. 1 (Blumenthal) and 13 (Robinson); cf. also *MO*, pp. 434, 468.

they immediately ate him up.¹³⁶ Why the mice pursued this man so cruelly, we do not know because the judgments of God are unfathomable. Sometimes God's judgments are clear, and other times they are hidden—but they are always just. Perhaps this rich and powerful man chewed up many others by destroying them with rumour, stealing their goods, or inflicting injuries upon their persons—so as he devoured others alive, it was fitting that he be eaten alive by mice, so the words of the book of Wisdom should be fulfilled: *For by what things a man sins, by the same shall he be tormented.*¹³⁷

Also, we read in the Old Testament that God chose to punish the proud Egyptians by the vilest creatures—a multitude of frogs, mosquitoes, and dogflies—so they would perceive their own inability to withstand these vilest creatures and should recognise their own vileness.¹³⁸ Similarly, perhaps this man proved proud, and God wished to humble his pride by means of these lowliest of creatures. Also, as the book of Wisdom says, God could have sent lions and bears to devour the Egyptians, but he wished to punish them little by little with these vile creatures so that they would have space for repentance.¹³⁹ In the same way God could have sent against this man a lion or a bear who would have devoured him immediately, but instead He chose mice to gnaw at him little by little to give him space for repentance. As we read in the book of Kings, a certain people called Philistines stole the ark of God from the sons of Israel, so God assembled a multitude of mice against them; they gnawed at them and all their belongings so the Philistines were compelled to return the ark.¹⁴⁰ Thus not by lions but by mice—who are the lowliest of creatures—did God choose to punish them and this man, so that they might know their own vileness and have space for repentance.

Also, Saint Augustine recounts how a certain Roman believed it a bad omen when mice gnawed something in his house. One night the mice gnawed his boots, and when he discovered it in the morning, he went to Cato, the wisest of men, to tell him what it meant. But Cato answered him scornfully, saying: 'It is not a marvel if mice have eaten your boots. On the contrary, it would be more astonishing and a worse omen if

---

136 William of Malmesbury, *Gesta regum Anglorum* 3.290; cf. *MO*, p. 468.
137 Wisdom 11.17 (previously cited in part 11.10 n. 94).
138 Exodus 8.1–24.
139 Wisdom 11.18–24.
140 1 Kings 5.1–10.

PART ELEVEN: GENOA UNDER THE BISHOPS   197

your boots had eaten the mice'.[141] Perhaps that man perceived omens in mice just like this Roman, so it was fitting that as a diviner of mice he should be punished by mice.

About the same time, as we read in the chronicles, all the fish in the waters died, while chickens and other domestic birds fled their homes and became wild, and many other portents occurred.[142] But it is hardly surprising if such unnatural things happened because in these times the schismatic Wibert was protected while Gregory—that very holy man—was put to flight.

Chapter sixteen: Regarding Ciriacus, sixteenth bishop. Ciriacus, the sixteenth bishop, took office around the year of the Lord 1090 and completed nine years in the episcopate.[143] In the time of this bishop the aforementioned pope Gregory died and pope Urban suceeeded him.[144] This Urban excommunicated Archbishop Wibert of Ravenna, who had usurped the papacy, and also Emperor Henry, who supported him; [Urban] then fled into France out of fear of the emperor.[145] From there he wrote to the Genoese and sent a legate to Genoa, asking them as devout sons of the church to rescue the Holy Land.[146] And when other communities refused to help, the Genoese armed an equal number of ships and galleys to create a large force, and went to Syria with forty galleys.[147] There they found many pilgrims wearing the cross and many nobles and barons under Godfrey of Bouillon, duke of Lotharingia.

141 Augustine, ridiculing pagan superstition in *On Christian doctrine* 2.20. See also *SD*, fol. 239r–v.
142 Sigebert of Gembloux, *Chronica* 1086, p. 365; Annalista Saxo 1083, p. 471. See also Vincent of Beauvais, *Speculum historiale* 25.82.
143 Ciriacus is not documented in *RC*, which contains no documents between 1087 and 1104 (p. 496), but his episcopacy is believed to have covered *c.* 1090–95: Polonio (2002a), p. 23.
144 In skipping directly to Urban II (1088–99), Jacopo omits Victor III (1086–87).
145 Since Wibert held Rome as Clement III (n. 135, above), Urban used the early years of his papacy to hold a series of councils in northern Italy and France. These included the famous 1095 council at Clermont, at which he preached the First Crusade: Robinson (1990), pp. 17–22, 124–6, 322–33.
146 Here Jacopo jumps directly into the middle of the First Crusade, noting only that the Genoese found many westerners already in the Holy Land when they arrived. On the First Crusade generally, see Phillips (1997) and Asbridge (2004); on the Genoese in the crusading movement, see *CMG*, pp. 471–95 (Mack), and the introduction to *HP*. See also Caffaro, *CGA* for 1099–1102 (pp. 3–14), and *LCO*.
147 According to the *LCO* (p. 102), the Genoese participated in 1097 with twelve galleys and one *sandanum* (on this term, see *HP*, p. 46).

They had all gone to Antioch, seeking to retake it from the Saracens. Then Saint Andrew the Apostle appeared to a faithful and pious man, saying, 'Come, I will show you the lance with which the side of our Lord Jesus Christ was pierced: carry this lance before the army and you will obtain victory'.[148] When this man found the place indicated by the apostle, he considered how to tell the army's leaders and other princes, so he dug in that place and found the lance. Once he had found it, he was certain of victory, so he carried that lance before the army with reverence: and attacking Antioch valiantly, they recovered it from the hands of the Saracens.[149] They also then defeated a great army of Saracens who returned to Antioch and besieged it. Thus, having put the Saracens entirely to flight, the Genoese and other pilgrims returned to their homes in the year of the Lord 1099.[150]

Moreover, when certain Genoese ships returning from the expedition to Antioch stopped at the port of Patara, they went to Myra—'Stramirra' in the vernacular—where the body of Saint Nicholas once lay, where the relics of Saint John the Baptist were also preserved.[151] And taking the aforesaid relics of Saint John the Baptist, the Genoese took them to Genoa.[152] Since the account of these relics' translation says that the pontifical seat of Genoa was then vacant, it seems that the relics were transferred when Ciriacus [was already] dead and Airaldus [was] not yet elected or confirmed, namely in the year of the Lord 1099.[153] But because—God willing—we intend to give special treatment to the translation of the aforesaid relics of Saint John the Baptist, here we have simply outlined a summary of the subject as we intend to portray it.

148 *LCO*, pp. 107–85.
149 Previously discussed in part 5.2, above.
150 *LCO*, p. 111. Cf. *MO*, pp. 435, 468.
151 In 1087 merchants from Bari stole the relics of Saint Nicholas from Myra in Anatolia, supposedly to protect them from destruction by the Turks, brought them home to Bari, and built a grand basilica in the saint's honour (San Nicola, 1087–1197): Otranto (1987), esp. pp. 37–43 (Corsi). On relic theft more generally, see William Purkis' 'Crusaders and their relics' in the forthcoming *Cambridge history of the crusades*. See also *GL*, p. 25; *MO*, p. 434.
152 Since the relics of Saint Nicholas had already been carried off to Bari when the Genoese arrived in Myra, they handily acquired John the Baptist's relics instead: Jacopo, *HLT*, pp. 483–5; also Bertini Guidetti (1997a); Polonio (2000). Scholars have thus far been unable to explain why Caffaro never mentions these relics, an omission lamented already by Giorgio Stella (*Annales genuenses*, p. 19).
153 Cf. *HLT*, p. 485, although Jacopo must mean an earlier account (now lost), since the next sentence suggests that at this point he had not yet written the *HLT*.

For the present it will suffice to say this: that it can be demonstrated in four ways that these relics the Genoese took away from Stramirra were the relics of John the Baptist.[154] In the first place, it is shown by written tradition: for in many ancient legends of Saint Nicholas we read that the aforementioned relics [of Saint John] were preserved there. Secondly, it is shown by oaths: for the monks of the aforesaid church swore to the Genoese that they had learned from the fathers who preceded them that these relics were certainly those of Saint John the Baptist. Thirdly, it is shown through miracles that occurred both while they were transporting [the relics] and after they had been brought [to Genoa]. Fourthly, it is shown by privileges of the Apostolic Seat: for popes Alexander III and Innocent IV confirmed it with privileges in which they announced to diverse provinces that Saint John's relics are at Genoa, exhorted all to come there, and granted indulgences for those who come.[155] Therefore regarding this translation or revelation we have composed both a history and metrical hymns which are chanted solemnly in the church of San Lorenzo.[156]

Chapter seventeen: Regarding Airaldus, seventeenth bishop. Airaldus Guarachus, the seventeenth bishop, took office around the year of the Lord 1099 and completed seventeen years in the episcopate.[157] In the year of his election the Genoese armed forty galleys with which they proceeded to Syria.[158] Along with an army of pilgrims, they then took Jerusalem, Acre, and Gibelet (*Gibellum minor*). In those days they also took Antioch, as we reported above; then they took *Cersona*, Arsuf, and Tartus, and made Godfrey of Bouillon king of Jerusalem.[159] Out of

154 On this paragraph: *HLT*, pp. 482–4.

155 *HLT*, p. 489; cf. *GL*, p. 521. Alexander's privilege was granted in 1179 and Innocent's in 1244: *HLT*; Polonio (2000). Both popes had close ties to Genoa.

156 While the *HLT* survives, the hymns do not.

157 According to Caffaro, Bishop Airaldus (or Airardus) was elected in 1097 or 1098—although not consecrated until 1099—and died in 1116: *GA* 1.93; Polonio (2002a), pp. 24–30. Jacopo does not include Bishop Ogerius (r. 1096–97?), a 'shadow' who is absent from *RC*: Polonio (2002a), pp. 23–4.

158 While based on Caffaro's accounts, this paragraph confuses the Genoese campaigns of the First Crusade and its aftermath: the first campaign of 1097–99 sent twelve galleys to assist in the capture of Antioch (1098) and Jerusalem (1099): *LCO*, pp. 101–11. In 1100–1, twenty-six Genoese galleys assisted in the capture of Arsuf and Caesarea: *CGA*, pp. 4–13; *LCO*, pp. 111–14. Later campaigns assisted with the capture of Tartus in 1102; Acre and Gibelet (now Jubayl) in 1104; and Beirut and Sidon in 1110: *CGA*, pp. 14–15; *LCO*, pp. 118–21; *RIBH*, p. 128. See part 5.2, above, and *CMG*, pp. 471–95 (Mack), esp. pp. 471–7.

159 *Cersona* is unclear: see part 5.2 n. 14, above.

humility, however, Godfrey did not want to wear a golden crown in the place where Christ wore a crown of thorns.[160] In those days the Genoese also took Beirut and Sidon. And it was written in letters of gold on the altar (*troina*) of the Holy Sepulchre how the Genoese had always contributed to these victories and offered their assistance, and also how in those cities the Genoese were accustomed to have many privileges and concessions.[161]

In the time of this bishop [Airaldus], namely in the year of the Lord 1101, an emerald dish (*vas smaragdinum*) commonly called the platter (*scutella*) of Saint Lawrence was brought to Genoa. Let us examine how this dish was found and brought to Genoa: in the year of the Lord 1100, twenty-six Genoese galleys and six ships sailed to Syria, where they remained for a full year.[162] When they discovered that Godfrey, king of Jerusalem, had died, all the Christians elected his brother Baldwin king.[163] Then the aforesaid Baldwin and an army of the Genoese, Franks, and other Christians who were in those parts boldly advanced to the Saracen city of Caesarea; they besieged it forcefully and captured it triumphantly. The Genoese also sailed to the port of Jaffa and pulled their galleys up on land, arriving at Caesarea with King Baldwin as well as Daimbert, patriarch of Jerusalem, and the entire army of Christians. Then Patriarch Daimbert advised them that on the following day they should all make confession and receive communion, and when this was done, they should scale the walls of the city. A Genoese consul by the name of William the Hammer (*Guillelmus Malii*) put the ladder from his galley up against the wall and with the [men] from his galley he began to climb.[164] As the ladder was quickly broken, the consul was left alone on the wall, but virtually all the Saracens had now abandoned the first wall and retreated to the second. So the consul went into one of the towers along the wall and called out boldly: 'Climb up, climb up, for the city is ours!' They climbed up and attacked the second wall, and

---

160 *RIBH*, p. 127.
161 *LCO*, pp. 113–14 (with image), 121–2; also *RIBH*, p. 129. On the Golden Inscription see *HP*, pp. 24–6, 173–6; also the summary in *CMG*, pp. 475–6 (Mack).
162 This paragraph summarises *CGA*, pp. 5, 9–13; *LCO*, pp. 112–13, 117. Cf. William of Tyre, *Chronicle* 10.15 (*CCCM* 63.471–2).
163 Godfrey's title was most likely 'prince and advocate': Murray (1990).
164 The leader of the Genoese force, consul Guglielmo Embriaco—known as 'Hammerhead' (Latin *Caputmallei* or Italian *Testa di Maglio*)—is considered the greatest Genoese hero of the First Crusade: *CMG*, pp. 474–5; Pessa (2016). (*Consul* here denotes a military appointment rather than a political office.)

with the help of a certain branch that was leaning against the wall they climbed that wall and thus they took the city. The patriarch and another legate of the apostolic seat who was there consecrated the larger mosque in honour of Saint Peter the apostle, and the other in honour of Saint Lawrence.

In the aforesaid city was this dish of rare emerald [stone] and inestimable price.[165] So once the aforesaid [Christians] had captured the city, they decided by common consent to divide all that they had taken into three shares. To the first share they assigned this aforementioned emerald dish. To the second share they assigned the bulk of the city with all its immovable goods. To the third share they ascribed all the city's treasure and all its movable goods, and they decreed that since the Genoese had played the largest part in the city's capture, they should receive the share which they preferred most, King Baldwin should take one of the two remaining shares, and the entire rest of the army should have the remainder. Thus the Genoese refused the other two shares and claimed the emerald dish as their share, and they carried it back to Genoa with much rejoicing.[166]

That the dish is very truly of emerald stone has been attested by all the jewelers (*gemmarii*) who have seen it, who have confessed that they have never seen such precious emerald. And it is demonstrated by the fact that at Caesarea it was assessed to be of such great value that it was considered equivalent to either the entire city or the city's entire treasury. For how likely is it that this emerald stone could by itself be considered equivalent to the value of an entire city or the entire treasury of a city, unless [the crusaders] themselves had established for a certainty that it was the very truest emerald? For the aforementioned emerald stone is of such brilliance and marvelous clarity that all other emeralds and precious stones, when placed next to it, fall short of its brilliance and pale before its great splendour and clarity. Just as all the stars of the heavens are obscured by the arrival of the light of the sun, so all

---

165 On emeralds: Isidore, *Etymologies* 16.7.1.
166 William of Tyre, *Chronicle* 10.15 (*CCCM* 63.471), claims the Genoese paid 'a great sum of money' for the dish rather than choosing it as their share of the spoils, a claim confirmed by *CGA* (p. 13). Of the spoils assigned to the Genoese, first the individual rewards due the ship-captains, consuls, and noblemen were distributed, then the galley crews received 15 percent of the remainder, while 85 percent was divided among the eight thousand infantry, each of whom received forty-eight silver *solidi* and two pounds of peppercorns (a commodity often used as currency).

other precious stones are eclipsed in the presence of this stone due to its brilliance.

Furthermore, this dish was made in the shape of a platter (*chatinus*), for which reason it is commonly said that this was the platter out of which Christ ate during supper with his disciples, because Christ said, *he who puts his hand with me into this platter will betray me*.[167] We do not know whether this is true—because nothing is impossible with God, we neither assert it absolutely nor deny it obstinately. Thus anyone who wishes to believe it must not be argued with out of fun, and anyone who does not wish to believe it must not be reproved out of rashness.

Some object strongly, however, arguing that in all His deeds Christ always presented an example of the greatest humility, and that in eating out of so precious an emerald dish he would not have seemed an example of humility but one of considerable vanity. We may rebut this reasoning easily, however. It is certainly true that to eat everyday food out of an emerald dish would represent a kind of vanity or pomposity. But the paschal and sacramental lamb which Christ ate at dinner with his disciples—to eat such a paschal lamb out of a gold or emerald dish, I affirm, would not be pomposity but piety and great reverence. For that lamb roasted in the fire represented Christ, who was a lamb by reason of his innocence and 'roasted' by his cruel punishment on the cross. For this reason—just as today it does not demonstrate arrogance to take the sacrament of Christ's body and blood from a chalice of gold or emerald, but piety and great reverence—so it would not then have been a sign of vanity to eat that paschal and sacramental lamb out of a gold or emerald dish, but an example of divine reverence and devotion.

Also, we must not pass over in silence that in certain books of the English it is reported that when Nicodemus took Christ's body down from the cross, he collected His blood—which was still fresh and had been dishonourably splashed about—in a certain emerald dish which had been divinely prepared for him by God. And the English in their books call this dish the Holy Grail (*Sangraal*).[168] Nicodemus preserved this dish for a long time with great reverence, but with the passing of time it was moved to Caesarea and taken from there to Genoa. Therefore it was right that this dish—in which the precious treasure of the blood of Jesus Christ was meant to be collected—should itself be precious.

---

167 Matthew 23.26 (which calls the dish a *parapsis*) conflated with Mark 14.20 (which uses the term *catinus*).

168 Helinand of Froidmont, *Chronica* 45 for 718 (*PL* 212.814–15); cf. part 8.3 n. 78.

For just as nothing visible or created can be considered the equal of the precious blood of Christ, so it was appropriate that it should be collected in a dish so precious that nothing could be found anywhere of equal or similar preciousness.

Also, we intend to demonstrate by a two-part argument that this dish was not made by human artifice but produced by divine power (*virtus*). One argument is that if it had been created by human artifice, this would suggest that many other similar things should have been created in the world at some point. But from the beginning of the world up to now no similar item has been discovered in all the lands of the earth.

We may advance another argument to prove this more forcefully: it is certain that that which nature produces is more perfect than that which human artifice produces. And that which divine power produces miraculously is more perfect than anything which human artifice or nature can produce. Thus we may say, for example, that those stones which are called 'precious' may be created in three ways: first, by human artifice, since the most skillful jewelers know by their art how to decorate glass or crystal so subtly and artfully that they seem to be precious stones. But such precious stones have neither perfection nor truth, only the appearance of truth. Secondly, precious stones can be created by nature, just as we see that precious stones are generated in the bowels of the earth and by the power of the sun's rays: such stones as these have some truth, but they do not have total perfection, because there is no stone so precious—that is, so brilliant and well-crafted—that it could not display even greater shine and artifice.[169] Thirdly, precious stones can be made miraculously and by divine power—as we read in Saint John the Evangelist, who had stones from the seashore brought to him, which he converted into gems and precious stones.[170] These precious stones contained both truth and total perfection, for no jeweler could have claimed that any of these stones was lacking in brilliance or beauty. Therefore we assert that if all the jewelers in the world agree amongst themselves and maintain publicly that this dish [is] emerald, that it is of such perfection in its material, form, brilliance, and artifice, that no one can claim that either its brilliance or artifice could be increased, nor that it could be improved in some other way. From this it seems clear that the dish was not the work of nature, nor of human artifice—because such works are imperfect—but rather that it was

---

169 On precious stones, see Albertus Magnus' *Book of minerals*.
170 Isidore, *De ortu et obitu patriarcharum* 71.3; cited in *GL*, p. 55.

created by divine power, because things made in this way are fully perfect to the point that neither nature nor human artifice can add anything to their perfection.

And in the time of this same bishop [Airaldus], in the year of the Lord 1113, the Genoese built the fortress at Portovenere (*Portus Venerii*), which is often written corruptly and referred to incorrectly when it is called the Port of Venus (*Portus Veneris*).[171] For it must have been called *Portus Venerii* after a certain saint called Venerius whose body lies near there on the island of Tino. It used to be called 'port of the moon' (*Portus Lune*), after the port city of Luni that was recently destroyed, but after this saint's body was brought there it was renamed Portovenere.

Also in that time the currency of those pennies which are called *bruni* was invented; before that Genoese citizens used the coins of Pavia.[172]

In the time of this bishop the Genoese took Cagliari and restored it to its lord, who was called Marianus; he promised loyalty to the commune of Genoa and vowed to give one pound of gold to the Genoese church every year as a sign of his obligation.[173] And Pope Paschal confirmed this by his own privilege.[174]

Also in the time of this bishop flourished the holy Bernard, abbot of Clairvaux, a man noble in ancestry, distinguished in knowledge, and outstanding in holiness.[175] Upon the death of Airaldus this distinguished scholar (*doctor precipuus*) Bernard was elected to the Genoese episcopate.[176] When the official messengers sent from Genoa presented him with the decree of his election, he neither consented nor refused, saying that he was not subject only to his own law, but to the order of the supreme pontiff. Thus the Genoese sent to the supreme pontiff for confirmation,

---

171 *CGA*, p. 15. The fortress was meant to defend communal interests against both the local nobility and Pisan expansionism: Guglielmotti (2005), pp. 43–6. Portovenere's name is actually ancient, significantly predating the sixth- or seventh-century Saint Venerius of Tino: *AASS* 44 (13 September, vol. 4), pp. 108–20. On the relationship between Luni and Portovenere, see part 10.2 n. 21.

172 *CGA*, pp. 13, 16. Technically all of these were 'coins of Pavia'; Jacopo refers here to the 1115 depreciation of Pavian *bruni* to *bruneti*: *HP*, p. 48. On the Genoese coinage, see part 12.1 n. 17.

173 In 1107 the ruler or 'judge' (*iudex*) of Cagliari, on Sardinia, gave six estates (*donnicalie*) to the cathedral of San Lorenzo in return for Genoese military assistance: *Liber privilegiorum*, docs. 33–4, pp. 49–53; *CMG*, pp. 501–2 (Origone).

174 Paschal II (1099–1118).

175 Saint Bernard, Cistercian abbot of Clairvaux (1090–1153).

176 This claim does not appear in Caffaro's work.

but the supreme pontiff did not wish to assent since [Bernard] was extremely useful and necessary to the church at large. Then this Bernard sent a beautiful letter full of love for the Genoese in which he commended them for their great faith, their great devotion to the church, and their works of piety, exhorting them that they must persevere in these things even to the end. He concluded in this manner: 'Hold fast to perseverance, so that obedience does not expect payment; nor service, thanks; nor fortitude, praise'.[177]

Chapter eighteen: Regarding Otto, the eighteenth bishop. The eighteenth bishop, Otto, took office around the year of the Lord 1117 and completed three years in the episcopate, and after his death the episcopate was vacant for three years.[178] He had been born of the royal line of France, and was previously abbot of Saint-Victor at Marseilles.[179]

In the second year of his episcopate the body of Saint Syrus was moved from its place at the gates to the choir of San Lorenzo and placed with great reverence beneath the altar of that same martyr. In that same year, Pope Gelasius was present at Genoa, and solemnly consecrated the church of San Lorenzo in the presence of the bishops of Piacenza, Asti, Acqui, and many other prelates.[180] This pope endowed the church through many indulgences and supported it through privileges. We have been unable to find in any written source [details of] the time in which this church of San Lorenzo was built, or who first constructed it—but we know for certain that it had already been built in the time of Bishop Sabatinus, who was the third bishop from Saint Syrus, because

177 The idea of Bernard's election to the Genoese episcopate probably derives from his letter 129 to the Genoese, which was probably written 1132–33: *Opera* 7.322–4; trans. James (1998) as letter 131, pp. 200–1. The Genoese made Bernard an official patron of Genoa in 1625. Cf. *CGA*, p. 26 (which mentions the truce); *GL*, pp. 484–93, at p. 489 (which repeats the claim about his election).

178 1117–20, with a *sede vacante* (empty seat) from 1120–23: Polonio (2002a), pp. 30–1. Cf. *CGA*, p. 93; *RC*, p. 56.

179 The late Roman abbey of Saint-Victor in Marseilles was refounded as a Benedictine house *c.* 1000 and rose to great prominence. The *Chronique de Saint-Victor* records that 'abbot Oddo, surnamed Alamannus, ruled as abbot for five years, and was afterward made bishop of Genoa' (p. 317), but incorrectly records his death as 1099; Otto also appears as abbot in Saint-Victor's cartulary in 1112–13 (*Cartulaire*, 1.xxv). Jacopo's claim of Otto's royal descent is not otherwise substantiated.

180 Pope Gelasius II (1118–19), who was in Genoa approximately 5–20 October 1118; see *Liber privilegiorum*, doc. 1 (pp. 3–4); *CGA*, p. 16. The pope's attendants on that occasion were Aldo, bishop of Piacenza, Landulf, bishop of Asti, and Azzo, bishop of Acqui: Cambiaso (1918), pp. 100–1; Di Fabio/Besta (1998), pp. 51–4; Calderoni Masetti/Wolf (2012), pp. 41–5.

we read in the legend of Saint Romulus and in the register of our [archiepiscopal] palace that this Sabatinus moved the body of Saint Romulus from Villa Matuciana and settled it honourably under the altar of San Lorenzo.[181] If the church of San Lorenzo already existed in Sabatinus' time, it is therefore very likely that it already existed in Saint Syrus' time, since between Saint Syrus and Sabatinus there was only Saint Romulus.[182] But the body of Saint Syrus was not buried in the church of San Lorenzo because it was not yet the episcopal seat: rather, Syrus was laid in the basilica of the Twelve Apostles, which today is called the monastery of San Siro [Saint Syrus].

We maintain furthermore that a work so sumptuous as the noble church of San Lorenzo [fig. 5] was created by the commune of Genoa rather than by any particular person.[183] This church of San Lorenzo is of great sanctity, dignity, and authority. Indeed, it is of such sanctity that many bodies of saints are preserved there—namely, the bodies of Saint John the Baptist and of Saints Syrus, Felix, and Romulus. Also, there are three crosses there which hold a great portion of the wood of the True Cross, along with many other precious relics which it would take a long time to describe.[184] Moreover, this church is of such dignity that it has produced many cardinals and supreme pontiffs, especially the lord Innocent IV and the lord Adrian [V], who both descended from the counts of Lavagna.[185] And it is of such authority that it obtained sovereignty as metropolitan of its entire province.

The reason that the aforesaid Pope Gelasius came to Genoa was this: he, Gelasius, had been elected without the consent of the emperor, and

---

181 *RC*, p. 424; *Codice diplomatico* 1.4–6 (doc. 2); see also part 11.2–5, above.

182 As discussed earlier in part 11, there were certainly other bishops between the protobishop Syrus and the ninth-century bishop Sabatinus. The existence of San Lorenzo is first attested with Sabatinus' translation of the relics of Saint Romulus into it in the late ninth century: *AASS* 54 (13 October, vol. 6), p. 209; Polonio (2002a), pp. 15–16; Poleggi/Grossi Bianchi (1980), p. 38.

183 An important point given Jacopo's civic agenda in writing his *Chronicle*; furthermore, not inaccurate given the commune's financial support of the cathedral. A communal decree dated 1140, for example, assigns some of the annual profits from the Genoese mint to San Lorenzo 'for the execution of works': *Codice diplomatico* 1.121–3 (doc. 102).

184 The cross of the patriarch of Jerusalem, the cross of Saint Helena, and the cross of the hospital of Saint Lazarus, all described in *RIBH* (pp. 140–2); see Bertini Guidetti (1997a), pp. 179–80.

185 Sinibaldo Fieschi (Innocent IV, 1243–54) and Ottobuono Fieschi (Adrian V, 1276). The prominent Fieschi family were the hereditary counts of Lavagna, in the Riviera di Levante. Both are discussed further below.

PART ELEVEN: GENOA UNDER THE BISHOPS

he did not wish to apply to him for consent. The emperor was annoyed by this and named a certain Spaniard by the name of Burdinus to the papal seat, calling him Benedict.[186] Fearing the emperor, Pope Gelasius went with his cardinals to Gaeta and sent a legate from there to Genoa, asking the Genoese to send galleys with which he could come to Genoa and from there travel into France. The Genoese immediately armed their galleys and brought Pope Gelasius to Genoa with joy. The Pisans, to the contrary, favoured the emperor and opposed Pope Gelasius in all things.

But this emperor's anger with Pope Gelasius was unjust and irrational, because the emperor has no law above him but the supreme pontiff; conversely, the highest pontiff exercises much jurisdiction over the emperor, because he first considers the man who has been elected and then confirms the man whom he has so considered. This is why the emperor is crowned with three crowns: first he is crowned king of Germany with the silver crown at Aachen. Second, he is crowned king of Italy with the iron crown at Monza, in the county of Milan. Thirdly, he is crowned emperor of the Romans with the gold crown at Rome by the supreme pontiff.

Thus it is the pope who has jurisdiction over the emperor, not the emperor over the pope. For God made two great lights in the firmament of heaven: the greater light to rule the day and the lesser light to rule the night.[187] Similarly, in the firmament of heaven that is the universal church, God [also] made two great lights, because he instituted there two authorities which are the pontifical authority and the royal or imperial power.[188] But that which rules the days—that is, spiritual matters—is the greater. And that which rules the nights—that is, earthly matters—is the lesser. Thus as much difference as we recognise between the sun and the moon, so great is the difference between the supreme pontiff and the emperor. Just as the moon contributes nothing to the sun while the sun pours out all its light upon the moon, so the emperor has no authority over the supreme pontiff but the supreme pontiff exercises much jurisdiction over the emperor. As the Apostle says, *the spiritual*

---

186 Maurice Bourdin (or Burdinus)—French, but archbishop of Braga, Portugal—crowned Henry V emperor in Rome in 1117. Henry then had him elected pope in 1118, although he took the name not of Benedict but of Gregory VIII (now antipope). He was deposed in 1121 and died in confinement in 1137: Anselm of Gembloux, continuation of Sigebert of Gembloux, *Chronica* 1118, p. 377; *MO*, pp. 435, 469.

187 Genesis 1.16; Lee (2018), chap. 6, esp. p. 247. Cf. *SS*, fol. 253r; *Mariale* 81/L8 (*luna*), p. 247.

188 Vincent of Beauvais, *Speculum doctrinale* 7.32.2; *MO*, p. 407.

*man judges all things, and he himself is judged by no one.*¹⁸⁹ Also, not only does the pope have [the right] to evaluate the election of an emperor, to confirm and crown him, but also in the event of his fault and disobedience he may depose him from the emperorship, as a certain pope named Gregory deposed Emperor Leo who had the images of Christ and all the saints burned everywhere.¹⁹⁰ Likewise, Innocent III deposed Otto [IV] when he violated the laws of the church, and Innocent IV deposed that Frederick [II] who exercised tyranny against the church.¹⁹¹

Furthermore, since we have mentioned the empire we must also note that the imperial seat and the right of empire lay first with the Romans and remained among them for 351 years, from the time of the first emperor Octavian until the age of Constantine.¹⁹² After Constantine was baptised and cured by the blessed Sylvester, he conceded the seat of the western empire with all its imperial dignities to Saint Sylvester and his successors.¹⁹³ He built Constantinople in the image of Rome, and went into Greece and called it Romania, which was a kind of new Rome, and he chose to locate his imperial seat there. The seat and the right of empire then remained among the Greeks for 460 years, from the first Constantine up to Charles the Great.¹⁹⁴ For that was when the empire was first divided between Greeks and Latins, and multiple emperors were created: one among the Greeks who was called the Constantinopolitan emperor, and the other among the Latins who was called the Roman emperor.¹⁹⁵ Thus the right of empire was transferred via Charles to the Franks, and they held it for one hundred years until a certain emperor by the name of Ludovicus, of Frankish descent and from Charles's line, died without heirs.¹⁹⁶ Then the Germans elected a

---

189 1 Corinthians 2.15.

190 Part 11.6, above.

191 November 1210 and July 1245 respectively; see part 12.4–5, below.

192 Fairly accurate, depending on the dates chosen: for example, from 27 BC, in which Octavian adopted the title of 'Augustus', to AD 330, when Constantine moved the imperial capital to Constantinople, is 357 years. See the similar discussion in part 11.9.

193 The so-called *Donation of Constantine*; see Noble (1984), pp. 134–7, and *GL*, pp. 64–5. A foundational document for politics and political thought in the European Middle Ages, it was only in the fifteenth century recognised as a forgery (probably from the eighth century).

194 470 years, if counting from 330 to 800 (the year of Charlemagne's imperial coronation in Rome).

195 Jacopo here claims for the west the venerable title of 'Roman emperor' against similar Byzantine claims; cf. *GL*, p. 763.

196 Louis 'the Child', the last Carolingian king of East Francia, died in 911 and was succeeded by Conrad I (r. 911–18): presumably these are the Ludovicus and Conrad

certain German named Conrad as king of Germany, whom the pope later crowned emperor. In this way the right of empire was transferred to the Germans around the year of the Lord 930, and they hold it to the present day.

In the time of Bishop Otto—specifically, in the year of the Lord 1120—a serious war between the Genoese and the Pisans began.[197] The Genoese armed eighty galleys, thirty-five cats (*gatae*[198]), and ships carrying [war] machines; there were rumoured to be two thousand men in the entire force. They arrived at Pisa via the Arno River, and so overcame the Pisans' army that in the month of September, on the feast of Saints Cornelius and Cyprian [16 September], the Pisans swore peace regarding the quarrel over Corsica according to the terms set by the commune of Genoa. They were later faithless in upholding that peace, however, so the Genoese destroyed Piombino.[199] Also, the following year the Genoese crossed the ridge [of the Apennines] with a great army of knights and infantry and took in battle Fiaccone, Pietrabissaria, and certain other fortresses, while they bought the fortress of Voltaggio from Alberto, marquess (*marchio*[200]) of Gavi.[201]

Chapter nineteen: Regarding Sigefredus, nineteenth bishop. Sigefredus, the nineteenth bishop, took office around the year of the Lord 1123 and completed six years in the episcopate, after which the episcopate was vacant for one year.[202]

---

mentioned. Conrad, however, was never emperor: during his reign the imperial crown was contested between Louis 'the Blind', king of Provence, and Berengar I, king of Italy. The imperial throne was then vacant from 924 until the coronation of Otto I in 962 (Otto had acceded to the German throne in 936, which may be the source for Jacopo's 930 date). See *NCMH* 3, esp. chaps. 9 (Müller-Mertens) and 14 (Sergi).

197 Part 5.2, above; cf. *CGA*, pp. 16–17.

198 The word *gata* or *gatha* appears in numerous medieval sources (see Du Cange, *Glossarium*, both *gatus*[1] and *gatus*[2]), but its origin and meaning remain obscure. When used in contexts such as this (Du Cange's *gatus*[1]), it indicates a type of ship (see introduction to *HP*, p. 46), and Pryor (2008), p. 133, connects it with the Arabic *qiṭ'a*, suggesting a large galley. Yet in other contexts (e.g. part 12.1, below) it suggests a form of siege machine (Du Cange's *gatus*[2]).

199 1125, when the annalist Caffaro himself was present: *CGA*, pp. 21–3.

200 The Latin term *marchio* is difficult to render in English, as its modern cognates—French *marquis*, Germanic 'margrave', and Italian *marchese*—all have cultural implications dating from much later centuries. I have therefore used the relatively rare English term 'marquess': *CMG*, pp. xix–xx.

201 *CGA*, p. 17. The Genoese paid four hundred *librae* (pounds) for the fort of Voltaggio.

202 Polonio (2002a), p. 31–2. Cf. Caffaro, *Notitia episcoporum ianuensium* (*GA* 1.93); *RC*, pp. 496–9.

In the time of this bishop the pope was Calixtus, who excommunicated the Pisans as rebels against the church. He also convened a synod where he pronounced judgment that the Pisan archbishop should not involve himself in any way with the consecrations of bishops on Corsica, and he removed all the churches of the island of Corsica from that archbishop's jurisdiction.[203]

In the year of the Lord 1124 twenty-two Pisan ships laden with much merchandise, accompanied by nine galleys for their protection, were coming from Sardinia when seven galleys of the Genoese pursued them. Seeing this, the Pisan galleys immediately fled in terror. So the Genoese galleys took the [Pisan] ships and brought them to Genoa, to the surprise and amazement of all at such a capture and an unheard-of victory.[204]

Also in the time of this bishop, in the year of the Lord 1125, another destructive war between the Genoese and the Pisans began; for this reason the Genoese armed eighty galleys, thirty-five cats (*gatae*), and four ships carrying [war] machines, and invaded Porto Pisano by force.[205] They then proceeded up the Arno to the city, where they set up their standards and their tents, and crushed the Pisan army on land. When the Pisans promised that they would do everything the Genoese wanted, the Genoese hastened to the prisons to release their imprisoned [compatriots], and took them with them. Then they took the fortress of Piombino, destroyed it utterly, and took its men, women, and children back to Genoa.[206]

The aforesaid Pope Calixtus finally made peace with the emperor. At Sutri he besieged the Spaniard Burdinus, who had usurped the papacy; having captured him, he mounted him on a camel facing backward, holding its tail in his hand as a rein and wearing the skin of a castrated sheep as a cloak. In this fashion he made Burdinus go all the way to

---

203 The First Lateran Council of 1123, during which Calixtus II (1119–24) issued the bull *Quot mutationes* revoking the concessions his predecessor Gelasius II had granted to the Pisans: Jaffé (1885), no. 7056, published as Imperiale di Sant'Angelo (1894), appendix 21, pp. 384–7. The council is narrated with great drama by Caffaro, who was present as a Genoese ambassador: *CGA*, pp. 18–20.

204 *CGA*, pp. 21–2.

205 *CGA*, p. 16; on *gatae*, n. 198 above.

206 Here Jacopo confuses two separate conflicts with the Pisans: the eighty galleys that sailed up the Arno pertain to the conflict of 1120 (*CGA*, pp. 16–17, just reported in part 11.18), but the destruction of Piombino pertains to that of 1125 (*CGA*, pp. 22–3).

Rome and shut him up in prison, where he finished his life.[207] We do not believe, however, that such a severe punishment pleased God, for woe to us if God avenges our own sins so severely! A judge ought to punish crimes, but he must nevertheless be mindful of mercy in that punishment, according to the prophet's words regarding God: *Even when you are angry, you will remember mercy.*[208] For although too great mercy may be foolish and too severe punishment may be cruel, it is nonetheless more prudent to render judgment with too much mercy than with too severe punishment.

In the time of this bishop Sigefredus, again in the year of the Lord 1125, the church of San Matteo was built by the noble man Martino Doria with the authority and permission of the lord pope Honorius [II], who had succeeded Calixtus.[209] More recently, in the year of the Lord 1278 the noble men of the Doria tore down that older church and built a more beautiful one in place of the former.[210] But an extremely beautiful image of Christ had been displayed from ancient times on the altar of the church, and they grieved at the notion of destroying such an image; such was their ingenuity that they removed the altar whole and saved it, lifting it with the strength of twenty-five men. Then they permanently relocated it to the [new] foundation, where it remains today.

In the year of the Lord 1129 the Genoese armed eighteen galleys against the Pisans, and went seeking them as far as Messina, but when the townspeople there aided the Pisans, the Genoese chased both the Pisans and the townspeople out of the town of Messina as far as the royal palace. They also captured there a ship laden with precious merchandise and brought it back to Genoa.[211]

---

207 On Burdinus (antipope Gregory VIII), see n. 186, above.

208 Habakkuk 3.2.

209 San Matteo served as the 'family church' for the noble Genoese Doria family: *CMG*, pp. 231–7. Martino Doria later became a Benedictine monk at San Fruttuoso del Capodimonte, an isolated foundation along the Riviera closely linked to both San Matteo and the Doria family; see *DGA*, p. 54.

210 In 1278 the twelfth-century edifice was torn down and moved backward (east) to create a larger piazza: *CMG*, pp. 231–7, and Gorse (1988).

211 *CGA*, p. 24.

PART TWELVE: THE HISTORY OF GENOA UNDER THE ARCHBISHOPS

Here follows part twelve, which contains the names, dates, and orders of all the archbishops who have presided in the city of Genoa up to our own time; this part has as many chapters [eight] as there are names of archbishops. Let us therefore lay out the names and dates of these archbishops in order.

Chapter one: Regarding Siro, last bishop and first archbishop.[1]
Siro, the last bishop and first archbishop, took office in the year of the Lord 1130 and completed thirty-three years in the episcopate and the archiepiscopate.[2] This Siro was first a cardinal; since Pope Innocent II was at Genoa while the episcopal seat was vacant, he consecrated [Siro] bishop of Genoa as the aforesaid Innocent was being transported by the Genoese into France.[3] And when [Innocent] returned to Genoa, he promised to give it an archbishopric for the great services he had received from the Genoese; and although the said Innocent had been expelled [from Rome] by the Romans, with the help of the Genoese he was restored to his seat (*cathedra*).[4] On his way to Rome, he also consecrated the church at Portovenere.[5] After he was restored to his seat, Innocent went to Corneto and there negotiated a peace between the Genoese and the Pisans.[6] While he was there, he sent for bishop Siro

---

1 Bishops' names in part 11 appear in Latin or their English equivalents (Valentine, Obertus) while archbishops' names in part 12 appear in Italian (Siro, Jacopo); while not fully satisfactory, this seems to provide the best balance between accessibility and correlation with existing scholarship.

2 Bishop 1130–33 and archbishop 1133–63: *RC*, pp. 15, 276; *CGA*, pp. 25–7, 75, 93; Polonio (2002a), pp. 31–3, 55–8, 126–7. Siro was an indefatigable advocate for the Genoese church and the (archi)episcopate, although Jacopo is the only author who reports that he was a cardinal.

3 Innocent II (1130–43), a member of the Roman Papareschi family, was forced to flee Rome shortly after his election when a group of cardinals declared his election invalid and elected Anacletus II (1130–38) from the rival Pierleoni family. En route to France via Genoa, Innocent presided over Siro's episcopal election and consecration: *CGA*, pp. 25–6.

4 As support for Anacletus ebbed, Innocent reclaimed the papal *cathedra* in 1133: *CGA*, p. 27.

5 1130: *CGA*, p. 26.

6 Negotiated by Bernard of Clairvaux: part 11.17, above.

PART TWELVE: GENOA UNDER THE ARCHBISHOPS   213

of Genoa, made him archbishop, and gave him the archiepiscopal insignia in the year of the Lord 1133.[7] He assigned Siro three bishoprics on the island of Corsica—Mariana, Nebbio, and Accia—while also giving him two bishops from these parts as suffragans, namely Bobbio and Brugnato.[8] Later Alexander III placed the bishop of Albenga under the archbishop of Genoa, while Innocent IV placed that of Noli under him.[9]

In the time of this archbishop, namely in the year of the Lord 1134, eight districts (*compagnie*) were established in Genoa, where earlier there had been only seven.[10] Also, this Archbishop Siro gave to the monastery of San Benigno of Fruttuaria the church of San Benigno Capodifaro—originally called the church of Saint Paul—with the stipulation that the abbot must always be chosen or deposed with the archbishop's advice and consent, and that the archbishop should be able to correct and transfer its monks.[11] All these things were confirmed by a privilege of the lord pope Innocent II.[12]

In the year of the Lord 1135 twelve Genoese galleys went to Bugia and captured many Saracens there.[13] Also, they captured a large and rich ship there and brought it to Genoa. It is said that each of those galleys carried seven hundred pounds of the coin and treasure that had been found there.[14]

---

7 At Grosseto, 20 March 1133: *CGA*, pp. 26–7; *HP*, p. 64 n. 69. The bull is Innocent II, *Epistolae et privilegia* (*PL* 179.9–732, at cols. 174–6), or *Libri iurium* 1/2, pp. 12–16 (no. 282). The insignia of an archbishop include the crosier or processional cross, the mitre, the archiepiscopal ring, and the pallium, a ceremonial garment signifying papal appointment (a circular band around the shoulders with long strips hanging down at front and back).

8 Mariana, Nebbio, and Accia were bishoprics on Corsica while Bobbio and Brugnato were bishoprics on the mainland: part 10.2, above. As Bertini Guidetti notes (*CCG*, p. 290 n. 494), from this moment onward Jacopo relies not only on the *GA* but also on the archiepiscopal registers (*RC*, *RC2*).

9 Also discussed in parts 10.2 and 12.2.

10 *CGA*, pp. 24–7; Epstein (1996), p. 33.

11 The reform abbey of Fruttuaria, north of Turin, had been founded by William of Volpiano in 1003.

12 29 October 1142: *RC2*, pp. 388–9.

13 Present-day Béjaïa, Algeria.

14 According to Caffaro, this campaign occurred in 1136: *CGA*, p. 28. The campaign also gained the Genoese a fondaco in Bugia. A fondaco (Latin *fundicum*, a westernisation of the Arabic *funduq*) was a building belonging to a merchant community abroad for the storage and sale of goods, i.e. a warehouse, but it often served as an inn and/or embassy. As a first foothold in northern Africa, the fondaco in Bugia substantially increased Genoese access to Muslim markets.

Also, in the year of the Lord 1143 four Genoese galleys captured Montpellier and returned it to William of Montpellier, to whom it belonged by law. This William then allowed the Genoese to travel freely throughout his entire land, exempted them from all tolls, and granted them the fondaco (*fundicum*) of Bruno of Toulouse.[15]

In the time of this archbishop, in the year of the Lord 1139, the coins called *bruneti* then circulating at Genoa were stopped, and the German king Conrad—recently elected emperor—granted to the Genoese the right of making *genovini* (Latin *ianuini*), which are used even today, and he presented this privilege to them with a golden bull.[16] For first in Genoa coins of Pavia (*pavesini*) were used; then *bruni*; then *bruneti*, which were smaller than *bruni*; and lastly *genovini*, which are used now.[17]

In the year of the Lord 1140 the people of Ventimiglia rebelled, so the Genoese went there with a great army of infantry, cavalry, and sailors. They besieged the city by both sea and land, took it by force, and made those in both the city and the surrounding area swear perpetual loyalty to the Genoese.[18]

In the year of the Lord 1146 the Genoese armed twenty-six galleys and many ships carrying [war] machines, with one hundred knights and their warhorses. Then they went to Minorca and besieged it for twenty-two days. But then as winter was arriving they returned to Genoa with many spoils. They sailed around the entire island seizing lands, killing Saracens, and carrying off spoils.[19]

In the year of the Lord 1148, when Saracens from Almería were inflicting many damages on Christians, at the request of the supreme pontiff [Eugenius III] the Genoese armed sixty-four galleys along with 163

---

15 *CGA*, pp. 31–2; *Codice diplomatico* 1.148 (no. 125).

16 Conrad III Hohenstaufen, king of Germany 1138–51. Due to struggles between Conrad and the house of Welf (heirs of emperor Lothar II, d. 1137), Conrad was never crowned emperor.

17 *CGA*, p. 29. The Genoese mint began operations in 1139 with coins based on those of Pavia (part 11.17 n. 172, above): Day/Matzke/Saccocci (2016), pp. 254–5. For Conrad's diploma: *Codice diplomatico* 1.106–7 (doc. 86); *Libri iurium* 1/2, pp. 16–18 (no. 283); or *MGH DD KIII* 9.24–5 (doc. 15).

18 *CGA*, p. 30.

19 An expedition to the Balearic islands, at that time part of the Muslim Almoravid empire (based in Morocco), a key preliminary to the later campaigns against Almería and Tortosa. This initial expedition was led by Caffaro himself, who was then consul: from Minorca the Genoese went to Almería, where they extracted a large sum from its inhabitants: *CGA*, pp. 33–5.

ships and other boats; having prepared all things necessary for war, they set out for Almería.[20] The count of Barcelona came to their assistance with many of his people. Then the Genoese pulled their galleys up on shore at Almería; they put together their machines (*machinae*), cats (*gathae*[21]), and siege engines (*castella*), and approached the city. After many skirmishes and much spilled blood, the Genoese finally gained the victory: on the twentieth day a thousand of the Saracens were killed and ten thousand—among them boys, men, and women—were taken back to Genoa. Thus, with victory won, the Genoese went with their galleys and ships to Barcelona, where they pulled their galleys and ships up on land, and spent the winter.

Refitting their galleys and ships and preparing all things necessary for war, they went with the count of Barcelona to Tortosa, and on the first of July they entered the river at Tortosa with their whole army. Setting up their tents on the ground, raising their standards, and assembling their machines, cats (*gathae*), and fortifications, they approached the city—and after many skirmishes here and there, they finally took the city in the month of December. Of all the goods found there the Genoese took one-third, while the count and his army claimed two-thirds. Having thus conquered two cities, the Genoese returned to Genoa with much glory.[22]

Also in the time of this archbishop, in the year of the Lord 1155, the emperor Frederick demanded [oaths of] fidelity, hostages, and many other burdens from the Genoese. When these were denied him, he was incensed to such a great furor that men and women, children and adults persevered day and night in erecting walls and fortifications [around the city]. In fact, they made as much progress on the wall in eight days as another city could scarcely have made in a year. Upon hearing this, the emperor abandoned his demands and contented himself with just their loyalty.[23] Later these city walls were happily completed in the year

20 Caffaro narrates the campaign against Almería and Tortosa in detail in *YCAT*. See also Epstein (1996), pp. 49–52, and the excellent notes and documents 5–7 (pp. 179–86) in *HP*.
21 While the context implies a siege machine, the meaning of *gathae* is unclear: see part 11.19 n. 198, above.
22 Glory, but also debt: documents 6 and 8a–b in *HP* (pp. 184–9) reveal the commune's efforts to recover financially from the campaign.
23 Here Jacopo conflates the negotiations between Frederick I Barbarossa and the Genoese during Frederick's first Italian campaign in 1154–55 (*CGA*, pp. 42–3) and his second in 1158–62 (*CGA*, pp. 49–52; Freed (2016), p. 239). An 1158 document of shows Archbishop Siro pawning the cathedral's treasures to contribute

of the Lord 1159, and by the hand of God they were perfected in the space of fifty-three days. Overall, the aforesaid city walls are 5,522 feet long and topped with 1,700 crenellations (*merli*), which serve for decoration as well as adding strength for the walls and contributing to the protection of the city and the citizens.[24]

Also in the time of this archbishop, in the year of the Lord 1155, the Genoese signed a peace with the emperor in Constantinople [Manuel I Komnenos] in which the emperor promised to give the commune of Genoa 500 *hyperpyra* and two lengths of precious cloth (*pallia*) every year.[25] He also promised to give the archbishop of Genoa sixty *hyperpyra* and one cloth embroidered with gold annually, because the archbishop had long been protected by the emperors.

At this time the third (*tercia*) was taken away from wives.[26] It had been the custom in Genoa that when a husband died his wife was entitled to one-third of all his goods, whether he had many or he had none: this was called the law of the third (*ius tercie*), or the third (*tercia*). Hence when these thirds were taken away from wives, women protested strenuously and claimed that they were much oppressed; thus to placate them it was ordered that they should have the *antefactum* [instead].

In the year of the Lord 1158, when the Milanese were rebelling against the emperor Frederick, the emperor assembled a great army of both Germans and Italians and besieged Milan. The terrified Milanese came at the emperor's summons, gave him nine thousand marks of silver, and promised to give him three hundred hostages for a fixed term.[27] After that the emperor called off the siege.

---

to the wall-building effort: *Codice diplomatico* 1.371–2 (no. 294). By contrast, the imperial chronicler Rahewin claims that the Genoese were so afraid of Frederick that they agreed to pay him one thousand silver marks and stop building their wall: Otto of Freising, *Gesta Friderici* 4.12, pp. 412–13. Jacopo previously narrated these events in part 5.3.

24 *CGA*, p. 54; *CMG*, pp. 195–6 (Beneš). The most visible remnant of the wall today is the Porta Soprana.

25 *HP*, doc. 12 (pp. 195–6); discussed in *CGA*, pp. 41–2. This crucial treaty significantly improved Genoese trading access to the Byzantine Empire, lowering their customs duties (10 percent) to that of the Pisans (4 percent): Epstein (1996), pp. 72–4; Day (1988), pp. 19–26. The *hyperpyron* was a Byzantine gold coin.

26 2 February 1143: *Codice diplomatico* 1.145 (no. 122); *Libri iurium* 1/1, pp. 105–6 (no. 64); narrated in *CGA*, p. 31, with a marginal sketch of two angry women. For the shift from *tercia* to *antefactum*, two different ways of calculating a widow's property rights: *CMG*, pp. 156–61 (Braccia).

27 At the beginning of Frederick's second Italian campaign: *CGA*, p. 49; Freed (2016), pp. 227–30. Jacopo's account of Milanese cowardice in the face of imperial

Finally, in the time of this archbishop, namely in the year of the Lord 1161, there was a great schism in the church that lasted for nineteen years.[28] For, the greater and wiser part of the cardinals elected Alexander, a man revered by all, but three of the cardinals elected another man by the name of Octavian from amongst themselves, and called him Victor.[29] When he died shortly thereafter, they elected another whom they called Paschal; and when he died suddenly, they created another whom they named Calixtus; and when he died too, they elected another whom they called Innocent.[30] Every one of these four was excommunicated by Pope Alexander and died a horrible death.[31] The Genoese always supported the lord Alexander, while the Pisans always opposed him; the emperor Frederick, too, supported these four schismatics and always opposed Alexander. Finally, after this controversy between the pope and the emperor had gone on a long time, by divine will they reached a peace and concord at Venice.[32] But when the emperor prostrated himself humbly at the pope's feet to ask pardon for his great offences, the pope placed his foot on the emperor's neck, saying: *You will tread upon the asp and basilisk, and you will trample the lion and dragon under foot.*[33] To this the emperor is said to have responded: 'Not to you, but to Peter'—meaning, 'I do not make this obeisance to you by reason of yourself, but by reason of Peter the apostle'.[34]

---

aggression contrasts starkly with the courage and resolution shown by the Genoese three paragraphs earlier. Both episodes echo the narrative in *CGA* (pp. 42–3, 49–50), but in eliminating most of Caffaro's detail Jacopo presents a much simpler moral picture.

28 Aquicinctina continuation of Sigebert of Gembloux's *Chronica*, pp. 409–18. It was actually twenty-one years from the election of antipope Victor V (1159) to the deposition of antipope Innocent III (1180).

29 Alexander III (1159–81), a great partisan of the Genoese: *CGA*, p. 63; Duggan/Clarke (2016), especially pp. 141–2 (Coleman). Against him: antipope Victor IV or V (Ottaviano dei Crescenzi, 1159–64).

30 Antipopes Paschal III (1164–8), Calixtus III (1168–78), and Innocent III (Lando di Sezze, 1179–80): while Calixtus formally submitted to Alexander in 1178, Innocent refused to do so and was banished to an island in the Tyrrhenian Sea in 1180.

31 Canon 1 of the Third Lateran Council of 1179 revised the rules for papal elections to avoid such schisms: Robinson (1990), pp. 84, 140; cf. also *MO*, p. 437.

32 24 July 1177: Aquicinctina continuation of Sigebert of Gembloux's *Chronica*, pp. 415–18.

33 Psalm 90.13.

34 This anecdote appears in several Venetian chronicles, the earliest being the 1292 chronicle of Marco: *Prima edificacio*, p. 262. The visual tradition that developed had a long afterlife during the Reformation as an exemplum of papal arrogance. See also *SS*, fol. 191r.

Also at this time, when the Milanese were again rebelling against the emperor Frederick in the year of the Lord 1162, the emperor assembled a very large army and besieged Milan for nearly three years.[35] He so wore [the Milanese] down through both hunger and warfare that they put themselves totally at his mercy, placing not only themselves but their city and all their belongings in his power. The emperor granted them their lives and restored their movable and immovable goods, but he totally destroyed the entire city, dividing it into four smaller settlements and ordering each separated from the others by two miles.

Chapter two: Regarding Ugo, the second archbishop. Ugo, the second archbishop, took office in the year of the Lord 1163 and completed twenty-five years in the archiepiscopate.[36] He was first archdeacon and was afterward elected to the archbishopric. He was a man of great wisdom; when a certain conflict between the Avvocati and the di Castello (*de Castro*) caused many slayings, he led them back to peace by his wisdom.[37] He gave the churches of San Marco al Molo and San Salvatore in Sarzano to the chapter of San Lorenzo.[38] Also, by his influence the monastery on the island of Gallinara was placed under the archbishop of Genoa.[39]

During the tenure of this archbishop Pope Clement III first conceded—and after him many other supreme pontiffs conceded—that the Genoese archbishop should have a perpetual overseas legation, where he should go every eight years along with another cardinal or bishop, and in this way he should have full authority there as a cardinal legate might

---

35 The culmination of Frederick's second Italian campaign, 1161–62: *CGA*, pp. 64–5; Freed (2016), pp. 281–9; Raccagni (2010), pp. 26–7.

36 *CGA*, p. 75; *GA* 2.26–7; Polonio (2002a), pp. 458–9. Ugo is responsible for large numbers of acts in both *RC* (pp. 524–35) and *RC2* (pp. 17–141). He may have been a member of the prominent della Volta family.

37 In 1169 Ugo's mediation ended a longstanding conflict (*GA* 1.160) between these two prominent families: *CMG*, p. 108 (Filangieri) and p. 124 (Musarra).

38 San Marco al Molo: a parish church erected in the 1170s on the harbour mole: Poleggi/Grossi Bianchi (1980), pp. 89, 96. (In the 1190s, it was contested by the canons of San Lorenzo and those of Santa Maria di Castello; Jacopo's account favours the San Lorenzo claim.) San Salvatore was built in the 1140s (*Codice diplomatico* 1.131–2, no. 109), and granted by Ugo to the canons of San Lorenzo in 1182 (*JDV* 2.346 n. 1).

39 An island off the coast of Albenga, in the western Ligurian Riviera. This actually occurred in 1162 under Ugo's predecessor Siro: *Codice diplomatico* 1.387–91 (no. 305), at p. 390.

have.⁴⁰ Regarding this many sealed privileges are preserved in the archiepiscopal palace.

Also in the time of this archbishop it was established by specially appointed judges that the monastery of San Bartolomeo del Fossato should be obedient to the archbishop in all deliberations of the Genoese church, as well as in processions and in consecrations of abbots or bishops.⁴¹ All the aforementioned matters are preserved in the archiepiscopal chancery.

Also, in the year of the Lord 1164 the emperor Frederick made Barisone, judge of Arborea, king of the whole island of Sardinia at the request of the Genoese, and crowned him king at Pavia over the objections of the Pisans.⁴² Barisone declared his loyalty to the commune of Genoa, and as a sign of his loyalty he promised to send one hundred pounds of pure silver every year to the commune of Genoa and one pound [of the same] to the archbishop.⁴³

In the year of the Lord 1165 the Pisans armed twenty-five galleys and went to Albenga, which they captured, destroyed, and razed by fire.⁴⁴ When they heard this, the Genoese were extremely upset, and armed forty-five galleys in the space of four days. They set out in pursuit of the Pisan galleys, but although they sought them on the high seas, they escaped. In addition, a fierce tempest set upon [the Genoese] such that thirteen galleys perished with all their men.

---

40 Jacopo is probably referring to a bull of Clement III (1187–91) confirming privileges first granted by his predecessors, since this provision was in Alexander III's bull of 1162 (*Codice diplomatico* 1.389–90).

41 San Bartolomeo del Fossato was founded by the Vallombrosan order near the western suburb of Sampierdarena before 1138: *CMG*, p. 377 (Polonio); it was originally subject directly to the pope.

42 *GA* 1.158–67. As Freed (2016, p. 313) notes, 'the legal status of Sardinia was, even by medieval standards, a muddle'. Medieval Sardinia was divided into four realms (*iudicati*) each ruled by a 'judge' (*iudex*); by the twelfth century, the papacy, the empire, Genoa, and Pisa all also claimed rights on the island: Hobart (2017), chaps. 4 (Zedda) and 8 (Haug). In 1164, Frederick Barbarossa invested Barisone, judge of Arborea (Sardinia's middle-southern kingdom, north of Cagliari) with the title of king of Sardinia in return for Barisone's fealty and four thousand silver marks. Barisone's allies the Genoese served as intermediaries in these negotiations, and also as Barisone's creditors for the four thousand silver marks: *Codice diplomatico* 2.5–15 (nos. 3–5, all dated 16 September 1164).

43 Epstein (1996, p. 83) hypothesises that the Genoese 'enticed Barisone into debts far beyond his ability to repay in order to subvert his kingdom and take over the island'.

44 *GA* 1.180–5.

In the following year [1166] the judge of Cagliari in Sardinia swore loyalty to the commune of Genoa and its archbishop, and promised to give one hundred pounds of the best silver annually to the commune of Genoa, and also one pound to the archbishop.[45]

In the time of this archbishop, namely in the year of the Lord 1168, Alessandria in Lombardy was rebuilt: it was originally called Caesarea, but its name was afterward changed in honour of Pope Alexander. For the said Pope Alexander was then in those parts, and gave his approval that the city should be built. In this way, a city that had previously been named Caesarea in honour of an emperor was afterward called Alessandria in honour of the pope.[46] The said Alexander also gave them a bishop, but once he died they had no bishop; instead, its church is subject to the bishop of Acqui.[47] Also, because the Pavians were rebelling against the Roman church, the said Pope Alexander solemnly stripped the bishop of Pavia of the dignities of the pallium and cross which he had been accustomed to use.[48]

In the year of the Lord 1170 the Pisans took from the Lucchesi the fortress of Motrone, but with the help of the Genoese the Lucchesi recovered it the following year, and together the Lucchesi and Genoese rebuilt it since it had been mostly destroyed by the Pisans.[49]

---

45 Peter (r. 1163–88) was judge of Cagliari, the southernmost judgeship in Sardinia. In 1168 a peace treaty was signed between Barisone and the Genoese on one side and Peter, the Pisans, and the judge of Logudoro (Barisone of Torres, r. 1153–86) on the other: *GA* 1.190; Hobart (2017), pp. 216–20; also *Codice diplomatico* 2.27–8 (no. 10).

46 Jacopo gets this reversed: the city was originally founded as Alessandria c. 1164–67 in the Tanaro valley between Genoa and Milan: Godfrey of Viterbo (*Pantheon* and *Gesta Friderici*, pp. 127, 268); *GA* 1.213; Robert of Torigny, *Chronicle*, pp. 239–40; *MO*, p. 437. It was named after Pope Alexander III as an insult to Frederick Barbarossa: Freed (2016), pp. 380–424. Frederick demanded the city's destruction several times between 1177 and 1183; while he eventually agreed to the compromise of renaming it Caesarea ('city of the emperor'), its citizens soon reverted to calling it Alessandria: Raccagni (2010), pp. 117–18; Coleman (2016), especially p. 149.

47 The diocese of Alessandria was formed in 1175 from territory in the diocese of Acqui, and the bishops of Acqui occasionally tried to control it. In 1213 the bishopric was suppressed by Pope Innocent III (Gams (1931), p. 811) as punishment for the city's support of Otto IV, although the gossip-loving Milanese chronicler Galvano Fiamma reports that the real reason was the citizens of Alessandria had killed their bishop and eaten his heart: *Chronicon maius*, p. 714.

48 On the bishop of Pavia's unusual privilege of the pallium and cross: Schoenig (2016), pp. 305–6.

49 *GA* 1.240, 244–5.

PART TWELVE: GENOA UNDER THE ARCHBISHOPS

In the year of the Lord 1172 Obizzo Malaspina, a vassal of the archbishop of Genoa, and his son Murruel, a vassal of the Genoese commune, assembled around 350 soldiers and 3,000 infantry and attacked the town of Chiavari and the port of Sestri.[50] When this was known in Genoa, all hastened there with one accord by both land and sea. When the marquess [Obizzo] heard this, he wanted to flee, but instead he was wounded and died. Many were captured and taken prisoner, but others fled and thus escaped the field of battle.

In the year of the Lord 1176, the Milanese, who were dispersed throughout their [new] settlements, returned to their city and enclosed it with towers, walls, and gates—which greatly displeased the emperor Frederick, who had dispersed them [in the first place].[51] But the people of Brescia, Como, and many other cities of Lombardy assisted them in the completion of this task, and the emperor of the Greeks, Manuel, sent them many *hyperpyra* and many [blocks of] marble.[52] Then the emperor assembled a large army and came to Legnano, where the people of Milan, Brescia, and Como engaged with him and ousted him shamefully from the field of battle.[53]

Also in this year the Pisans broke the peace they had made with the Genoese. Advancing to Sardinia with an army, they expelled all the Genoese from the whole judgeship of Cagliari and confiscated all their goods. On account of this the Genoese armed twenty galleys against them and inflicted much damage on the Pisans. They also took the fortress of Bonifacio, which the Pisans had built, and destroyed it utterly.[54]

50 The Malaspina were local marquesses who had sworn fidelity to the commune of Genoa: Epstein (1996), p. 42; *CMG*, pp. 57–8 (Guglielmotti) and 96 (Filangieri). *GA* annalist Oberto Cancelliere gives a detailed account of this conflict (*GA* 1.255–61), but Monleone complains that Jacopo does not seem to have read it very carefully (*JVC* 2.353 n. 5). Peace was concluded with the Malapina in March 1174: *GA* 2.5–6; *Codice diplomatico* 2.184ff.

51 Frederick had Milan destroyed and its citizens dispersed in 1162 (part 12.1, above), but resettlement and reconstruction began as early as 1167: Raccagni (2010), pp. 37–40; Freed (2016), p. 289.

52 Raccagni (2010), pp. 31–2. The Byzantine *hyperpyron* remained the standard gold coin into the mid-fourteenth century. See Galvano Fiamma, *Chronicon maius*, pp. 707–9.

53 The battle of Legnano on 29 May 1176: *GA* 2.10. See Raccagni (2010), pp. 88–92, and Freed (2016), pp. 390–1, esp. n. 15, which lists other contemporary accounts.

54 Jacopo conflates two different conflicts with Pisa here: according to Ottobono *scriba* (*GA* 2.8–9), the 1175 conflict with Pisa occurred at the northern rather than the southern end of Sardinia. The peace settled that year was broken twelve years later in 1187, when Bonifacio was destroyed (*GA* 2.24–5).

And in the time of this archbishop, in the year of the Lord 1177, the emperor Frederick made peace between the Genoese and the Pisans and gave the whole middle part of the island of Sardinia to the commune of Genoa. Furthermore, this emperor came to Genoa with his wife Beatrice and his son Henry, and there they were received with honour in the year of the Lord 1178.[55]

Also in these times the daughter of the king of England, who had been given as wife to the king of Sicily, came to Genoa, and was borne honourably onward to her husband on Genoese galleys.[56] Later the daughter of the French king also came to Genoa; she had been promised in matrimony to the son of Manuel, emperor of the Greeks, and she was similarly borne honourably to her husband by Genoese galleys.[57]

Also in the time of this archbishop, in the year of the Lord 1179 a general council was celebrated by the lord pope Alexander III in the church of the Lateran, in which council the aforementioned Archbishop Ugo took part.[58] He was accompanied by the provost of San Lorenzo, the [cathedral] schoolmaster, and the noble men Enrico Doria, Nivellono di Camilla, Ansaldo Golia, and Arduino di Lavagna, who all made full oath and presented sufficient proof to the lord pope and the cardinals that the relics of Saint John the Baptist had been carried to Genoa from Myra. Accordingly the pope approved and confirmed that the body of Saint John the Baptist was held in the city of Genoa, ordering that this revelation should be solemnly celebrated. He also wrote to distant provinces that all should participate in the said feast, and he decreed a

---

55 Frederick came through Genoa on his way to Burgundy in 1178: he was crowned king of Burgundy at Arles on 30 July, and his wife Beatrice was crowned queen at Vienne on 15 August: *GA* 2.11–12; Freed (2016), pp. 419–20.

56 *GA* 2.11–14: Princess Joan or Joanna (1165–99), daughter of Henry II of England and Eleanor of Aquitaine, sailed from England on 27 August 1176; she married William II (r. 1166–89) and was crowned queen of Sicily in Palermo on 13 February 1177: Matthew (1992), pp. 273–5.

57 Agnes (1171–after 1204), youngest daughter of Louis VII and Adèle of Champagne, came through Genoa in 1179 on her way to marry Alexios II Komnenos (r. 1180–83), son of Emperor Manuel I Komnenos (r. 1143–80). The two were apparently betrothed but never married, so when Alexios was overthrown by his cousin Andronikos I Komnenos in 1183, Agnes found herself Andronikos' wife instead: *NCMH* 4.2, pp. 626–30 (Magdalino).

58 The Third Lateran Council, attended by more than three hundred prelates from across western Christendom, met three times in March 1179: *GA* 2.12–13; *NCMH* 4.1, pp. 329–36 (Robinson).

great indulgence for those who came.[59] Pope Alexander also conceded to the [cathedral] schoolmaster in Genoa and his successors the right to wear a mitre on occasions of great solemnity.[60] Finally, he placed the bishop of Albenga under the archbishop of Genoa, and made him its suffragan.[61]

Also in the time of this archbishop, in the year of the Lord 1187, the holy cross which is called the Cross of the Hospital of Saint Lazarus was brought to Genoa.[62] At that time Saladin took Jerusalem and the whole kingdom of Syria, with the exception of the city of Tyre.[63] He also took captive the reigning king Guy and William the aged marquess of Montferrat along with many other barons in Damascus, and he seized the True Cross which is said to be the cross of the hospital of Saint Lazarus.[64] When Marquess Conrad of Montferrat, who was then at Constantinople, heard this, he went in a Genoese ship to Syria to defend the city of Tyre.[65] With the assistance of the Genoese, the aforesaid Marquess Conrad defended that city forcefully, and for this reason he sent the aforementioned cross, which he recovered from the aforementioned Saladin, to the commune of Genoa as a great gift.[66]

59 *HLT*; see also part 11.16, above.
60 Ogerio Galletta: *GA* 2.13; *RC*, p. 412.
61 *GA* 2.12–13; also discussed in part 10.2 (n. 16).
62 Mentioned in part 11.18: see *RIBH*, p. 141; Bertini Guidetti (1997a), pp. 179–80.
63 An-Nasir Salah ad-Din Yusuf ibn Ayyub, better known in English as Saladin, founder of the Muslim Ayyubid dynasty of Egypt. After taking over Egypt in 1171, he began a grand programme of expansion into crusader territory. Beginning with his massive victory at the Battle of Hattin on 4 July 1187, where he destroyed most of the crusader army and took King Guy of Jerusalem prisoner, he then conquered most of the rest of the Crusader Kingdom, capturing Jerusalem on 2 October: Tyerman (2006), chaps. 11–12; *CMG*, pp. 481–4 (Mack).
64 Guy of Lusignan, king of Jerusalem 1186–92, and William of Montferrat, then about seventy. On the complex politics of the Kingdom of Jerusalem in this period—exacerbated by young Baldwin IV's leprosy—see Hamilton (2000); Jotischky (2017), pp. 97–110, 167–83. Cf. also *GA* 2.23–4.
65 William's second son, who succeeded to the title on his father's death in 1191. By marriage to the heiress Isabella, he became *de facto* king of Jerusalem from 1190; while formally elected in April 1192, he was assassinated only a few days later: Jotischky (2017), p. 172. After the loss of Jerusalem, Tyre became the crusaders' *de facto* capital. While the Genoese had not previously held trading privileges there, their alliance with Conrad gained them valuable concessions that equalled or surpassed those of their rivals the Venetians: *CMG*, pp. 485–6; *HP*, docs. 19–24 (pp. 215–25).
66 Contemporary sources for the Third Crusade all suggest that the True Cross was lost or destroyed after Saladin's capture of Jerusalem, although the crusaders negotiated hard for its return: Murray (1998), esp. p. 238.

Chapter three: Regarding Bonifacio, the third archbishop. Bonifacio, the third archbishop, took office in the year of the Lord 1188 and completed fifteen years in the archiepiscopate.[67] He was first archdeacon and afterward he was elected to the archiepiscopate. In the first year of his archiepiscopate, in the presence of the lord Pietro Piacentino, cardinal priest of the *titulus* of Santa Cecilia and legate of the apostolic see, this archbishop had the body of Saint Syrus raised from underneath the altar of San Lorenzo and piously relocated in a marble coffer over the same altar, where the bones of Saint Felix and Saint Romulus were also found in other coffers.[68]

In the time of this archbishop, in the year of the Lord 1189, Emperor Frederick was in the lands beyond the sea with a noble army seeking to recover the Holy Land; he was traveling through the lands around Antioch, and while crossing the Faro River, which was fairly narrow, he fell from his horse and drowned.[69] Also in the year of the Lord 1190 Philip, king of the French, came to Genoa with Richard, king of England, and the duke of Burgundy, and set out to rescue the Holy Land; with them eighty Genoese ships laden with pilgrims [i.e. crusaders] departed for Syria from the port of Genoa.[70]

In the time of this archbishop, in the year of the Lord 1190, there ceased to be consuls in the city of Genoa; because all aspired to the consulate many jealousies and hatreds had grown up in the city, so

---

67 1188–1203: *GA* 2.27–8, 87; numerous acts in *RC* and *RC2*; Polonio (2002a), p. 149; *DBI* 12.116.

68 *GA* 2.28–9; *RC*, pp. 411–12. Felix, Syrus, and Romulus were all saintly early bishops of Genoa: see parts 11.2–4 above; also part 11.5 on the translation of Romulus' relics into San Lorenzo. Cardinal Pietro (d. 1208), cardinal priest of Santa Cecilia, was a native of Piacenza whom Clement III appointed papal legate and charged with mediating conflicts between cities in Lombardy.

69 The Third Crusade is often called the Kings' Crusade for the number of monarchs who took the cross after news of Jerusalem's fall reached Europe (n. 63, above): Frederick I Barbarossa, Richard I of England, and Philip II Augustus of France, as well as Hugh III of Burgundy (r. 1162–92): Tyerman (2006), chaps. 11–12. Barbarossa chose an overland route to Palestine, while the others went by sea from Italy; as Jacopo reports, he died crossing a river in Cilicia in 1190: see *GA* 2.33; *GL*, p. 770; *Crusade of Frederick Barbarossa*. His death threw the German army into disarray; by some estimates, only 5 percent of Frederick's original force made it to the crusaders' rendezvous in Acre.

70 *GA* 2.33–6. The Genoese participated in the Crusade with expeditions in both 1189 and 1190. In February 1190 the Genoese committed the city's entire fleet to transport the French army to the Holy Land, causing the entire city's trade to suffer when Philip II Augustus kept postponing the agreed-upon sailing date: *RIBH*, pp. 141–2; *CMG*, pp. 481–6 (Mack).

the citizens wished to be ruled by podestà instead.[71] Accordingly they elected a certain citizen of Brescia by the name of Manegold as first podestà of Genoa.[72] About the time the rule of this podestà began, some of the di Castello maliciously killed Lanfranco Pipere. Filled with shame and grief, the podestà called together a great assembly. Then, taking up his weapons, he bravely mounted his horse and valiantly rode to assault the malefactors' houses, seized them forcefully, and totally razed them.[73]

In the time of this archbishop, in the year of the Lord 1191, when a certain man named Tancred made himself king of Sicily, the Genoese armed thirty-three galleys against him in service to Emperor Henry.[74]

In the following year and the next, there were many civil wars in the city of Genoa such that murderers and thieves ruled throughout the city. For this reason the consuls, who had resumed rule, abandoned the government, and Oberto di Olevano, a noble citizen of Pavia, was elected as podestà; by his wisdom and diligence he removed all seditions and scandals and brought all conflicts back to peace.[75]

In that year Emperor Henry came to Genoa, seeking assistance from the Genoese to help him recover the kingdom of Sicily, and promised the Genoese many great things. The Genoese thus armed a great fleet of galleys in his service and valiantly went to his aid.[76] This fleet's admiral was the aforementioned podestà Oberto, who died later that year. Then the aforesaid Emperor Henry confirmed to the commune of Genoa the city of Siracusa with all its appurtenances by a privilege

---

71 Podestà were magistrates hired from outside Genoa for terms of six months or a year (as opposed to consuls, who were citizens). On the shift from a consular to a podestarial regime, see Epstein (1996), p. 88; *CMG*, pp. xxii, 108–10 (Filangieri), 484–5 (Mack).

72 Manegoldo da Tettuccio of Brescia, who took office in 1191.

73 *GA* 2.36–7.

74 *GA* 2.38–40. Here Jacopo reports the correct *Tancredus* where the *GA* gives an incorrect *Tanclerius*, demonstrating that Jacopo did not simply copy unthinkingly from the *GA*. Tancred of Lecce, king of Sicily 1189–94, was an illegitimate cousin of William II of Sicily. When William died without an heir, Tancred had himself crowned king in 1190 against the claims of his aunt Constance and her husband Emperor Henry VI. After several years of fraught negotiations, Tancred died before he could secure the realm for his own sons: Matthew (1992), chap. 10.

75 *GA* 2.42–5 on the civil conflicts; see also *CMG*, pp. 109–10 (Filangieri), 122–5 (Musarra). Oberto di Olevano, an intimate of Emperor Henry VI (*GA* 1.159), was elected podestà in 1194.

76 *GA* 2.45–7; Matthew (1992), pp. 288–90.

secured with a golden seal. He also confirmed to them the castle of Gavi, and gave them the promontory of Monaco.[77]

Also in the time of this archbishop, in the year of the Lord 1195, the True Cross of Christ which is antonomastically[78] called the 'Holy of Christ' (*sancta Christi*) was brought to Genoa. The patriarch of Jerusalem always carried this Holy Cross in battles and thereby gained victory. For it happened that, as [our] sins necessitated, Saladin captured Jerusalem together with its patriarch and the Holy Cross. But with the passing of time the emperor of the Greeks came to terms with Saladin, and Saladin sent the cross back to the same emperor of the Greeks in a certain ship, but Genoese and Pisan galleys seized the ship by force of arms. When they were dividing the spoils, a certain Pisan named Fortis secretly stole this cross and hid it for safekeeping in the fortress of Bonifacio, which the Genoese had once destroyed but the Pisans had rebuilt. Three ships and certain galleys of the Genoese took the said fortress. Seeing this and trusting in the virtue of the Holy Cross, Fortis placed it in his breast, crossed safely through the midst of his enemies, left the fortress, and escaped into a nearby forest. But in the end he returned to the fortress, handed over the cross to the commune of Genoa and was made a citizen of Genoa. It is also said, however, that the said Fortis, having taken up the cross and trusting in its power, undertook to walk on top of the sea as if it were solid ground—but while he was still thinking of fleeing and getting far away from the fortress, by the will of God he suddenly found himself back within the fortress, and thus the Genoese took the cross from him and brought it to Genoa.[79]

Around the same time, in the year of the Lord 1197, Drudo Marcellino—citizen of Milan and podestà of Genoa—ordered that towers that were

---

77 30 May 1191: *Codice diplomatico* 3.4–12; *MGH Const.* 1.479–83. In return for Genoese naval assistance to unseat Tancred in Sicily (*GA* 2.38–9, 45–6, 58–9), Henry VI agreed to uphold the concessions granted by his father Frederick I and recognise Genoese sovereignty over the entire Ligurian coast, along with numerous other promises. Ottobono *scriba* comments crossly that 'afterward he upheld these promises poorly and dishonestly, contrary to his own honour and the good faith he had sworn' (*GA* 2.39); see Abulafia (1977), chap. 7.

78 Antonomasia: the substitution of any epithet or descriptive phrase for a proper name.

79 *RIBH*, pp. 140–1: Jacopo omits Fortis's Genoese accomplice to place greater emphasis on the Cross's miraculous powers. The Genoese retook Bonifacio, which the Pisans had rebuilt, in 1195 (*GA* 2.55–7), but the *GA* doesn't mention such a cross among the booty: Bertini Guidetti (1997a), pp. 179–81. See also the curious report of Vincent of Beauvais, *Speculum historiale* 30.43.1.

PART TWELVE: GENOA UNDER THE ARCHBISHOPS   227

too tall should be shortened and reduced to a height of eighty feet.[80] Also in the time of this podestà it was decreed that eight noble men should always be elected to assist the podestà, and this [custom] was observed all the way up to the times of the *capitani*.[81] We read elsewhere, however, that the aforesaid eight noble men were first elected under the lord Rambertino di Bovarello, a citizen of Bologna and later podestà of Genoa in the year of the Lord 1218.[82]

This podestà, lord Drudo, was reappointed the following year. Because he had forbidden anyone to go to Sicily but certain nobles were going there with their galleys anyway, the said podestà had their houses destroyed.[83] When they returned, great discord arose between them and the podestà, to the point that they dared to erect a bridge to the podestà's house by night. But as soon as the podestà learned of this, he convened an assembly early in the morning and had the entire people armed. Then [the nobles] were terrified and submitted to the decrees of the podestà.

Also in the time of this archbishop, specifically in the last year of his reign, the commune of Genoa bought the fortress of Gavi from the marquesses, giving them 3,200 pounds (*librae*) for all their rights in that place. Then the marquesses were made citizens [of Genoa].[84]

Chapter four: Regarding Otto, fourth archbishop. Otto, a native of Alessandria and the fourth archbishop, took office in the year of the

80 Actually 1196: *GA* 2.61. Factional strife and high population density in Italian cities meant that tall, defensible towers were a favoured form of urban residence for those who could afford them. Although relatively few survive today (the most famous being in Bologna and San Gimignano), medieval skylines bristled with them, and civic authorities often ordered their height reduced either for symbolic reasons (to reprove their owners) or on practical grounds (to reduce the risk of collapse): Dean, *Towns of Italy*, pp. 39–41; Jansen/Drell/Andrews, *Medieval Italy*, pp. 230–3.

81 *GA* for 1196 (2.60). On the Council of Eight: *CMG*, pp. 109–10 (Filangieri), 126 (Musarra). *Capitani del popolo* ('captains of the people') were instituted in 1257: see part 12.6, below.

82 *GA* for 1218 (2.145).

83 *GA* 2.71–2: after Drudo had the house of Nicolò Doria (*DBI* 41.409–12) destroyed for defying the ban, Doria and his supporters built their bridge to the 'new archbishop's palace', which was being used to house municipal officials.

84 *GA* 2.83–4. While many other Italian communes gained control of the surrounding countryside (their *contado*) by military means, the Genoese often bought such properties outright—as here, in a treaty dated 18 September 1202: *Libri iurium* 1/3, pp. 203–5 (no. 527). See Epstein (1996), p. 90; *CMG*, chap. 2 (Guglielmotti), esp. pp. 56–7.

Lord 1203 and completed thirty-six years in the archiepiscopate.[85] He was first bishop of Bobbio, but he was transferred to the episcopal throne because he was strong in virtue and reputation, as well as endowed with venerable old age and maturity.

In the second year of his archiepiscopate the count of Flanders and Boniface the marquess of Montferrat besieged Constantinople along with the doge of the Venetians, and afterward seized the city itself.[86] The marquess sent the [Byzantine] emperor, together with his wife and children, to Montferrat, where they were held captive.[87] After the capture of the city of Constantinople the holy cross called the Cross of Saint Helena was transported to Genoa. It is called the cross of Saint Helena because when Saint Helena discovered the cross of the Lord, she decorated part of it with silver and gold plate and pearls and took it to Constantinople for her son Constantine. Then, when the Venetians were taking the cross to Venice along with many other relics, it happened that a certain Genoese citizen of the dei Fornari [family] by the name of Dondedeus Bos armed two galleys against the Venetians, since great discord then existed between Genoese and Venetians.[88] The aforesaid Dondedeus Bos captured that ship and brought the Holy Cross and the other relics to Genoa, where he presented the cross to the Genoese commune and the church of San Lorenzo as a great gift. The other relics he kept for himself, hoping to acquire later a not-inconsiderable treasure from some prince in exchange for them. But because God did not want the city of Genoa to be despoiled of such treasures, after some time the aforesaid relics were obtained by us and came to the Friars Preacher. They are preserved with great reverence in the friars' church,

---

85 *GA* 2.87, 3.94–5; also numerous acts in *RC* and *RC2*.

86 *GA* 2.88–9. The Fourth Crusade (1202–4), led by Baldwin of Flanders; Boniface of Montferrat (younger brother of Conrad of Montferrat, above), and Doge Enrico Dandolo: diverted from its original goal of Jerusalem, the crusaders sacked Constantinople in April 1204 and established the Latin Empire of Constantinople (1204–61): Phillips (2004); Tyerman (2006), chaps. 15–17. These events obstructed Genoese trade in the east since the Venetians now controlled access to Constantinople and the Black Sea: *CMG*, pp. 456 (Kirk), 488 (Mack).

87 The besieged emperor Alexios III (r. 1195–1203) escaped Constantinople on 17 July 1203 with only his daughter Irene and a small retinue. Despite attempting to organise opposition to the new Latin regime in Constantinople, he was eventually captured by Boniface of Montferrat, Thessalonica's new ruler, and spent four years as Boniface's prisoner in Montferrat: Villehardouin, *Memoirs* 182, 309 (Smith, *Chronicles*, pp. 48, 83); also Phillips (2004), pp. 182–4, 286–7.

88 Jacopo gives Dondedeus more dignity than the *RIBH*, which describes him as 'practising the art of piracy' (p. 141); also *GA* 2.89.

where we have had them honourably mounted on two silver-plated panels.[89]

In the year of the Lord 1205 the noble man Folco di Castello was elected as podestà of Genoa; he was the first and last podestà elected from the bosom of the city.[90] And in the time of this archbishop, when Emperor Henry died, Duke Otto of Saxony was elected as emperor and solemnly crowned by Innocent III in the year 1208.[91] He swore himself to defend the rights of the church, but afterward acted totally to the contrary.[92] Furthermore, he went into Campania, first to Capua and then to Naples, attempting against the will of the church to usurp the kingdom of Apulia from Emperor Henry's son Frederick. For this reason Innocent III excommunicated him and all his supporters, and then—as Otto's contumacy grew—Innocent deposed him and arranged for Henry's son Frederick to be elected [instead].[93] In service to the aforesaid Otto the Pisans armed forty galleys that they sent as far as Naples, but the Genoese, fearing excommunication, gave him no assistance.[94]

In that year the Genoese natives Count Alamanno and Count Henry of Malta went to Siracusa with twenty Genoese ships coming from

---

89 Referring to San Domenico, Genoa. A pastoral letter written upon Jacopo's election as archbishop invites the faithful to venerate these relics (*JVC* 1.66–8).

90 That is, a Genoese citizen; see *GA* 2.94.

91 After Henry VI's death in 1197, the imperial crown was disputed between Henry's brother Philip of Swabia and the duke of Saxony, Otto of Brunswick. Philip and Otto spent the next ten years in a conflict that occupied much of western Europe, since Philip was allied with Philip Augustus of France and Otto with kings Richard and John of England. Philip's murder cleared the way for Otto's coronation as king of Italy in 1208 and emperor (as Otto IV) in 1209: Huffman (2000), chaps. 4–5.

92 Otto made numerous promises to gain Innocent's support for his claim to the empire, most of which he broke immediately after his imperial coronation as he tried to reassert imperial rule in Italy: *NCMH* 5.380–1 (Toch); Moore (2003), pp. 187–9.

93 After Innocent III excommunicated Otto in 1210, Otto claimed southern Italy and Sicily as imperial fiefs against the claim of Henry VI's son Frederick (later Frederick II), then a minor in Innocent's guardianship. Eventually the German princes—exasperated by Otto's Italian focus—colluded with Innocent and Philip of France to have young Frederick (then seventeen) elected king of Germany and recognised as emperor-elect at the Diet of Nuremberg in 1211. Otto was forced to abdicate the imperial throne in 1215 and died in 1218, while Frederick was crowned emperor by Honorius III in 1220: Abulafia (1988), pp. 137–9.

94 1210–11: *GA* 2.119–20.

Oltramare as well as certain galleys; they besieged [the city] forcefully and captured it triumphantly.[95] Then this Alamanno was made count there, swearing to hold the city for the honour of the Genoese commune and to offer one cloth (*pallium*) annually on the altar of San Lorenzo.[96] In the following year Count Henry took the island of Crete in battle, and afterward came to Genoa to ask for help.[97] The commune of Genoa gave him eight galleys and three ships with all their armaments as well as three thousand *lire* and one hundred soldiers, so he left Genoa rejoicing and waged many wars. When he took Crete in battle, he also captured the doge of the Venetians, Rainerio Dandolo, and put him in prison.[98]

Because the aforementioned Frederick did not dare to leave Sicily—fearing the Pisans, who favoured [emperor] Otto—at Pope Innocent's request the Genoese armed galleys and brought him to Genoa, where he made a stay of three months at the commune's expense.[99] And because the Pisans were rebels against the church, Innocent confiscated all their fiefs, privileges, and dignities, and solemnly deprived the Pisan archbishop of the primacy he held on the island of Sardinia.[100]

In the time of the same Archbishop Otto a general council was celebrated under Pope Innocent III in the year of the Lord 1216; it is said that more than 1,300 patriarchs, archbishops, bishops, and other prelates were present there.[101] The aforesaid Archbishop Otto also went to this

---

95 Actually 1204, when the Genoese took the city from an occupying Pisan force. Alamanno da Costa (fl. 1193–1229; *DBI* 1.574–5) became count of Siracusa, and Count Henry of Malta (Enrico Pescatore; fl. 1203–30; *DBI* 42.746–50), a member of the di Castello family, became admiral of Sicily: *CMG*, pp. 489 (Mack), 502 (Origone); Abulafia (1975), esp. pp. 110–19. The Pisans attempted to retake the city in 1205 without success: *GA* 2.91–2, 96–8.

96 *GA* 2.92.

97 Having conquered Crete in 1206, Henry did not return to Genoa himself in 1208 but sent a messenger requesting the commune's support: *GA* 2.104, 109.

98 Not the doge but 'admiral and lord of the army in Crete', Dandolo died shortly after capture: *GA* 2.109–10. Henry's hold on Crete was a major source of friction with the Venetians: *CMG*, p. 489 (Mack); Abulafia (1975); Otten-Froux (2011).

99 Frederick II, who *c.* 1210 was already king of Sicily but not yet king of Germany or emperor, spent 1 May–15 July 1212 in Genoa as the guest of Nicolò Doria: *GA* 2.122. On 9 July 1212 (*MGH DD FII* 1.54–6) he granted the Genoese new concessions while confirming those previously made in 1200; he later revoked most of these after his imperial coronation in 1220.

100 Moore (2003), pp. 189–90. Innocent also ordered the judges of Sardinia to resist and hinder the Pisans, who were supporting Otto: Potthast (1874) no. 4303, p. 371.

101 The Fourth Lateran Council, which met in November 1215: *GA* 2.136–7, and Moore (2003), chap. 9.

council, and when he returned he celebrated a provincial council where he announced those things which had been decreed and ordered them to be upheld.[102]

Also in the time of this same archbishop, two orders were begun: the orders of Preachers and Friars Minor.[103] While Innocent confirmed the Order of Friars Minor, his successor Honorius confirmed the Order of Preachers, specifically in the year of the Lord 1216. Innocent had actually promised that he would confirm it himself, but he was prevented by death that year and was unable to fulfill his promise.

Also in the time of that archbishop, in the year of the Lord 1211, a certain very cunning thief came to Genoa. Unbeknownst to the guards, he concealed himself among the vaults where the crosses of the Lord are kept. Then with crowbars he broke open the box in which the aforesaid crosses were preserved and carried them away from the city of Genoa. When this was known, great sorrow came upon all and great sadness engulfed everyone. But after messengers had been sent to various places the thief was captured and the crosses recovered, with universal thanks given to God. In fact, the thief had surrendered the crosses for safekeeping to a certain Alessandrian named Niger, and the commune of Genoa redeemed them from him for more than fifty *lire*.[104]

In the year of the Lord 1214 Otto, marquess of Carretto, freely gave to the commune of Genoa the fortress of Cairo with all its appurtenances. Then the commune of Genoa returned the same to him in fief and he swore fidelity to the commune of Genoa for it.[105] In the following year the Genoese constructed a castle at Monaco and fortified it with very solid towers and walls.

In the year of the Lord 1218 the men of Capriata gave themselves to the commune of Genoa, which accepted that fortress and reinforced it.[106]

102 April 1216: *GA* 2.140; Cambiaso, *Sinodi genovesi*, pp. 12–13.
103 Better known as the Dominicans and Franciscans: Innocent III approved the Order of Friars Preacher (OP) in 1215, but the official bull was issued by his successor Honorius III in 1216. Likewise, while Innocent had approved the Franciscan rule in 1209, the Order of Friars Minor (OFM) was not approved until 1223: Lawrence (2013). Cf. *MO*, p. 438; *GL*, pp. 430–44 (Dominic), 606–16 (Francis); *SS*, fols. 222–5, 282–91, 383–9.
104 *GA* 2.120, 123.
105 Cairo Montenotte, in the hills above Savona. Sworn by Ottone del Carretto and his son Ugo, 25 July 1214: *GA* 2.134–5; *Libri iurium* 1/1, pp. 408–10 (no. 273).
106 *GA* 2.149–50. The delegation from Capriata came to Genoa in October 1218: *Libri iurium* 1/3, pp. 180–6 (nos. 517–18).

In the year of the Lord 1220 the Saracen city of Damietta was captured by an army of Christians to which the Genoese had contributed ten galleys.[107]

Also around this time, in the year of the Lord 1221, a very grave disagreement arose between the archbishop and the commune of Genoa, because it seemed that the commune had unlawfully usurped the rights of the archbishopric in Sanremo. So the archbishop laid an interdict on the land and went to Pavia, but afterward the pope entrusted the case to the bishop of Parma and the abbot of Tiglieto. Thus the case was settled and the archbishop returned to his seat and recovered his rights.[108]

In this year the people of Ventimiglia, who had rebelled against the commune of Genoa, came barefoot and with ropes around their necks [to beg] for mercy from the commune of Genoa.[109]

In the year of the Lord 1222, in the month of August, a German youth called Nicholas arrived in Genoa in a pilgrim's habit, followed by a great crowd of pilgrims, both adults and children, even infants. They numbered over seven thousand, and all had cloaks marked with crosses as well as pilgrims' staffs and purses. They claimed the sea would dry up at Genoa and in this way they would walk to Jerusalem. Many among them were sons of the nobility who travelled with their tutors. The Genoese wanted them to leave the city, not only because they believed they were led more by whimsy than by truth, but also because they feared such a great multitude [of pilgrims] would bring famine into the city; they also feared danger to the city, especially because the emperor was then a rebel against the church and the Genoese were supporters of the church against the emperor. But after some time all this business came to nothing, because it was founded upon nothing.[110]

---

107 The Fifth Crusade (1217–22) against the Egyptian Ayyubids: *GA* 2.153–4, 159–61. The Christians managed to capture Damietta, on the Egyptian coast, in November 1219, but the crusade was a dismal failure and they held it less than two years: Mylod et al. (2017); Bird (2018), chaps. 7–10.

108 This dispute was settled in 1222: *GA* 2.177–8, 181–2.

109 First subjected to Genoese authority *c.* 1140, the city of Ventimiglia in the far western Riviera rebelled numerous times over the years, sometimes assisted by the Provençals and Pisans: *GA* 2.161–77; Epstein (1996), pp. 110–11.

110 Not 1222 but 1212 (25 August, per *GA* 2.123): the famous 'children's crusade', which may or may not have consisted mainly of children. The group in Genoa came from across France and Germany, but reportedly the Genoese refused to give them ships to get to the Holy Land. Some went on to Pisa, where the inhabitants were less scrupulous; many went home; many died along the way; and most of those who ultimately reached the Holy Land were sold into slavery: Dickson (2008).

PART TWELVE: GENOA UNDER THE ARCHBISHOPS 233

In the year of the Lord 1222, on the day of the nativity of the Lord, there was such a tremendous earthquake in Genoa and in nearly the whole of Italy that buildings fell and the earth was torn into many pieces, so that men deserted the cities and lived in the fields.[111] After Honorius died, he was succeeded by Gregory IX, who helpfully compiled books of decretals by his chaplain, Brother Raymond of the Order of Preachers.[112] This Gregory also canonised blessed Dominic, blessed Francis, and Saint Elisabeth.[113]

In the year of the Lord 1227, the Savonese and Albengans rebelled against the commune of Genoa, but the Genoese assembled a great army against them and the Albengans and Savonese came [to Genoa] with crosses in their hands at the command of the Commune.[114]

In the time of this archbishop, in the year of the Lord 1230, four pirates were captured—namely Recupero of Portovenere, Guglielmo of Ventimiglia, Durando of Portovenere, and Rubeo of Morinello—who were all condemned to hanging by the lord Spino, podestà of Genoa.[115] But such a multitude assembled on the piazza of San Lorenzo, especially of ladies who wished to free the said pirates, that they could not be led to the gibbet. Accordingly the podestà mounted his horse and rode about here and there [to clear space], but his horse became completely terrified and carried him over onto the stones next to the door of San Lorenzo; there he fell, breaking his leg and hip, an injury from which he later died. In the end the four pirates were hanged. But two of them, Recupero and Guglielmo, commended themselves to the relics of Saint John the Baptist which were kept in the church of San Lorenzo, and more than an hour after the other two were already dead, they still had not died. Eventually a messenger went to the commune and announced these things to the podestà, who had not yet died, and to the council. And

---

111 *GA* annalist Marchisio *scriba* reports that after the initial shock the Genoese went to San Lorenzo, took out the relics of the Baptist and other saints, and processed with them around the city: *GA* 2.187–8. Cf. Coleman (2007), p. 9; Alberic of Trois-Fontaines, *Chronicle* 1222, p. 912, who also reports that the damage was worst in Brescia.

112 Gregory (1227–41) is perhaps best known for his compilation of canon law—the *Decretals* of Gregory IX—which he commissioned from his confessor Raymond of Peñafort in 1230. Raymond, a prominent jurist who served as master general of the Dominican order 1238–40, lived into his nineties (d. 1275) and was later canonised: Kuttner (1982).

113 In 1234, 1228, and 1235 respectively. See introduction, pp. 16–17, esp. n. 55.

114 *GA* 3.19–24, at p. 23. The crosses signify penitence.

115 Spino da Soresina of Milan, podestà for 1230 (*GA* 3.54).

when the messenger returned, they were still found to be alive. They were therefore cut down; they explained how they had commended themselves to the blessed John the Baptist, who kept them alive, and thus they were sent away totally free.[116]

In the year of the Lord 1232, the Genoese elected the lord Pagano di Pietrasanta of Milan as podestà, contrary to the order of the emperor.[117] The emperor was so furious that he ordered all the Genoese who were in his realm to be taken prisoner. In addition, he ordered his marshal, who was in the lands beyond the sea, that all the Genoese there should be taken prisoner as well. But the Genoese sent ten galleys and two ships there and took total dominion over the sea. Afterward the emperor allowed all who had been taken captive in his realm to leave.[118]

In the year of the Lord 1237 the Milanese were defeated and conquered at Cortenuova by Emperor Frederick II; they lost their battle-wagon (*carroccio*[119]) and many nobles were taken prisoner into Apulia.[120]

In the following year the Ventimiglians, the Albengans, and the Savonese rebelled against the commune of Genoa. But the Genoese armed fourteen galleys, went to Ventimiglia, went ashore and took the city.[121] In that year Emperor Frederick sent his ambassadors to Genoa with letters seeking an oath of loyalty and homage, but the Genoese absolutely refused to make such an oath and sent the messengers of the emperor away unsatisfied.[122]

116 *GA* 3.52–4: one of numerous miracles the relics reportedly performed after their installation in San Lorenzo.

117 Frederick II (emperor 1220–50): this followed a pattern of increasing distance between Frederick and the Genoese, as Frederick had repealed their trading privileges in Sicily and their sovereignty over Siracusa after his imperial coronation in 1220. *GA* 3.62–6 gives the text of the two letters.

118 Here Jacopo omits the Genoese expedition to Ceuta in 1231–35 (*GA* 3.75–6), discussed above in part 5.3.

119 The *carroccio* or battle-wagon that carried an army's standard was an important military symbol. Like the eagle of an ancient Roman legion, its capture in battle was considered shameful: Dean, *Towns of Italy*, pp. 48–50; Raccagni (2010), pp. 88–91.

120 27 November 1237: *GA* 3.81. While Cortenuova was a massive victory for Frederick, it did not have the desired effect of quickly re-imposing imperial sovereignty in northern Italy: Abulafia (1988), pp. 305–12.

121 *GA* 3.83–6.

122 *GA* 3.87–8: the occasion of a 'great assembly' (*maximum parlamentum*) of citizens in San Lorenzo, echoing the similar exchange between the Genoese and Frederick I in part 12.1.

PART TWELVE: GENOA UNDER THE ARCHBISHOPS   235

And in the time of this archbishop, namely in the year of the Lord 1239, there was such an eclipse of the sun that no one of any age could remember such a great darkness ever occurring before.[123] The stars appeared in the heavens just as they usually appear in the quiet air at night. We, too, although we were then of childish years, saw the stars shining in the heavens in just this way.[124] In this same year the aforesaid Archbishop Otto, of reverend memory and illustrious renown, was similarly eclipsed: while he lost his earthly light, he found his celestial light.[125]

Chapter five: Regarding Giovanni, fifth archbishop. Giovanni da Cogorno, fifth archbishop, took office in the year of the Lord 1239 and completed twelve years in the archiepiscopate.[126] This man had been an archdeacon of Genoa, and was unanimously elected to the archbishopric. After his election he departed for the curia on an armed galley together with two ambassadors from the commune of Genoa, to obtain the gift of consecration from the supreme pontiff. He found such favour in the sight of the pope and cardinals that to the honour of the commune of Genoa he was entirely set free [to return home] by Pope Gregory IX within the space of three days.[127] This archbishop was a very learned man, and especially skilled in the art of medicine.

In the time of this archbishop, in the year of the Lord 1241, the imperial party in Genoa, who were known as the Mascherati, withdrew from the city, and the lord Ansaldo de Mari was named chief admiral by

123 3 June 1239: *GA* 3.93–4. Cf. *MO*, p. 439.
124 This is the first of several instances where Jacopo contributes his personal recollections. Although—as discussed in the introduction—he gives readers of the *Chronicle* relatively little information about his own life, his own perspective, experience, and analysis come through more frequently from this point in the chronicle.
125 *GA* 3.94–5.
126 A renowned doctor and scholar who had previously been provost of Santa Maria di Castello and archdeacon of San Lorenzo. Salimbene of Parma, who was then living in Genoa, describes Giovanni as 'a small man, who was very old and avaricious. Moreover, there was a very evil rumour circulating about him that he was not a good Catholic': *Chronicle* 461, p. 482. See also *GA* 3.95, 4.10; *RC*, p. 474; *RC2*, pp. 391–6; also the *Kalendarium* of the cathedral chapter: Cambiaso (1917), p. 345.
127 As the *GA* notes: 'he was examined on the first day, consecrated on the second, and awarded the grace of the pallium on the third' (3.95).

Emperor Frederick.[128] Then Pope Gregory convened a council against Emperor Frederick, persecutor of the church, but while prelates were being brought to Rome on Genoese galleys, this Frederick secretly had a multitude of galleys armed in his own realm and by the Pisans; then he captured those prelates and imprisoned them.[129] When the Genoese heard this, they armed forty-eight galleys powerfully in the space of only a few days and went eagerly to search out and attack their enemies.[130] Then the aforesaid Frederick so corrupted the Romans with money that they sought to expel the pope from the City and bring in the emperor. Learning of this, the pope gathered the heads of the apostles to his bosom; in bare feet and accompanied by the cardinals he carried them to the church of Saint Peter the Apostle, where he convened the Roman people. There he displayed the uncovered heads of the apostles to the people with many tears, so rousing them with his fervent words that almost all had themselves marked with the cross against the emperor. And when the emperor approached Rome with his army, hoping to be granted easy entry, he heard of this enormous change in the people and retreated. Also, after the galleys of the emperor and the Pisans had captured the aforementioned prelates, they came often to the Genoese Riviera and did much damage. For this reason the Genoese powerfully armed ninety-six galleys and chased all of [the Pisans'] galleys so far that they never dared to return.[131]

In the time of this archbishop, in the year of the Lord 1243, the lord Sinibaldo of the counts of Lavagna was elected to the papacy and called

---

128 A good example of how civic conflict was tied to broader political debates such as that of papacy (the Guelfs) v. empire (the Ghibellines). Here the city's prominent Ghibellines, known as the Mascherati, left the city in protest against the commune's pro-papal policies. See *CMG*, chap. 5 (Musarra), on such conflicts in Genoa, and *NCMH* 5.433–4 on the effects of Frederick's actions in Genoa.

129 The battle of Giglio, 3 May 1241, in which the fleet of the Genoese commune, which the pope had commissioned to bring prelates from western and northern Europe to his council, was trapped near the island of Giglio (in the Tuscan archipelago) by the imperial fleet (consisting of ships belonging to the kingdom of Sicily, Pisa, and the Genoese Ghibellines, commanded by the Genoese Ghibellines Ansaldo de Mari and his son Andreolo), which captured or sank almost the entire papal-Genoese fleet (three galleys sunk and twenty-two captured): *NCMH* 5.433–4 (Pryor). Captured prisoners included three papal legates, three archbishops, six bishops, and six abbots, including those of Cîteaux, Clairvaux, and Cluny. An interdict on Pisa proclaimed in response by Gregory IX lasted for sixteen years.

130 *GA* 3.114, which notes that they worked around the clock, even by candlelight, to outfit the ships.

131 *GA* 3.104–14.

Innocent IV.[132] Indeed, when he was surrounded near Sutri by the said Frederick and his soldiers in the year of the Lord 1244, the Genoese armed twenty-two galleys and brought him to Genoa with rejoicing. Afterward he went overland to Lyons, where he deposed Frederick from the imperial seat.[133] This Innocent was the first to ordain that cardinals should wear red hats.[134]

In the same year in which Pope Innocent came to Genoa, by the grace of the Savior I was inspired to enter the Order of Preachers, where from adolescence up to old age I have been nourished and taught by its maternal breasts.[135]

In the year of the Lord 1248 the aforesaid Frederick besieged the city of Parma in such force that he built another city next to it which he called Victoria.[136] And the Genoese sent many crossbowmen to the aid of the Parmesani. Finally Frederick was shamefully expelled from there and all his treasures were seized, for the Parmesani, the Piacenzans, the Milanese and the Genoese crossbowmen who had assembled in the city of Parma made such an attack on Victoria that the emperor was put to flight with his entire army and only recovered himself at

---

132 Pope Innocent IV (Sinibaldo Fieschi, of the Genoese Fieschi family, counts of Lavagna) was elected on 25 June 1243 after nearly twenty months of vacant see (*GA* 3.148). Previously a professor of law at Bologna, he was made cardinal priest of San Lorenzo in Lucina in 1227, and in 1235 he was bishop of Albenga. A great supporter of his native city, he wrote to the Genoese immediately after his election to assure them of his favour (*GA* 3.148). The author of a brilliant and influential commentary on Gregory IX's *Decretals*, he died in December 1254.

133 As Bertini Guidetti points out, Pope Innocent IV's rescue by the Genoese in spring 1244 (*GA* 3.153–60) was crucial for the final defeat of Frederick II in 1250, since from Genoa Innocent went on to Lyons, where he announced Frederick's excommunication and deposition in the third session of the Council of Lyons, 17 July 1245 (also discussed in part 5.3, above). Innocent also granted numerous privileges and concessions to the Genoese in a decree of 14 July: Potthast (1874), no. 11724, p. 995; *Libri iurium* 1/6, p. 44 (no. 953).

134 The cardinals' privilege of wearing a *galero*—a bright red hat with tassels—was announced at the same Council of Lyons in 1245.

135 A short and unusual insertion of Jacopo's own life into the general narrative; while vague, it implies that Jacopo was then in Genoa, and in the range of 10–15 years old (useful as his precise birthdate is unknown). The characterisation of the Order as a lactating mother—with spiritual sustenance or doctrine as her milk—is not uncommon.

136 The siege of Parma (1247–48), to which the Genoese contributed three hundred crossbowmen for Parma's defence: *GA* 3.170–2, 178–80, 188. The Genoese were renowned for the skill of their crossbowmen, who not only served in communal campaigns but also hired themselves out as mercenaries: Lane (1969).

Cremona.[137] They found there imperial crowns and great and precious treasures, by which many were enormously enriched, while the city which Frederick had built and called Victoria was totally destroyed. Meanwhile the emperor hurried back into Apulia and finished his life with a miserable death.

In the same year the lord Louis, king of the Franks, crossed over to the regions of Oltramare on Genoese galleys and ships; he had in his army two noble Genoese admirals, the lord Ugo Lercari and the lord Jacopo di Levanto. Although they captured Damietta, in the end the king was captured by the Saracens and many of the Christians were captured or wounded. Because of this the queen and the remaining Christians returned Damietta [to the Saracens] and recovered the king.[138]

In the year of the Lord 1249 King Enzo, the son of the emperor, was captured by the Bolognese and put in prison, where he remained for many years and eventually finished his life.[139]

In the year of the Lord 1251 the Savonese, who were rebelling, acceded to the demands of the commune, and the Genoese [Ghibellines] who were called Mascherati were recalled, and the lord pope Innocent IV came back to Genoa on his return from Lyons and was received in great glory.[140] Passing through Lombardy, he consecrated the church of the Blessed Dominic in Bologna, then he went into Apulia, where he died.[141]

137 The Cremonese were Frederick's allies: *GA* 3.179.

138 In August 1248 an enormous fleet, including many Genoese ships, assembled at Sampierdarena under the leadership of King (later Saint) Louis IX and set off to make another attempt to conquer Damietta: *GA* 3.178, 185–7; also Joinville, *Life of Saint Louis* 377 (Smith, *Chronicles*, p. 238), who mentions the Genoese. This was the Seventh Crusade, which ended in total and humiliating defeat: Tyerman (2006), chap. 24. Louis was captured at the battle of Fariskur in March 1250; to retrieve him, the crusaders were forced to give up Damietta and agree to a ransom of 800,000 bezants.

139 Enzo (*c.* 1218–72; *DBI* 43.1–8) was an illegitimate son of Frederick II, who appointed Enzo king of Sardinia in 1238. He was captured at Fossalta on 26 May 1249 (*GA* 3.185) and died in prison in Bologna after more than twenty years in captivity: Kleinhenz (2004), pp. 317–18. While Enzo's captivity was honourable, the collapse of the Hohenstaufen side after Frederick's death in 1250 left no one to ransom him.

140 *GA* 4.5–8. Innocent IV received a triumphal reception in Genoa on 18 May 1251 and stayed over a month (*GA* 4.5). Salimbene (*Chronicle* 646, p. 674) describes the magnificent wedding of one of the pope's Fieschi nephews during his visit: 'if the Queen of Sheba had seen it, she would have marvelled'. On the factional conflict between the Mascherati and their opponents the Rampini, see part 12.8 at n. 215, below.

141 San Domenico was consecrated on 17 October 1251. Innocent IV died at Naples on 7 December 1254; cf. *GA* 4.15.

PART TWELVE: GENOA UNDER THE ARCHBISHOPS   239

Chapter six: Regarding Gualterio, sixth archbishop. Gualterio da Vezzano, sixth archbishop, took office in the year of the Lord 1253 and completed twenty-one years in the archiepiscopate; after his death the archiepiscopate was vacant for two years.[142] He was made archbishop by the lord pope Innocent IV, to whom he was connected by great intimacy; for earlier he had been archdeacon of Luni, then the aforesaid pope made him marquess of the march of Ancona and later gave him the archbishopric of Genoa.[143] He was a man of great integrity, piety, and grace, and although he was of noble birth, he displayed [even] greater nobility in his habits. Also, he was skilled in the law and distinguished in all goodness and virtue. He was of such renown among the Roman curia that once when the Apostolic See was vacant, there was a great consensus among the cardinals that he should be elected to the supreme pontificate.

In the year of the Lord 1256 the marquess of Cagliari sent [a message] to the commune of Genoa that they should send galleys and fortify the fortress of Cagliari, because he wished to pledge himself to the commune of Genoa.[144] Therefore six galleys and one ship were sent along with many soldiers and crossbowmen, and they reinforced the fortress. Then, because the Pisans were harassing the same fortress of Cagliari, the Genoese armed twenty-four galleys and captured the eight Pisan galleys which were there.[145]

In the same year the Genoese armed eighty-four galleys and assembled many soldiers; then they besieged the fortress of Lerici and captured it.[146] Also in that year the galleys of the Genoese took six ships of the Pisans.

In the time of this archbishop, in the year of the Lord 1257, Guglielmo Boccanegra was made *capitano* of the Genoese *popolo* and held the

---

142   1253–74. The *GA* records his death in 1274 (4.171), but not his election *c.* 1252–53. This may be related to the fact that Gualterio was the first archbishop appointed directly by the pope rather than elected by the cathedral canons of San Lorenzo. While he was from a local noble family (Vezzano is near La Spezia in the eastern Ligurian Riviera), he had been papal chaplain to Innocent IV, who appointed him.

143   Probably papal rector; see Waley (1961).

144   *Libri iurium* 1/6, pp. 207–15 (nos. 1053–4, dated 20 April and 25 May 1256).

145   *GA* 4.21–3. Cagliari is at the southern tip of Sardinia; the Pisans had been trying to extend their hegemony over the area for some time.

146   *GA* 4.19–21. The conquest of Lerici, which controls the entrance to the gulf of La Spezia, gave the Genoese near-total domination of the Ligurian Sea.

captaincy for five years.¹⁴⁷ In the second year of his captaincy he armed four ships and forty galleys against the Venetians and Pisans and sent them across to Acre with the lord Rosso della Turca as admiral.¹⁴⁸ But they were badly equipped because they were filled with people from Lombardy—so that which was done badly came to a bad end, and twenty-six of the Genoese galleys were lost.¹⁴⁹ After a long conflict, the parties compromised through the mediation of the lord pope Alexander IV, who proclaimed a truce between them. But during the truce the Venetians and Pisans totally destroyed an extremely noble and beautiful tower the Genoese had built in Acre.¹⁵⁰

This archbishop [Gualterio] obtained a grant from the Apostolic See that no cleric of the Genoese diocese, especially in time of war, should be able to be removed from the territory (*districtus*) of Genoa for any reason on the pretext of certain letters; the privilege regarding this is preserved in the archiepiscopal palace.¹⁵¹

In the time of this archbishop, in the year of the Lord 1261, there was mass flagellation through nearly the whole of Italy.¹⁵² For great and small, noble and ignoble removed their clothes and went naked from the belt upward in procession through the cities, villages, and fortresses, whipping themselves and entreating the glorious Virgin and other saints with angelic songs. Among them, certain nobles and commoners came to Genoa from Tortona, and when they began whipping themselves through the city everyone mocked them as foolish and delirious. But suddenly by the will of God the entire city was moved—that is, great and small, noble and ignoble began whipping themselves day and night from church to church, singing heavenly and angelic songs. And those who had been the first to ridicule them were afterward first in constant

---

147 *GA* 4, pp. 25–8. On the office of *capitano del popolo* ('captain of the people'), see part 6.1 n. 4. Boccanegra was a wealthy non-noble citizen and military hero, yet his policies were unpopular and his regime collapsed in 1262: *CMG*, pp. 111–15 (Filangieri); Epstein (1996), pp. 135–8.

148 The war of Saint Sabas (1256–58) between Genoa and Venice: *GA* 4.28–36; *CMG*, pp. 489–90 (Mack); Musarra (2009). While the Pisans were originally allies of the Genoese, they switched sides in 1257 and a Venetian-Pisan coalition inflicted catastrophic defeat on the Genoese at Acre in 1258.

149 On Lombards as sailors, see part 5.3, above.

150 *CMG*, p. 486 (Mack); Wardi (1997).

151 Probably referring to a 1255 grant of Alexander IV, extending a concession originally granted by Innocent IV (part 12.5 n. 133, above).

152 On the flagellant movement of 1260–61: Dickson (1989).

PART TWELVE: GENOA UNDER THE ARCHBISHOPS 241

self-flagellation. Furthermore, many enmities and both old and new conflicts in the city of Genoa and in nearly all of Italy were led back to peace and concord.

This devotion was begun by certain poor and simple people in Tuscany and disseminated through all of Italy; it was observed by both children and adults, as much by nobles as by common people. They went about in society, two by two, whipping themselves, with clerics and members of the religious preceding them with crosses and banners. Many who had committed murder went with bare swords to their enemies and placed their naked swords in their hands, willing to accept any revenge from them that they wished. But their enemies threw the swords to the ground and prostrated themselves at their adversaries' feet, with weeping and tears by all concerned out of devotion and heartfelt exultation. Additionally, some beat themselves with whips made for this purpose, some with spines, and some with iron fetters. Miraculously, although this great flagellation occurred in the middle of winter and men went about naked above the belt from dawn to the hour of terce, it was nonetheless never reported that anyone was affected by the cold; rather, if they whipped themselves zealously at daybreak, on the following day they whipped themselves more zealously and more forcefully. But it is no wonder if they did not feel the external cold, because the fierce ardour of love which burned internally in their minds kept exterior cold from their whole bodies.[153]

Also in the time of this archbishop, in the year of the Lord 1264, a shining comet star appeared, dragging behind it an enormous fiery tail, rising from the western horizon and moving toward the eastern one. This became visible on the first day of August and appeared to grow continuously for nearly forty days. We often saw this comet and wondered what God wished to signify by so unusual and unprecedented a portent, or what great future event he wished to presage by it.[154]

Also in this year the kingdom of Sicily and Apulia was given by the church to Charles, count of Provence. Going to Rome, he accepted the crown and then went into Apulia, where he totally overcame Manfred, a son of Emperor Frederick, who had made himself king and rebelled

---

153 The flagellant movement clearly touched a social nerve: accounts of the event by Jacopo and the *GA* (4.39–41) on which it is based are unusually vivid.
154 *GA* 4.57–8, where its appearance is linked to the death of Urban IV (2 October 1264) and other contemporary events. Jacopo, unusually, confirms his own sighting of the comet, but does not attribute any particular significance to it.

against the church.¹⁵⁵ Then, after some time, Conradin, Emperor Frederick's grandson, went with a large army to Pisa intending with the help of the Pisans and nearly all the Ghibellines to enter Apulia by force and take the kingdom out of Charles' hands.¹⁵⁶ Indeed, when all feared this, the lord pope Clement [IV] was solemnly celebrating the feast of Pentecost and preaching at Viterbo in the church of the Friars Preacher.¹⁵⁷ I was then prior of the province of Lombardy for the Friars Preacher, and I was present on that occasion at our general chapter, when he said publicly to us all: 'Do not fear, because we know that this youth will be led like a sheep to his death by evil men. We know this through logic, and there is nothing greater than that after the articles of faith'.¹⁵⁸ He persuaded us with these words to the greatest admiration. But words offered by the spirit are proved by effect: when the aforesaid Conradin entered Apulia, he and all his army were overcome by King Charles and entirely crushed, and Conradin was punished with a capital sentence.¹⁵⁹

In the year of the Lord 1268 the Genoese armed twenty-seven galleys to go to Acre to fight the Venetians and Pisans, and Lanfranco Borborino was made admiral.¹⁶⁰ The Venetians had twenty-four galleys. This Borborino was fearful in his heart and inexperienced in military matters, however, so it was a great mistake to make him admiral in this way—for

---

155 Charles of Anjou (b. 1226/7), count of Provence and youngest brother of King Louis IX of France. The popes had been seeking someone to clear the remnants of the Hohenstaufen party from southern Italy since Frederick II's death in 1250. In 1263 Charles, a seasoned soldier, accepted Urban IV's offer to seize the kingdom of Sicily (consisting of Sicily and southern Italy); Urban accordingly declared a crusade against Frederick's last remaining son Manfred, who had seized the throne of Sicily. Charles defeated Manfred at Benevento and was crowned king in Rome in 1266: Dunbabin (1998), esp. chap. 5; Runciman (1958).

156 After Benevento, Charles turned his attention to Frederick II's grandson Conradin (1252–68), whose claim to Sicily was supported by the German princes, northern Italian cities, and Castile, all of whom were concerned about the papal-French alliance. Arriving in Verona in March 1268, Conradin travelled to Pisa via Pavia and Vado: *GA* 4.106–9. See also *Annales placentini gibellini*, p. 526, and Runciman (1958), chap. 7.

157 Clement, who was on poor terms with the Romans, used the papal palace at Viterbo as his chief residence: Brentano (1974), pp. 99, 110, 162.

158 Jacopo was elected Dominican prior for Lombardy at Bologna in 1267: Epstein (2016), p. 3. This is Jacopo's personal recollection of Clement IV's address to the Dominican general chapter at Viterbo in 1268.

159 Conradin was defeated at Tagliacozzo in August 1268 and executed in October. See also *MO*, p. 441.

160 Actually 1266: *GA* 4.89–91.

the leader of an army must be generous of heart, thoughtful in spirit, and stout of both body and spirit. Once the galleys of the Venetians had been sighted near Trapani, [Borborino's] spirit was quickly broken and his strength dissolved; he climbed into a sloop, fled, and deserted the squadron. And thus the galleys were scattered and captured since their leader had fled. Nonetheless, although some have accused him of treason, we believe it to have been more cowardice of heart than betrayal.[161] In any case, when this was known in Genoa, without delay they armed twenty-five galleys of which the lord Oberto Doria was made admiral.[162] He sought the enemy everywhere, and finally captured in battle a certain Venetian city called Terranova on the island of Crete; he totally destroyed it by iron, fire, and blood, and the men whom they took there he brought captive to Genoa.[163]

In the time of this archbishop, in the year of the Lord 1270, the noble men lord Oberto Spinola and lord Oberto Doria were made *capitani del popolo* of Genoa, and they maintained the captaincy and the regime for twenty-two years. The single exception is that lord Oberto Doria resigned in the fifteenth year, against the will of the people of Genoa; but he appointed in his place his son lord Corrado, who held the office of *capitano* for seven years.[164]

After this the aforesaid lord Gualterio, beloved of God and esteemed by men, full of days, virtues, and good works, and enfeebled by a good old age, went to rest with a blessed end. His fragrant renown remains in the world as his blessed spirit rules in heaven.[165]

Chapter seven: Regarding Bernardo, seventh archbishop. Bernardo, a native of Parma and seventh archbishop, took office in the year of the Lord 1276 and completed ten years in the archiepiscopate; after his

161 Afterward Borborino was convicted of treason; he was exiled and his possessions were confiscated: Ferretto, *Codice diplomatico di Liguria*, p. 56.
162 At this time in his thirties, Oberto Doria (before 1230 to 1295; *DBI* 41.424–31) went on to a brilliant naval and political career. In 1270 (n. 164, below) he was elected co-*capitano del popolo* (a position he held for fifteen years), and in 1284 he led the Genoese fleet to victory over Pisa at Meloria, which led to Pisa's decline as a maritime power.
163 *GA* 4.91–2, which correctly identifies the city as Chania.
164 *GA* 4.140–1; *GA* 5 (*DGA*), pp. 70–1, 136. Spinola and Doria were co-*capitani* 1270–85; Spinola then continued with Oberto's son Corrado as co-*capitani* until 1291, when the city reverted to rule by a non-Genoese podestà and *capitano*: Epstein (1996), pp. 155–6, 181.
165 *GA* 4.171.

death the archiepiscopate was vacant for two years.[166] He was first archdeacon of Narbonne, then he was made marquess of the march of Ancona, and finally he was promoted to the honour of the archiepiscopate in the Genoese church by the lord Pope Innocent V.[167]

In the time of this archbishop, in the year of the Lord 1288 [actually 1284], the Pisans armed seventy-two galleys against the Genoese, believing that the Genoese would be unable to arm so many.[168] Then they went across to the Ligurian Sea, intending to despoil the Riviera, but in the end they did not dare to land anywhere nor to inflict any damages. But when the Genoese learned of this, they valiantly armed ninety-six galleys and set out in force to search out and discover their enemies with both speed and strength. Then, when they found the Pisan galleys at Porto Pisano, they attacked them so daringly that they took thirty-three galleys, and of the others some were sunk while others fled shamefully. Thus [the Genoese] returned to their homes in great triumph. From that time onward the Genoese so humiliated and overpowered the Pisans that up to the present day [i.e. 1296] they have kept their galleys in port and prohibited other vessels from entering there.[169]

This archbishop was greatly skilled in canon law, and very careful and wise in all his doings. He was also attentive and focused on advancing all things [related to the] archbishopric.[170] At Genoa he greatly improved the palace of the archbishop; at Molassana he built a large and beautiful palace; at Sanremo he expanded and improved a noble palace begun by lord Gualterio, and he accomplished many other useful works besides.[171] Then he was called to the Roman curia by the lord Gerardo, bishop of Sabina, who retained him, and it was hoped that he would be made a

---

166 The canon lawyer Bernardo degli Arimondi of Parma, appointed by Innocent V in 1276: *GA* 4.176–7; Cambiaso (1917), pp. 344–5.

167 The Dominican theologian Peter of Tarentaise (January–June 1276), later beatified.

168 Jacopo's chronicle is unusually short for Bernardo's archiepiscopate and the administratorship of Opizzo Fieschi, recording only the battle of Meloria and the papal succession: see the introduction, p. 15.

169 Referring to the great Genoese victory at Meloria on 6 August 1284 and its aftermath: *DGA*, pp. 51–7; *CMG*, pp. 464–6 (Kirk).

170 Contrariwise, the *GA* comments that 'this archbishop was agreeable to neither the commune nor the people' (4.177).

171 These commissions honoured his saintly predecessors: Saint Syrus was a native of Molassana, and Saint Romulus died at Sanremo: part 11.3–4, above.

cardinal.[172] But as he was travelling to the city of Parma, he felt himself grow gravely ill, so he abandoned his journey and returned to Genoa—not without great cost to his body—preferring to die in the city where he had been made spiritual father than in the one where he had been carnally created. When he reached Genoa, his illness worsened, and he was raised by death from earthly mediocrity and honourably entombed.

Around these times three cardinals were elected to the supreme pontificate in succession, all of whose brief lives were extinguished and finished within only a very few days. The first was Innocent V of the Order of Preachers, who ruled for five months. This man was very famous and very distinguished in theology; he taught theology at Paris for many years. He had a special fondness for the city of Genoa and made peace between this city and King Charles.[173] The next [was] Adrian [V] of the counts of Lavagna, who ruled for one month and a few days.[174] Although he was of great wisdom and experience, he was nonetheless unable to accomplish anything important or noteworthy due to the brevity of [his] tenure. Indeed, when his friends and relatives rejoiced at his elevation, he said to them, 'Why do you rejoice? It was better for you to have a live cardinal than a dead pope'. Indeed, after a short time he fell ill and rested in peace. The next [was] John [XXI], a native of Spain, who ruled for eight months.[175] For when he was having a certain house built, the house suddenly fell down, taking him with it, and thus his life ended. The church did not greatly suffer by his death because, while he was full of the knowledge of the physical and natural [world], he was simultaneously very much empty of discernment and natural sense.

Regarding Opizzo, the patriarch of Antioch. Opizzo Fieschi, of the counts of Lavagna, began to rule the Genoese church in the year of the Lord 1288, and reigned over it for three and a half years. He was a relative of the lord popes Innocent IV and Adrian [V]. And it is to

---

172 Gerardo Bianchi of Parma, cardinal bishop of Sabina (d. 1302).
173 On Innocent V: n. 167, above. For his letter to the Genoese urging them to reconcile with Charles of Anjou: Potthast (1874), no. 21099, p. 1704; *GA* 4.173–4.
174 Adrian V (Ottobono Fieschi, 11 July–16 August 1276)—son of Tedisio Fieschi, count of Lavagna, and nephew of Innocent IV, who had named him cardinal deacon of Sant'Adriano *c.* 1251—died before he could be ordained priest and crowned pope: *GA* 4.174–5. Dante placed him among the avaricious in *Purgatorio* 19.100–2.
175 John XXI (Peter of Toledo, 8 September 1276–20 May 1277), previously archbishop of Braga and cardinal bishop of Tusculum.

[that family's] great honour and immense renown that within the space of thirty-six years or thereabouts that these two aforementioned supreme pontiffs came from the same house.[176] Furthermore, many cardinals arose similarly from the same house.[177] The aforementioned lord Innocent made this Opizzo patriarch of Antioch, and he held and ruled over that patriarchate for a long time, and was of the highest and greatest dignity there. But at last its sins were weighed (*peccatis exigentibus*[178]), and the city of Antioch—so noble and famous—was captured by the Saracens, and all the goods of the patriarchate were seized and laid waste. And thus it was necessary for the patriarch to return to the lands on this side of the sea. Sympathetic and wishing to provide for him, the Roman church [i.e. the pope] therefore gave him the care (*cura*) of the church of Trani.[179] And after a number of years it entrusted to him the care of the Genoese church—as much in temporal as in spiritual things.[180]

Later the commune of Genoa sent official ambassadors to the lord pope Nicholas IV regarding certain items of business of the commune of Genoa.[181] The aforesaid ambassadors humbly requested that the supreme pontiff condescend to give them an archbishop according to custom. The supreme pontiff wished to agree to their petition, so he provided fully and honourably for this patriarch, and gave the city of Genoa an archbishop.

Chapter eight: Regarding Brother Jacopo, the eighth archbishop.

Brother Jacopo da Varagine of the Order of Preachers, eighth archbishop,

---

176 Thirty-three years, from the election of Innocent IV in 1243 to that of Adrian V in 1276.

177 The staunchly Guelf Fieschi may have contributed as many as five cardinals to the thirteenth-century college, but the only well-documented one is Guglielmo (d. 1256), bishop of Ferrara and nephew of Innocent IV (who made him cardinal deacon of Sant'Eustachio in 1244). On Guglielmo and his two papal relatives, see Paravicini Bagliani (1972), pp. 61–71, 329–40, 358–79.

178 A conventional phrase for explaining Christian setbacks in the Holy Land: Siberry (1985), pp. 69–89.

179 *Cura* suggests responsibility without formal office, much as a curate might perform the responsibilities of an absentee priest.

180 Opizzo Fieschi was named patriarch of Antioch in 1247, but fled the city in 1268 in the face of a Muslim siege. In 1280 Martin IV named him bishop-administrator of Trani; similarly, in 1288 Nicholas IV named him administrator, but not archbishop, of Genoa after the death of Archbishop Bernardo—but he remained in that post less than four years due to conflict with the commune and died in 1292: *DBI* 47.508–10; Hamilton (1980), pp. 231–5.

181 Pope Nicholas IV (Girolamo Masci), 22 February 1288–4 April 1292 (*DBI* 78.357–60).

PART TWELVE: GENOA UNDER THE ARCHBISHOPS   247

took office in the year of the Lord 1292 and will live as long as it pleases God.[182] He was named archbishop by Pope Nicholas IV, of the Order of Friars Minor, who had called him into his presence by means of letters, intending to bestow upon him the gift of consecration and give him the pallium.[183] But when Jacopo arrived in Rome on Palm Sunday [30 March 1292], he found the same supreme pontiff labouring under a dangerous illness so grave that Nicholas returned his soul to God that Friday [4 April], and, so we believe, has entered into the heavenly palace.[184] Then the venerable college of cardinals, forming a consistory during the octave of Easter [6–13 April], ordered that for the honour of the commune of Genoa its archbishop ought to be appointed very quickly. Accordingly, Jacopo was consecrated on the octave of Easter by the venerable father Lord Latinus, bishop of Ostia, and adorned with the pallium in that same week, and thus he returned to his city with joy and was received with reverence by the people.[185]

Here, previously as a member of his order and afterward as archbishop, he composed many works. He compiled a single-volume *Legends of the saints*, adding many legends to those in the *Ecclesiastical history*, the *Tripartite history*, the *Scholastic history*, and the chronicles of many different authors.[186] After the prologue, this work begins, 'The Advent of the Lord' (*Adventus Domini*), etc.[187] He also wrote two volumes of sermons on all the saints, by which their feasts are celebrated according to the cycle of the church year.[188] One volume is very wide-ranging; the other is extremely brief and constrained. Both volumes begin: 'My foot follows

182 Jacopo Doria, who presented his completed section of the *GA* (*DGA*) to the commune in 1294, does not mention Jacopo da Varagine's election as archbishop (*DGA* for 1292, pp. 137–65).

183 A ceremonial garment signifying papal appointment (see part 12.1 n. 7).

184 Jacopo uses the Greek *Parasceve*, a term used in the Gospels and by the church fathers for the Sabbath eve (Friday), and more particularly for Good Friday. The word emphasises the fact that—like Christ—Nicholas IV died on Good Friday.

185 Latino Malabranca Orsini, O.P. (*c.* 1235–94; *DBI* 67.699–703), then dean of the college of cardinals.

186 The *GL* (*Golden legend* = *Legenda aurea, c.* 1260), a compilation of saints' legends for which Jacopo is best known: on the *GL* and the rest of Jacopo's works detailed in this paragraph, see the introduction, pp. 1–2, 16–19. Other references are to Bede's *Historia ecclesiastica* (*c.* 731); the *Historia ecclesiastica tripartita* compiled by Cassiodorus and his student Epiphanius Scholasticus *c.* 510 (*CSEL* 71); and Peter Comestor's twelfth-century *Historia scholastica* (part 1.1 n. 4, above).

187 Lacking official titles, medieval works were often identified in library catalogues by *incipit* ('it begins'), that is, the first few words of the text.

188 *Sermones de sanctis* (*SS*).

in his footprints' (*Vestigia eius secutus est pes meus*[189]). He also wrote sermons for all the Sunday Gospel readings that are read in church throughout the course of the year, creating three sermons for each Gospel reading in honour of the indivisible Trinity.[190] This work, after the prologue, begins: 'Prepare to meet your God, O Israel' (*Preparare in ocursum Dei tui, Israel*[191]). He also wrote sermons on all the Gospels which are read on each weekday during Lent, namely from Ash Wednesday until the Tuesday after Easter, making two sermons for each Gospel reading.[192] This work begins: 'Daughter of my people, put on a hair shirt' (*Filia populi mei, induere cilicio*[193]), etc. He also wrote a book called the *Mariale*, which is entirely about the Blessed Mary and arranged according to the order of the letters of the alphabet.[194] This book, after the prologue, begins: 'Various forms of abstinence' (*Abstinencia multiplex*). In addition, he compiled the present *Chronicle*.[195]

Here in the second year of his pontificate, namely in the year of the Lord 1293, he celebrated a provincial council in the church of San Lorenzo, where the bishop of Albenga, the bishop of Brugnato, the bishop of Noli, the bishop of Mariana, and the bishop of Nebbio were present.[196] The bishop of Bobbio excused himself, being oppressed by infirmity and old age, but he sent his procurator and syndic in his place; the bishopric of Accia was then vacant.[197] Many mitred abbots also attended, specifically the abbots of San Siro, Santo Stefano, San Fruttuoso,

---

189 Job 23.11.

190 *Sermones de omnibus Evangeliis dominicalibus* (*SD*).

191 Amos 4.12.

192 *Sermones quadragesimales* (*SQ*).

193 Jeremiah 6.26.

194 *Liber Marialis* (*Mariale*).

195 *Chronicle of the city of Genoa* (*JVC*, *CCG*).

196 Niccolò Vaschone di Ceva, OFM, bishop of Albenga (1292–after 1302; Polonio (2002a), pp. 91–2); Arduino Franchi, bishop of Brugnato (1288–after 1292); Ugolino, bishop of Noli (dates unknown); Adamo, bishop of Mariana (before 1283–after 1298); and Giovanni, bishop of Nebbio (1283–1311): respectively Eubel (1960), pp. 81, 148, 358, 325, 360. For more on the Genoese archbishopric, see parts 10.2 and 11.1.

197 Bobbio: Not the abbot of the monastery, but the bishop of the city; see part 10.2 n. 15, above. On Accia: Eubel (1960), p. 67. Brugnato, Bobbio, and the Corsican bishoprics had all been placed under the authority of the archdiocese of Genoa by Innocent II in 1133, while the bishoprics of Albenga and Noli were added to its jurisdiction in 1162 and 1239 respectively: parts 10.2, 11.1, and 12.2, above.

and Tino.[198] The abbot of Borzone and the abbot of the island of Gallinara excused themselves, being burdened with illness and old age; they also sent their procurators and syndics.[199] A great assembly of priors, archpriests, and ministers of the church were also present—and at that council many useful things were established and many constitutions announced which are still observed today.[200]

Among other things, it seemed that some doubt had arisen as to whether the body of Saint Syrus was actually in the marble sarcophagus located above the altar of San Lorenzo, so we wished to know the full truth of this matter.[201] For this reason, we had the tomb opened in the presence of the council and the podestà, the *capitano*, the abbot of the people, and many other nobles of the city of Genoa; in it we found a wooden sarcophagus closed up and carefully sealed.[202] Upon opening this, we found there a lead cover, a marble tablet, and a card placed on a pyx. And on both sides it was noted in writing that the bones of Saint Syrus were deposited in this box. We ordered the box to be placed on the altar of San Lorenzo, and upon examining its contents with our own

---

198 The Benedictine monastery of San Siro had been the cathedral of Genoa before the episcopal seat was transferred to San Lorenzo (part 11.11 n. 100, above), while Santo Stefano was a dependency of the abbey of Bobbio. San Fruttuoso di Capodimonte is a Benedictine foundation patronised by the Doria family near Portofino: part 11.19 n. 209. The 'abbot of Tino' was the abbot of San Venerio on Tino, an island off the Mediterranean coast near La Spezia: see part 11.17, n. 171. On the religious orders in Genoa, see *CMG*, chap. 13 (Polonio).

199 Sant'Andrea di Borzone, ten kilometres inland from Chiavari, and San Martino on Gallinara, a small island just off Albenga.

200 This is the only surviving notice of this provincial council; no mention of it appears in the contemporary annals of Jacopo Doria (*DGA*), and no record of its proceedings has survived.

201 Saint Syrus was a saintly early bishop of Genoa: part 11.3, above; *GL*, pp. 600–10. The church dedicated to him served as Genoa's cathedral from the fifth or sixth century until the diocesan seat—and the saint's relics—were transferred to San Lorenzo in the eleventh century: see parts 11.3 and 11.11, above. In 1283, during renovations in San Lorenzo, the monks of San Siro reclaimed Syrus' relics along with those of Saints Felix and Romulus. The facts and legitimacy of this reclamation/theft were hotly disputed; hence the official investigation arranged by Jacopo in 1293.

202 After the end of the Doria-Spinola double captaincy (part 12.6 n. 164, above), Genoa had a podestà and a *capitano del popolo* as its chief magistrates, both foreigners elected annually (*DGA*, p. 121). In July 1293 the podestà was Pietro Carbone of Bologna (*DBI* 19.703–4), and the *capitano* was Beltramo de' Ficeni of Bergamo: *DGA*, pp. 147, 165–70. On the (secular) office of 'abbot of the people', see part 6.1 n. 5.

hands, we found all the bones required for the composition of the human body.²⁰³ Moreover, a few days later, with the arrival of the feast of the same Saint Syrus, we ordered that the box with the bones should be placed over the great pulpit of the church of San Lorenzo and there we clearly displayed the epitaphs and the bones to the people, and they were viewed by all with the greatest devotion and venerated humbly.²⁰⁴ Then we ordered that the head of Saint Syrus should be kept in the sacristy and enclosed within a silver casket.

Also in our times—that is, in the year of our Lord 1294—there was a certain hermit from the area of the Abruzzo by the name of Brother Peter Morrone, who for fifty years had led the life of a hermit; he was a man of great asceticism and holy repute. Therefore when the Apostolic Seat had lain vacant for two years and more since the cardinals were unable to agree, on a certain day when they were gathered together for some other great business, the fame of this same Brother Peter the Hermit came amongst them. Then one of the cardinals is said to have pronounced the following words: 'Why should we not make this hermit pope?' Immediately all votes were united in his favour, and they unanimously elected him and called him Celestine.²⁰⁵ And after he had been made supreme pontiff, one day when he was going to L'Aquila he rode on an ass as an example of humility.²⁰⁶ And again, when going from L'Aquila to Naples he did not wish to use a palfrey but only a humble little ass.²⁰⁷

203 Unfortunately, Jacopo's confirmation that the relics in the cathedral were those of Saint Syrus was contested by Brother Raimondo, a monk of San Siro, and the dispute over the saint's true resting place continued for almost two centuries: in 1457, a committee of mediators concluded that Bishop Landulf had only transferred part of Saint Syrus' relics to the new cathedral, while the rest had remained at San Siro: Ferretto (1907), pp. 238–47.

204 Saint Syrus's feast day is 29 June, but Genoese churches more often celebrate the translation of his relics on 7 July: Macchiavello (1997), pp. 21–36.

205 Celestine V (Pietro da Morrone), 5 July–13 December 1294: *DBI* 23.402–15. The papal seat had been vacant for nearly two years before Celestine's election in July 1294, when he was about seventy-nine. He reigned about six months before abdicating in December of that year: Potthast (1874), pp. 1921–2. Until 2013, Celestine was the only pope ever to have resigned; virtually his only legacy as pope was an edict in which he confirmed the pope's right to abdicate: Potthast (1874), no. 24019, p. 1921. He was canonised in 1313.

206 Celestine was elected in Perugia on 5 July 1294 and consecrated in L'Aquila on 29 August; travelling through Abruzzo and Campania, he reached Naples on 13 November.

207 A palfrey is a valuable horse bred for riding: that is, Celestine refused the type of horse a pope would usually ride to follow the example of Christ, who entered Jerusalem riding an ass (John 12.14–15).

PART TWELVE: GENOA UNDER THE ARCHBISHOPS 251

In the first year of his pontificate, this pope in his full power (*de plenitudine potestatis*) created twelve cardinals. After that, in his full simplicity (*de plenitudine simplicitatis*) he created another cardinal without attending to appropriate time and protocol—namely the archbishop of Benevento, whom he made cardinal priest not at the appropriate moment nor with the counsel of the cardinals, but at the suggestion of others.[208] Indeed, in handing out dignities, prelacies, offices, and benefices, he did not follow the custom of the curia, but more often followed the suggestions of others and his own ignorant simplicity. And he did many other things in which he did not follow in the footsteps of earlier fathers or their statutes. Although he acted not out of malice, but more out of his own simplicity, nonetheless these resulted in great injury (*preiudicium*) to the church.[209] For this reason, seeing his own incompetence and inexperience and having been led by good counsel, he issued a constitution that if any pope should find himself incapable of the papal office he might freely resign it.[210] With this done, when he had held the papacy for about six months or thereabouts, he freely resigned on the feast of Saint Lucy [13 December] and, resuming his eremitical habit (*habitus*[211]), returned to his previous solitude.[212] After his resignation, namely on the vigil of the Nativity of the Lord, Lord Benedetto of Anagni, certainly a man of great knowledge and experience, was elected as supreme pontiff and called Boniface VIII.[213]

---

208 Giovanni Castrocoeli, OSB, archbishop of Benevento 1282–94 (d. 22 February 1295). Although there was some precedent for this practice, a major objection to Castrocoeli's appointment was that he remained administrator of his archdiocese after being appointed cardinal, instead of joining the curia in Rome.

209 In the professional Latin of the late medieval courts, *preiudicium* ('injury') has a technical meaning of 'legal disadvantage', which underlines Jacopo's point that Celestine was a good hermit but a poor administrator.

210 Potthast (1874), pp. 1921–2.

211 Like the English 'habit', *habitus* may refer either to a practice or to a form of monastic dress.

212 Jacopo is reckoning from Celestine's July election rather than from his August consecration. Celestine lived out his remaining days at the castle of Fumone in Campania and died in 1296; historians disagree as to whether this was imprisonment (lest his successor's enemies rally around him as an antipope) or a kind of harmless supervised solitude: Gigliotti (2008).

213 Boniface VIII (Benedetto Caetani), 24 December 1294–11 October 1303 (*DBI* 12.146–70). As pope, Boniface made aggressive claims for the temporal and spiritual supremacy of the papacy—most notably in the Bull *Unam sanctam* (1302). These ideas brought him into conflict with secular rulers, including the Holy Roman Emperor Albrecht I, King Philip IV of France, and the influential Colonna family of Rome, mentioned by Jacopo below: Canning (2011), pp. 11–59.

In addition, in that same year eighteen galleys and two ships of some merchants of Genoa fought against twenty-eight galleys and four ships of the Venetians; this was discussed previously in part five, chapter three.[214]

In the year of the Lord 1295, in the month of January, a general and universal peace was made in the city of Genoa between those who were called Mascherati, or Ghibellines, and those who were called Rampini, or Guelfs.[215] Between them there had long been great animosities, many divisions, and dangerous disagreements: these dissensions, divisions, and factions persisted for fifty-five years and more. But, acting by the grace of the Savior, all were brought back to peace and concord, so that among them was made one fellowship, one brotherhood, one body. At this so much joy followed that the entire city was full of rejoicing, full of dancing, full of immense joy. And in the public assembly at which the peace was sworn, robed in pontificals, we expounded the word of God and there with our clergy sang the *Te Deum laudamus* in a loud voice, having among us four mitres between bishops and abbots.[216] After eating dinner, we rode happy and rejoicing through our whole city on a palfrey draped in linen, dressed in pontificals and followed by the entire militia, bestowing on all God's benediction as well as our own, and giving thanks to God.[217]

Also, as a sign of the joy of this so-noble-and-glorious peace, the commune of Genoa then made the noble man Lord Jacopo di Carcano, a citizen of Milan who was then podestà of Genoa, a belted knight, and heaped many honours and gifts upon him. But since in this present life no good

---

214 See also *NCMH* 5.445–6 (Pryor).

215 A famous example of the factionalism that divided many central and northern Italian communes in the later Middle Ages; see the examples in Dean, *Towns of Italy*, pp. 141–50, 156–88. On the riots see Epstein (1996), pp. 182–3; Di Fabio/Besta (1998), pp. 223–53; Calderoni Masetti/Wolf (2012), pp. 75–82 (Novello). The division to which Jacopo refers goes back to the reign of Frederick II (1194–1250), if not further. The Rampini were a faction of Genoese families who refused to render the homage demanded by Frederick II after his victory at Cortenuova in 1237, allying themselves first with the papacy and then the Venetians. Their rivals the Mascherati favoured Frederick and were mostly exiled by the Rampini during these years. See Epstein (1996), pp. 124–8; *NCMH* 5.433 (Pryor).

216 *Te deum laudamus* (We praise you, O God): a canticle of thanksgiving. Jacopo's point about having 'four mitres' present underscores the importance of the occasion (in this case, the presence of bishops and other high-ranking clerics who wore mitres as part of their official robes).

217 Unlike Celestine V (nn. 206–7 above), Jacopo does not scorn the use of a palfrey as a symbol of his office.

things are pure, because pure good exists in heaven, pure evil exists in hell, and in truth good and evil are mixed in this world, thus—what sorrow!—*our harp is quickly turned to mourning and our organ is changed to a voice of weeping.*[218] For that same year, in the month of December—namely, five days after the Nativity of the Lord—while our citizens rejoiced in the aforementioned peace, the enemy of the human race, begrudging the peace, threw our citizens into such discord and tumult that they clashed in hand to hand combat through the alleys and piazzas, and for many days they contended angrily against one another. From this followed the slaying of men, the wounding of many, the burning of houses, the looting and plunder of many things.[219] And because an angry madness refuses the bridle of reason, the frenzied chaos proceeded so far that certain people who were attempting to take possession of the tower of San Lorenzo dared to set a fire in that same church of San Lorenzo and thus burned up its roof entirely. This very dangerous sedition lasted from the fifth day after the Nativity of the Lord up to the seventh day of February.[220] Finally two *capitani* were created, namely lord Corrado Spinola and lord Corrado Doria, and thus the city was calmed from its battles, and the *capitano* who had been elected from outside [the city] was dismissed.[221] Also, the glorious and magnificent fleet which the Genoese armed against the Venetians in the year of the Lord 1295 was discussed earlier in part five, chapter three.

In the following year the Venetians armed a fleet of galleys and set off for Romania [Byzantium]; there they destroyed a certain Genoese territory by the name of Pera near Constantinople, which was totally undefended, as well as a certain territory by the name of Phocaea, belonging to the lords Benedetto and Emanuele Zaccaria.[222]

---

218 Job 30.31.

219 These riots did not spare the archbishop's palace, and Jacopo was forced to apply to Pope Boniface VIII for funds to replace lost furniture and books. These were granted by Boniface in a letter of 12 June 1296, which allowed Jacopo 'to receive up to the sum of two hundred silver marks for things looted and villainously taken': *JVC* 1.69–70, 2.412.

220 30 December 1294–7 February 1295.

221 Corrado Doria (*c.* 1250–1321/3; *DBI* 41.318–22), Genoese *capitano del popolo* and admiral, and Corrado Spinola (1269–99), another Genoese *capitano*—the sons of former *capitani* Oberto Doria and Oberto Spinola respectively. See part 12.6 n. 164, above.

222 Benedetto Zaccaria, Genoese admiral and diplomat, had been made ruler of Phocaea (Italian *Focea*; now Foça, Turkey) in 1275: *DGA*, pp. 51, 75; also *CMG*, pp. 408–16, 509–12.

In the year of the Lord 1297 the Venetians armed sixty-five galleys, and the Genoese seventy-five galleys, but they were not able to meet up with the galleys of the Venetians. And when the galleys of the Genoese heard falsely that the galleys of the Venetians had returned to Venice, they went back to Genoa with their own galleys. But then they heard that the Venetian galleys, which had been lying low, had set out for Sicily, and they took and destroyed by fire many ships of the Genoese which were there. Because of this there was great tumult in Genoa.[223]

Also in that year the lord Pope Boniface laid serious charges against some of the Colonna, both clerical and lay, on account of their serious excesses, stripping two cardinals of those same Colonna of their titles.[224] The [Colonna] barricaded themselves in certain cities, rebelling against the church, but the army of the church took two of these cities, so they retreated to the city of Palestrina, which is said to be very strong.[225]

223 This phase of the Venetian–Genoese wars ended the following year with the Battle of Curzola (8 September 1298), in which the Venetians (under Andrea Dandolo, son of Doge Giovanni Dandolo) suffered a major defeat by the Genoese (led by Lamba Doria, Oberto's younger brother) near the island of Curzola (off modern Croatia): see appendix, pp. 255–7. For an overview of the Genoese-Venetian wars, see *CMG*, pp. 466–9 (Kirk); also Rose (2008), chaps. 25–6 (Dotson).

224 Cardinal Giacomo Colonna (*c.* 1250–1318; *DBI* 27.311–14), cardinal deacon of S. Maria in Via Lata, and his nephew Cardinal Pietro Colonna (1260–1326; *DBI* 27.399–402), bishop of Verona and papal legate to France. Boniface's involvement with the Colonna came from intervening in an inheritance dispute: after Cardinal Giacomo disinherited his three brothers in favour of his nephews (including Pietro) and the brothers appealed to Boniface, Boniface ordered Cardinals Giacomo and Pietro to restore the disputed lands to the three brothers; to return the consignment of papal treasure that their kinsman Stefano had seized and deliver Stefano up as a prisoner; and lastly, to hand over many of the Colonna lands around Rome, including their stronghold of Palestrina. When Giacomo and Pietro refused to comply, Boniface deprived them of their offices, excommunicated them, and ordered the forfeiture of their property by the bull *In excelso throno* (10 May 1297). Cf. the account in the slightly later *Chronicle* of the Dominican Francesco Pipino (*RIS* 9.737); also Rehberg (1999), pp. 42–56. This dispute led most of the Colonna family (with the exception of Giacomo's three brothers) to side against Boniface as his conflict with Philip IV of France grew more serious. On 7 September 1303 Boniface was attacked by a combined French–Colonna force at his retreat in Anagni outside Rome; although he was released from captivity after three days, he died about five weeks later, probably as a result of the humiliation and the injuries he sustained: Le Pogam (2007).

225 The 'cities' taken by papal forces were the castles of Colonna and Zagarolo, but the Colonna stronghold of Palestrina held out until September 1298, when it surrendered after Boniface promised the city would be spared. Boniface later ordered its destruction regardless, reputedly sowing salt on the site as the Romans had been said to do at Carthage in 146 BC.

APPENDIX

The following passage detailing the events of 1298—specifically, Jacopo's death and the Genoese triumph over the Venetians at Curzola—appears at the end of part 5 of some manuscripts of the Chronicle *(text, JVC 2.109–11).*[1]

In the year of the Lord 1297 [actually 1298], the aforesaid father [Jacopo], archbishop of Genoa, died; the lord Porchetto Spinola, a brother of the Order of Friars Minor, was elected to the archiepiscopate the following year with apostolic approval.[2] In June of that year the commune of Genoa elected the distinguished man Lamba Doria as general admiral against the aforesaid Venetians; by order of the Credenza, the lord admiral left Genoa with a resolute mind in the month of August with eighty-seven galleys.[3] Having embarked, however, when they came to a certain island which is called Gherba, they left three galleys there on the advice of certain sage men of the company.[4] Then they sailed to Messina, where certain Catalans became overconfident in their stupidity and presumed to attack them with arms out of envy and shame for the honour or dignity—that is, the magnificence—of the Genoese fleet. But in a moment of cleverness the Genoese vanquished them. These Catalans then fled into the city of Messina and the Genoese pursued them; they attacked the gates of the city with constant fire, and entering the city valiantly and powerfully they claimed victory over the same Catalans.

Then the aforesaid lord admiral waited with his fleet for the Venetian galleys for the space of eight days, during which time he heard no news of them at all. Finally, seeking to put an end to this war—not to mention

1 *CMG*, pp. 466–7 (Kirk). Curzola is best known as the battle in which the Venetian Marco Polo was captured; his resulting imprisonment in Genoa led to his collaboration with Rustichello of Pisa on the *Description of the world* (also known as the *Travels*). Marco's capture at Curzola 'now seems unlikely', however: see Kinoshita's introduction to Marco Polo, *Description*, p. xviii.
2 1299–1321: Polonio (2002a), pp. 93–4, 100, 104.
3 Oberto Doria's younger brother (*c.* 1250–1317; *DBI* 41.396–9). The Credenza was a council in charge of military matters: Epstein (1996), p. 158.
4 Djerba, off the coast of Tunisia: *GA* 5.60.

the idleness of his city—he chose rather to penetrate the Venetians' borders than to return home; so he crossed the seas of Calabria and Apulia and went up into the Gulf of Venice with more than four thousand men, leaving the many Venetian cities and castles behind as of no account, so much did he wish to meet the enemy fleet. And when he had reached a certain island known as Curzola, he landed there and totally devastated it.[5] But because meadows do not always produce flowers, it happened fortuitously that by some immense luck six Genoese galleys were unable to follow their admiral, so that only seventy-eight galleys remained with the lord admiral. They destroyed [the city of] Curzola on the fifth of September; and after they had pillaged and looted it, the entire army landed and rested there for an entire day and the following night.

When morning appeared in the east [on 7 September], with the blessing of God, they saw the galleys of the Venetians in the distance, which were ninety-six in number, with sixty boats with three [rows of] oars. These galleys of the Venetians, when they had seen the galleys of the Genoese, immediately all put out their gangplanks and landed so that they could more effectively prepare for battle. Meanwhile the galleys of the Genoese were on the other side of the channel on a certain outcropping, preparing themselves profitably and with the greatest anticipation. When they saw this, each one boarded the galleys in an orderly manner, rejoicing, and prepared himself speedily for battle. But the Venetians refused to engage [in battle] that day.

With the coming of the next day, however, a Sunday which was the eighth of September and the feast of the mother of all good things [the Nativity of the Virgin Mary], the Venetians came out against us. Then the aforesaid lord admiral of Genoa, who had with him the True Cross—of which we will speak further below—held it erect, inspired by great zeal for the motherland, and hastened toward them with great exultation and energetic noise from his own [people].[6] Then, once the terrible conflict had begun by unheard-of scalings, you would have seen everywhere arrows flying through the air like clouds; you would have seen the abilities of steadfast men standing ready; you would have seen galleys crash into galleys; you would have seen innumerable men tossed into the sea with no hope of life. What more should we say? It is a mercy to write it, for on either side the men did their duty manfully and equally

---

5 Curzola, on the coast of Dalmatia between Split and Ragusa (now Dubrovnik), was then controlled by the Venetian Zorzi family.

6 Probably one of the crosses detailed in part 11.18 n. 184, above.

until a little past the third hour [9:00 am]. But then by the decree of divine judgment the galleys of the Venetians succumbed and from shortly after the hour of nones [3:00 pm] they were defeated without any hope of recovery. Eighty-four of the Venetian galleys were captured there, while the rest took themselves off, seeking refuge in flight. And in this conflict eight thousand men from the Venetian side were captured, of which eight hundred wounded were left on the mountain of Ragusa. The rest were taken as captives to Genoa. In this terrible deadly conflict, seven thousand of these Venetians perished.

Then the aforesaid lord admiral, giving boundless thanks to God for such an incredible and unheard-of victory, returned safely to Genoa with his aforesaid distinguished fleet without any arrogance for such a victory. And in the next year the Genoese, moved by the requests and urging of the lord Matteo Visconti of Milan as well as by mercy, and wishing to recognise God for such a blessing, signed a peace with the said Venetians and freed all the Venetian captives.[7] And in that same year they similarly made peace with the Pisans and freed their captives as well.[8]

---

7 Matteo I Visconti (1250–1322), *signore* (lord) of Milan and imperial vicar in Lombardy. The 'eternal peace' signed in 1299—*Libri iurium* 1/6, pp. 325–35 (no. 1226, dated 25 May 1299)—lasted until the next breakout of hostilities in 1350.

8 *Libri iurium* 1/6, pp. 282–308 (no. 1220, dated 31 July 1299).

REFERENCES

Primary sources

This reference list omits entries for classical and late antique works with standardised book and chapter divisions (Livy's *Ab urbe condita*, Augustine's *City of God*, etc.).

Alberic of Trois-Fontaines, *Chronica*, ed. P. Scheffer-Boichorst, *MGH SS* 23, pp. 631–950.

Albertino Mussato, *Ecerinis*, ed. L. Padrin and trans. J.R. Berrigan (Munich, 1975).

Albertus Magnus, *Book of minerals*, trans. D. Wyckoff (Oxford, 1967).

Annales placentini gibellini, ed. G.H. Pertz, *MGH SS* 18, pp. 457–581.

Annalista Saxo, *Der Reichschronik des Annalista Saxo*, ed. K. Naß, *MGH SS* 37.

Anonimo genovese, *Poesie*, ed. L. Cocito (Rome, 1970).

Avicenna, *Canon of medicine*, trans. L. Bakhtiar, 5 vols. (Chicago, 1999).

Bede, *De temporum ratione*, ed. C.W. Jones in *Opera didascalica*, CCSL 123 (Turnhout, 1975), pp. 263–544; trans. F. Wallis as *The reckoning of time* (Liverpool, 2012).

———, *Expositio Actuum apostolorum*, ed. M.L.W. Laistner and D. Hurst in *Opera exegetica 2.4*, CCSL 121 (Turnhout, 1983), pp. 6–104.

———, *Historia ecclesiastica*, ed. B. Colgrave and R.A.B. Mynors (Oxford, 1992).

Beno, cardinal, *Gesta romanae ecclesiae contra Hildebrandum*, in *Benonis aliorumque schismaticorum contra Gregorium VII et Urbanum II scripta*, ed. K. Francke, *MGH SS Ldl* 2, pp. 369–80.

Benzo d'Alessandria, *Chronicon* [excerpts], ed. and trans. J.R. Berrigan in 'Benzo d'Alessandria and the cities of northern Italy', *Studies in medieval and Renaissance history* 4 (1967): 125–92.

Bernard of Clairvaux, *The letters of St Bernard of Clairvaux*, trans. B.S. James (Stroud, 1998).

———, *On the Song of songs I (Works of Bernard of Clairvaux, 2)*, trans. K. Walsh (Kalamazoo, 1981).

———, *Opera*, ed. H. Rochais, C.H. Talbot, and J. Leclercq (Rome, 1957).

REFERENCES

Bernardo Maragone, *Annales pisani*, ed. M.L. Gentile, *RIS2* 6.2 (Bologna, 1930).

Boccaccio, Giovanni, *Genealogy of the pagan gods*, ed. and trans. J. Solomon (Cambridge, MA, 2011).

Boniface VIII, 'Breve ai Veneziani del dì 13 febbraio 1295 per la loro pacificazione coi Genovesi', ed. F. Bonaini, *Archivio storico italiano* 9 (1853): 389–95.

———, *Gloriosus et mirabilis* (24 January 1295), in *Foedera, conventiones, literæ et cujuscunque generis acta publica, inter reges Angliæ et alios*, ed. T. Rymer, 3rd ed. (London, 1745), 1.2.141–2.

Bonvesin da la Riva, *De magnalibus Mediolani*, ed. P. Chiesa (Milan, 2009); excerpts translated in Dean, *Towns of Italy*, pp. 11–16.

Brunetto Latini, *Li livres dou tresor*, ed. S. Baldwin and P. Barrette (Tempe, AZ, 2003).

Cambiaso, D., ed., *Sinodi genovesi antichi* (Genoa, 1939).

Cartario genovese ed illustrazione del registro arcivescovile, ed. L.T. Belgrano, *ASLSP* 2.1 (Genoa, 1870).

Cartulaire de l'abbaye de Saint-Victor de Marseille, ed. B.E.C. Guerard, repr. 1857 ed. (Cambridge, 2010).

Charlemagne (Charles the Great), *Admonitio generalis*, ed. H. Mordek, K. Zechiel-Eckes, and M. Glatthaar, *MGH Fontes iuris* 16.

Chronicon parmense, ed. G. Bonazzi, *RIS2* 9.9.2 (Città di Castello, 1904).

La chronique de Saint-Victor de Marseille, ed. M.J.H. Albanès, *Mélanges de l'École française de Rome* 6 (1886): 64–90, 287–326, 454–65.

Codice diplomatico della repubblica di Genova, ed. C. Imperiale di Sant'Angelo, *FSI* 77, 79, 89 (Rome, 1936–42).

Le cronache di Todi (secoli XIII–XVI), ed. G. Italiani (Spoleto, 1991).

The crusade of Frederick Barbarossa: The history of the expedition of the Emperor Frederick and related texts, ed. and trans. G.A. Loud (Farnham, 2012).

Dante Alighieri, *De monarchia*, ed. P. Chiesa and A. Tabarroni (Salerno, 2013); trans. P. Shaw (Cambridge, 1996).

———, *Divine comedy (Inferno, Purgatorio, Paradiso)*, trans. R. Durling and R. Martinez (Oxford, 1996, 2004, 2013).

Dean, T., ed. and trans., *The towns of Italy in the later Middle Ages* (Manchester, 2000).

Dino Compagni, *Chronicle of Florence*, trans. D.E. Bornstein (Philadelphia, 1986).

Donation of Constantine = Constitutum Constantini, ed. H. Fuhrmann, *MGH Fontes iuris* 10.

Donizo of Canossa, *Vita Mathildis*, ed. L. Bethmann, *MGH SS* 12, pp. 348–409.

Eneas: A twelfth-century French romance, ed. J.A. Yunck (New York, 1974).

Excidium Troiae, ed. E.B. Atwood and V.K. Whitaker (Cambridge, MA, 1944).

Ferreto de' Ferreti, *Historia rerum in Italia gestorum*, in *Opere*, vol. 1, ed. C. Cipolla, *FSI* 42 (Rome, 1908).

Ferretto, A., ed., *Codice diplomatico delle relazioni fra Liguria, Toscana e Lunigiana ai tempi di Dante, parte prima (1265–74)*, *ASLSP* 31 (Genoa).

Francesco d'Andrea, *Cronica*, ed. P. Egidi (Manziana, 2002).

Galvano Fiamma, *Chronicon maius*, ed. A. Ceruti in *Miscellanea di storia italiana* 7 (Turin, 1869), pp. 598–773.

———, *Manipulus florum*, *RIS* 11.531–740.

Giovanni Balbi, *Catholicon* (Cologne, 1506).

Giovanni Mansionario, *Brevis adnotatio de duobus Pliniis*, in E.T. Merrill, 'On the eight-book tradition of Pliny's letters in Verona', *Classical philology* 5.2 (1910): 175–88; trans. C.E. Beneš as 'Short note (*Adnotatio*) on the two Plinys of Verona' (2018), https://bit.ly/2pKYaH4.

Godfrey of Viterbo, *Pantheon* and *Gesta Friderici*, ed. G. Waitz, *MGH SS* 22, pp. 107–307 and 307–44.

Gratian, *Decretum*, ed. A.L. Richter and E. Friedberg, repr. 1879 ed. (Union, NJ, 2000).

Hanna, R. and T. Lawler, eds., *Jankyn's book of wikked wyves, vol. 1: Primary texts* (Athens, GA, 1997).

Helgaud of Fleury, *La vie du roi Robert*, ed. F. Guizot and M. Tailhac (Clermont-Ferrand, 2011).

Herman of Reichenau, *Chronicon*, ed. G.H. Pertz, *MGH SS* 5, pp. 67–133; partly translated in Robinson, *Eleventh-century Germany*, pp. 58–98.

Hillenbrand, C., ed., *The crusades: Islamic perspectives* (New York, 2000).

Huguccio (also Uguccio), *Derivationes*, ed. E. Cecchini (Florence, 2004).

Istorietta trojana, ed. E. Gorra in *Testi inediti di storia trojana preceduti da uno studio sulla leggenda trojana in Italia* (Turin, 1887), pp. 371–403.

Jacques de Vitry, *The exempla or illustrative stories from the Sermones vulgares of Jacques de Vitry*, trans. T.F. Crane (London, 1890).

———, *Lettres*, ed. R.B.C. Huygens (Leiden, 1960).

Jansen, K.L., J.H. Drell, and F. Andrews, eds., *Medieval Italy: Texts in translation* (Philadelphia, 2009).

John of Salisbury, *Policraticus sive de nugis curialium libri VIII*, ed. C.C.J. Webb (Oxford, 1909); partly translated in C.J. Nederman, *Policraticus: Of the frivolities of courtiers and the footprints of philosophers* (Cambridge, 2009).

Landolfus Sagax, *Historia romana*, ed. A. Crivellucci, *FSI* 49–50 (Rome, 1912).

Landulf Senior, *Historia Mediolanensis usque a 1085*, ed. D.L.C. Bethmann and W. Wattenbach, *MGH SS* 8, pp. 32–110.

Lanfranc of Pavia, *De corpore et sanguine Domini adversus Berengarium Turonensem*, *PL* 150.407–42; trans. M.G. Vaillancourt, *On the body and blood of the Lord* (Washington, DC, 2009).

Liber pontificalis, trans. R. Davis as *The lives of the eighth-century popes: The ancient biographies of nine popes from AD 715 to AD 817* (Liverpool, 1992).

Liber privilegiorum ecclesiae ianuensis, ed. D. Puncuh (Genoa, 1962).

I Libri iurium della repubblica di Genova, ed. A. Rovere, D. Puncuh, et al. (Genoa, 1992–2002).

Liudprand of Cremona, *Antapodosis*, ed. P. Chiesa, *CCCM* 156, pp. 1–150; trans. P. Squatriti as *Retribution* in *Complete works of Liudprand of Cremona* (Washington, DC, 2007), pp. 41–202.

Marco, *Prima edificacio civitatis Venetorum*, in A. Pertusi, 'Aspetti della cronachistica veneziana nei secoli XIII e XIV', in Carile (ed.), *La storiografia veneziana fino al secolo XVI: Aspetti e problem* (Florence, 1970), pp. 121–6.

Marco Polo, *The description of the world*, trans. S. Kinoshita (Indianapolis, 2016).

Martino da Canal, *Les estoires de Venise*, ed. A. Limentani (Florence, 1973); trans. L.K. Morreale (Padua, 2009).

Memoriale temporum, in *Il* Chronicon veronense *di Paride da Cerea e dei suoi continuatori 1.1: La cronaca parisiana (1115–1260) con l'antica continuazione (1261–77)*, ed. R. Vaccari (Legnago, 2014), pp. 193–4.

Mirabilia urbis Romae, in *Codice topografico della città di Roma*, vol. 3, ed. R. Valentini and G. Zucchetti, *FSI* 90 (Rome, 1946), pp. 3–65; trans. F.M. Nichols and E. Gardiner, 2nd ed. (New York, 1986).

Otto of Freising, *Gesta Friderici I imperatoris*, *MGH SSrG* 46; trans. C.C. Mierow, *The deeds of Frederick Barbarossa* (repr. New York, 2004).

Paul the Deacon, *Historia Langobardorum*, ed. D.L.C. Bethmann, *MGH SSrG* 48, pp. 49–242; trans. E. Peters, *History of the Lombards* (Philadelphia, 1974).

———, *Historia romana*, ed. A. Crivellucci, *FSI* 51 (Rome, 1914).

———, *Liber de episcopis Mettensibus*, ed. D.I. von Arx, *MGH SS* 2, pp. 260–88.

Pseudo-John of Damascus, 'Letter to the emperor Theophilus', in *The letter of the three patriarchs to Emperor Theophilus and related texts*, trans. J.A. Munitiz (Camberley, 1997), pp. 141–205.

Pseudo-Methodius, *Revelationes*, ed. M.W. Herren in G. Guldentops, C. Laes, and G. Partoens, eds., *Felici curiositate: Studies in Latin literature and textual criticism from antiquity to the twentieth century in honour of Rita Beyers* (Turnhout, 2017), pp. 409–18.

Ptolemy of Lucca, *Annales* = *Die Annalen des Tholomeus von Lucca*, ed. B. Schmeidler, *MGH SSrG NS* 8.

———, *On the government of rulers* = *De regimine principum*, trans. J.M. Blythe (Philadelphia, 1997).

Ralph of Caen, *Gesta Tancredi in expeditione Hierosolimitana*, in *Recueil des historiens des Croisades, occidentaux* 3 (Paris, 1866), pp. 587–716; trans. B.S. Bachrach and D.S. Bachrach, *The Gesta Tancredi of Raoul of Caen: A history of the Normans on the First Crusade* (Aldershot, 2005).

Rees, B.R., *Pelagius: Life and letters* (Woodbridge, 1988).

Riccobaldo da Ferrara, *Cronica parva Ferrariensis*, ed. G. Zanella (Ferrara, 1983).

Robert of Torigny, *Chronicle*, ed. R. Howlett, *Chronicles of the reigns of Stephen, Henry II, and Richard I, vol. 4* (London, 1889).

Robinson, I.S., trans., *Eleventh-century Germany: The Swabian chronicles* (Manchester, 2008).

———, trans., *The papal reform of the eleventh century: Lives of Pope Leo IX and Pope Gregory VII* (Manchester, 2004).

Rolandino of Padua, *Cronica in factis et circa facta marchie Trivixane (ca. 1200–1262)*, ed. A. Bonardi, *RIS2* 8.1 (Città di Castello, 1905); trans. J.R. Berrigan, *Chronicles of the Trevisan march* (Lawrence, KS, 1980).

Salimbene de Adam, *Cronica*, ed. G. Scalia, *CCCM* 125–125A (Turnhout, 1999); trans. G. Baglivi, J.L. Baird, and J.R. Kane (Binghamton, NY, 1986).

Salutati, Coluccio, *Epistolario*, ed. F. Novati, *FSI* 15–18 (Rome, 1891–1905).

Sedulius Scottus, *Collectaneum miscellaneum*, ed. D. Simpson, *CCCM* 67 (Brepols, 1988).

Sextus, *The sentences*, trans. W.T. Wilson (Atlanta, 2012).

Sigebert of Gembloux, *Chronica*, ed. D.L.C. Bethmann, *MGH SS* 6, pp. 268–474.

Smith, Caroline, trans., *Chronicles of the crusades* (London, 2008).

Stella, Giorgio and Giovanni Stella, *Annales genuenses*, ed. G. Petti Balbi, *RIS2* 17.2 (Bologna, 1975).

Thomas Aquinas, *De regimine principum*, ed. and trans. J.M. Blythe, in Ptolemy of Lucca, *On the government of rulers*; also trans. R.W. Dyson as *On the rule of princes* in *Aquinas: Political writings* (Cambridge, 2002), pp. 5–51.

———, *Summa theologiae*, ed. and trans. T.C. O'Brien, T. Gilby, et al. (London, 1964–76).

The Vatican mythographers, trans. R.E. Pepin (New York, 2008).

Villani, Giovanni, *Nuova cronica con la continuazioni di Matteo e Filippo Villani*, ed. G. Porta, 2nd ed. (Parma, 2007); partly translated by R. Selfe and P. Wicksteed, *Villani's chronicle* (rev. ed., London, 1906); by P. Clarke, 'The Villani chronicles', in Dale, Lewin, and Osheim (eds.), *Chronicling history: Chroniclers and historians in medieval and Renaissance Italy* (University Park, PA, 2007), pp. 113–44; and by R. Diakité and M.T. Sneider, *The final book of Giovanni Villani's New chronicle* (Kalamazoo, 2016).

Vincent of Beauvais, *Speculum doctrinale*, *Speculum naturale*, and *Speculum historiale* (together, *Speculum maius*), version SM trifaria (Douai, 1624:

electronic edition), SourcEncyMe: Sources des encyclopédies médiévales (accessed 21 November 2018). http://sourcencyme.irht.cnrs.fr/encyclopedie/voir/165; http://sourcencyme.irht.cnrs.fr/encyclopedie/voir/133; http://sourcencyme.irht.cnrs.fr/encyclopedie/voir/134.

Vita beati Romuli episcopi, ed. F. Ughelli, *Italia sacra* 4 (Rome, 1652), cols. 1153c–1156d.

Walther, H. and P.G. Schmidt, eds., *Proverbia sententiaeque Latinitatis medii aevi = Lateinische Sprichwörter und Sentenzen des Mittelalters und der frühen Neuzeit*, 9 vols. (Gottingen, 1963).

Wenzel, S., ed., *The art of preaching: Five medieval texts and translations* (Washington, DC, 2013).

William Durandus, *Rationale divinorum officiorum*, books 7–8, ed. A. Davril and T.M. Thibodeau, *CCCM* 140B (Turnhout, 1995).

William of Malmesbury, *Gesta regum Anglorum = The history of the English kings*, ed. and trans. R.A.B. Mynors, R.M. Thomson, and M. Winterbottom (Oxford, 1998).

William of Tyre, *Chronicon*, ed. R.B.C. Huygens, *CCCM* 63–63A (Turnhout, 1986); trans. E.A. Babcock and A.C. Krey, *A history of deeds done beyond the sea* (New York, 1943).

Secondary sources

Abulafia, D. (1975), 'Henry count of Malta and his Mediterranean activities: 1203–1230', repr. in Abulafia, *Italy, Sicily, and the Mediterranean 1100–1400* (London, 1987), art. III.

—— (1977), *The two Italies: Economic relations between the Norman kingdom of Sicily and the northern communities* (Cambridge).

—— (1988), *Frederick II: A medieval emperor* (Oxford).

—— (2004), *Italy in the central Middle Ages, 1000–1300* (Oxford).

Airaldi, G. (1988), *Jacopo da Varagine: Tra santi e mercanti* (Genoa).

Allen, M.I. (2003), 'Universal history 300–1000: Origins and western development', in Deliyannis (ed.), *Historiography in the Middle Ages* (Leiden), pp. 17–42.

Andrews, F. (2004), 'Albertano of Brescia, Rolandino of Padua and the rhetoric of legitimation', in Antón, Kennedy, and Escalona (eds.), *Building legitimacy: Political discourses and forms of legitimacy in medieval societies* (Leiden), pp. 319–40.

Angeli Bertinelli, M.G. (1999), 'Le origini: L'età romana e tardoantica', in Puncuh (ed.), *Il cammino della chiesa genovese: Dalle origini ai nostri giorni*, *ASLSP NS* 39.2 (Genoa), pp. 33–75.

Aron-Beller, K. (2017), 'Byzantine tales of Jewish image desecration: Tracing a narrative', *Jewish culture and history* 18.2: 209–34.

Asbridge, T.S. (2004), *The First Crusade: A new history* (London).

Balzaretti, R. (2013), *Dark age Liguria: Regional identity and local power, c. 400–1020* (London).

Beneš, C.E. (2011a), *Urban legends: Civic identity and the classical past in northern Italy, 1250–1350* (University Park, PA).

────── (2011b), 'Noble and most ancient: Catalogues of city foundation in fourteenth-century Italy', in Baswell (ed.), *Medieval manuscripts, their makers and users* (Turnhout), pp. 263–78.

Bertini Guidetti, S. (1997a), 'Contrastare la crisi della chiesa cattedrale: Iacopo da Varagine e la costruzione di un'ideologia propagandistica', in Airaldi (ed.), *Le vie del Mediterraneo: Idee, uomini, oggetti (secoli XI–XVI)* (Genoa), pp. 155–81.

────── (1997b), 'Iacopo da Varagine e le *Ystorie antique*: Quando il mito diventa exemplum della storia', in Montanari and Pittaluga (eds.), *Posthomerica 1: Tradizioni omeriche dall'antichità al Rinascimento* (Genoa), pp. 139–57.

────── (1998a), *I sermones di Iacopo da Varazze: Il potere delle immagini nel duecento* (Florence).

────── (1998b), *Potere e propaganda a Genova nel Duecento* (Genoa).

────── , ed. (2001a), *Il paradiso e la terra: Iacopo da Varazze e il suo tempo* (Florence).

────── (2001b), 'Scrittura, oralità, memoria: La *Legenda aurea* fonte e modello nei *Sermones* e nella *Chronica civitatis ianuensis* di Iacopo da Varagine', in Fleith and Morenzoni (eds.), *De la sainteté a l'hagiographie: Genèse et usage de la Légende dorée* (Geneva), pp. 123–38.

Bettini, M., ed. (2010), *Miti di città* (Siena).

Bird, J.L., ed. (2018), *Papacy, crusade, and Christian–Muslim relations* (Amsterdam).

Brentano, R. (1974), *Rome before Avignon: A social history of thirteenth-century Rome* (London).

Calderoni Masetti, A.R. and G. Wolf, eds. (2012), *La cattedrale di San Lorenzo a Genova = The cathedral of St. Lawrence in Genoa* (Modena).

Cambiaso, D. (1917), 'L'anno ecclesiastico e le feste dei santi in Genova nel loro svolgimento storico', *ASLSP* 48: 1–418.

────── (1918), 'La consecrazione della cattedrale, 10 ottobre 1118', in *Cattedrale di Genova, 1118–1918* (Genoa), pp. 87–104.

Campopiano, M. (2014), 'The problem of origins in early communal historiography: Pisa, Genoa and Milan compared', in Mostert and Adamska (eds.), *Uses of the written word in medieval towns* (Turnhout), pp. 227–50.

Canning, J. (2011), *Ideas of power in the late Middle Ages, 1296–1417* (Cambridge).

Cary, G. (1956), *The medieval Alexander*, ed. D.H. Ross (Cambridge).

Cassidy, B. (2007), *Politics, civic ideals and sculpture in Italy c. 1240–1400* (London).

Cigni, F. (2006), 'Copisti prigioneri (Genova, sec. XIII)', in *Studi di filologia romanza offerti a Valeria Bertolucci Pizzorusso* (Pisa), pp. 425–39.

Coleman, E. (2007), 'Lombard city annals and the social and cultural history of northern Italy', in Dale, Lewin, and Osheim (2007), pp. 1–28.

—––– (2016), '"A city to be built for the glory of God, Saint Peter, and the whole of Lombardy": Alexander III, Alessandria, and the Lombard League in contemporary sources', in Duggan and Clarke (2016), pp. 127–51.

Conklin Akbari, S. (2012), *Idols in the east: European representations of Islam and the orient, 1100–1450* (Ithaca, NY).

Corbari, E. (2013), *Vernacular theology: Dominican sermons and audience in late medieval Italy* (Berlin).

Cornish, A. (2011), *Vernacular translation in Dante's Italy: Illiterate literature* (Cambridge).

Cowdrey, H.E.J. (1977), 'The Mahdia campaign of 1087', *The English historical review* 92.362: 1–29; repr. in France (ed.), *Medieval warfare, 1000–1300* (London, 2016), pp. 494–521.

—––– (1998), *Pope Gregory VII, 1073–1085* (Oxford).

Dale, S., A.W. Lewin, and D.J. Osheim, eds. (2007), *Chronicling history: Chroniclers and historians in medieval and Renaissance Italy* (University Park, PA).

Dauverd, C. (2015), *Imperial ambition in the early modern Mediterranean: Genoese merchants and the Spanish crown* (Cambridge).

Day, G.W. (1988), *Genoa's response to Byzantium, 1155–1204: Commercial expansion and factionalism in a medieval city* (Urbana-Champaign).

Day, W.R., M. Matzke, and A. Saccocci (2016), *Medieval European coinage 12: Northern Italy* (Cambridge).

Destefanis, E. and P. Guglielmotti, eds. (2015), *La diocesi di Bobbio: Formazione e sviluppi di un'istituzione millenaria* (Florence).

Dickson, G. (1989), 'The flagellants of 1260 and the crusades', *Journal of medieval history* 15.3: 227–67.

—––– (2008), *The children's crusade: Medieval history, modern mythistory* (Houndmills).

Di Fabio, C. (1978), 'Le reliquie di S. Agostino a Geneva: Dalle cronache altomedievali al formarsi di una tradizione', *Romanobarbarica* 3: 39–61.

—––– and R. Besta, eds. (1998), *La cattedrale di Genova nel medioevo: Secoli VI–XIV* (Genoa).

Doran, J. and D.J. Smith, eds. (2016), *Pope Innocent II (1130–43): The world vs. the city* (London).

Du Cange, C. du F., ed. (1883–87), *Glossarium mediae et infimae latinitatis* (Niort).

Duggan, A.J. and P.D. Clarke, eds. (2016), *Pope Alexander III (1159–81): The art of survival* (London).

Dunbabin, J. (1998), *Charles I of Anjou: Power, kingship and state-making in thirteenth-century Europe* (London).

Epstein, S.A. (1996), *Genoa and the Genoese, 958–1528* (Chapel Hill).

——— (2016), *The talents of Jacopo da Varagine: A Genoese mind in medieval Europe* (Ithaca, NY).

Eubel, C. (1960), *Hierarchia catholica medii aevi*, rev. ed. (Padua).

Ferretto, A. (1907), *I primordi e lo sviluppo del Cristianesimo in Liguria ed in particolare a Genova*, ASLSP 39 (Genoa).

Fichtenau, H. (1998), *Heretics and scholars in the high Middle Ages, 1000–1200* (University Park, PA).

Filangieri, L. (2006), 'The chapter of San Lorenzo in Genoa: Institutional dynamics and social relations (10th–12th centuries)', *Reti medievali rivista* 7: 1–37.

Freed, J.B. (2016), *Frederick Barbarossa: The prince and the myth* (New Haven).

Frugoni, C. (1991), *A distant city: Images of urban experience in the medieval world*, trans. W. McCuaig (Princeton).

Gabriel, A.L. (1988), '*Translatio studii*: Spurious dates of foundation of some early universities', in *Fälschungen im Mittelalter*, MGH Schriften 33, 1.601–26.

Gams, P.B. (1931), *Series episcoporum ecclesiae catholicae* (Leipzig).

Gigliotti, V. (2008), *Fit monachus, qui papa fuit: La rinuncia di Celestino V tra diritto e letteratura* (Florence).

Gilchrist, J.T. (1965), '*Simoniaca haeresis* and the problem of orders from Leo IX to Gratian', repr. in Gilchrist, *Canon law in the age of reform, 11th–12th centuries* (Aldershot, 1993), article IV.

Goez, W. (1958), *Translatio imperii: Ein Beitrag zur Geschichte des Geschichtsdenkens und der politischen Theorien im Mittelalter und in der frühen Neuzeit* (Tübingen).

Gorse, G. (1988), 'A family enclave in medieval Genoa', *Journal of architectural education* 41: 20–4.

Guglielmotti, P. (2005), *Ricerche sull'organizzazione del territorio nella Liguria medievale* (Florence).

Hamilton, B. (1980), *The Latin church in the crusader states: The secular church* (Farnham).

——— (2000), *The leper king and his heirs: Baldwin IV and the Crusader Kingdom of Jerusalem* (Cambridge).

Hamilton, L.I. (2003), 'Memory, symbol, and arson: Was Rome "sacked" in 1084?' *Speculum* 78.2: 378–99.

Hamilton, S. (1997), 'A new model for royal penance? Helgaud of Fleury's *Life of Robert the Pious*', *Early medieval Europe* 6.2: 189–200.

Haug, H. (2015), *Annales ianuenses: Orte und Medien des historischen Gedächtnisses im mittelalterlichen Genua* (Göttingen).

Hay, D.J. (2008), *The military leadership of Matilda of Canossa, 1046–1115* (Manchester).

Hertter, F. (1973), *Die Podestàliteratur Italiens im 12. und 13. Jahrhundert* (Hildesheim).

Hiley, D. (1993), *Western plainchant: A handbook* (Oxford).

Hinnebusch, W.A. (1966), *History of the Dominican order*, 2 vols. (Staten Island, NY).

Hobart, M., ed. (2017), *A companion to Sardinian history, 500–1500* (Leiden).

Huffman, J.P. (2000), *The social politics of medieval diplomacy: Anglo-German relations, 1066–1307* (Ann Arbor).

Hyde, J.K. (1966), 'Medieval descriptions of cities', *Bulletin of the John Rylands library* 48: 308–40.

Imperiale di Sant'Angelo, C. (1894), *Caffaro e suoi tempi* (Turin).

Inguscio, A. (2015), *Reinterpreting Genoese civil conflicts: The chronicle of Ottobonus Scriba* (New Orleans).

Jaffé, P. (1885), *Regesta pontificum romanorum*, 2nd ed. (Leipzig).

Jansen, K.L. (2018), *Peace and penance in late medieval Italy* (Princeton).

Jotischky, A. (2017), *Crusading and the crusader states* (London).

Kempshall, M.S. (1999), *The common good in late medieval political thought* (Oxford).

Kleinhenz, C., ed. (2004), *Medieval Italy: An encyclopedia* (New York).

Kumhera, G. (2017), *The benefits of peace: Private peace-making in late medieval Italy* (Leiden).

Kuttner, S. (1982), 'Raymond of Peñafort as editor: The *Decretales* and *Constitutiones* of Gregory IX', *Bulletin of medieval canon law* 12: 65–80.

Lane, F.C. (1969), 'The crossbow in the nautical revolution of the Middle Ages', in Herlihy, Lopez, and Slessarev (eds.), *Economy, society, and government in medieval Italy* (Kent, OH), pp. 161–72.

Lawrence, C.H. (2013), *The friars: The impact of the early mendicant movement on Western society* (London).

Lee, A. (2018), *Humanism and empire: The imperial ideal in fourteenth-century Italy* (Oxford).

Le Goff, J. (2014), *In search of sacred time: Jacobus de Voragine and the* Golden Legend, trans. L.G. Cochrane (Princeton, NJ).

Le Pogam, P.-Y. (2007), 'La lutte entre Boniface VIII et les Colonna par les armes symboliques', *Rivista di storia della chiesa in Italia* 61.1: 47–66.

Lilley, K.D. (2009), *City and cosmos: The medieval world in urban form* (London).

Little, L.K. (1983), *Religious poverty and the profit economy in medieval Europe* (Ithaca, NY).

Liva, A. (1981), 'Il potere vescovile in Genova', in *Storia dei genovesi* 1 (Genoa), pp. 49–71.

Longo, U. and L. Yawn, eds. (2012), *Framing Clement III (anti)pope 1080–1100*, *Reti medievali rivista* 13.1: 115–208.

Loud, G.A. (2007), *The Latin church in Norman Italy* (Cambridge).

Macchiavello, S. (1997), 'Per la storia della cattedrale di Genova: Percorsi archeologici e documentari', *ASLSP NS* 37.2: 21–36.

Maggioni, G.P. (1997), *Ricerche sulla composizione e sulla trasmissione della 'Legenda aurea'* (Spoleto).

Maiolo, F. (2007), *Medieval sovereignty: Marsilius of Padua and Bartolus of Saxoferrato* (Delft).

Mandonnet, Pierre, O.P. (1948), 'Domini canes', in *Saint Dominic and his work*, trans. M.B. Larkin (St Louis), pp. 447–59. http://opcentral.org/blog/domini-canes-by-pierre-mandonnet-o-p/.

Mannucci, F.L. (1904), *La cronaca di Jacopo da Varagine* (Genoa).

Mansi, G.D. and P. Labbe, eds. (1901), *Sacrorum conciliorum: Nova et amplissima collectio* (Paris).

Matthew, D. (1992), *The Norman kingdom of Sicily* (Cambridge).

Mattison, W.C. (2007), 'Jesus' prohibition of anger (Matthew 5:22): The person/sin distinction from Augustine to Aquinas', *Theological studies* 68.4: 839–64.

McLynn, N.B. (1994), *Ambrose of Milan: Church and court in a Christian capital* (Berkeley).

Melli, P. (1996), *La città ritrovata: Archeologia urbana a Genova, 1984–1994* (Genoa).

Miller, M.C. (2000), *The bishop's palace: Architecture and authority in medieval Italy* (Ithaca, NY).

Milner, S.J. (2011), 'Communication, consensus, and conflict: Rhetorical precepts, the *ars concionandi*, and social ordering in late medieval Italy', in Cox and Ward (eds.), *The rhetoric of Cicero in its medieval and early Renaissance commentary tradition* (Leiden), pp. 365–468.

Moore, J.C. (2003), *Pope Innocent III (1160/61–1216): To root up and to plant* (Leiden).

Morton, N.E. (2017), *Encountering Islam on the First Crusade* (Cambridge).

Mulchahey, M.M. (1998), *'First the bow is bent in study—': Dominican education before 1350* (Toronto).

Müller, W.P. (1994), *Huguccio: The life, works, and thought of a twelfth-century jurist* (Washington, DC).

Murphy, J.J. (1974), *Rhetoric in the Middle Ages: A history of rhetorical theory from Saint Augustine to the Renaissance* (Berkeley).

Murray, A.V. (1990), 'The title of Godfrey of Bouillon as ruler of Jerusalem', repr. in *The Franks in Outremer, 1099–1187* (Farnham, 2015), art. VII.

——— (1998), '"Mighty against the enemies of Christ": The relic of the True Cross in the armies of the Kingdom of Jerusalem', repr. in *The Franks in Outremer, 1099–1187* (Farnham, 2015), art. XV.

Musarra, A. (2009), *La guerra di San Saba* (Ospedaletto).

Mylod, E.J., G. Perry, T.W. Smith, and J. Vandeburie, eds. (2017), *The Fifth Crusade in context: The crusading movement in the early thirteenth century* (London).

Niermeyer, J.F., ed., with C. van de Kieft and J.W.J. Burgers (2002), *Mediae Latinitatis lexicon minus = Medieval Latin dictionary = Lexique latin médiéval = Mittellateinisches Wörterbuch* (Leiden).

Noble, T.F.X. (1984), *The republic of St Peter: The birth of the papal state, 680–825* (Philadelphia).

——— (2009), *Images, iconoclasm, and the Carolingians* (Philadelphia).

——— (2013), 'Why Pope Joan?' *Catholic historical review* 99.2: 219–38.

Otranto, G. (1987), *San Nicola di Bari e la sua basilica: Culto, arte, tradizione* (Milan).

Otten-Froux, C. (2011), 'Identities and allegiances: The perspective of Genoa and Pisa', in Herrin and Saint-Guillain (eds.), *Identities and allegiances in the eastern Mediterranean after 1204* (Farnham), pp. 245–64.

Paravicini Bagliani, A. (1972), *Cardinali di Curia e familiae cardinalizie dal 1227 al 1254* (Padua).

Parish, H.L. (2010), *Clerical celibacy in the west, c. 1100–1700* (London).

Pavoni, R. (1992), *Liguria medievale: Da provincia romana a stato regionale* (Genoa).

Perry, B.E. (1952), *Aesopica: A series of texts relating to Aesop or ascribed to him* (Urbana, IL).

Pessa, L., ed. (2016), *Genova nel medioevo: Una capitale del Mediterraneo al tempo degli Embriaci* (Genoa).

Petrucci, A. (1995), *Writers and readers in medieval Italy*, trans. C. Radding (New Haven).

Phillips, J., ed. (1997), *The First Crusade: Origins and impact* (Manchester).

——— (2004), *The Fourth Crusade and the sack of Constantinople* (London).

Poleggi, E. and L. Grossi Bianchi (1980), *Una città portuale del Medioevo: Genova nei secoli X–XVI* (Genoa).

Polonio, V. (1999), 'Tra universalismo e localismo: Construzione di un sistema (569–1321)', in Puncuh (ed.), *Il cammino della chiesa genovese: Dalle origini ai nostri giorni, ASLSP NS* 39.2 (Genoa), pp. 77–210.

―――― (2000), 'L'arrivo delle ceneri del Precursore e il culto al Santo a Genova e nel Genovesato in età medioevale', in Paolocci (ed.), *San Giovanni Battista nella vita sociale e religiosa a Genova e in Liguria tra medioevo e età contemporanea* (Genoa), pp. 35–66.

―――― (2002a), *Istituzioni ecclesiastiche della Liguria medievale* (Rome).

―――― (2002b), 'Identità ecclesiastica, identità comunale: La memoria a Genova', in Puncuh (ed.), *Comuni e memoria storica: Alle origini del comune di Genova, ASLSP NS* 42.2, pp. 449–82.

Potthast, A. (1874), *Regesta pontificum romanorum* (Berlin).

Pryor, J. (2008), 'A view from a masthead: The First Crusade from the sea', *Crusades* 7: 87–152.

Purkis, W. (forthcoming), 'Crusaders and their relics', in *Cambridge history of the crusades* (Cambridge).

Raccagni, G. (2010), *The Lombard League, 1167–1225* (Oxford).

Rehberg, A. (1999), *Kirche und Macht im römischen Trecento: Die Colonna und ihre Klientel auf dem kurialen Pfründenmarkt (1278–1378)* (Tübingen).

Richardson, E.C. (1935), *Materials for a life of Jacopo da Varagine*, 2 vols. (New York).

Riché, P. (1987), *Gerbert d'Aurillac, le pape de l'an mil* (Paris).

Robinson, I.S. (1990), *The papacy, 1073–1198: Continuity and innovation* (Cambridge).

―――― (2003), *Henry IV of Germany, 1056–1106* (Cambridge).

Rose, S. (2008), *Medieval ships and warfare* (Aldershot).

Rouse, M.A. and R.H. Rouse (1979), *Preachers, florilegia and sermons: Studies on the* Manipulus florum *of Thomas of Ireland* (Toronto).

Rubin, M. (1999), *Gentile tales: The narrative assault on late medieval Jews* (Philadelphia).

Runciman, S. (1958), *The Sicilian Vespers: A history of the Mediterranean world in the later thirteenth century* (Cambridge).

Salonia, M. (2017), *Genoa's freedom: Entrepreneurship, republicanism, and the early modern Atlantic world* (London).

Scarfe Beckett, K. (2008), *Anglo-saxon perceptions of the Islamic world* (Cambridge).

Schoenig, S.A. (2016), *Bonds of wool: The pallium and papal power in the Middle Ages* (Washington, DC).

Siberry, E. (1985), *Criticism of crusading, 1095–1274* (Oxford).

Smalley, B. (1974), *Historians in the Middle Ages* (New York).

Sperling, J.G. (2016), *Roman charity: Queer lactations in early modern visual culture* (Bielefeld). http://oapen.org/download?type=document&docid=624848.

Starn, R. and L. Partridge (1992), *Arts of power: Three halls of state in Italy, 1300–1600* (Berkeley).

Stegmüller, F. (1950), *Repertorium biblicum medii aevi* (Madrid).

Stone, H.S. (2002), *Saint Augustine's bones: A microhistory* (Amherst, MA).

Taylor, F. (2016), 'Catharism and heresy in Milan', in Roach and Simpson (eds.), *Heresy and the making of European culture: Medieval and modern perspectives* (London), pp. 383–401.

Tyerman, C. (2006), *God's war: A new history of the Crusades* (Cambridge, MA).

Van Houts, E.M.C. (1995), *Local and regional chronicles* (Turnhout).

Waley, D.P. (1961), *The papal state in the thirteenth century* (London).

——— and T. Dean (2013), *The Italian city-republics*, 4th ed. (London).

Wardi, E. (1997), 'The Monçoia of the Genoese at Acre', *'Atiqot* 31: 201–7.

Wickham, C. (2015), *Sleepwalking into a new world: The emergence of Italian city communes in the twelfth century* (Oxford).

Witt, R.G. (2000), *In the footsteps of the ancients: The origins of humanism from Lovato to Bruni* (Leiden).

——— (2012), *The two Latin cultures and the foundation of Renaissance humanism in medieval Italy* (Cambridge).

Zanna, P. (1991), '*Descriptiones urbium* and elegy in Latin and vernaculars in the early Middle Ages: At the crossroads between civic engagement, artistic enthusiasm and religious meditation', *Studi medievali*, 3rd series 32: 523–96.

INDEX

Note: Figures with recognisable family names (Doria, Spinola, etc.) are alphabetised by family name; all others by first name.

Aachen 191, 207
abbot (*abate del popolo*), civic official 100–1, 249
Abraham 46, 48, 57–8, 66
Abruzzo 250
Accia, diocese 10, 163, 213, 248
Acqui, diocese 205, 220
Acre 8, 34, 85, 199, 224n.69, 240, 242
Adam 5–7, 130, 187
Adamo, bishop of Mariana 248
Adrian V, pope (Ottobuono Fieschi) 206, 245–6
Adriatic Sea *see* Gulf of Venice
adultery 147, 152, 168
  see also lust
Aeneas 52–3, 59
Aesop, 'The belly and the feet' 108
Africa, Africans *see* Carthage; Muslims
Agilulf, king of the Lombards 172, 175n.47
Agnes, daughter of Louis IX, later Byzantine empress 222
Ahab, biblical king 73
Ahasuerus, biblical king 127–8, 132
Airaldus Guarachus, bishop of Genoa 199–204
Alamanni, tribe 170
Alamanno da Costa, count of Siracusa 229–30
Alba 59
Alba Longa 52–3, 59
Albano 53
Albaro, hill 53–4, 77
Albenga, city 219, 233–4
  diocese 10, 164, 213, 223, 237n.132, 248
Alberto, marquess of Gavi 209

Albertus, bishop of Genoa *see* Obertus
Albuin, king of the Lombards 170–2
Alcuin, scholar 180
Aldo, bishop of Piacenza 180
Alessandria 220, 227, 231
Alexander II, pope 191
Alexander III, pope 89, 164, 199, 213, 217, 220, 222–3
Alexander IV, pope 240
Alexander the Great 114, 118, 129–31, 135
Alexandria 160
Alexios II Komnenos, emperor 222
Alexios III Angelos, emperor 228
All Saints, feast 176
Almería 90, 214–15
alphabet 53, 172
Alps, Cottian 164–5, 171
Amandus, saint 175
ambassadors 88–9, 95–6, 121, 163, 234–5, 246
Ambrose, saint 16, 31, 77n.23, 122, 127, 136n.63, 137–8, 195
  Ambrosian office 181–2
Anacharsis, Greek philosopher 110
Anacletus II, antipope 162–3, 212
Ancona, march of 239, 244
Andrew, apostle and saint 75, 198
Andronikos I Komnenos, emperor 222n.57
angels 45, 73, 77, 170, 174, 177
anger 89, 105, 126–7, 130–1, 155, 171, 207
Anianus, saint 160
Annalista Saxo 180–1, 186, 197
Anselm, saint 192–3
Antenor 34, 52, 59, 70n.25
Antigonus, tutor to Alexander 131

INDEX

Antioch 7, 87, 174, 198–9, 224, 245–6
Apollinaris, saint 160
Apollo 50, 122
Apostles' Creed 74–5
Apulia 193, 229, 234, 238, 241–2
   see also Naples, Angevin kingdom
Aquileia 71, 76, 160, 171
Aragon, kingdom 11, 95
Arborea, Sardinia 219
Arduino di Lavagna, Genoese citizen 222
Arduino Franchi, bishop of Brugnato 248
Arianism 169–70, 173–5, 181–2
Aristotle 126, 154
Armenia 75, 93–4
Arno River 87, 90–1, 209–10
arrogance *see* pride
ars praedicandi 17, 19, 42n.7
Arsuf 34, 85, 199
assembly (*parlamentum*) 225, 227, 234, 252
Asti 13, 205
astrology 66, 168
Athens 114, 118–19, 136
Augustine, bishop of Hippo and saint 29–31, 36, 57n.2, 60n.13, 81, 115, 147–50, 152–3, 178, 181
   City of God 59, 62–3, 67, 114, 120–1, 126, 129–30, 133–42
   On Christian doctrine 101, 196
Augustus Caesar, emperor 125, 208n.192
avarice *see* greed
Avvocato family 218

Babylon 46–7, 58, 171
Balbi, Giovanni 31, 69
Baldwin IX, count of Flanders, later Latin emperor of Constantinople 228
Baldwin of Boulogne, king of Jerusalem 86, 200–1
Balearic islands 34, 214
Barcelona 215
Barisone, judge of Arborea 219–20
Barnabas, apostle and saint 76

basilisks 173, 217
beasts v. human beings 50, 105–6, 129, 153
Beatrice, empress 222
Bede the Lesser 177
Bede the Venerable 31, 44n.9, 55n.58, 58, 177, 247
Beirut 199–200
Béjaïa *see* Bugia
Belshazzar, biblical king 116
Beltramo de' Ficeni, *capitano* 249
Benzo d'Alessandria, historian 20
Berengar of Tours 192–3
Bergamo 5, 67, 249n.202
Bernard, uncle of Charlemagne 180
Bernardo degli Arimondi, archbishop of Genoa 243–5
Bernard of Clairvaux, theologian 31, 64, 204–5, 212
Bernardo Maragone 5
Bisagno River 173
Black Sea, Genoese trade in 8, 228
Bobbio, abbey 175, 249n.198
   diocese 10, 163–4, 213, 228, 248
Boccanegra, Guglielmo, *capitano* 9, 100n.4, 239–40
Boethius 129, 169
Bologna 13, 227, 237n.132, 242n.158, 249n.202
   San Domenico 238
Boniface I, marquess of Montferrat 228
Boniface IV, pope 176
Boniface VIII, pope 15, 94–5, 251–4
Bonifacio, archbishop of Genoa 174, 224–7
Bonifacio, fortress 221
Bonvesin da la Riva, author 24
Borborino, Lanfranco, admiral 242–3
Bordeaux 13
Borzone, abbey 249
Bourdin, Maurice *see* Gregory VIII
breastfeeding 157, 237
Brenta River 34, 52
Brescia 5, 67, 100, 184, 221, 225, 233n.111
bribery 94, 113, 141
Brugnato, diocese 10, 164, 213, 248
Brunetto Latini 25, 28

Budapest 13
Bugia, north Africa 213
Byzantine Empire 28, 92, 178, 185,
  208, 216, 221–2, 226, 228,
  253
  see also empire, western v. eastern;
  Romania; *translatio imperii*

Cadalus, bishop of Parma *see* Honorius II, antipope
Caesar, Gaius Julius 32, 66n.10, 139
Caesarea 7, 23, 36, 86, 199n.158, 200–2
Caesarea (Alessandria renamed) 220
Caffaro di Caschifellone, consul and annalist 8, 22–3, 86, 90n.34, 209n.199, 210n.203, 214n.19
Cagliari 204, 220–1, 239
Caiaphas, high priest 128
Cain 45–6
Cairo Montenotte 231
Calixtus II, pope 210–11
Calixtus III, antipope 89nn.28–9, 217
Camillus, Roman consul 138–9
Campania, region 229, 250n.206, 251n.212
canon law 45n.1, 190, 244
capitano del popolo (captain of the people), civic official 9–10, 26, 36, 91, 97, 100–2, 239–40, 243, 249, 253
Capriata 231
Capua 229
cardinals
  cardinal legates 193, 218
  college of 134–5, 162, 182, 190, 206–7, 212, 236, 245–6, 251, 254
  galero (red hat) 237
  as papal electors 162, 191, 217, 239, 247, 250
Carignano, hill 54, 173
Carmadino, Guido di 189
Carmenta 53, 172
carroccio (battle wagon) 234
Carthage, Carthaginians 43, 57, 59–63, 135–6, 254n.225
  see also Hannibal; Mago

Cassian, saint 19
Cassiodorus 32, 247
Castello, hill 54
Catalonia, Catalans 94, 255
Cato the Elder 62–3, 139–40
Cato the Younger 139, 196–7
Celestine V, pope (Pietro da Morrone) 250–1
Celsus, saint *see* Nazarius
Ceriana 173, 191
Ceuta, north Africa 90
Chaldea, the Chaldeans 66
Chania, Crete 243
Charlemagne, emperor 181, 208
Charles I of Anjou, count of Provence, later king of Sicily and Naples 242
Charles II of Anjou, king of Naples 95, 245
Chiavari 221
children *see* parents and children
chimera 117
Christ, personal characteristics 179, 202
chronicle, genre 3–7, 23–5, 32, 35, 41, 44
Chronicon parmense 6, 32
Cicero, M. Tullius 25, 32, 106, 111n.11, 116, 134–40
Ciriacus, bishop of Genoa 197–9
citizenship 4, 6, 10–11, 22, 24–5, 28, 32, 120–42
city (*civitas*), features of 4–6, 36, 83, 161
Civitavecchia 90
Clement III, antipope 195, 197
Clement III, pope 218, 224n.68
Clement IV, pope 242
Clotilde, queen of the Franks 169–70, 172
Clovis, king of the Franks 169–70
Codrus, king of Athens 136
Cologne 14
Colonna family 15, 251, 254
Columbanus, saint 175
comet of 1264 12, 241
Commodus, emperor 79
commonwealth, the 6, 101–8
  see also governance

INDEX 275

commune, Genoese 7–9, 11, 20, 22, 36–7, 89n.26, 92, 94, 100, 163, 204, 206, 209, 216, 219–20, 222–30
  see also Genoese annals
Como 5, 221
compagna 8
  see also commune
compilation as authorial practise 23, 29
concessions see privileges
concubinage see nicolaism
Conrad I, bishop of Genoa 191–3
Conrad II, bishop of Genoa 195–7
Conrad II, emperor 190–1
Conrad III, emperor 214
Conrad, count of Ventimiglia 191
Conrad, marquess of Montferrat 223
Conradin, king of Sicily 242
conspicuous consumption 130–1
Constantine I, emperor 79, 135, 208, 228
  see also Donation of Constantine
Constantinople 8, 92n.46, 182, 208, 216, 223, 228, 253
consul, civic official 9, 26–7, 36, 100–2, 120, 224–5
conversion, religious 170–2, 174, 189–90
  see also Genoa, Christianisation; Jews
Corneto 163, 212
Corsica 10, 163, 209–10, 213, 248
Cortenuova, battle of (1237) 234, 252n.215
Cottius, Roman client king 164, 171
  see also Alps, Cottian
Council, Lateran
  First (1123) 210
  Third (1179) 217n.31, 222
  Fourth (1215) 193n.123, 230
Council of Brixen (1080) 195
Council of Clermont (1095) 197n.145
Council of the Credenza 94, 97, 255
Council of Eight Nobles 100, 227
Council of Lyons (1245) 90, 237
council, provincial (1293) 14–15, 174, 248–9
cowardice 110–11, 115, 216n.27, 243

creed see Apostles' Creed
Cremona 5, 94, 237–8
Crete 49–51, 64, 160, 230, 243
crosses, reliquary 35, 206, 223, 226, 228, 231, 256
Crusades 7–8, 32, 34, 51n.34
  Children's (1222) 232
  First (1095–1101) 23, 34, 36, 85–6, 197–201
  Third (1189–92) 223–4
  Fourth (1202–4) 228
  Fifth (1217–21) 90, 232
  Seventh (1248–54) 238
currency 41, 201n.166, 204, 214
Curzola, battle of (1298) 99, 255–7
Cyprian, saint 159

Dacia 172
Dagobert, king of the Franks 175
Daimbert, patriarch of Jerusalem 200
Damascus 223
Damietta 90, 232, 238
Dandolo family 228, 230, 254–7
Daniel, prophet 112, 116, 124
Darius, king 132n.44, 157
David, king 102, 111, 132
decadence see wealth
Decretum see Gratian
dei Fornari family 228
del Carretto family, marquesses 231
della Turca, Rosso, admiral 240
de Mari, Ansaldo and Andreolo, admirals 235–6
Democritus, Greek philosopher 132
demons 56, 72–4, 115, 120, 122
Demosthenes, Greek orator 119, 141–2
Desiderius, king of the Lombards 180
desire see lust
devil, the 85, 104, 120, 146, 168–9, 174, 185–6, 193
  see also demons
di Camilla, Nivellono 222
di Castello/de Castro family 218, 225
  Folco 229
  see also Henry, count of Malta
Diet of Nuremberg (1211) 229n.93
Diogenes, bishop of Genoa 166n.1

Diogenes, Greek philosopher 129–30
Dionides, pirate 114
Dionysius, bishop of Genoa 180–2
discord, evils of 50, 94–5, 102–4, 118–19, 253
Distichs of Cato 139
Djerba, island off north Africa 255
Dominic, saint 1n.5, 12–13, 17, 118, 233, 238
Dominican order 1, 12–14, 231, 233n.112
  see also *ars praedicandi*; San Domenico
Dominio (the 'Dominion', Genoa's trading empire) 84, 88, 161–2
Domitian, emperor 79
Donation of Constantine 76n.19, 134n.54, 208
Dondedeus Bos 228
Doria family
  church patronage see San Fruttuoso; San Matteo
  Corrado, *capitano* 9, 253
  Enrico 222
  Jacopo, annalist 14, 22–3, 42n.5, 84n.111, 247n.182
  Lamba, admiral 254n.223, 255–6
  Martino 211
  Nicolò 227n.83, 230n.99
  Oberto, admiral and *capitano* 9, 91, 94, 98, 100, 243
dowry law 216
Drudo Marcellino, podestà 226–7
Duilius, Roman admiral 147–8

earthquakes 27, 174, 233
eclipse of 1239 12, 235
effeminacy 128–32
Egypt, the Egyptians 51, 66, 172, 196
  see also Alexandria; Damietta; Saladin
elders or *anziani* (civic officials) 100–1
Eli, prophet 155
Elisabeth of Hungary, princess and saint 17, 233
Elpes, wife of Boethius 169
Embriaco, Guglielmo 36, 200–1
Emilia, region 171

empire 180, 207, 229, 236
  eastern see Byzantine Empire
  Genoese see *Dominio*
  Roman 133–4
  western v. eastern 181, 208
  see also Gelasian dualism; Investiture Contest; *translatio imperii*
encyclopedias 29–31, 75n.12
envy 46, 105, 134, 146, 151, 224, 255
Enzo, king of Sardinia 238
Ephesus 160
Epiphanius, monk 179
Epiphanius Scholasticus see Cassiodorus
Epirus, the Epirotes 47, 55, 121
equality 158–9
Eris, goddess of discord 50
Ermengild, Visigothic prince 174
Esther, biblical queen 67, 127
etymology 23–4, 53n.47, 64–71, 106, 154
Eugenius III, pope 214
Eve 130, 146

Fabricius, Roman consul 121, 138
factionalism see discord; Guelf– Ghibelline conflict
Faro River 224
Felix, Genoese bishop and saint 166, 170–3, 176, 206, 224, 249n.201
Ferrara 6, 94, 192, 246n.177
Fiaccone 209
Fiamma, Galvano, Milanese chancellor and historian 6, 24, 220n.47
Fieschi family 206, 238n.140, 246n.177
  Opizzo, patriarch of Antioch 14, 245–6
  Ottobuono see Adrian V
  Sinibaldo see Innocent IV
fire 10, 46, 55–6, 66, 85–6, 130, 170, 253
flagellants 28, 240–1
Florence 2, 5–6, 71n.29
Florentius, saint 19
Florus, Roman historian 138
Foça, Turkey see Phocaea

INDEX

fondaco 213–14
Fontanella 28, 86–7, 184
Formosus, pope 185
Fortis, Pisan thief 226
fortitude 111, 144, 189, 205, 216n.27
Francia, France, the Franks or French 89–90, 95n.56, 162, 169–70, 172, 184–5, 187–8, 197, 200, 205, 208, 212, 222, 224, 229, 238, 254n.224
  see also French (language); Gaul
Francis, saint 17, 233
Franciscan order 17n.55, 92, 231
  see also Nicholas IV; Salimbene; Santa Caterina di Luccoli
Frederick I 'Barbarossa', emperor 9, 33, 35, 88–90, 215–22, 224
Frederick II, emperor 47n.11, 90, 208, 229–30, 234–8, 241–2, 252n.215
free will 96, 168
French (language) 7n.28, 25, 28–9
Fruttuaria, abbey see San Benigno

Gabriel, archangel 170
Gaeta 207
Galla (Gisela), queen of Hungary 172, 189
Gallinara, island 218, 249
gates and portals see ianua
Gattilusio, Luchetto 95
Gaul, the Gauls 66n.10, 67, 168, 172, 185
  see also France
Gavi 209, 226–7
geese 67–8
Gelasian dualism 207–8
Gelasius II, pope 173, 205–7, 210n.203
Gelibalds 170
Genoa
  archbishopric 33, 232, 244
  genesis 10–11, 88, 161–5, 212–13
  palace 10, 15, 54, 178, 227n.83, 244, 253n.19
  see also San Silvestro
  registers 30, 83, 184, 191, 206, 219, 240
  battle standard 87, 96, 98

  bishopric 10, 160–1, 166–7
  cathedral see San Lorenzo; San Siro
  Christianisation 43, 74–81, 160–1
  city walls 12, 54, 89, 187, 215–16
  climate 70
  compagnie (districts) 213
  districtus (contado, territory) 10–11, 33, 164–5, 240
  empire see Dominio
  growth 82–99
  political autonomy 4, 25–6, 33, 161–2
  riots of 1295 10, 15, 252–3
  Roman 56, 59–63, 68–9
  sack 28, 60–2, 83, 86–7, 184, 187
Genoese, the
  honour 34, 36–7, 81, 85, 91, 95–7, 176, 206, 222, 229–30, 235, 246–7, 255
  piety 33–5, 76–81, 88–91, 97–8, 224
  renowned as crossbowmen 237, 239
Genoese annals 2, 5, 14, 22–3, 30, 32, 37, 42n.6, 84n.11
genovini 214
Genua (classical form) 20, 43, 62, 70–1
genua (knees) 70–1
Gerardo Bianchi, cardinal bishop of Sabina 244–5
Gesta Romanorum 134
Gibelet (Gibellum minor, also Byblos; now Jubayl) 34, 85, 199
Gideon, biblical hero 133
Giglio, battle of (1241) 236
Gildardus, saint 168
Giovanni, bishop of Nebbio 248n.196
Giovanni Castrocoeli, archbishop of Benevento 251
Giovanni da Cogorno, archbishop of Genoa 235–8
Gisela of Bavaria, queen of Hungary see Galla
gluttony 111, 129, 133
Godfrey of Bouillon, duke of Lorraine 34, 85–7, 197, 199–200
Golden Inscription 200
Golia, Ansaldo, Genoese citizen 222
Gorgias, Greek philosopher 140
governance 100–22
Gratian, Decretum 31, 142n.79, 195

Greece, the Greeks 47, 49, 51–2, 75,
    79–80, 84, 126, 140, 179–80,
    185, 208
  see also Byzantine Empire
greed 46, 48, 63, 74, 105, 109, 112,
    114–22, 129–30, 134, 141–2,
    144
Gregory I 'the Great', pope and saint
    17, 31, 120, 149, 166–7, 170
  Dialogues 166, 169, 174
  Gregorian office 181–2
Gregory II, pope 178, 208
Gregory IV, pope 176
Gregory VI, pope 190
Gregory VII, pope 191, 195–7
Gregory VIII, antipope 207, 210–11
Gregory IX, pope 164n.16, 233,
    235–6
Gregory of Nazianzus 195n.131
Gregory of Nyssa, saint 168
Gregory of Tours, saint 32, 169–70
Grosseto 213n.7
Gualterio da Vezzano, archbishop of
    Genoa 239–43
Guelf–Ghibelline conflict 9, 15, 26, 33,
    235–6, 238, 242, 252
  see also Frederick I; Frederick II;
    Investiture Contest
Gulf of La Spezia 11, 165, 239n.146,
    240
Gulf of Venice (Adriatic Sea) 98, 256
Guy of Lusignan, king of Jerusalem
    233

Hadrian, emperor 79
Haman, biblical prince 127–8
Hannibal, Carthaginian general 60–2,
    134
Hebrew (language) 46–7
  see also Jews
Hecuba, queen of Troy 50
Helen, wife of Menelaus 50–1
Helena, mother of Constantine 228
Helgaud of Fleury 187–8
Helinand of Froidmont 141n.78,
    202
hell 65, 75, 121, 153, 253
Henry, count of Malta (Enrico
    Pescatore), admiral 229–30

Henry II, emperor 189
Henry III, emperor 190–1
Henry IV, emperor 195, 197
Henry V, emperor 207
Henry VI, emperor 222, 225–6, 229
Henry II, king of England 222
heresy 12, 33, 79n.30, 81, 115, 193,
    195
  see also Arianism
Hermagoras, saint 160
Herman of Reichenau 188
Hieronymus de Bursellis, chronicler
    13n.51
Hildebrand see Gregory VII
Historia scholastica see Peter Comestor
Holy Grail see *sacro catino*
Holy Lance 198
Holy Land 95, 97, 197, 224, 232n.110,
    246
  see also Oltramare; Syria
Holy Spirit 74, 75, 170, 188, 194
Honoratus, archbishop of Milan 171
Honorius II, antipope 191n.117
Honorius II, pope 211
Honorius III, pope 1n.5, 229n.93, 231,
    233
Horace, Roman poet 155
Hugh, archbishop of Embrun 193–4
Hugh III, duke of Burgundy 224
Huguccio, *Derivationes* 31, 56, 66, 69
humility 59, 71, 91, 106, 174, 179,
    190, 192, 196, 199–200, 202,
    250
humoural theory 70, 123, 154
Hungary, the Hungarians 172, 189–90
  see also Elisabeth; Galla; Stephen
hymns 181–2, 199
hyperpyron (Byzantine gold coin) 216,
    221

Iacopo, Iacobus see Jacopo
ianua (gate or portal) 38, 65n.8, 69–70
  janitrix (gatekeeper) 84
iconoclasm 178–9, 208
idolatry 66–9, 72–4, 76, 81, 178–9
  see also statues
impartiality 9, 100n.2, 139, 141
  see also justice
indulgences 199, 205, 223

INDEX 279

Innocent II, pope 162–4, 212–13
Innocent III, antipope 89nn.28–9, 217
Innocent III, pope 208, 220n.47, 229–31
Innocent IV, pope (Sinibaldo Fieschi) 90, 199, 206, 208, 213, 236–9, 245–6
Innocent V, pope 244–5
interdict 232, 236n.129
Investiture Contest 8–9, 195, 206–7, 210
Isidore of Seville, bishop and saint 29, 31, 44n.9, 46, 49–50, 53, 55–6, 70, 72–3, 115, 123
Isis 172

Jableh (*Gibellum maior*, city in Syria) 86
Jacobus de Voragine *see* Jacopo da Varagine
Jacopo da Varagine
  beatification 16
  career 13, 16, 237, 246–53
  Chronicle of the city of Genoa
    manuscripts 19–20, 99, 255
    organisation 21–8
    sources 28–32
    themes 32–7
  Golden legend 1–2, 16–17, 247
  Legend of John the Baptist (*HLT*) 18–19, 30n.85, 198–9, 223n.59
  Legend of Saint Syrus (*LSS*) 18, 30, 173–4, 177
  Mariale 18, 248
  other hagiographical works 19
  sermons 17–18, 247–8
Jacopo di Carcano, podestà 252
Jacopo di Levanto, admiral 238
Jacques de Vitry, bishop and theologian 81n.34, 118n.47, 121n.57, 157n.72
Jaffa 200
James, apostle and saint 51, 60n.13, 75–6, 153n.50, 185
'Janicula' 48–9, 54, 57–8, 64, 83–4
Janiculan hill *see* Rome

Janua, medieval Latin form of Genoa 20, 38, 43, 48–9, 57n.3, 64–70, 83–4, 101
  see also Genua; *ianua*
January 51, 176
Janus 20, 42–5, 64–5
  king of Epirus 55–6
  king of Italy 47–50, 57–8
  prince of Troy 20, 33, 50–5, 59
  Roman god 56, 66, 68–9
Jericho 188
Jerome, saint 23, 31–2, 44n.9, 58, 78, 119, 127n.19, 140, 144–51, 176
Jerusalem 7, 34, 85–6, 186, 199–200, 223, 224n.69, 226, 228n.86, 232
  ancient 23, 76, 80, 128n.28
  Kingdom of 8, 223
  New Jerusalem 188
Jesus Christ *see* Christ
Jews, Jewish people 46, 51–2, 57–8, 66, 104–5, 127–8, 147, 169, 180
  see also Hebrew
Joan or Joanna, English princess, later queen of Sicily 222
John, bishop of Genoa 189–91
John I, pope 169
John XXI, pope 245
John Chrysostom, saint 29, 31, 115, 126, 143–4, 146, 149–50
John of Damascus, saint 31, 179
  see also Pseudo-John of Damascus
John of Salisbury, scholar 31, 114n.24, 129n.34
John the Baptist, saint 35, 234
  feast 95, 222–3
  relics 16, 18–19, 198–9, 206, 222, 233–4
John/Torchitorio V, judge of Cagliari 239
Josaphat, biblical king 111
Joshua, prophet 109, 188
Judas Iscariot 75n.13, 119
Judas Maccabeus 93
Juno 50
Jupiter 49–50, 106
justice 26, 93, 98, 102–3, 107, 109–22
Justina, empress 181–2

Justinus *see* Pompeius Trogus
Juvenal 32, 140nn.72–3

Laiazzo 93
Landolfus Sagax, historian 32, 49n.25
Landulf, bishop of Asti 205n.180
Landulf, bishop of Genoa 173, 187–9, 250n.203
Landulf Senior, historian 5, 32, 181n.74
Lanfranc of Pavia, theologian 31, 192–3
language acquisition 47
L'Aquila 250
La Spezia *see* Gulf of La Spezia
Last Judgment 159
Lateran church *see* Rome, San Giovanni
Lateran Councils *see* Council
Latinus, king of Italy 53, 172
Latium, region 49
laus civitatis tradition 23–4, 28
Lavagna, counts of *see* Fieschi family
Lawrence, saint 200–1
  see also San Lorenzo
Lazarus 65, 206n.184, 223
Legnano, battle of (1176) 89n.29, 221
Leo III, emperor 178, 208
Leo III, pope 181
Lercari, Ugo, admiral 238
Lerici 239
Liber privilegiorum ecclesiae Ianuensis 30
Libri iurium 30
Liguria, region 10–11, 33, 164–5, 171
  see also Genoa, *districtus*
lions 106, 113, 117, 129, 196, 217
Liudprand, king of the Lombards 178
Liudprand of Cremona 32, 86n.19, 185n.89
Liuvigild, Visigothic king 174
Livy 20, 25, 27, 31–5, 52–3, 60–2, 83, 107, 134n.54, 161
Lodi 5
Lombard League 8, 221
Lombards, tribe 16, 170–2, 178, 180, 184
Lombardy, the Lombards (its inhabitants) 34–5, 69–70, 81, 92, 191–2, 220–1, 224n.68, 240, 257n.7
Lothar III, emperor 162–3
Louis III 'the Blind', emperor 184n.87, 208n.196
Louis IV 'the Child', emperor 208
Louis IX, king of France, saint 238, 242n.155
Lucca, the Lucchesi 6, 14, 220
Lucius II, pope 163
Luni 165, 204, 239
lust 51, 63, 117, 122, 129–32, 139, 145, 148–50
Lyons 13, 90, 180, 237–8

Maccabees *see* Judas Maccabeus
Mago, Carthaginian general 60–2, 83
magic 185
Magra River 164
Malaspina family 221
Manegold of Brescia, podestà 100, 225
Manfred, king of Sicily 241–2
Manto *see* Mathys
Mantua 64, 191n.117, 192
Manuel I Komnenos, emperor 221–2
Marco, Venetian chronicler 34, 52n.38, 217n.34
Marcus Aurelius, emperor 79
Marcus Curtius 137
Margaret of Provence, queen of France 238
Mariana, diocese 10, 163, 213, 248
Marianus of Cagliari 204
Mark, apostle and saint 76, 160, 181
Marseilles 61, 205
Martino da Canal 6, 28–9
Martin of Opava 23, 31
martyrs, martyrdom 17, 33, 76n.21, 78, 173, 176, 189, 205
Mary, Blessed Virgin, saint 16, 18, 75, 169, 176, 178–9, 182, 188–90, 240, 248
Mascherati, Ghibelline faction 15, 235–6, 238, 252
  see also Guelf–Ghibelline conflict
mass 15, 170, 186, 195
Mathys, queen and founder of Mantua 64
Matilda, countess of Tuscany 192

INDEX 281

Matuciana 175–6, 206
Medardus, saint 168
medicine 138, 148, 235
Meloria, battle of (1284) 8, 28, 36, 91, 243n.162, 244
Menenius Agrippa, Roman consul 108
Mercury 50, 66
mercy 70–1, 111, 126, 185–7, 211, 232, 257
Merula River 164
Messina 95, 98, 211, 255
Methodius *see* Pseudo-Methodius
mice 195–7
Michael VIII Palaiologos, emperor 8
Midas, king 122
Milan, the Milanese 5, 13, 20, 23–4, 32–4, 67, 71n.29, 76–9, 81, 164n.17, 171, 182, 207, 221, 226, 233–4, 237, 252, 257
  archbishopric 10, 33, 163n.12
  siege and destruction 216–18
Minorca 214
miracles 17, 34–5, 85–7, 173–5, 179–80, 184, 188, 199, 233–4, 241
  see also omens
misogyny *see* effeminacy; wives; women
mitres 134–5, 213n.7, 223, 248, 252
Modena 192
Mohammed, prophet 85, 170
Molassana 173, 244
Monaco 11, 226, 231
Montferrat *see* Conrad; William V
Montpellier 13, 214
Monza 207
Mordecai, biblical hero 127–8
Moses 48, 54, 57–9, 109, 147, 188
Motrone, fortress 220
Muratori, Ludovico 6, 21
Muslims, Muslim empires 7, 66, 83–8, 90, 175–6, 180, 193, 213–15, 246
  sack of Genoa (934–5) 28, 86–7, 184, 187
  see also Balearics; Bugia; Carthage; Ceuta; Crusades; Djerba; Egypt
Myra 198, 222

Naples, Angevin kingdom 11, 95, 242, 245
  see also Charles I; Charles II
Naples, city 229, 238n.141, 250
Narbonne 244
Nazarius, saint 33, 76n.21, 77–8, 161
Nebbio, diocese 10, 163, 213, 248
Neptune 49–50
Nero, emperor 77–9, 121–2
Niccolò Vaschone di Ceva, bishop of Albenga 248n.196
Nicholas IV, pope 14, 246–7
Nicholas of Myra, saint 198–9
Nicodemus 202
nicolaism 195
Nimrod, biblical king 46–8, 66
Nineveh 47, 64
Ninus, biblical king 47, 64, 67
Noli, diocese 10, 164, 213, 248
Numa Pompilius, Roman king 134

Oberto, viscount 189
Oberto di Olevano, podestà 225
Obertus, bishop of Genoa 193–5
Octavian *see* Augustus
Ogerius, bishop of Genoa 199n.157
Oltramare 7, 79–80, 84, 86–7, 197, 199–200, 223–4, 229–30, 238
  see also Holy Land; Syria
omens 196–7
Order of Friars Minor *see* Franciscan order
Order of Friars Preacher *see* Dominican order
Orosius, Paulus 67, 121–2, 128
Orsini, Latino Malabranca, cardinal bishop of Ostia 14, 247
Osbergerius, Manuel, Genoese jurist 95
Otto I, bishop of Genoa 173, 205–9
Otto II, archbishop of Genoa 11, 227–35
Otto IV, emperor 89, 220n.47, 229–30
Ovid 32, 50–1, 122, 130n.35

Padua 34, 52, 59, 94
Pagano da Pietrasanta, podestà 234

Palestine 80
  see also Holy Land; Oltramare; Syria
Palestrina see Colonna family
pallium (episcopal or archepiscopal
    stole) 163, 213, 220,
    235n.127, 247
pallium (length of precious cloth) 216,
    230
Pannonia 170, 172
papacy
  abdication see Celestine V
  conflict with empire see Guelf–
    Ghibelline conflict;
    Investiture Contest
parents and children 143–4, 149,
    153–7
Paris, son of Priam 50–1
Paris, university of 13, 179–80, 192,
    245
parlamentum see assembly
Parma, the Parmesani 191–2, 232,
    237–8, 243, 245
  chronicle see Chronicon parmense
Parthia 51
Paschal II, pope 204n.174
Paschal III, antipope 89n.28, 217
Patara 198
Patrimony of Saint Peter 9, 192
Paul, apostle and saint 46, 75–6, 78,
    104–5, 149, 158, 160, 166,
    169, 174
Paul the Deacon 32, 49n.25, 164n.17
  Historia romana see Landolfus
    Sagax
Pavia 67, 169, 171, 178, 180, 219–20,
    225, 232
  coinage 204, 214
peace 10, 15, 21, 35–6, 62–3, 92, 95,
    104, 140–1, 150–2, 188, 209,
    212, 216–18, 221–2, 225,
    241, 245, 252–3, 257
Peace of Venice (1177) 217, 222
Pera, Genoese outpost at
    Constantinople 92, 253
persecution of Christians 79–80
Peter, apostle and saint 16, 75–6, 78,
    80, 87, 102, 104, 129, 158,
    160, 166, 169, 183, 192, 194,
    201, 217

Peter Comestor 23, 29, 31, 46n.4, 118
Peter/Torchitorio III, judge of
    Cagliari 220
Phalaris of Agrigento 128
Pharisees 105, 115
Philip II 'Augustus', king of France
    224, 229n.91, 229n.93,
    251n.213, 254n.224
Philip, king of Macedon 118–19,
    141–2
Philip, saint 14, 19, 75
Philip of Swabia, king of Germany
    229n.91
Philistines 196
Phocaea 253
Phocas, emperor 176
Piacenza 5, 19, 205, 237
Piedmont, region 11, 164n.17
Pietrabissaria 209
Pietro Carbone, podestà 249
Pietro di Ugolino, Genoese jurist 95
Pietro Piacentino, cardinal legate 224
Pietro Pierleone see Anacletus II
pigs 53, 85, 131, 145, 183
Piombino 91, 209–10
Pipere, Lanfranco, Genoese citizen
    225
piracy 35, 114, 226, 228n.88, 233–4
Pisa, the Pisans 2, 5, 7–10, 27–8,
    33–5, 87–8, 90–2, 163, 191,
    204n.171, 209–12, 219–22,
    226, 239–40, 242–4, 257
  Ghibelline affiliation 9, 33, 195, 207,
    210, 217, 229–30, 236, 242
  see also Porto Pisano, Piombino
Pliny the Elder 164–5
Pliny the Younger 164–5
Pluto 49
podestà, civic official 9–10, 26, 36, 97,
    100–2, 225–7, 229, 233–4,
    249, 252
Polcevera River 165
Pompeius Trogus, Roman historian
    135
Pompey (Gn. Pompeius Magnus) 139
Pope Joan 27, 182
popolo 9, 100–1, 239–40
  see also *capitano del popolo*
Po River 94, 164n.17

INDEX 283

portents *see* omens
Porto Pisano 90–1, 210, 244
Portovenere 11, 165, 204, 212, 233
precious stones 131, 201–3
pride 60, 91–3, 98–9, 106, 114–17,
    130, 155, 171, 196, 202,
    217n.34, 226, 257
privileges and concessions 30,
    199–200, 205, 219, 223n.65,
    226, 230, 237n.133
Provence 69, 89n.19, 241
prudence 96, 102, 111, 123–5, 143,
    162, 211
Pseudo-John of Damascus 62
Pseudo-Methodius 7
Ptolemy of Lucca, Dominican scholar
    6, 24n.71
Punic Wars 23, 30, 59–63
    see also Carthage; Hannibal; Mago
Pyrrhus 138
Pythagoras 131

Ragusa 256–7
Ralph of Caen 32
Rambertino di Bovarello, podestà 227
Ramon Berenguer IV, count of
    Barcelona and king of
    Aragon 215
Rampert, bishop of Genoa 178n.57,
    185–7
Rampini, Guelf faction 15, 252
    see also Guelf–Ghibelline conflict
Ravecca 173
Ravenna 48, 71, 79, 160, 171, 186
Raymond of Peñafort 233
Reggio Calabria 95
Reggio Emilia 192
Regulus, Roman consul 134n.53, 135,
    138
Reims 185
relics *see* Augustine; John the Baptist;
    Syrus; True Cross
Richard I, king of England 224,
    229n.91
Riviera 10, 35, 96–7, 171, 236, 244
    see also Liguria
Robert 'the Pious', king of France
    187–8
Romagna, region 171

Romania (Byzantium) 92, 208, 253
    see also Byzantine Empire
Rome, the Romans 14, 23–4, 47, 52,
    55–68, 70n.25, 71, 89, 106–8,
    120–1, 134–7, 162–3, 169,
    180–2, 197n.145, 207–8,
    211–12, 236, 241, 247,
    254n.224
Capitoline Hill 67–8, 106
Janiculan hill 48–9, 56n.60
origin as 'Romula' 48
Pantheon 176
San Giovanni in Laterano 186, 222
San Pietro 181, 185, 236
San Salvatore 180
Santa Croce in Gerusalemme 186
virtuous citizens 106, 120–1, 134–7
    see also Janus; Punic Wars; triumph
Romulus 48, 53, 64–5, 68, 134
Romulus, bishop of Genoa and saint
    83, 166–7, 173, 175–6, 206,
    224, 244n.171, 249n.201
    see also Sanremo
Rosamund, Gelibaldian princess 170–1

Sabatinus, bishop of Genoa 175–80,
    205–6
sacro catino 200–4
Sadducees 105
Saint-Victor, Marseilles, abbey 205
Saladin 35, 223, 226
Salimbene de Adam 11–12, 32, 47n.11,
    235n.126, 238n.140
Sallust 133–4, 139n.70
Salutati, Coluccio 20–1
Salvago, Porchetto 95
Sampierdarena 219n.41, 238n.138
Samson 59, 132
San Bartolomeo del Fossato 219
San Benigno di Capodifaro 177, 213
San Domenico 11–12, 16, 228–9
San Fruttuoso di Capodimonte 211,
    248
San Lorenzo (cathedral) xv, 10, 15,
    35–6, 173–4, 176, 187, 199,
    204–6, 218, 222, 224, 228,
    230, 233, 239n.142, 248–50,
    253
San Marco al Molo 218

San Martino 173
San Matteo 211
San Nazario, Albaro 77
Sanremo 173, 175, 191, 232, 244
San Salvatore 218
San Silvestro 54n.53, 178
San Siro 11, 15, 166, 173, 187, 206, 248, 249n.201, 250n.203
Santa Caterina di Luccoli 11
Sant'Agostino 178
Santa Maria delle Vigne 11, 189
Santa Maria di Castello 11, 16, 218n.38, 235n.126
Sant'Egidio 12
San Teodoro 178
San Thoma 178
Santi Giacomo e Filippo 14, 19
Santo Stefano 173, 248–9
San Venerio (Tino), abbey 204, 249
Saracens *see* Muslims
Sardinia 11, 28, 86, 91, 178, 210, 219–22, 230, 239
  see also Arborea; Barisone; Cagliari; Enzo
Sarzano 54, 218
Saturn 47–50, 66
Saul, biblical king 102
Savona 165
Scandinavia 172
schism 89–90, 103, 162, 191n.117, 195–7, 217
  see also Investiture Contest
Scipio, Gn. Cornelius 61
Scipio, P. Cornelius 61, 131
Scipio Africanus, P. Cornelius 61n.20, 62
Scipio Nasica, P. Cornelius 63, 120, 141
Scythia, Scythians 157
seamanship 53, 92
Secrona 85n.14
Sedulius Scottus 31
Seneca the Younger 32, 146, 149
Sergius II, pope 183
Sergius III, pope 185
Sergius IV, pope 183
servants and slaves 157–9
Sestri Levante 164, 221

sexual intercourse 149–50, 152
ships, importance to Genoese 50, 80, 192
Sicily 11, 52, 95, 98, 168–9, 222, 225–7, 230, 234n.117, 241, 254
  see also Naples, city
Sidon 199–200
siege machinery 209–10, 214–15
Siena 25
Sigebert III, king and saint 175
Sigebert, bishop of Genoa 182–4
Sigebert of Gembloux 29, 32, 86n.19, 184
Simon Magus 194
simony 193–5
Siracusa 225–6, 229–30, 234n.117
Siro [Syrus II], bishop and archbishop of Genoa 162–3, 173n.34, 212–18
  see also Syrus
slaves *see* servants
sloth 41, 129, 158
Socrates 124–6, 146
Sodom 174
Solinus 29, 32, 48–9, 57–8, 64, 83
Solomon, biblical king 82, 96, 99, 105–6, 110–13, 124, 128, 132, 135, 143–7, 154–5, 158, 189
Spain 7–8, 34, 60n.16, 61, 75, 84, 90, 120, 131, 174, 245
  see also Almería; Balearics; Muslim empires; Tortosa
Spino da Soresina, podestà 233
Spinola family
  Corrado 253
  Nicolino 92
  Oberto 9, 100, 243
  Porchetto 253
statues 56, 66–9, 72–4, 137, 193
Stella, Giorgio, Genoese chronicler 20, 70n.26, 76n.22, 198n.152
Stephen I, king of Hungary 189
Stephen VI, pope 185n.89
storks 157
Sturla River 173
summa, genre *see* encyclopedias

Sutri 49, 90, 190n.112, 210, 237
Swabia 67, 90n.31
Sylvester I, pope 208
  see also Donation of Constantine
Sylvester II, pope 185–6
Syria 75, 94, 180
  see also Holy Land; Oltramare
Syrus, bishop of Genoa and saint 30n.85, 166–7, 170, 173–6, 224n.171
  relics 11, 15, 18, 173–4, 176, 187, 205–6, 224, 249–50
  see also San Siro; Siro

Tancred of Lecce, king of Sicily 225–6
Tartus 34, 85, 199
  see also Tortosa
Te Deum 15, 252
temperance 100–11, 123–4, 177
tempests 77, 144, 219
tercia 216
theft 46, 114, 120, 168, 190, 198, 231
Themistocles, Athenian statesman 145
Theodelinda, queen of the Lombards 172
Theodoric, king of Italy 169
Theodulf, bishop of Genoa 87, 166–7, 176n.52, 184–5, 189n.109
Theodulf, bishop of Orléans 183–4
Theophilus of Adana, saint 168–9
Theophrastus 144–51
Thomas Aquinas 13, 25, 30–1, 102n.11
Tiglieto 232
Timothy, apostle and saint 160
Tino see San Venerio
Titus, apostle and saint 160
Titus, emperor 128
Todi 6
tonsure 87
Tortona 240
Tortosa, Spain 85n.14, 90, 214–15
  see also Tartus
Tower of Babel 46
towers 54, 90, 125, 162, 183, 200, 221, 226–7, 231, 253
  see also factionalism; walls
Trajan, emperor 79, 164

Trani 246
translatio imperii (translation of empire) 71n.29, 184–5, 208–9
translatio studii (translation of studies) 179–80
  see also universities
transubstantiation 192–3
Treaty of Anagni (1295) 95
Treviso 94, 171
Tripoli, Lebanon 86
triumph, Roman 106
Troy 50–2, 59
  see also Aeneas; Antenor; Janus
True Cross, the 35, 98, 206, 223, 256
Tullus Hostilius, Roman king 130
Turnus 52–3
Tuscany 49, 69, 192, 241
tyranny 105–6, 114, 128, 163, 208
Tyre 223

Ugo, archbishop of Genoa 218–23
Ugolino, bishop of Noli 248
universities 13, 31, 75n.12, 179–80
Urban II, pope 197
Urban IV, pope 241n.154, 242n.155
Ursula, saint 14
usury 11, 41, 153

Vado 165, 242n.156
Valentine, bishop of Genoa and saint 161, 166–8
Valerius Maximus 29–30, 32, 36, 156–7
vanity 65, 113, 130–1, 202
  see also effeminacy; greed; lust
Varazze 1, 12
Varro 31–2, 125
Vegetius 31–2, 121, 133
Venerius of Tino, saint see San Venerio
Venetia, the Veneto 52, 171
Venice, the Venetians 2, 11, 14, 32, 34, 52, 70n.25, 88, 217, 228
  conflict with the Genoese 7–9, 14–15, 27, 34–5, 91–9, 223n.65, 230, 242–3, 252–7
  see also Gulf of Venice
Ventimiglia 11, 164, 191, 214, 232–4

Venus 50–2, 66, 204
Verona 4n.16, 23, 67, 164n.18, 171, 242n.156, 254n.224
Vespasian, emperor 128
Viator, bishop of Genoa 178–80
Victor IV/V, antipope 89n.28, 217
Victoria, city founded by Frederick II 237
Villani, Giovanni 5–6, 10n.41
Vincent of Beauvais 30–1, 141n.78
Virgil 50, 60n.13
Visconti family, lords of Milan 6, 257
Viterbo 6, 242
Voltaggio 209
vultures 157

walls 4, 12, 46, 54–5, 68, 83, 140–1, 187–8, 200–1, 215–16, 221, 231
    see also towers
War of Saint Sabas (1256–58) 7, 240
wealth 83, 114, 121, 144
    dangers of 114, 121–2, 129–30, 140
    treasure 86–7, 184, 193, 201, 213, 215n.23, 237–8, 254n.224
Wibert of Ravenna see Clement III

William II, king of Sicily 222n.56
William V, marquess of Montferrat 223
William VI of Montpellier 214
William of Tyre 32, 201n.166
wine 67, 132, 193n.123
wisdom 41, 50–1, 72, 74, 96, 112, 119, 123–8, 134–8, 141, 143–6, 154–5, 158, 172, 182, 187, 218, 225, 244–5
wives and husbands 143–52
    see also adultery; parents; sexual intercourse; tercia
women 56, 69, 144–52, 172–3, 189–92, 215–16
    alluring 51, 131–2, 145, 148–9
    angry 144–6, 151, 171
    presumptuous 182–3
    virtuous 53, 67, 143, 147–8, 152, 156–7, 170, 172–3, 189–92
    weak 146, 148, 154, 173, 189
works of mercy 71
wrath see anger

Xenocrates 114

Zaccaria family 91, 253

EU authorised representative for GPSR:
Easy Access System Europe, Mustamäe tee 50,
10621 Tallinn, Estonia
gpsr.requests@easproject.com

www.ingramcontent.com/pod-product-compliance
Lightning Source LLC
Chambersburg PA
CBHW070234240426
43673CB00044B/1793